HOW TO
cheat IN PHOTOSHOP
Elements 9

Discover the magic
of Adobe's
best kept secret

David Asch and Steve Caplin

ELSEVIER

AMSTERDAM • BOSTON • HEIDELBERG • LONDON • NEW YORK • OXFORD
PARIS • SAN DIEGO • SAN FRANCISCO • SINGAPORE • SYDNEY • TOKYO
Focal Press is an imprint of Elsevier

Focal
Press

Focal Press is an imprint of Elsevier
The Boulevard, Langford Lane, Kidlington, Oxford, OX5 1GB, UK
30 Corporate Drive, Suite 400, Burlington, MA 01803, USA

First edition 2011

British Library Cataloguing in Publication Data
A catalogue record for this book is available from the British Library

Library of Congress Control Number: 2010939692

ISBN: 978-0-240-52238-8

For information on all Focal Press publications visit our website at www.focalpress.com

Book design and cover by Steve Caplin

Printed and bound in Canada

10 11 12 11 10 9 8 7 6 5 4 3 2 1

Contents

How to cheat, and why vi

How to use this book viii

Essential keyboard shortcuts 1

Getting up to speed 2

1 Selection techniques 4

Marquee selections 6

More selection tools 8

The Magnetic Lasso tool 10

Quick selection + refine edge 12

Magic extraction 14

Working with selections 1 16

Working with selections 2 18

Interlude: Setting up Elements 20

2 Working with layers 22

Three card tricks 24

Divide and multiply 26

Importing layers 28

Think smart! 30

Adding a little style 32

Protect your work 34

The power of adjustment 36

Exploring blend modes 38

Banqueting arrangements 40

Cut-up collage 42

Interlude: Keep up, no slacking 44

3 Hiding and showing 46

Exploring layer masks 48

Smudge masking 50

On golden pond 52

Part of the scene 54

Polaroid-style photos 56

Spectacular fireworks 58

Fairy gets her wings 60

Extending the scene 62

Reusable images 64

Panorama power 66

Interlude: Digital cameras 68

4 Image adjustments 70

Adjusting images with Levels 72

Shadows and highlights 74

Bee flat to bee sharp 76

RAW adjustment 78

Photomerge: exposure 80

All that glitters... 82

The perfect respray 84

Shifting seasons 86

Photomerge: style match 88

A splash of color 90

Contents

Smart bling. 92

Changing skies 94

Miracle healing 96

Making rainbows 98

Catching the drops. 100

0-60 in ten minutes. 102

Real world modeling 104

Sunset silhouette. 106

That's snow business 108

Interlude: But is it art? 110

5 Light and shade 112

Shadows on ground and wall 114

Painting soft shadows 116

Turning day into night. 118

Making fire .120

Instant candlelight. 122

Stage lighting. 124

Divine light. 126

Shading using Hard Light 128

Deceiving the eye. 130

Flashlight illumination. 132

Cooking up a storm 134

Interlude: Can I get a job doing this? . 136

6 Transformation and distortion 138

The science of transformation 140

Distorted field of vision. 142

Simple perspective distortion 144

Tricky selections 146

Locket and load 148

Wrapping around surfaces 150

Making curls and folds 152

The ripple effect. 154

A flag for all nations 156

Not so extreme close-up. 158

Smoke without fire 160

Troublesome perspective 162

It's a kind of magic 164

Keep your composure 166

Interlude: Drawing comparisons 168

7 Materials and textures 170

Conjuring curtains 172

Quick and easy wood grain. 174

Pattern forming 176

Lying on a bed of satin 178

Making notepaper 180

The art of paper tearing 182

Creating old paper 184

Ageing a photo in minutes 186

A quick repair job. 188

Letting the dust settle. 190

You spin me round. 192

A little light relief 194

Stamp duty. 196

Finger-friendly stained glass. 198

Blueprint for design. 200

Unfinished illustration. 202

Interlude: Finding images for free.... 204

8 Working with text 206

Carving in stone.................. 208
Neon signs with layer styles........ 210
Instant chrome................... 212
No mess pumpkin carving......... 214
Write on the button.............. 216
Three-dimensional text 218
Writing in the sand 220
Chop and change................ 222
Elements of design............... 224

Interlude: Image size............... 226

9 People and animals 228

Heads on bodies.................. 230
Photomerge: faces 232
Cosmetic surgery: healing......... 234
Cosmetic surgery: weight loss 236
Age and youth 238
Adding people to the scene 240
Cleaning up the scene............ 242
Eyes wide shut 244
Warhol-style pop-art............. 246
Hollywood glamor 248
Bobblehead caricature............ 250
All in the mind.................. 252
Dog in a basket 254

Interlude: TIFFs, JPEGs and the rest... 256

10 Shiny surfaces............... 258

Upon reflection 260
Complex reflections............... 262
Window reflections 264
From railway to waterway 266
Goo, slime... and molasses 268
Preserving the occasion........... 270

Interlude: Keeping it real........... 272

11 The third dimension 274

Lifting the lid 1 276
Lifting the lid 2 278
Tiling the floor 280
Opening doors 282
Using perspective................. 284
Make your own jigsaws............ 286
Out of bounds................... 288

Interlude: RGB or CMYK?........... 290

12 Print and the internet...... 292

Saving files for the internet 294
Presenting your work.............. 296
Animated GIFs 298
Easy print matching.............. 300
Glossary....................... 302
What's on the DVD 306
Index......................... 308

How to cheat, and why

The truth about cheating

We've used the word 'cheating' in the title of this book in two ways. The most obvious is that we're describing how to make images look like photographs, when they're not. In this sense, it simply means creating photographic work without the need for a studio.

The other sense of 'cheating' is finding shortcuts to help you work more quickly and more economically. Wherever possible, we've used the quickest solutions we can find to achieve the results.

Each workthrough in this book is designed as a double page spread. That way, you can prop the book up behind your keyboard while going through the associated file on the DVD.

At the end of each chapter you'll find an Interlude, in which we discuss an issue of relevance to the Elements artist. Some cover essential information about file sizes and types, color mode, and so on; others take a broader view. Think of them as light relief, and read them to save eye strain from staring at the screen for too long.

Who is the book for?

As the 'baby brother' to the full Photoshop CS5, Photoshop Elements has long suffered the stigma of being a cheap, unprofessional product. Cheap it may be, but it contains 90% of the features found in the full Photoshop and, as we've seen from user-created artwork, it's anything but unprofessional.

It's true that Elements is rarely used in a graphics studio or publishing company. But this is mainly because it doesn't include the high-end prepress features found in Photoshop: using Elements doesn't mean that you're working with a substandard application.

Some Elements users simply want to enhance their digital captures, perhaps adding a caption or two. But there are also those who want to take their work further: to explore the field of photomontage, and to make reality from the dreams locked in their heads. It's for these users that *How to Cheat in Photoshop Elements 9* will be of most benefit, helping them to release that potential and get their ideas out of their heads and onto the screen.

As a montage application, Elements is only as limited as your imagination. It can realize any montage you can conceive, as long as you have the technical skill required. We aim to provide you with that skill set, enabling you to unleash your creativity. Whether you're montaging missing family members into a group portrait, or creating a complex work of art, Elements can help you achieve your goal.

What's on the DVD?

We've included all the photographic images from the workthroughs in this book on the DVD, so that after reading about them you can open up the original files and experiment with them for yourself. There are also a number of QuickTime movies showing specific techniques in action: sometimes it's better to see how to achieve an effect than merely to be told about it.

The DVD also includes a set of layer styles and custom shapes that we've created in Photoshop. Although you can't create these effects in Elements, you can import them and apply them to your own artwork – and modify them to quite a large degree.

Many things have changed in Elements since we started writing this series and some of its features have been removed or replaced. We do, however, want to keep the book as compatible with older versions as possible. To avoid confusion, we have moved old projects and those that refer to these features to the DVD as PDF files.

Going further

Visit the book's website at www.howtocheatinphotoshopelements.com and you'll find the Reader Forum. This is where you can post questions or problems, and exchange ideas with other readers: we'll also do our best to solve any Elements-related issues that may be troubling you. If you get stuck, either on a tutorial in the book or elsewhere in Elements, this is your first place to look for a solution.

Steve Caplin and David Asch
London and Brighton, 2010

How to use this book

We doubt if any readers of this book are going to start at the beginning and work their way diligently through to the end. In fact, you're probably only reading this section because your computer's just crashed and you can't follow any more of the workthroughs until it's booted up again. This is the kind of book you should be able to just dip into and extract the information you need.

But we'd like to make a couple of recommendations. The first four chapters deal with the basics of photomontage: making selections, working with layers, and adjusting your images. There are many Elements users who have never learnt how to make layer masks, or picked up the essential keyboard shortcuts. Because we talk about these techniques throughout the book, we need to bring everyone up to speed before we get to the harder stuff.

Although the book is designed for users of Elements 9, most of the tutorials will apply to those who have earlier versions of the program as well. We've indicated on each page where Elements 9 is specifically required to perform the task in hand.

The techniques in each chapter build up as you progress through the workthroughs. Frequently, we'll use a technique that's been discussed in more detail earlier in the same chapter, so it may be worth going through the pages in each chapter in order, even if you don't read every chapter in the book.

The DVD icon on each tutorial page indicates that the source file for that tutorial is on the DVD, so you can open it up and try it out for yourself. The Movie icon indicates that there's an associated QuickTime movie on the DVD.

If you get stuck anywhere in the book, or in Elements generally, visit the Reader Forum, accessed through the main website or directly via this address:

www.howtocheatinphotoshopelements.com/htcbb

This is where you can post queries and suggestions. We visit the forum every day, and will always respond directly to questions from readers. But expect other forum members to weigh in with their opinions as well!

Essential keyboard shortcuts

Elements is full of keyboard shortcuts that help you to work more efficiently. Here are the more essential ones that every Elements user should know.

Tools

Larger/smaller brush	`[` / `]`
Harder/softer brush	`Shift` `[` / `]`
Temporarily access Move tool	`ctrl` `⌘`
Temporarily use Dodge with Burn tool	`alt` `⌥`
Move, Marquee, Lasso tools	`V` `M` `L`
Brush, Stamp, Burn, Smudge tools	`B` `S` `O` `R`
Change opacity:10%, 20%...100%	`1` , `2` ... `0`
Change opacity to e.g. 35%	`3` then `5`

Layers

Move layer up/down	`ctrl` `⌘` `[` / `]`
Select layer up/down	`alt` `⌥` `[` / `]`
Nudge layer 1 pixel (Move tool)	`←` `→` `↑` `↓`
Nudge layer 10 pixels	`Shift` `←` `→` `↑` `↓`
Cycle through layer modes	`Shift` `+` / `−`
Fill, foreground color	`alt` `Backspace` `⌥` `Backspace`
Fill, background color	`ctrl` `Backspace` `⌘` `Backspace`
Open Fill dialog	`Shift` `Backspace`
Set colors to default black/white	`D`
Swap foreground/background colors	`X`
Lock layer transparency	`/`

Selections

Feather selection	`alt` `ctrl` `D` `⌘` `⌥` `D`
Copy merged	`ctrl` `Shift` `C` `⌘` `Shift` `C`
Move copy of selection	`alt` `ctrl` `⌥` `⌘`
Constrain to square/circle	`Shift`
Transform from center	`alt` `⌥`
Add new selection to old	`Shift`
Subtract new selection from old	`alt` `⌥`
Interect new selection with old	`ctrl` `alt` `⌘` `alt`
Load layer as selection	`ctrl` `⌘` click thumbnail

Artwork views

Hide all palettes	`Tab`
Fit to screen	`ctrl` `0` `⌘` `0`
Actual size pixels	`ctrl` `alt` `0` `⌘` `⌥` `0`
Zoom in/out	`ctrl` `⌘` `+` / `−`

Working with dialogs

Load previous settings	`alt` `⌥` + menu
Repeat last filter	`ctrl` `F` `⌘` `F`
Increase/decrease values	`↑` / `↓`
Increase/decrease values x10	`Shift` `↑` / `↓`

MAC WIN BOTH

Getting up to speed

REGARDLESS OF YOUR SKILL LEVEL it's always useful to have a refresher on the basics. We've used these two pages to not only document some of Elements' standard features but also to illustrate how they are used and referred to throughout the book.

The Layers panel

We use the Layers panel all the time when we're editing images in Elements. It displays all sorts of information about how layers interact with each other. It's worth taking the time to get to know how it works, and how to use the icons and settings to make our layers behave as we want them to.

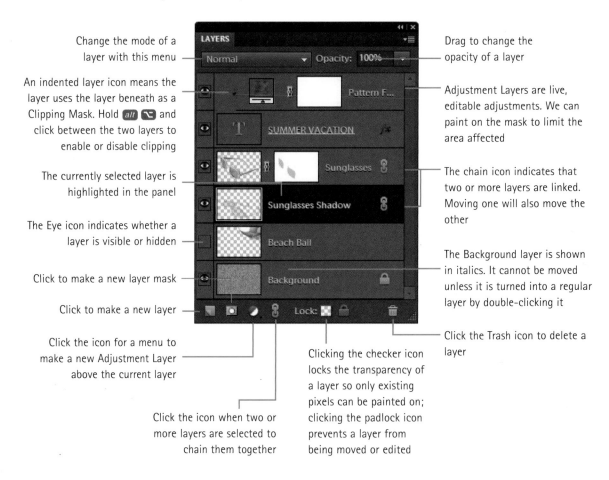

Change the mode of a layer with this menu

An indented layer icon means the layer uses the layer beneath as a Clipping Mask. Hold **alt** ⌥ and click between the two layers to enable or disable clipping

The currently selected layer is highlighted in the panel

The Eye icon indicates whether a layer is visible or hidden

Click to make a new layer mask

Click to make a new layer

Click the icon for a menu to make a new Adjustment Layer above the current layer

Click the icon when two or more layers are selected to chain them together

Drag to change the opacity of a layer

Adjustment Layers are live, editable adjustments. We can paint on the mask to limit the area affected

The chain icon indicates that two or more layers are linked. Moving one will also move the other

The Background layer is shown in italics. It cannot be moved unless it is turned into a regular layer by double-clicking it

Click the Trash icon to delete a layer

Clicking the checker icon locks the transparency of a layer so only existing pixels can be painted on; clicking the padlock icon prevents a layer from being moved or edited

The Toolbox

The Toolbox is the most important part of the Elements editor. Tools can be selected by either clicking their icons or pressing their corresponding keyboard shortcut.

Many of the tools have two or more options – denoted by a small black triangle next to its icon. These can be selected by clicking and holding the mouse to display the sub-menu or by pressing the shortcut key repeatedly to cycle through them.

The various settings for each tool appear in the Options bar. This is found at the top of the Elements window under the menus.

Here is a list of the tools along with their shortcuts. These are mainly the same for both the Windows and Mac versions – differences are shown in color.

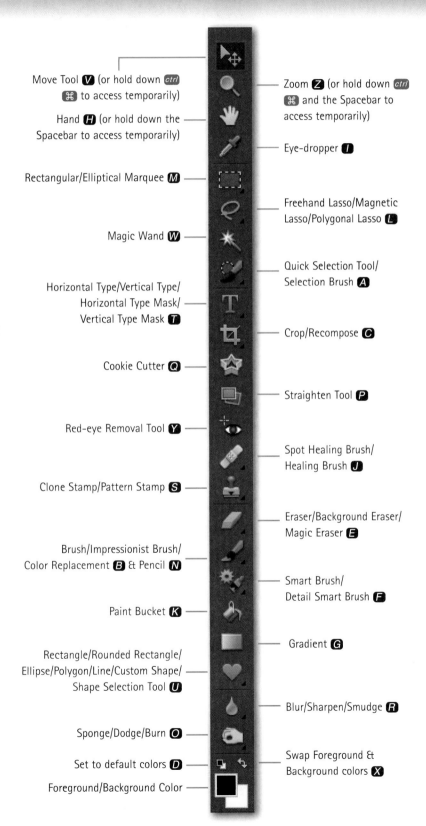

Move Tool **V** (or hold down *ctrl* ⌘ to access temporarily)

Hand **H** (or hold down the Spacebar to access temporarily)

Rectangular/Elliptical Marquee **M**

Magic Wand **W**

Horizontal Type/Vertical Type/ Horizontal Type Mask/ Vertical Type Mask **T**

Cookie Cutter **Q**

Red-eye Removal Tool **Y**

Clone Stamp/Pattern Stamp **S**

Brush/Impressionist Brush/ Color Replacement **B** & Pencil **N**

Paint Bucket **K**

Rectangle/Rounded Rectangle/ Ellipse/Polygon/Line/Custom Shape/ Shape Selection Tool **U**

Sponge/Dodge/Burn **O**

Set to default colors **D**

Foreground/Background Color

Zoom **Z** (or hold down *ctrl* ⌘ and the Spacebar to access temporarily)

Eye-dropper **I**

Freehand Lasso/Magnetic Lasso/Polygonal Lasso **L**

Quick Selection Tool/ Selection Brush **A**

Crop/Recompose **C**

Straighten Tool **P**

Spot Healing Brush/ Healing Brush **J**

Eraser/Background Eraser/ Magic Eraser **E**

Smart Brush/ Detail Smart Brush **F**

Gradient **G**

Blur/Sharpen/Smudge **R**

Swap Foreground & Background colors **X**

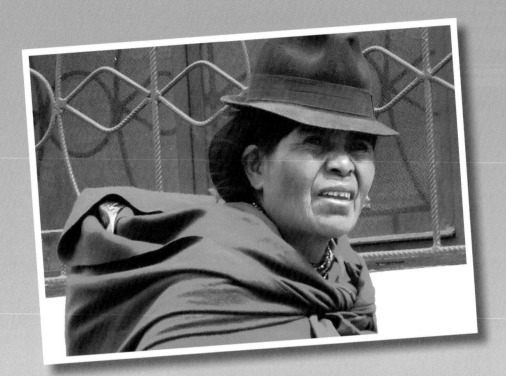

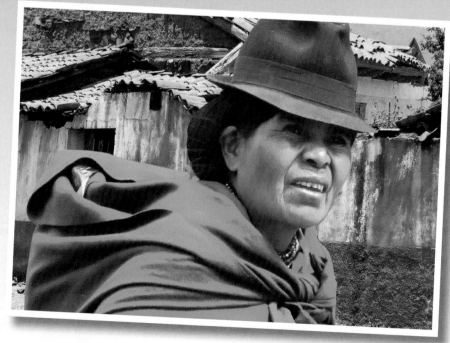

■ The photograph of a woman in Ecuador, above, shows a strong face, brightly colored clothes and a neatly incongruous hat. But that background is just confusing: how much better it is when we change it for the view across the street. Removing the woman from her background is easier than you might think!

1

Selection techniques

WORKING IN PHOTOSHOP ELEMENTS almost always involves making selections. Whether you're combining images from several sources into a single montage, or simply replacing an overcast sky with a bright sunny one, you need to make selections within your image.

Elements offers a range of tools for the purpose. Some are automatic, and will find areas of similar color; some involve tracing around an object's edge; some combine the two methods, making complex selections easy to do.

Whether you're new to Elements, or an old hand, it's worth your while going through this chapter to make sure you're up to speed on the selection methods that are available to you.

Marquee selections

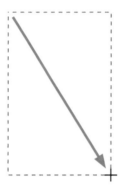

T HE MARQUEE TOOL is the basic tool for making selections in Elements. Pressing **M** is the keyboard shortcut for this tool: pressing the key again will toggle between the standard rectangular Marquee, and the Elliptical Marquee.

Every Elements user should be aware of the ability to hold the **Shift** key to draw a square or a circle, rather than a rectangle and an ellipse, and to hold **alt** **⌥** to draw a selection from the center out.

We're not limited to just one selection at a time, however; by holding combinations of the **alt** **⌥** and **Shift** keys, we're able to add and subtract additional selections – and we can even create intersections of the old and the new.

1 By default the Marquee Tool draws selections from corner to corner. Hold the tool as you drag, and when you release you'll have a rectangular selection, with the start and end points of the drag at opposite corners.

2 If you hold **alt** **⌥** *after* you start to drag with the tool, it will draw a selection from the center out. This can be useful when you want, for instance, a circular selection centered on a point in the image.

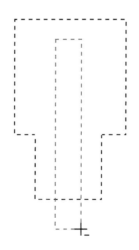

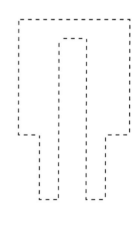

5 As well as adding to our existing selection, we can also subtract from it. This time, rather than the **Shift** key, hold down **alt** **⌥** before starting to draw the new selection. This time, the thin vertical selection (above

left) is drawn on top of the existing selection. Note how now the crosshair cursor has a – sign next to it to show subtraction. Once this selection is removed from the original, we're left with the selection shown above right.

 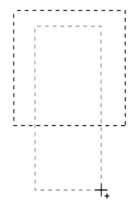 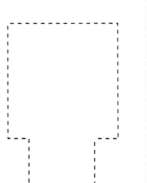

3 Holding **Shift** after you start to drag will turn a rectangle into a perfect square, and an ellipse into a perfect circle. This is essential for starting to draw square floor tiles, or even moons and suns.

4 Different things happen if you hold keys down *before* you begin to draw a selection. Here, the square is our initial selection; if we hold **Shift** before we make a new selection, the effect is to add the new selection

to the old one. Note how the cursor crosshair now displays a tiny + sign next to it to indicate an additional selection. The result of making the two selections, above left, is shown on the right.

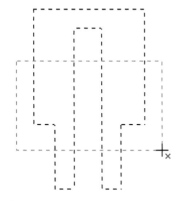 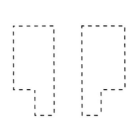

6 The final key combination is a mixture of the two previous ones. If you hold **alt** **Shift** **⌥** **Shift** before making a new selection, the result will be the intersection of the new with the old: in other words, the area where the

two selections overlap. The cursor now shows a tiny x with the crosshair. The result of making an intersection of the original selection, above left, is shown in the selection above right.

7 All these key combinations work for elliptical as well as rectangular selections, and can be used in combination. To make this ring selection, above, we first painted a tiny dot to mark the center. An elliptical selection was made, holding **alt** **⌥** to draw from the center out, and then adding **Shift** to make the ellipse into a circle. Next, we held **alt** **⌥** before drawing to subtract from the selection, then released this key and held **alt** **Shift** **⌥** **Shift** to draw another circle from the center out.

SHORTCUTS
MAC **WIN** **BOTH**

More selection tools

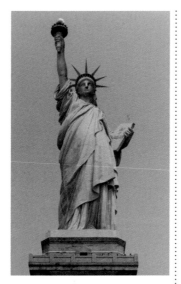

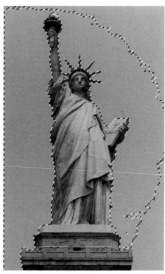

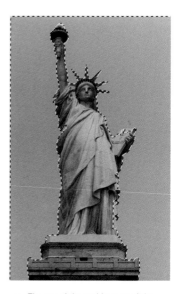

W E LOOKED AT the Marquee tools on the previous pages – but what if you want to make a selection that isn't rectangular or round? There are several other tools we can use for this purpose.

Here, we'll look at the Lasso, Magic Wand, and Selection Brush tools. While the Magic Wand selects a range of colors, the other two select only those regions you trace. They're three quite different tools, but they each have their uses, as we'll see here.

We're going to use all these tools to remove the sky from this photograph of the Statue of Liberty, beginning with the Magic Wand to select the bulk of the sky.

1 To select all the sky in this image, first use the Magic Wand tool (**W**). You can change the tolerance to select a smaller or wider range of colors: a setting of 32 works well. Click once to the left of Liberty's body, and you'll see a selection something like this.

2 The top right and bottom right corners weren't included in the selection, as the color there is just outside the range. To add to the selection, hold **Shift** and click with the Magic Wand in the top right corner. These colors are now added.

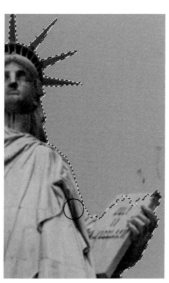

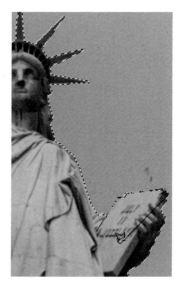

6 There's a problem with 'leakage' on the other shoulder as well, and we can use the Selection Brush to fix that. The book, however, has straight edges to it; even if we made the Selection Brush really tiny, we'd find it hard to trace those straight lines.

7 Instead, let's go back to the Lasso tool: this time, we'll use the Polygonal Lasso instead. Holding **alt** before we drag once more, click from inside the body onto each corner of the book to add it with a straight line selection.

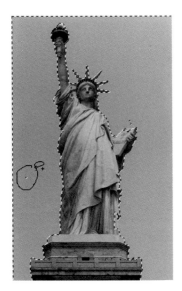

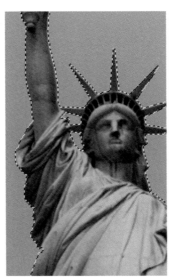

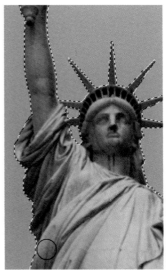

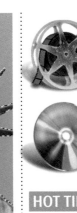

3 We can see a few stray pixels – most probably dirt on the lens – above the book, and to the left. Rather than use the Magic Wand, switch to the Lasso tool (**L**). Hold **Shift** once more and draw a loop around the stray dots to add them to the selection.

4 We can add the sky between the crown and the shoulder with the Magic Wand, holding **Shift** as before. Now that we're zoomed in, we can see a problem: part of the pale green statue has inadvertently been selected along with the sky.

5 The best tool to use here is the Selection Brush (**A**). Since we want to subtract from the sky selection, hold **alt** ⌥ as you drag over the area: everywhere within the radius of the tool will be removed from the selection.

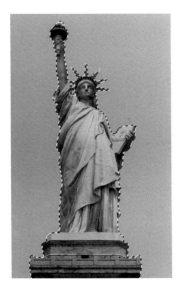

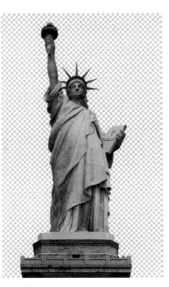

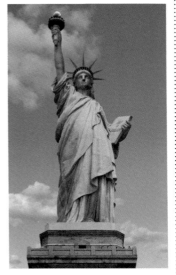

8 Once we've done a little further tidying up, our statue is selected. Except, of course, that it's the sky that we've selected rather than Liberty herself. We need to inverse that selection, by pressing **ctrl Shift I** ⌘ **Shift I**.

9 With Liberty now properly selected, we can make a new layer from her by pressing **ctrl J** ⌘ **J**. When we hide the original layer by clicking on the eye icon in the Layers panel, we see Liberty just cut out against a checkerboard background.

10 Once the original background has gone, we can replace it with anything we choose – such as this more appealing sky, for example. See the following chapter for more about working with layers.

The Magnetic Lasso tool

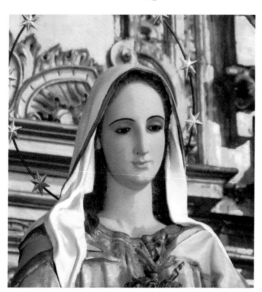

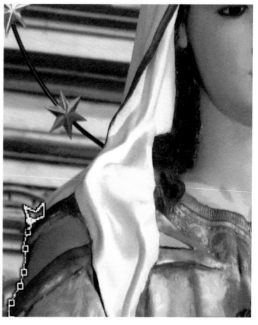

ALTHOUGH THE LASSO TOOL is useful for tracing outlines, it can be tricky to draw accurately with it. There is another method: the Magnetic Lasso is a variant. As its name implies, this tool sticks to the edges of shapes as you draw around them, making the process of cutting objects or people from their backgrounds very much simpler.

The tool isn't perfect, by any means; it's almost impossible for any computer program to figure out the difference between foreground and background objects with any degree of accuracy. But it's a real time saver, and can be used to make quick selections with ease.

To choose the tool, click on its icon in the Options bar when the Lasso tool is selected, or simply select it from the pop-up Lasso icon in the toolbar.

1 Start in one corner of the statue and trace along the edge of the object, sticking as close as you can to it. We've zoomed in here and enhanced the Magnetic Lasso edge to show it more clearly. The tool places square 'anchor points' each time it marks a change in direction.

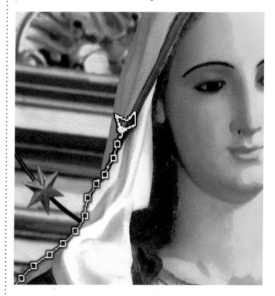

4 We'll hit a few more of these snags as we work our way around the figure; they occur each time Elements finds a strong line to follow. Once again, it's not a problem; simply delete the misplaced points, and then click the mouse button to add your own.

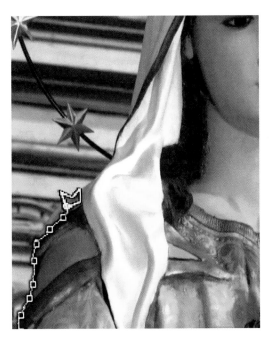

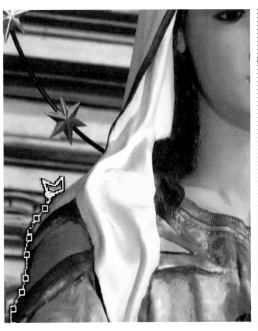

2 Right away, we hit a problem: when we get to the shoulder, the Magnetic Lasso wants to follow the gold bar, rather than the paler white cloth. No need to start again; simply press *Backspace* to remove the last placed points, backtracking along the traced line.

3 We can now force the tool to go in the direction we want. Drag a little way up the perimeter, and before Elements places another point, get in first by clicking the mouse button to place one of your own. Continue doing this until the tool recognizes the direction in which you're going.

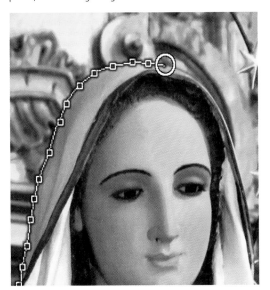

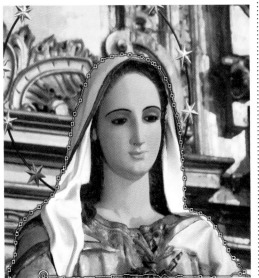

5 To make it easier to trace the outline, press the *Caps Lock* key on your keyboard. This will change the Magnetic Lasso icon to a circle, which shows the perimeter of the area in which it searches for boundaries.

6 When you get to the end of the object – in this case, the bottom right corner – it can be tricky to trace back along the bottom to the start, as the tool will think you're still looking for edges. Rather than get this wiggly line, press *Enter* to turn the path you've drawn into a selection.

HOT TIP

In step 5, we change the icon from a standard Magnetic Lasso to a circle showing the radius. You can make this larger and smaller using the Width setting on the Options bar; make it bigger for straightforward images, smaller for lots of fiddly edges.

The Edge Contrast and Frequency settings determine how much variation the tool looks for, and how often points are added to the path. In practice, you'll rarely need to change these from their default values.

SHORTCUTS

Quick selection + refine edge

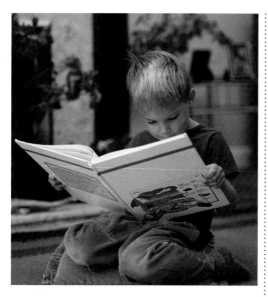

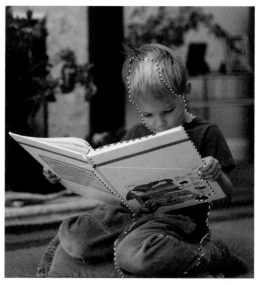

THE Quick Selection tool may well be the fastest method yet for cutting a person or object away from the background.

We've seen several selection methods already in this chapter, but they all involve a fair amount of work on the part of the user. The Quick Selection tool can help the process of lifting a complex subject from a complex background, quickly and painlessly.

The companion to this tool is the Refine Edge dialog, which processes the image after a selection has been made. Here, we can adjust the selection for an even better fit.

The image we'll work with here is of a boy reading in his living room. It's a tricky selection to make: both the boy and his surroundings include a range of colors and tones, making it harder for automatic selection to take place. But even in cases like this, we can perform the function with ease.

1 Begin by switching to the Quick Selection tool (**A**) and drag a single stroke from the center of the boy's head, across the book and down to his knee. We can see how the selection process guesses our intent: it's selected his face, most of the cover of his book, but stopped short at the pillow he's kneeling on.

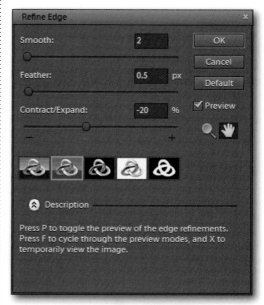

4 With our initial selection made, we can fine tune it by pressing the Refine Edge button on the Options bar above the image. This brings up the Refine Edge dialog: here we can smooth the selection, feather it (adding soft edges), and contract or expand it. This latter control is useful in cases where some background has inadvertently crept in.

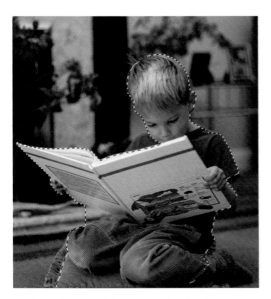

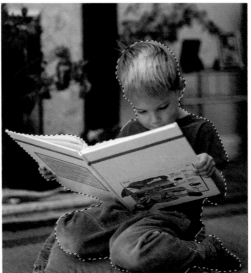

2 Let's add in the missing areas by dragging the tool over them. We don't have to do this all in one go: by default, any new strokes with this tool will add to the existing selection. As we can see here, we've now captured all but his right shoulder, his elbow and his sock; but we've also included a small piece of background below the book.

3 Reduce the size of the brush, and drag over the missing parts to include them in the selection. We can now remove the unwanted portions as well, by holding `alt` ⌥ as we drag over them: as with all selections, holding this key removes the new selection from the original. With a little work, we can create a perfect selection.

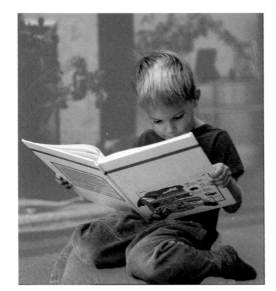

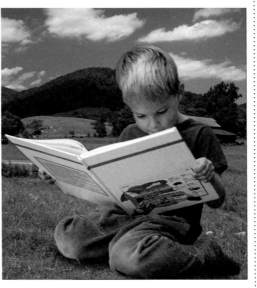

5 While we're working with the Refine Edge dialog open, we can choose to view our image either with standard 'marching ants' selection borders, or with one of four other modes. The black or white background modes are particularly useful for checking that no stray areas of background are being included.

6 Once the selection is complete, we can either delete the background or make a new layer from the selection. Adding a little smoothing can give unnaturally soft edges when seen against a plain white background, but by the time we've added a new background – such as this pastoral scene – the montage works well.

HOT TIP

The Refine Edge dialog works with all selections, not just those made with the Quick Selection tool. Use it with the Magic Wand to eliminate rough edges, or with the Lasso to remove hard lines. It's a superior selection technology that becomes useful for just about every type of selection you're likely to make.

SHORTCUTS
MAC **WIN** **BOTH**

Magic extraction

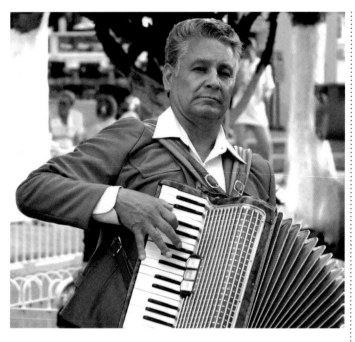

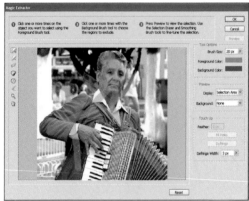

1 Use the Foreground Brush **B** to drag within the area you want to keep. Make sure the brush touches areas like the hair, which could be mistaken for background.

SOME TYPES OF IMAGE are just too complex to cut out with the Quick Selection tool, or the Magic Wand; photographs such as this accordionist, with his complex instrument photographed against a busy background, would be tricky to trace with the Lasso or Selection Brush.

The Magic Extractor, however, offers a relatively quick and painless solution to this problem. It works within its own dialog, using a range of tools that combine to make difficult object selection far easier.

The precise order in which you use the tools depends on the image you want to cut out, but you always start with the Foreground and Background brushes, before moving on to fine tuning. Begin by choosing Magic Extractor from the Image menu.

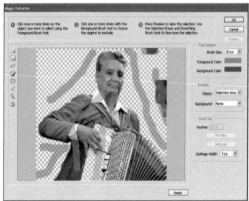

4 Use the Foreground Brush once more to drag a line over the keyboard, and the Background Brush to drag over those extra background elements.

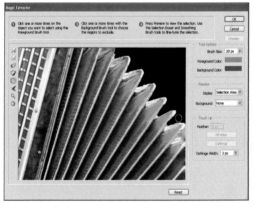

7 The Add To Selection Tool **A** is used to paint missing parts back in. Use a very small brush for fiddly areas, such as the edge of the accordion's bellows.

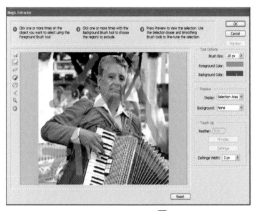

2 Switch to the Background Brush 🅟 and drag in areas you want removed. This brush paints a blue stroke, in contrast with the red of the Foreground Brush.

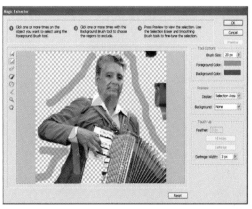

3 Now hit the Preview button to see how the extraction looks so far. There are some problems – pieces of stray background, and the keyboard is missing – which we can fix.

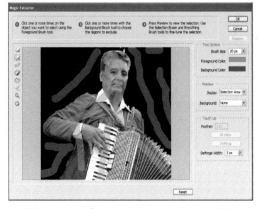

5 When we press Preview again, we can see a much better result. This is also a good time to change the preview background from None to Black, so we can see it clearly.

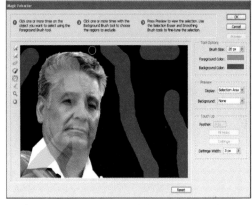

6 One or two stray background elements remain. We can remove these with the Remove From Selection Tool 🅓, which works like an eraser.

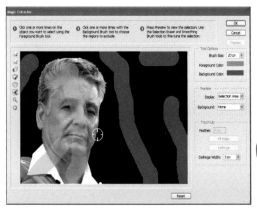

8 The extraction process does leave some ragged edges. Trace over the edge with the Smoothing Brush 🅙 to soften out the jaggies; hit OK when you're done.

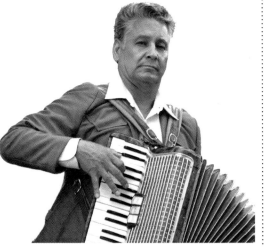

HOT TIP

You can view the entire photo at any point by choosing Original Photo from the Display pop-up. The 'touch up' section of the dialog includes useful tools: Feather will soften the edge of the whole image; Fill Holes will make sure there are no stray pieces missing by accident; and Defringe will smudge the colors at the edge of the selection to make the edges crisper.

15

Working with selections 1

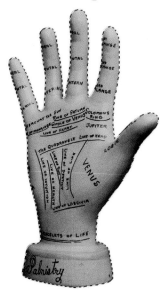

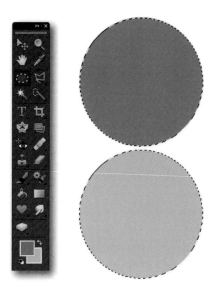

S O FAR IN THIS CHAPTER we've looked at how to make selections using a variety of methods. Here, we'll look at what we can do with those selections when we've made them.

As well as being used to extract areas of an image from their background, selections can be used to contain, isolate and protect an area; for painting and filling localized parts of the image with color, for example. They can also be used in conjunction with filters and other effects.

Note: Each of the steps on these pages are individual actions to demonstrate the different methods of filling the selections. After trying each one, go to Edit > Revert to restore the example image back to its default state.

1 We'll work mainly with circular selections here, for clarity – although any selection will work. To fill a selection with the current foreground color, press `alt` `⌥` `Backspace`; to fill it with the current background color, press `ctrl` `⌘` `Backspace`.

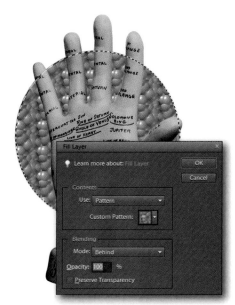

4 We can also change the blend mode of the fill (more on these in Chapter 2). One of the more useful ones, shown at the bottom of the dialog, is Behind. This fills the selected area behind the pixels already present on the current layer: the hand here remains fully visible.

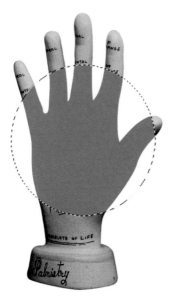

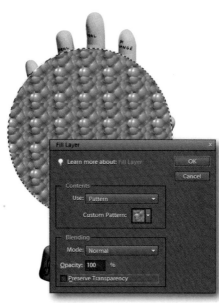

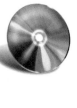

2 If you hold down **Shift** along with either of the keys we used in step 1, it will fill with color but preserve the transparency of the current layer – as we can see here with this palmistry hand, which is on a layer of its own. Only the areas that already contain pixels are affected.

3 Pressing **Shift Backspace** will open the Fill dialog. There are several options: here, we're filling the circle with a pattern, as chosen from the 'Use' pop-up menu. Press OK to complete the fill process. The Preserve Transparency feature would have the same function as holding **Shift** in step 2.

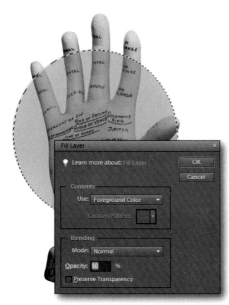

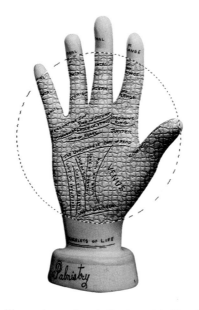

5 We can also vary the opacity, or the strength of the fill. Here, we're filling with the current foreground color, but we're choosing to fill with an opacity of just 50%, so we can still see the hand through the filled circle. The lower the percentage, the more we see through the filled area.

6 We can also use the selection to contain filter effects. Here we've used the Mosaic Tile filter; it only affects the pixels within the selection. If we wanted to apply the filter to the area of the hand outside of the circle, we would inverse the selection first by pressing **ctrl Shift I** **⌘ Shift I**.

Working with selections 2

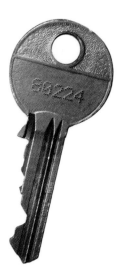

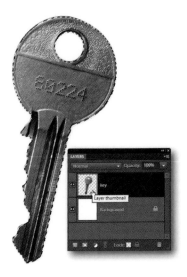

W E EXPLORED THE MANY WAYS to fill areas using selections on the previous pages. In this project we'll put them to practical use and create a shadow that's directly attached to an object. We'll also look at another feature of selections: the ability to duplicate the selected object on the same layer.

This technique is great for creating repeating patterns and effects and keeps the document tidier than if you were to create the objects on separate layers; particularly useful if you know that you won't need to edit the individual copies at a later date.

1 This key has previously been selected and placed on a separate layer. We can recall its selection by holding *ctrl* ⌘ and clicking its thumbnail in the Layers Panel. This is known as 'loading up' the selection and we'll be referring to this in the techniques throughout the book.

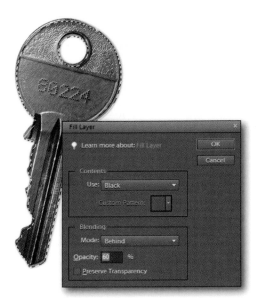

4 Now we have the selection in place, we can create the shadow. Press *Shift Backspace* to open the Fill dialog. We'll set the Contents to Black and the Blending to Behind; this will only fill the empty pixels within the selection. Finally, lower the Opacity to around 60% and click OK.

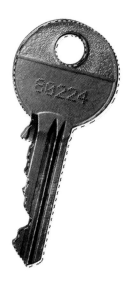

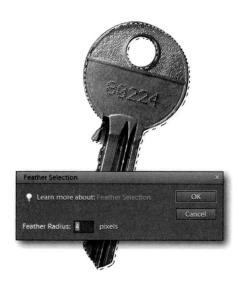

2 Make sure you have one of the selection tools active. Using the cursor keys, tap three or four times to the right and down to nudge the selection away from the key slightly; we could have also dragged the selection with the mouse but it's far more accurate this way.

3 We'll need to soften the outline a little. Go to Select > Feather, or press *ctrl* *alt* D ⌘ ⌥ D*, and choose a fairly low value. A radius of around 4 pixels is sufficient here. This will vary depending on the size of the image you are working on. We don't see any difference yet, of course.

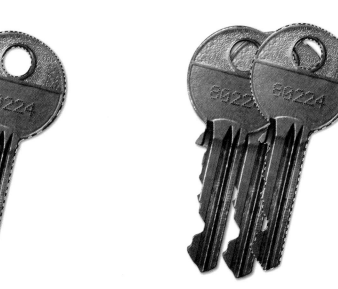

5 We now have a soft shadow. Before we start making our duplicates, however, we will need to reload the selection as it's still offset; otherwise the left edge of the key will be feathered and cut off. Press *ctrl* D ⌘ D to deselect, then load it up again to surround the entire object.

6 Hold down *ctrl* *alt* ⌘ ⌥. Click and drag inside the selection. This will create a copy on the same layer; if the selection wasn't active it would create a new layer each time. Release the mouse but keep the keyboard shortcuts held. Click and drag again to make another copy.

19

Setting up Elements

WHEN YOU BUY MOST APPLICATIONS, you can just install them and run them straight out of the box. (Or out of the zip archive in which you downloaded them, if you prefer.) And so, to some extent, you can with Elements; but there are a few tricks you can do to make the experience more comfortable.

It isn't that Elements is a particularly awkward program, but that since it involves working with images, it's memory hungry. It will happily gobble up all the RAM (memory) you allocate to it, and then sit panting for more. If it can't find any more real memory, it will settle for virtual memory, using vast chunks of your hard disk to store temporary files while you're working. These 'scratch' files, as they're called, are slotted in around the other files on your hard disk, and are then deleted when you quit Elements. The more fragmented your hard disk, the more pieces these files will end up in, and the slower Elements will run. In the Interlude following Chapter 2, we'll look at the best way of coping with scratch files.

The Elements interface can be customized in a number of ways. Normally, you probably wouldn't bother to mess around with the interface of your applications – after all, the people who designed the program probably know it better than you do, so why not just trust their judgment and leave things as they are? Well, believe it or not, the people who designed Elements don't seem to spend that much time actually working in it. If they did, they wouldn't have the Project Bin turned on by default. Sure, it gives you access to all your currently open files, but it uses up an inch or more of valuable real estate. And that's an inch you could be using to view your pictures that much larger. Turn it off: you don't need to have it permanently on view. You can always pop it open when you need it.

The Palette Bin, down the right-hand side of the screen, contains your most frequently used panels. Store your favorites here, but collapse them to just their title bars when you're not using them: they take up a lot of space, and you want to give the maximum amount of space to the Layers panel. When you have a document with a lot of layers in it, consider reducing the size of the thumbnails (using the pop-up menu at the top of the panel) to fit more in.

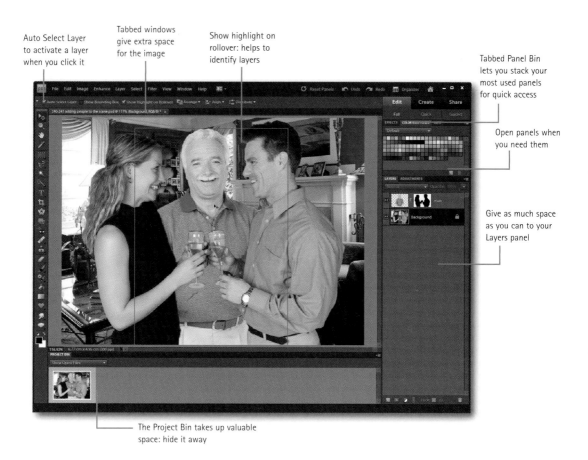

Auto Select Layer to activate a layer when you click it

Tabbed windows give extra space for the image

Show highlight on rollover: helps to identify layers

Tabbed Panel Bin lets you stack your most used panels for quick access

Open panels when you need them

Give as much space as you can to your Layers panel

The Project Bin takes up valuable space: hide it away

When the Move tool is active, the Options bar will display a number of choices. Checking Auto Select Layer will mean that a layer is activated when you click on it, but this can happen by accident; when this is unchecked, you need to hold the Ctrl/Cmd key when clicking on a layer to select it. You can also check the Show Highlight on Rollover box, which will pop up a blue rectangle surrounding each layer as you roll over it. This can help to identify layers, but can quickly become irritating. If you don't find the feature useful, turn it off. Similarly, the Show Bounding Box option will place handles around each selected layer. Again, this prevents you from seeing the image clearly; don't use it unless you find it helpful.

The tabbed window view is a great space-saver, giving you as much viewing area as possible. If, however, you prefer to work with the classic floating window setup, you will need to initially enable it in preferences. This is found under General > Allow Floating Documents in Full Edit Mode.

21

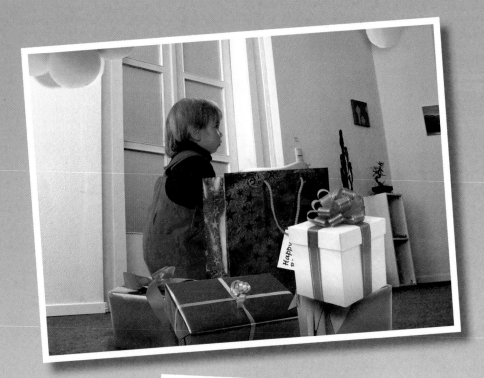

This little chap seems overwhelmed by all the gifts. If they had all been placed directly onto the photo, it would be stuck like that. Using layers in our image means we can freely move them around. Now we can clearly see that, like most children, he's not really interested in the gifts at all; he's perfectly happy playing with one of his balloons.

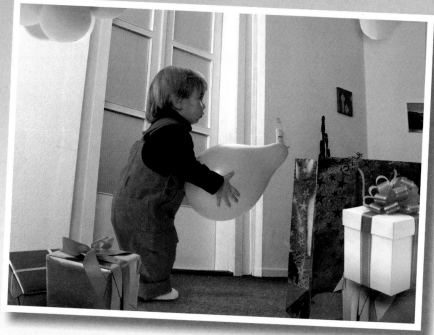

Working with Layers

WHEN CREATING A MONTAGE, layers are probably the most important part of the process. Aside from the design itself, of course. Without them, creating complex composite images would be a slow and difficult process. Think of layers as individual celluloid sheets: each one can be laid on top of (or beneath) another to build up the artwork. These can be manipulated independently without affecting the rest of the picture. There are many different types of layer, too, as we'll see.

We'll be exploring techniques that demonstrate the many functions and abilities of the main layer types. Beginning with the basics and on through to more advanced concepts, we'll see how layers are created, controlled and can be made to interact with each other in a variety of different ways.

Three card tricks

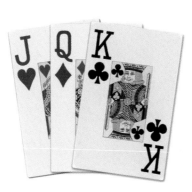

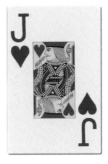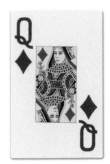

1 Opening the example image, we have a document containing four separate layers – the background and three playing cards. In effect, we have four different images inside the same file. They can all be moved and edited independently of one another. We can see the separate

WHEN YOU CREATE A NEW DOCUMENT, it consists of a single layer: the background. This is your blank canvas. You can paint on it, run most filters and perform many other operations. But working on a single layer is very limiting, and you'll probably find yourself continuously reaching for the Undo command. Although a painter will create his art directly on the canvas, we don't have to. Using layers allows us to add, remove and arrange pieces of our artwork, making as many changes along the way as we need.

The following example demonstrates the fundamentals of building a simple montage of playing cards using layers. We'll see how layout of the artwork can be changed simply by altering the order in which the layers appear and by either adjusting their visibility or hiding them completely.

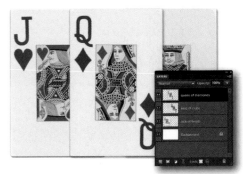

3 The order of the layers is not fixed, of course. Click and hold the queen layer's thumbnail in the Layers panel. Now drag it up above the king's layer. An indicator line will appear over its thumbnail. Release the mouse. The queen is now sitting on top of the other two cards.

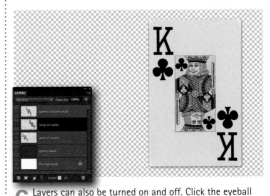

6 Layers can also be turned on and off. Click the eyeball next to the layer you wish to hide. If you hold *alt* ⌥ and click, it will toggle the visibility of the other layers (including the background). This is particularly useful when you need to remove the clutter temporarily.

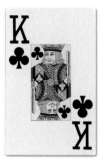

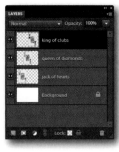

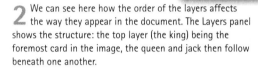

layers in the Layers panel. Each has its own thumbnail representation that shows a miniature version of the layer. We can customize the appearance of this thumbnail using the pop-up menu at the top of the the Layers panel and choosing Panel Options.

2 We can see here how the order of the layers affects the way they appear in the document. The Layers panel shows the structure: the top layer (the king) being the foremost card in the image, the queen and jack then follow beneath one another.

Although it's easy to see which layers are which in a simple montage such as this, it's always good practice to give your layers meaningful names as they are added: Finding *Jack of Hearts* will be far easier than *Layer XX* when working on a complex piece of artwork with dozens of layers. Simply double-click the layer's label and replace it with your own.

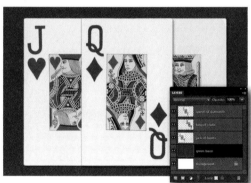

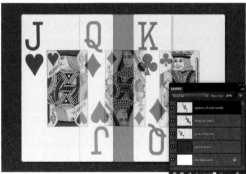

4 You can, of course, add blank layers. We've made the background layer active by clicking its thumbnail. A new layer is added by clicking the New Layer icon at the bottom of the Layers panel. Here it's been filled with color and some Gaussian Noise to represent the fabric of a card table.

5 The transparency of a layer can be adjusted. This is achieved with the opacity slider in the Layers panel. This ranges from invisible (0%) to completely solid (100%). The queen's opacity has been lowered to 50%. The rest of the image can now be seen through it.

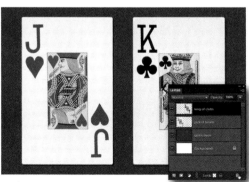

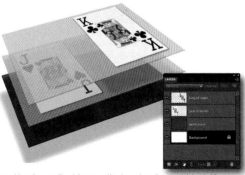

7 For a more permanent solution, you can delete unwanted layers. This is done either by selecting the layer and clicking the Trash icon or by clicking and dragging the layer's thumbnail onto it. Here we've made all the layers visible again and disposed of the queen.

8 Here's our final image displayed as it would look if you could view its component layers in three dimensions. Although the background layer appears as the same size as the other layers in the panel, it is represented here as an infinite base on which the rest of the images sit.

25

Divide and multiply

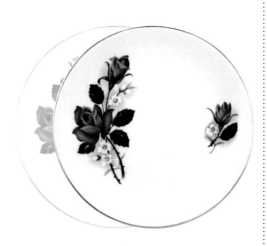

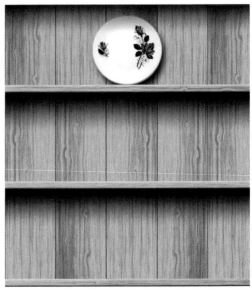

O N THE PREVIOUS PAGE, we created a piece of artwork by importing individual images as layers. The composition was altered simply by reordering the structure and changing their visibility. In the following tutorial we'll go a stage further. Using the Move tool and a combination of keyboard shortcuts we'll reposition and duplicate a single layer to quickly create multiple copies of the same object. This is similar to the technique we used in Chapter 1, except when we duplicate the objects here, they are placed on a new layer.

In the most recent versions of Elements, multiple layers can be selected to form a temporary group, allowing us to manipulate them as a single item. This is a much better way of working as there is no need to merge the layers into one before duplicating them, as was the case with earlier revisions of the program.

1 Here's our single plate. Its shadow has been created using a layer style; we'll be covering these later in the chapter. Notice how the shadow from the shelf falls across the plate. This is because both the shelves and their shadows are on a separate layer in front of the rest.

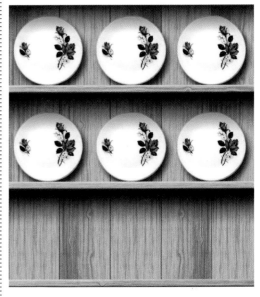

4 Go to the Layers panel. Hold **Shift** and click the first plate layer. This will highlight all three layers and in doing so, temporarily group them together. Use the same keyboard shortcut as before; this time, drag the cursor straight down to create a copy of the entire row.

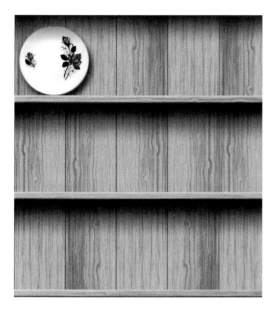

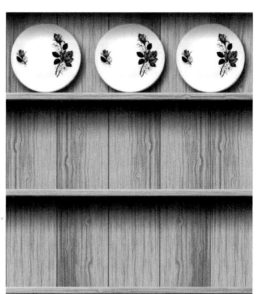

2 Make sure the plate layer is active by clicking its thumbnail in the Layers panel. Select the Move tool **V**. Click and hold the cursor over the plate. Now drag it across to the left edge of the shelf. Additionally, you can hold **Shift** to constrain the movement.

3 Holding **alt** **Shift** **⌥** **Shift**, click and drag the plate over to the right. Instead of simply moving it, this action has created a copy of the plate on a new layer. Release the mouse but keep the keys held. Now click on the new plate and drag once more to create the third.

HOT TIP

Make sure the Move tool's Auto Select Layer option is disabled in the Options bar. Whilst this feature can be useful for finding a layer buried deep in your artwork, it can also cause chaos. You may find yourself moving or copying the wrong part of your image if you accidentally click another layer instead of your intended target. You can mimic this function at any time by holding **ctrl** **⌘** and clicking the layer in the document.

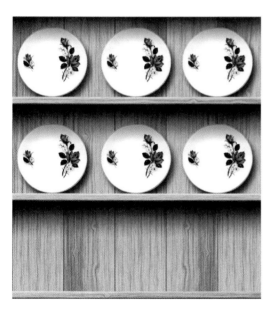

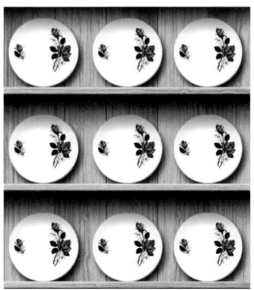

5 Leave the previous grouping enabled. Create a duplicate set for the final row. If you need to retain the group on a more permanent basis, click the chain icon at the top of the Layers panel. An icon will appear to the right of each layer denoting that it is part of a linked set.

6 Currently there are nine separate plate layers. If you don't intend to make changes on an individual basis, you can flatten them into three rows or even one single layer. To do this, use the multiple select feature to group the layers together. Finally, press **ctrl** **E** **⌘** **E** to merge them.

SHORTCUTS
MAC **WIN** **BOTH**

27

Importing layers

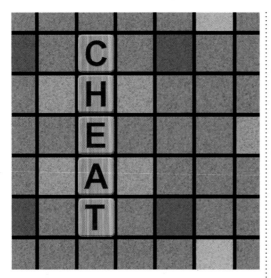

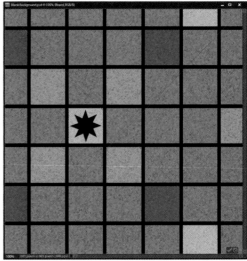

S O FAR WE'VE SEEN HOW LAYERS can be duplicated, moved around, and placed over and under one another inside of a single image. These layers have all been included in the example files, however. So, how do we go about getting them into the document in the first place?

As we'll discover here, there are several ways to do this, each with their own merits. To demonstrate we'll build up an image in six stages, each one using a different technique. You'll find the three .psd files used here in their own folder inside the Tutorial Files folder on the accompanying DVD.

1 Begin by opening the Blank Background document. Now go to File > Place and choose the Board file. It opens as a new layer within the document. Notice how we also get a bounding box; at this point we could scale but we'll accept the default by pressing *Enter*. Notice the small icon in the corner of the layer's thumbnail. This denotes the layer is a Smart Object. We'll cover these later in the book.

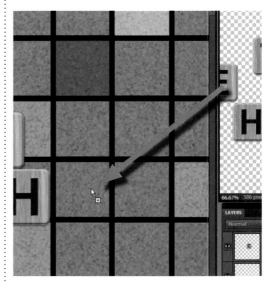

4 We can also drag layers between documents. There are three ways to do this: the first is directly from the document itself. Select the Move tool *M*, click and hold on the layer and drag it across to the other document. If, as with the example, we have many layers, holding *ctrl* *⌘* when clicking the object will automatically select it.

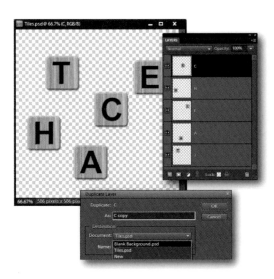

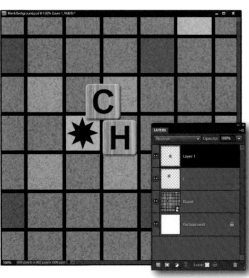

2 Now go to File > Open and choose the Tiles file. This contains five layers, each containing a letter. Click the top layer's thumbnail to make it active, now go to Layer > Duplicate layer. Currently, the destination is set to the same document; we'll choose the Blank Background from the drop-down list. When we click OK, a copy of the tile will appear as a new layer in our other document.

3 We can also copy and paste between documents. Make sure the H tile's layer is active, hold *ctrl* ⌘ and click its thumbnail to load its selection. Press *ctrl* C ⌘ C to store it in the clipboard, now switch to the other document and press *ctrl* V ⌘ V to paste a copy. We'll need to rename the layer as it wasn't carried across. Remember to deselect *ctrl* D ⌘ D in the original document too.

HOT TIP

Although we've used only a single layer to demonstrate each of the different ways of importing, we can – with the exception of the Place command and dragging from the Project Bin – just as easily perform the same tasks on multiple layers.

It's also important to note when importing with the Place command or from the Project Bin that multi-layer files will be flattened, so make sure you have all the necessary elements of your document visible (or hidden) beforehand.

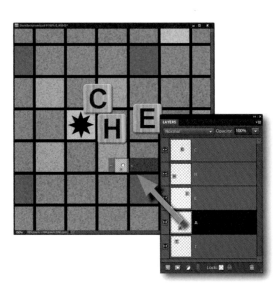

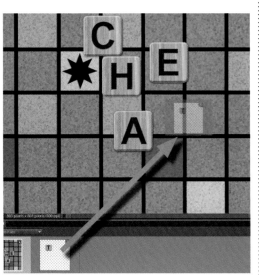

5 The second approach is similar to the last but instead of dragging from the document, we'll copy the layer across from the Layers panel. With this and the previous method we also have control of where the object will be placed in the document. We can also force the layer to be placed in the center of the document by holding *Shift* as we drag.

6 Lastly, we can drag the document in from the Project Bin. First, hold *alt* ⌥ and click the T layer's visibility icon to hide the other layers. If we didn't do this, we would end up with all the letters duplicated on the layer. Now drag the thumbnail from the bin onto our board to add the final layer to our image.

SHORTCUTS
MAC WIN BOTH

29

Think smart!

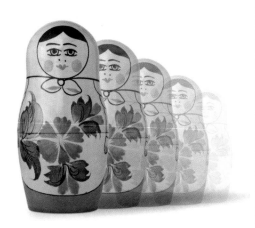

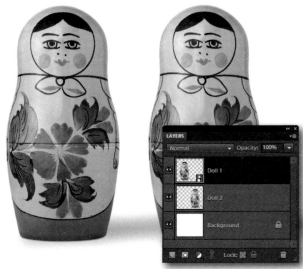

O N THE PREVIOUS PAGE WE TOUCHED briefly on the subject of Smart Objects. So what do we mean by this term and what is the difference between them and regular layers?

Outwardly, aside from a small icon which sits in the bottom corner of their thumbnails, Smart Objects appear to be no different to a standard layer. Behind the scenes, however, is a different story: they are resolution independent, which means they can be scaled up and down and, unlike their raster counterparts, never lose their original integrity.

This is incredibly useful when we're experimenting with different layouts in a montage, as we never have to be concerned about the degradation which occurs when continually scaling an object.

1 Here we have two seemingly identical Russian dolls. They're both on separate layers but looking at the left-hand doll's thumbnail in the Layers panel, we can see that it has the small icon in the corner which tells us that it's a Smart Object that has been created using the Place command. Over the next few steps we'll be able to see the advantages this type of layer has.

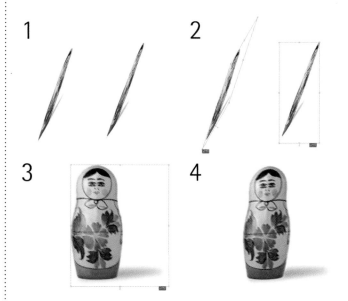

4 Here image 1 shows the two layers after being heavily distorted with Free Transform. Image 2 shows how the Smart Object's transform frame has kept its shape whereas the standard layer is square. Image 3 shows how simple it was to restore and it will, of course, be perfectly smooth when we commit the changes. Image 4 is the regular layer after a lot of battling; the result speaks for itself.

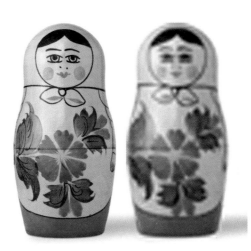

2 To demonstrate the way in which Smart Objects can be resized and then returned to their original size with no loss of quality, we've shrunk both layers down to 10% of their original size using the Scale command. Both objects still look good, just as we'd expect them to.

3 After scaling them back up to their original size, however, we can clearly see the difference. The Smart Object layer on the left is exactly as it was before we resized it. The standard layer, on the other hand, looks awful; it's detail is blurred and the edges are horribly jagged.

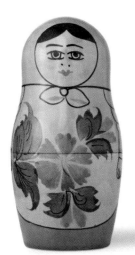

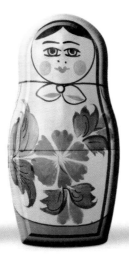

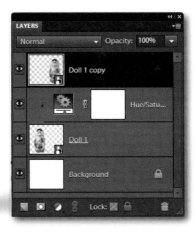

5 It's worth pointing out that Smart Objects are not without their drawbacks: they cannot be edited or added to once they have been imported into the document. This, however, is a small price to pay when compared to the benefits. They can still be distorted, scaled and rotated like a regular layer. As we can see from the image and the Layers panel inset, we can duplicate the object, add layer styles, masks and Adjustment Layers (we'll be covering these later in the book) to change their appearance; and it's all done non-destructively.

HOT TIP

Once you have the project you are working on looking right, you can, of course, convert the Smart Object back to a regular layer using the Simplify Layer command, which will allow you to edit and apply filters directly to it. It may be worthwhile making copies first though, just in case you need to alter something at a later stage.

Adding a little style

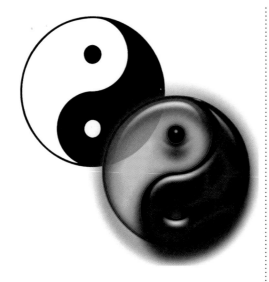

L AYER STYLES ARE VERSATILE, REUSABLE
effects. With them you can quickly place
shadows under objects, create metal textures,
add embossing and much more. Unlike filters,
however, they are non-destructive; once
applied, they can be altered, added to or
removed without the need to undo previous
changes or recreate parts of the artwork.
Styles are not limited to regular image layers
either; in fact, they show their worth far better
when applied to objects which themselves are
changeable such as shape or text layers.

From version 6 and later the program comes
with a much better Settings dialog with which
to fine tune the styles. Previous editions still
gave you control over the attributes but these
were fairly rudimentary in comparison. If you're
using an older version, you will, of course, still
be able to follow the majority of this tutorial.

1 Styles can be added to a layer by double-clicking their
thumbnail in the Effects panel, dragging their thumbnail
across to the layer itself, or by highlighting them and clicking
Apply. In the example, we've added the Simple Sharp Inner
Bevel and Low Drop Shadow presets to our text object.

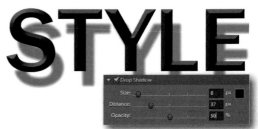

4 We'll adjust the shadow next. Start by lowering the size.
This makes it sharper, as though the light source were
closer to the text. Increasing the distance value gives the
appearance of the text being further from the background.
You can also lower the opacity if required.

7 Because the style affects the layer as a whole, you have
the ability to change the content of the layer without
the need to apply the style again. In the example, the color
and wording of the text has been changed; the style is added
as we type. This even works when painting on a layer.

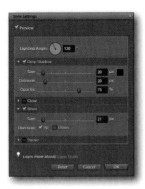

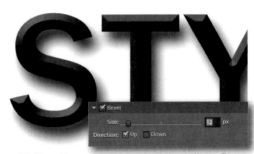

2 The default settings of the styles may not always be right for the image you are working on. Double-click the *fx* icon to the far right of the layer thumbnail to open the settings dialog. Here you'll see the adjustments that can be made to the style's attributes.

3 We'll start by making the bevel a little smaller to fit the text better. Use the slider to lower the value; you'll see the effect change as you do so. Bring it down enough to make the bevel's ridges straight with a slight flatness on top. Here a value of around 12 pixels is sufficient.

5 The Lighting Angle controls the highlight and shadow of the bevel effects as well as the direction of the drop shadow. The default is top-left. This can be changed within the dialog. You can also click and drag within the document itself. This allows you to set the angle visually.

6 We can also copy styles: right-click the layer style icon and select Copy Style. Now when we right-click on another layer's label we can paste a copy. The text adopts the exact same effect. This is useful when you have customized the style and want to match it across the artwork.

8 The effects also operate independently to the layer. Here both layers have been flipped vertically. You'd expect the bevels and shadows to follow suit. Instead, they retain their original direction. One more thing to note: altering the Lighting Angle will affect all layers with a style applied.

9 Now you've set up your styles, what if you want to remove them? You can hide/show all styles from the Layer Styles sub-menu under the main Layer menu. You can also clear them from there (the same as deleting). This is also available from the More fly-out in the Layers panel.

HOT TIP

Although styles are normally cumulative, you can force the current effect to be replaced outright by holding *Shift* when applying the new style. Be aware that many of the more complex built-in presets will override your effects as they already contain compound settings. It's also worth noting that patterned styles on surfaces in perspective may not look right, particularly those which contain strong horizontal or vertical lines. Such effects are generally designed to be applied to flat objects. You'll need to simplify (flatten) the style, then create the distortion on the object.

SHORTCUTS
MAC WIN BOTH

33

Protect your work

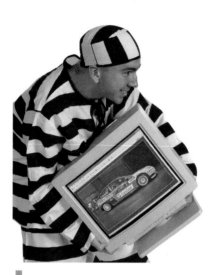

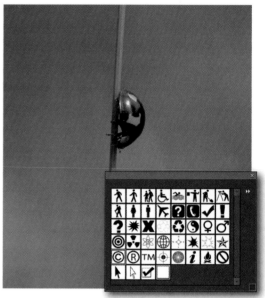

IF YOU'RE PLANNING on putting your images up for sale online or sending them somewhere for evaluation, the last thing you want is for some unscrupulous person to stroll in and steal them for themselves.

One of the most common ways to prevent this is to add a watermark to the image; this will often be your website address or logo because they also serve as good advertising. The problem we can have is knowing where to place it: if we put it along the edges, it could easily be cropped or cloned away, and having something that covers up too much of the image is defeating the purpose.

There is a compromise, of course: we'll be using a shape layer and layer styles to create a way of protecting the image quickly and effectively by filling the document whilst leaving it almost completely visible beneath.

1 First of all, we need to decide what to use as our watermark: for simplicity, we'll use the copyright symbol. Select the Custom Shape tool **U**. From the Options toolbar open the Shape Picker; our shape isn't in the default set so go to the fly-out menu and choose Symbols from the list.

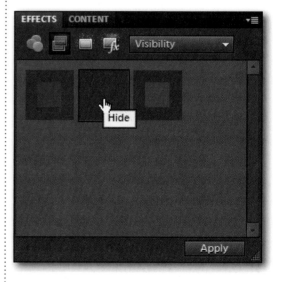

4 We can't use the opacity control to remove the color as we'd have to drop it to 0%, which would also remove the bevel. Instead, go back to the Styles panel and choose Visibility from the Layer Styles menu. From the three available options, double-click Hide.

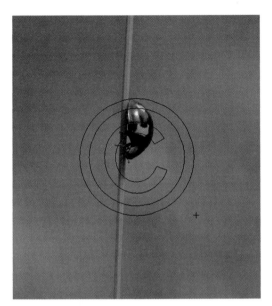

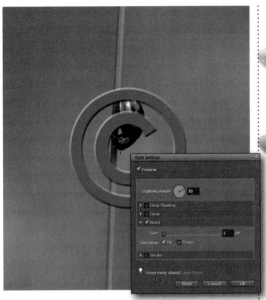

2 Holding *Shift* to retain the shape's proportions, click and drag out the shape. Make sure as much of the important detail is covered; if we also hold the spacebar, we can move it into the correct position. Here, it's just the insect that matters so we've scaled the symbol down to suit.

3 Don't worry about the color as it will be removed later. We'll give it some styling: from the Effects panel, select Layer Styles and choose Bevels. Double-click Simple Sharp Outer. It's too large so we'll double-click the layer style icon to open the settings and reduce the size slightly.

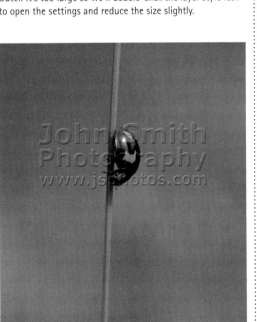

5 We've removed all the color but kept the layer style. This lets us see the image without too much obstruction but also makes sure we protect it from being used without our consent. It would be difficult and time-consuming to restore the image convincingly, and more-so on a complex image.

6 We're not restricted to simple shapes, of course. We can also use text: here we've used the company name and its website address; now it becomes a passive advertisement as well as preventing theft. As it's using live text and styles, it can easily be altered, too.

SHORTCUTS

The power of adjustment

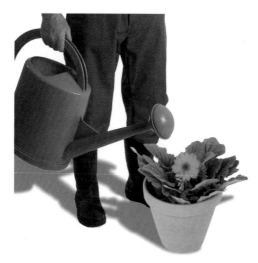

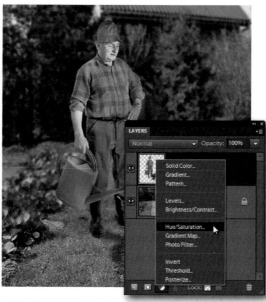

1 Our image comprises two layers: the garden background and the man watering the plant. Make sure the gardener layer is active by clicking its thumbnail. Click the split circle icon at the bottom of the Layers panel and select Hue/Saturation from the Adjustments menu.

WHEN YOU APPLY AN ADJUSTMENT such as Levels to an image, the affected pixels are permanently altered. If at a later stage you decide you no longer want that effect, unless you made a backup, you have a problem. It would, of course, be really helpful if you could create the same effect but have the ability to turn it on and off, alter its settings and have it apply to only certain areas of the image and, most importantly, be able to return to the image at any stage to do so. With Adjustment Layers you can do just that. Anything beneath them in the layer stack will be affected unless, of course, you don't want it to be. They are just like regular layers. You can alter their opacity and change the blend mode. Most importantly, however, they can be toggled on and off, disabling the effect.

In the following tutorial we'll use a Hue/Saturation Adjustment Layer to remove the color from the entire image, and then from only a single layer.

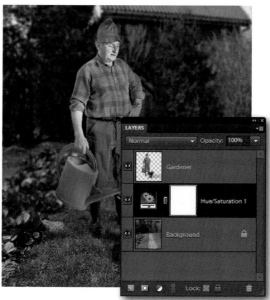

4 If we wanted to reverse the effect, having the gardener in color and the background in black and white, we simply need to drag the Adjustment Layer down between the two layers. The color is restored to the gardener's layer as it is now above the Adjustment Layer.

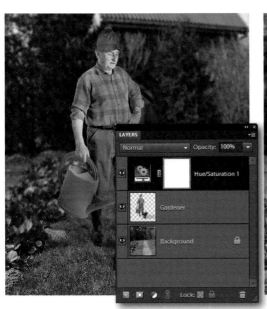

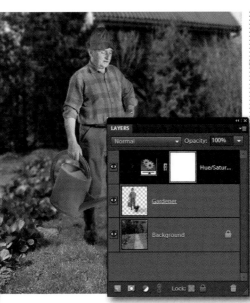

2 Drag the Saturation slider to 0 in the Adjustments panel. This has removed all the color from both the gardener and the background as it sits above both layers. As we can see from their thumbnails, the layers beneath are physically unaffected and still have their color.

3 If we wanted the adjustment to only affect the gardener, we can create what is known as a clipping group (more about these in the next chapter). Make sure the Adjustment Layer is highlighted. Now press *ctrl* G ⌘ G. The background is now unaffected and its color has returned.

HOT TIP

You can use Adjustment Layers to make temporary alterations to an image. For example, you may be having difficulty selecting and separating your subject from its background because there are areas of low contrast or it's simply too dark in places. Create a Brightness/ Contrast Adjustment Layer above it. You can take the values to their extremes for the duration of the task. Afterwards, you can simply turn the layer off or discard it completely.

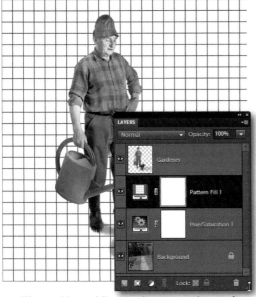

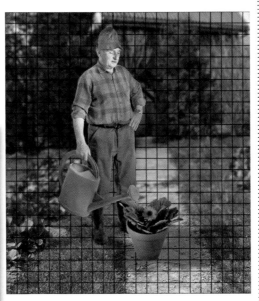

5 We can add more Adjustment Layers to our image, of course. Here, for example, we've added a pattern fill layer that gives us a black and white grid. It's still beneath the gardener's layer so he appears above it. Being a solid layer, it covers up the original background.

6 We can change the blend mode of the Adjustment Layer. We've set the pattern layer's mode to Multiply which makes the white areas transparent, allowing us to see through to the background. We've also edited the original Hue/Saturation layer, setting it to Colorize with a green hue.

SHORTCUTS
MAC WIN BOTH

37

Exploring blend modes

EVEN IF YOU'VE NEVER USED THEM you will no doubt be familiar with the term 'blend modes'. These determine how layers interact with the other layers in the artwork. In our example, we'll change the graffiti layer's mode which will affect the way it blends with the wall, our background layer. There isn't space to show every mode but the examples should serve as a guide; the results you get will vary greatly depending on the colors and tones of the component layers in your image.

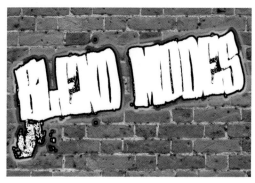

1 The default is Normal. Technically this isn't really a blend mode at all as the top layer does not interact with the base layer, apart from its transparency. Almost all layer types can use blend modes. Individual tools such as the paint brush and gradients use them as well.

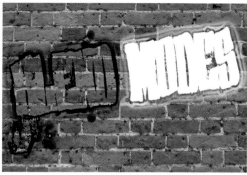

4 Here we have Multiply on the left and Screen on the right. Multiply produces rich, darker tones. Again, white has no effect and is cancelled out. The opposite, Screen, produces a much brighter blend. White is completely opaque. Any black in the image has no effect and is not displayed.

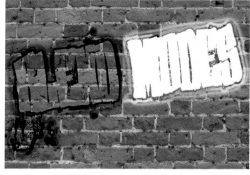

5 Color Burn (left) and Color Dodge (right) produce similar results to Multiply and Screen. The colors, however, appear far more exaggerated using these modes. Following on from these are Linear Burn and Linear Dodge (not shown). These produce slightly stronger results.

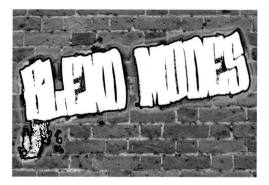

8 Hard Light, Vivid Light (shown here on the left) and Linear Light all produce strong color tones, Linear being the deepest. Pin Light (right) uses the tones of the base image to shift the color of the top layer, depending on lightness. 50% gray is invisible in all of these modes.

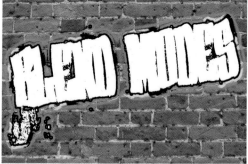

9 Hard Mix limits the blending image to eight colors – white, black, red, green, blue, yellow, cyan, and magenta; the mix depends on the blending colors of both layers. This produces a result similar to that of posterize. It is a brash, aliased effect and therefore has limited use.

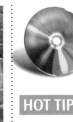

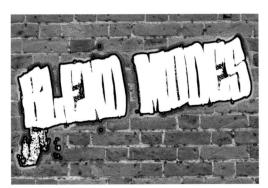

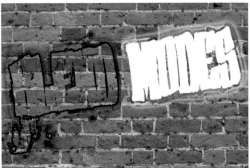

2 This is Dissolve. On a crisp, fully opaque image this mode has no effect. However, when you add some blur or start to lower the opacity, random pixels will start to disappear. The more the image is blurred, the stronger the effect becomes. You can see this on the sprayed green edge.

3 On the left we have Darken. This blends any pixels that are lighter than the wall: white becomes transparent. There's little change in the color. On the right is its counterpart, Lighten. This has the opposite effect, blending where the wall is darker. The color is a little washed out.

Because using blend modes can produce very different results depending on the number of blended layers, their tonal values and many other factors, it's often easier to cycle through the individual modes until you find one that fits the effect you're looking for. There's a keyboard shortcut for this: press Shift + to drill down the list and Shift − to drill up. Make sure you're not in one of the painting modes as that will result in changing the mode for that tool, rather than the layer.

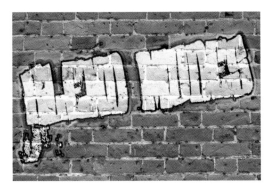

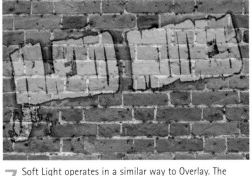

6 This is Overlay. It's a combination of Multiply and Screen. It darkens lighter pixels and vice versa. In areas of midtones there is little or no effect, 50% gray being completely invisible. The highlight and shadows are retained, giving it a slightly blown out appearance.

7 Soft Light operates in a similar way to Overlay. The difference being it combines Darken and Lighten. As you can see, this produces a somewhat muted blend. This mode is often used for creating reflections because of its already slightly translucent qualities.

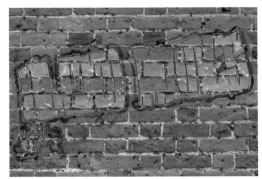

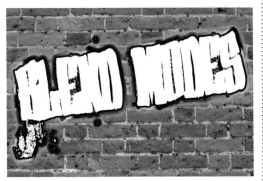

10 In Difference mode color is subtracted from either the base layer or the blend layer, depending on brightness. Pure white inverts the blending colors; black has no effect. This can be used for comparing images for slight changes. Exclusion (not shown) gives a less contrasted effect.

11 The four remaining modes: Hue, Saturation, Color, and Luminosity, work by combining the named attribute of the top layer with the remaining two attributes (excluding Color) from the base layer. Here we have Luminosity, which discards the color, leaving only the layer's brightness values.

SHORTCUTS
MAC WIN BOTH

Banqueting arrangements

A FEATURE INTRODUCED in Elements 5 was the ability to automatically align and distribute layers within the document. In earlier versions, this would have needed to be done by hand, either by sight alone or by setting up and aligning to a grid – a somewhat messy business. Now you can accurately space out and arrange components evenly across your artwork with just a few clicks of the mouse. This is great for making precise designs such as navigation bars on web pages or for laying out and ordering text and images for scrapbook pages.

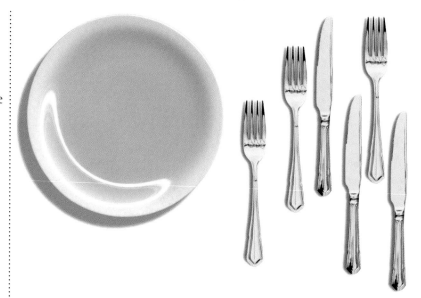

1 Here we have the all the pieces of our place setting on separate layers. We could, of course, select and position each individual layer manually, but this is time consuming and not altogether accurate. Instead, let's make use of

Elements' ability to select and work with multiple layers simultaneously. By grouping the sets of cutlery together we can then use the new Align/ Distribute feature of the Move tool to space them out neatly either side of the plate.

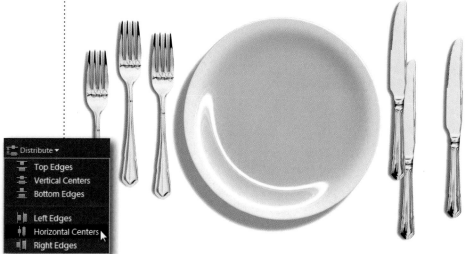

3 Now we can space the cutlery out. The Distribute function works by spacing the central layer(s) evenly between the two outer ones. Start by arranging the knives and forks into two rough groups. The forks have already

been tidied in the example. Select all the knives by holding ctrl ⌘ and clicking on their name labels. Now click the Horizontal Centers option in the Distribution menu. They will now all be evenly spaced out.

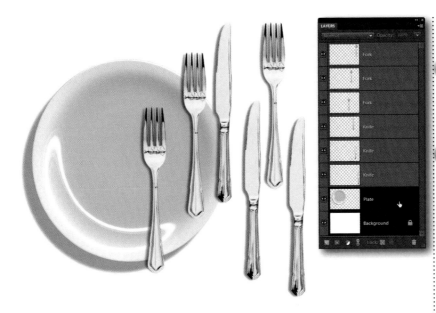

2 The first task is to bring the plate into the center of the canvas. Select the Move tool 🅥. Click the background layer in the Layers panel to make it active. Now hold *ctrl* ⌘. Click on the plate layer's name (not the thumbnail) to group the two layers. Start by selecting Horizontal Centers from the Align menu in the Options toolbar. This will shift the plate across to the middle. Now use the Vertical Centers option to move it down.

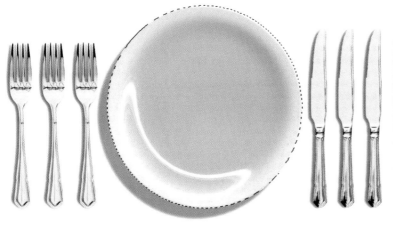
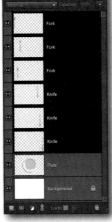

4 Press *ctrl* ⌘ and click the plate layer's thumbnail to load its selection. Now group all the cutlery layers together. You can do this by holding *ctrl* ⌘ and dragging a bounding box across the document to encompass the knives. You'll see the layers highlighted in the panel. Release the mouse and do the same for the forks. Go back to the Align menu. This time select Bottom Edges. All the cutlery will move down to align with the bottom of the plate.

HOT TIP

You can also align layers to selections as well. We've used this method in the final step to match the cutlery to the baseline of the plate. If we had only used a layer group, everything would have been aligned to the base of the entire document.

SHORTCUTS
MAC WIN BOTH

41

Cut-up collage

WE CAN USE LAYERS to create interesting image effects too. The British artist, David Hockney, creates artworks by taking photos of his subject in sections, he then assembles them in a slightly offset arrangement. The result is a slightly abstract version of the original scene.

We can recreate this effect from a single image by slicing it into several layered sections that we can rotate and reposition. To make sure our sections are of equal sizes, we'll use one of the less prominent new features of Elements 8, user-defined guides. We can specify the exact position of the guides as units of measurement (inches, picas, etc.) or as a percentage of the document's dimensions, which we'll be using in this project. Once defined, we can use the snap-to feature to create perfect selections to slice up our photo.

If you're using an earlier version, you can still create the guides using a different method: see pages 224-225.

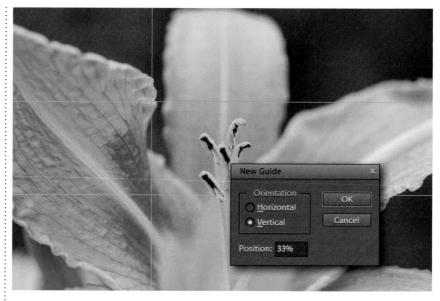

1 We'll begin by creating our guides. For this project we'll divide it up into a simple 3x3 grid. Go to View > New Guide. We'll leave the orientation on Vertical to start with. Type 33% (one third of the image) in the Position box and click OK. Create another new guide, this time setting the Position to 66% (two thirds). This gives us three columns. Repeat the process of 33% increments, but this time set the orientation to horizontal to create the three rows.

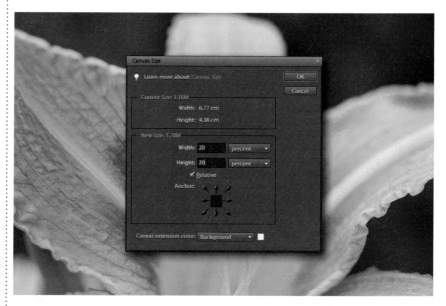

3 We've finished with the guides now so we can remove them. Go to View > Clear Guides. We also need to add some extra working space to the document to enable us to rotate and move the pieces around. Go to Image > Resize > Canvas Size. Make sure Relative is checked. Set both the width and height to 20% and click OK. Now Select the Move tool **V**. Make sure Auto Select Layer and Show Bounding Box are enabled in the Options toolbar.

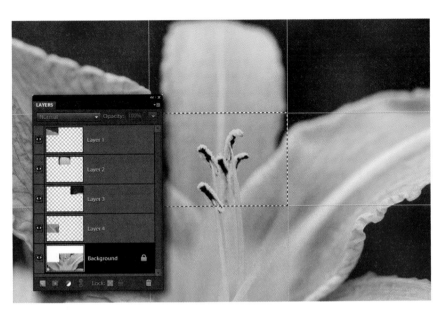

2 Make sure Snap To > Guides is set in the View menu. Grab the Rectangular Marquee tool **M**. Click and drag the selection out in the top-left corner of the image. It will snap to the guides and document edges. Press *ctrl* *Shift* *J*

⌘ *Shift* *J* to cut the selection to a new layer. Click the background layer to make it active again. Make a selection in the next section and cut it. Repeat this for each piece, remembering to switch back to the background each time.

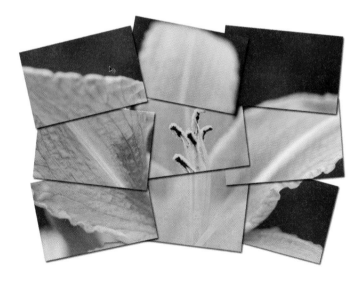

4 Click to select one of the layers. Move the cursor outside of the bounding box until it becomes a curved arrow. Click and drag to rotate it. Press *Enter* to accept the change. Move to another section, click again to select the layer and

rotate it. Repeat this for the whole image. We can also go back and move the pieces around to fill some of the gaps. Finally we can add a small Drop Shadow layer style to each of the pieces to make them appear more three-dimensional.

HOT TIP

Instead of having to specify that the value is a percentage each time you create a new guide, you can change the default unit of measurement by opening the Info panel (Window > Info) and clicking the little disclosure arrow next to the crosshair icon. You'll get a menu showing all the available units. Select percent and you'll now only have to type the value in the box without the percentage sign. This works for most tools and also the Status Bar at the bottom of the document window.

SHORTCUTS
MAC WIN BOTH

43

Keep up, no slacking

THERE'S ONLY ONE THING FASTER than the speed of light: the computer industry. It seems that no sooner do you remove the shrink-wrap from your software or prize the new PC from its snug Styrofoam packaging, than you expect to see a little fortune cookie-style note congratulating you on your purchase being out of date. That groaning, creaking sound you hear becoming progressively louder is not your antiquated computer about to keel over in a spectacular shower of sparks, but the heavy cogs of the corporate machine trundling toward you, decimating all but the newest of technologies in its path.

As with the fashion industry, it seems you're nobody unless you're first in line for this season's must have accessory. As the glossy adverts in magazines will imply and the even glossier sales people in computer stores will tell you (the prospect of a sales commission instantly makes you an expert, of course), your current system is already half way to the scrap heap and not fit for anything other than being the basis for a retro art statement.

You should not be too despairing of the seemingly decrepit piece of hardware chugging away beneath your desk, or that your copy of Whizz-Bang 3000 Professional Gold Edition SP5 is now 'so last Tuesday'. Before you rush out to part with a month's salary, you have to ask yourself: *is it good enough for my purposes and, if it lacks a certain area of functionality, can I achieve the same thing in a different way?* Unless the latest hardware or software is offering something completely revolutionary, the answer will almost certainly be yes.

There will, of course, come the time where an upgrade is necessary. Perhaps support for your current operating system is being dropped and its replacement will not run efficiently on your computer. It may also be that certain components, such as graphics cards, need replacing. This doesn't involve replacing the whole system.

Ask anybody in the world of digital imaging – unless they're trying to sell you a completely new computer – what, above all, are the most important system components and you'll generally get the same answer: memory and hard disk space. Even if you have the latest AMTEL liquid-cooled, 50 megagiga-googleplex processor, it is still very much at the mercy of these two commodities. The computer needs memory to run the graphics program itself and store the image(s) you are currently working on, not to mention everything else that's going on in the background. Adobe recommends 1Gb+ for the current version of Elements to run smoothly. The more complex the document becomes, however, the more memory it needs to use to hold that information. Images can often bloat out to hundreds of megabytes in size, especially when you start creating multiple layers. Add to that the history (undo) states and the space used by copying and pasting to the clipboard and you'll soon be pushing the resources to their limits.

There's no way to second-guess how much memory you will need. Presently the average PC comes with around 1-2 Gb which is ample for most tasks. When the system starts running low on physical memory, it starts to free it up by using virtual memory, referred to as 'scratch' space in Elements. This is a temporary area on the hard disk set aside for storing the overflow. Think of it as writing things down on a scrap of paper when you begin to become overwhelmed with information. This is where you need to make sure you have a large enough hard disk. Remember, the operating system, programs and your data all share this space. If it's full to bursting, trying to cram in this transient file will at best slow things down to a crawl; at worst it can cause the program (or the entire system) to crash, taking whatever you are working on with it.

Enhancing your system needn't be expensive. A large external hard drive will set you back around $100-200; you just plug them in and they're ready to go with no fuss. An internal drive could be half that amount. You can add an extra gigabyte of memory for less than $50. If you're not technically minded and unwilling to delve into the arcane world that is the inside of your computer, there will usually be someone you know who can help. If not, there will be no shortage of people advertising in the classified section of the newspaper who will be able to do the work – usually for a reasonable price, too. If it keeps you up and running for a year or two more, it's certainly money well spent.

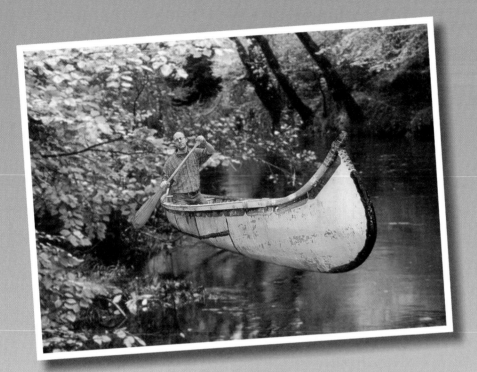

■ This photograph of a man rowing has been removed from its original background and placed into a tranquil river setting. It looks far more part of the scene when it's partially hidden behind the foliage; that, and the reflection in the water, really bring the scene to life.

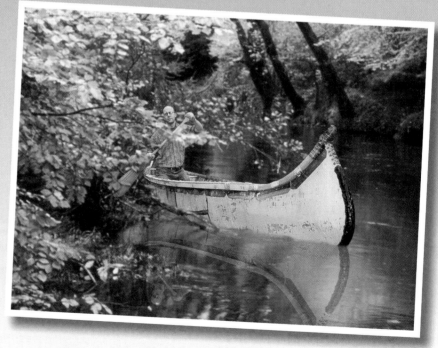

3 Hiding and showing

CREATING EFFECTIVE PHOTOMONTAGES is all about making layers interact with each other. And more often than not, this entails making layers partially hidden behind existing objects in the scene.

The standard way to do this is to erase the parts you don't want. But this is an irrevocable step; instead, we'll look at the tools that give Elements users some of the power of Photoshop CS5, with the ability to selectively hide and show regions of layers.

We'll also see how to blend layers together in a convincing manner, and how to arrange our montages so that they look that bit more convincing.

Exploring layer masks

ELEMENTS 9 sees the very welcome addition of custom layer masks; previously they have only been available when using Adjustment Layers.

If you're not familiar with the concept, a mask allows us to selectively hide areas of a layer non-destructively, as unlike the eraser, we can restore the hidden parts whenever we want.

As we'll see here, and in the rest of the book, masks have many practical uses and are an essential part of the montage artist's repertoire.

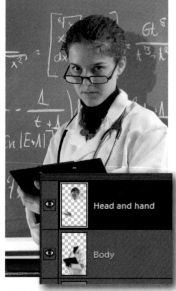

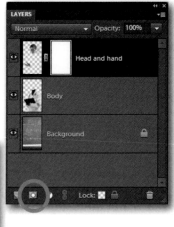

1 This medical scientist has been experimenting with invisibility. We'll see how masks can make her disappear. To begin, we've placed her head and hands on a separate layer.

2 Make sure the head and hands layer is active by clicking its thumbnail. Now click the Add Layer Mask icon at the bottom of the Layers panel. We won't see any change yet.

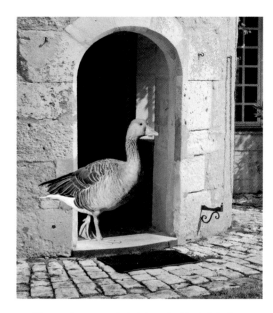

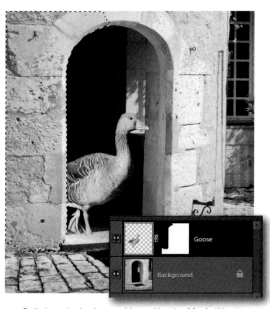

1 We can also use masks to integrate objects into the image. Here we have a goose in a doorway. It's not particularly convincing, as it appears to be both in front and behind the entrance at the same time. We can use a mask to hide the goose where it should be inside the building.

2 Switch to the background layer. Use the Magic Wand or Quick Selection tool to make a selection around the left side of the doorway. Click the goose layer's thumbnail. Now go to Layer > Layer Mask > Hide Selection. This creates a mask and fills it based on the selection we made.

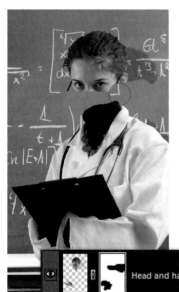

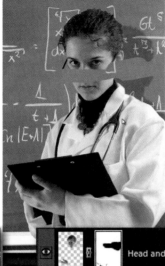

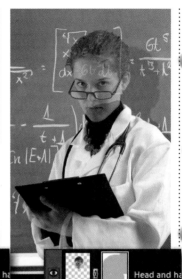

3 Make sure we're working on the Layer Mask. Grab a large black brush. When we paint over the woman's hands and head they vanish. We can see the areas showing up on the mask.

4 If we switch the foreground color to white, we can start to paint the areas back in again. Here we've brought her hand and mouth back. The image is never affected directly.

5 Masks work on grayscale shades. Black is completely transparent, white is totally opaque. If, then, we choose a mid-gray we get something in between: a ghostly transition.

HOT TIP

We can quickly clear a mask by selecting the whole document, *ctrl* A ⌘ A, and filling it with white. We could also have done this in the last step of the invisible woman but used gray. The mask only affects the layer it's attached to.

If you don't have Elements 9 you won't have layer masks in this form. There are two workarounds on the DVD in the Old Techniques folder.

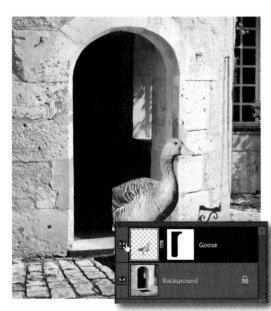

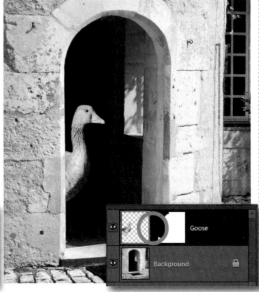

3 Although we have added the mask to the goose layer, because it fills the space taken up by the doorway it gives the appearance that the goose is behind the wall. If we move the goose, however, we have a problem. As we can see, the mask moves as well leaving the poor goose tailless.

4 We'll undo the previous move step. Between the goose's thumbnail and the mask is a small chain icon. If we click it, it disappears. This means the mask is no longer linked to the image. Now we can move our goose and the mask stays in place. Here we've moved it further inside the doorway.

SHORTCUTS
MAC WIN BOTH

Smudge masking

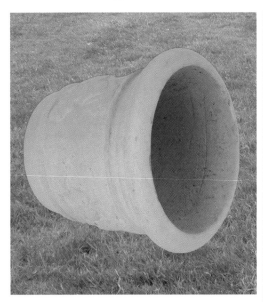

S O FAR, WE'VE LOOKED AT CREATING and editing layer masks by painting on them with the Brush tool. It works well: we can paint on a layer's mask to hide and show the object it's attached to.

But we can use any of the painting tools, not just the brush. Here, we'll look at how we can use the Smudge tool to create a convincing grass effect, using a technique that's far easier than painting each blade.

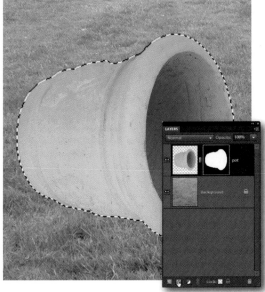

1 Make sure you are working on the pot layer. Hold *ctrl* ⌘ and click on the pot's thumbnail to load up its selection. Click the Add Layer Mask icon at the bottom of the Layers panel. The selection ensures that only the area around the pot is masked. We don't see any change yet, of course!

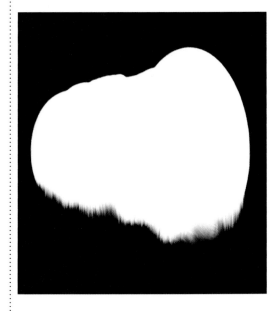

4 Here's how the finished layer's mask looks on its own. Smudging the mask in from the edges in this way is very much easier than painting the mask, as the smudging creates a natural, fading look that matches the growth style of the grass.

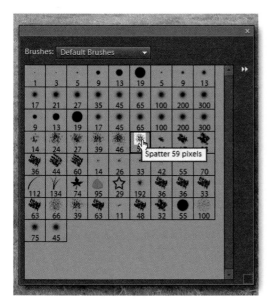

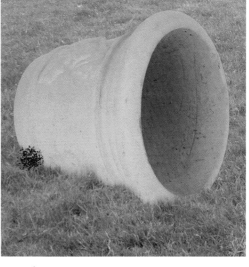

2 Select the Smudge tool **R** from the toolbox. Go to the brush picker in the Options bar and select one of the spatter brushes. Now set the tool's strength to somewhere around 60-70%; this controls how much of the area is affected with each stroke.

3 Pick an area at the base of the pot and start making short upward strokes with the brush. What we're doing is dragging the mask over the pot which starts to reveal the grass beneath, making it look as though it's growing up around the pot. Continue around to complete the effect.

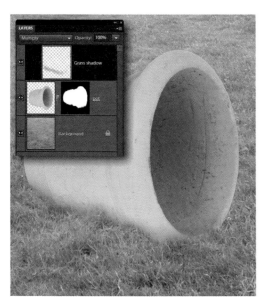

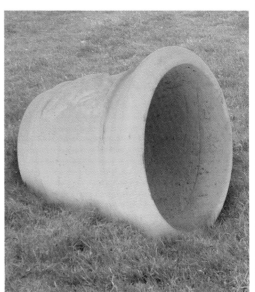

5 Now let's add some shading. Make a new layer above the pot, press *ctrl* **G** ⌘ **G** to group it with the pot; set the layer's blend mode to Multiply. Now sample a dark color from inside the pot with the Eye-dropper **I**, and use a soft-edged brush to paint shadows on the pot's lower edges.

6 Finally, make a new layer above the grass. This is where we'll paint the shadows cast by the pot. Use a soft-edged brush again, with black as the foreground color. Set the brush to a low opacity, and build up the shadow behind the pot in small stages until it looks convincing.

HOT TIP

Try changing the size of the brush to vary the density of the grass clumps. To make finer areas with only a few strands, use the outer edge of a fairly large brush, dragging up from the very edge of the mask.
If you are not happy with the way an area looks, simply reverse the stroke, using the brush to push the area back down again.

SHORTCUTS

51

On golden pond

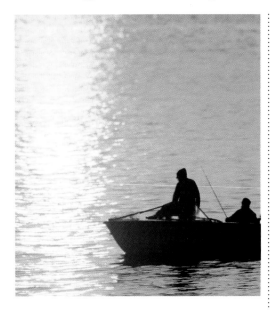

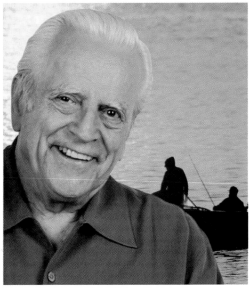

1 Having chosen our background, the next step is to place our figure in front of it. Since he's the main figure in our composition, make him as large as possible within the frame, while leaving space top right for a caption.

BLENDING TWO IMAGES TOGETHER is a technique that has many uses. Here, we'll look at a specialized use: making a composite of a man with his favorite hobby.

It's a technique that's reminiscent of the poster for the Henry Fonda movie, *On Golden Pond* – and that's why we've chosen this particular subject.

Blending the portrait into the background is straightforward enough, using the techniques outlined earlier in this chapter. But what makes this image work is blending the color as well, rather than simply relying on the colors in the original pictures. This is the secret to creating a montage that looks unified, rather than two disparate elements.

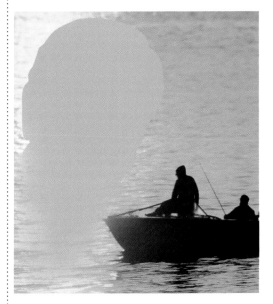

4 By default, a Solid Color Adjustment Layer appears as the current foreground color: black in the example. Changing this to a warm orange better suits the background. As we can see, because the Adjustment Layer is grouped with the figure, it only shows up where it overlaps the man.

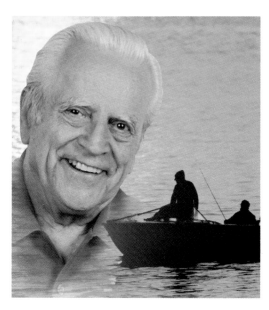

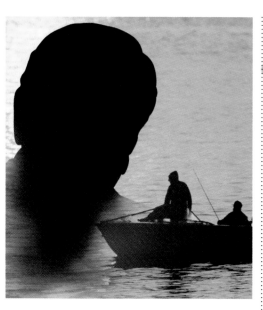

2 To fade him out, make sure his layer is active by clicking the thumbnail in the Layers panel, then create a layer mask. Use the Brush tool to paint in black on the mask to hide the layer, and paint in white to reveal it again. We'll paint out around his shirt, leaving his face intact.

3 At the end of the previous step, our image was working well as a composition, but the color didn't match the warm orange glow of the background. Create a new Solid Color Adjustment Layer using the pop-up menu at the top of the Layers panel, and group it with the figure layer.

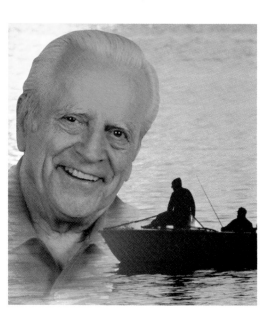

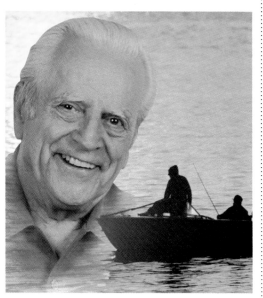

5 In order to be able to see the man through the Solid Color, we need to change the layer's mode from Normal to Multiply. Now we can see the man clearly, and the color is having its effect. But it's much too strong: we need to lower the opacity of the layer.

6 Taking the opacity of the Solid Color layer down to 50% gives us the effect we want. He now has a coloring that matches the background far more closely: the two separate images are now unified into a single montage that works as a whole.

HOT TIP

By creating a layer mask in step 2, rather than simply erasing the figure around the boat, we have the flexibility we need to move him around and adjust the mask as required. It's important that the man doesn't hide the prow of the boat, for example, but needs to wrap around it smoothly. This would be hard to achieve by simply erasing parts of the layer.

Hiding and showing

Part of the scene

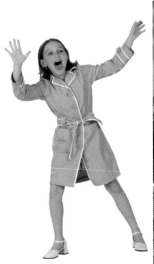

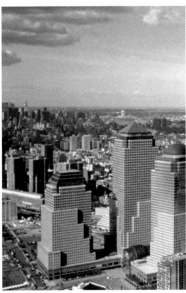

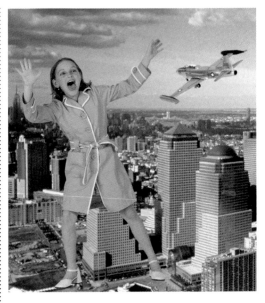

BIG KIDS, LITTLE KIDS: how about giant kids? It's easy to turn a straightforward photograph into a King Kong creation by simply changing the background and adding a plane or two.

But we can go further than this. Placing a child in front of a scene may be the first step, but it's a long way from the finished montage. The trick is to bring picture elements from the background in front of any people or objects we've placed in the scene. By doing this, we're integrating our placed items in such a way as to make them appear to be genuinely part of the background, rather than merely floating on top. It makes all the difference between a straightforward montage, and a truly compelling scene.

1 We've placed the girl on the view of New York, and her feet fit neatly into the space in front of the buildings; the toy plane has been added to give her something to look at. But we can integrate her into the scene better than this.

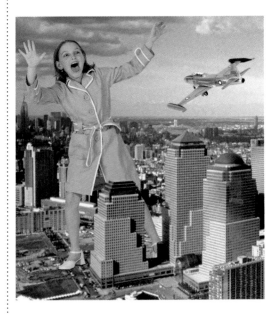

4 In the last step, we left part of the girl's shoe showing beneath the new buildings layer, so we need to move her up. Judge where she fits best within this scene, positioning her so that her feet seem to be firmly planted behind the buildings.

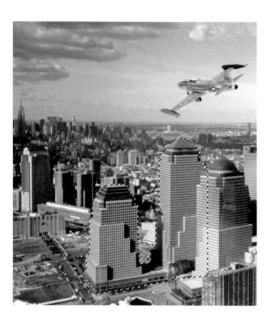

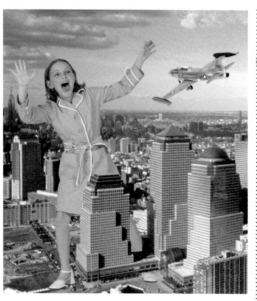

2 Hide the girl's layer, and make a selection of the two buildings in the middle. With straight edges such as this, the Polygonal Lasso tool works best; you can also hold *alt* with the regular Lasso to trace straight lines.

3 Make the buildings' layer active and create a new layer using *ctrl* J ⌘ J. Move this layer above the girl's layer, so that she appears behind the buildings. She now looks like she's in the middle of the buildings.

HOT TIP

This trick of moving background elements to the front will help in just about any kind of montage. If there aren't any suitable background objects that can be 'promoted' in this way, then create your own: an out-of-focus bush, for example, can help an outdoor montage to look that much more realistic.

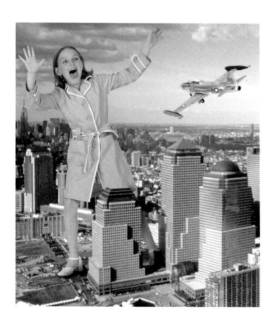

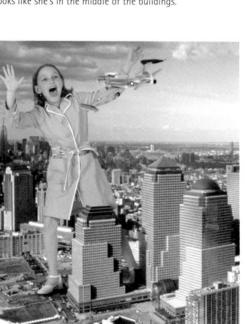

5 To integrate her further, we need to add some shadows. First, on a new layer, paint shadows beneath her foot on the ground below. Then make another layer just above the girl, grouped with her layer; paint shadows here on her leg, as if the building is adding shading to it.

6 Finally, we can move the plane so it's right in her line of sight. Also, by positioning it slightly in front of her hand, we further help to create the illusion that she's really standing in the middle of downtown New York, batting away an attacking air force.

SHORTCUTS
MAC WIN BOTH

Polaroid-style photos

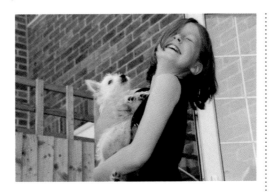

POLAROID INSTANT CAMERAS may be somewhat out of favor since digital photography became so accessible, but the familiar shape of the photos they produce remains a popular way of framing images, particularly if you're looking to create a retro theme.

The following tutorial serves not only to explain the steps to create a great Polaroid effect, but also demonstrates the use of clipping groups to crop a photo down to fit the frame; this gives us the freedom to position, scale and rotate the image within the window before commiting to any permanent changes.

1 Start by opening up the paper background file from the DVD. Create a new layer by pressing `ctrl` `alt` `Shift` `N` `⌘` `⌥` `Shift` `N`. Now use the Rectangular Marquee tool `M` to mark out the shape of the frame. Fill the selection with white. Press `ctrl` `D` `⌘` `D` to deselect.

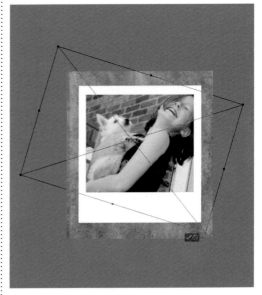

4 Press `ctrl` `T` `⌘` `T` to enter Free Transform. The image is quite large so you'll need to zoom out to see the whole of the bounding box. Now you can scale and rotate the photo within the frame – remember to keep the proportions constrained so it doesn't become distorted.

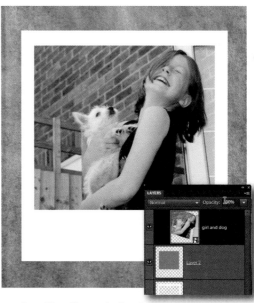

2 Draw an almost square selection inside the frame and offset it towards the top. Press *ctrl* *Shift* *J* *⌘* *Shift* *J* to create a new layer from the selection. We've filled the new layer with 50% gray here to make it visible, as it is also white, but this is not necessary for the technique.

3 Go to File > Place and select the Girl and Dog file from the DVD. Press *Enter* to accept the default size, we'll be able to alter it later. Now press *ctrl* *G* *⌘* *G* to create a clipping group with the smaller layer beneath. Now we can only see that portion of the photo.

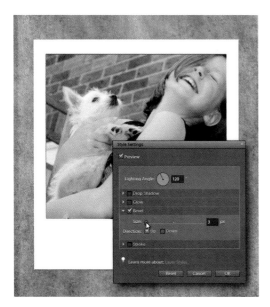

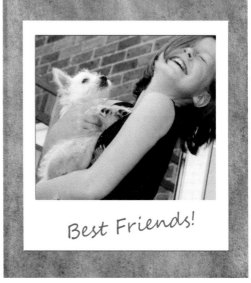

Best Friends!

5 Polaroid photos are thicker than normal prints so we'll add a Bevel layer style. Click the white frame layer's thumbnail to make it active, and apply the Simple Inner Bevel. The default is too large so open the Style Settings dialog and adjust the bevel's size to suit.

6 To finish off the effect a texture has been applied to the frame using the Texturizer filter. Setting the texture to canvas with a very low relief gives us a rough but subtle effect, breaking up the solid white. A text layer has also been added; that's why the extra space is there, after all.

HOT TIP

You don't, of course, have to leave the Polaroid image square on the page once it's complete: multi-select the component layers (or link them if you have an older version of the program) and use Free Transform to make further changes. This way you still have the option to edit the text or adjust the photo a little.

SHORTCUTS
MAC WIN BOTH

Spectacular fireworks

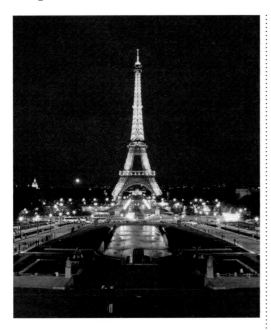

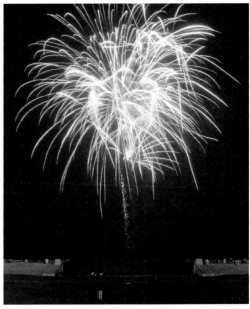

FIREWORK DISPLAYS ARE FANTASTIC to watch but notoriously difficult to photograph, especially when there are other elements in the scene to consider; the camera has to be perfectly steady to prevent the foreground from becoming horribly blurred – not to mention the problem of timing the shot to capture the moment at its best.

With Elements, of course, we can add our own pyrotechnic delights. Although merging something as complex as fireworks into a photo might seem like an arduous task, it's surprisingly simple: using a blend mode to knock out the dark areas, allowing the background to show through, enables us to place the fireworks into the scene precisely where we want them.

1 We've placed our first firework into the scene which has, of course, hidden most of the background. There's far too much going on to be able to select it or mask it out, and lowering the opacity would cause it to become washed out.

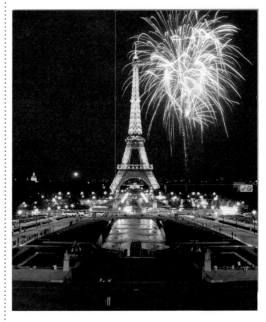

4 The firework is too large so press *ctrl* T ⌘ T to invoke Free Transform; now you can position and scale the firework down so it fits into the scene – remember to hold *Shift* to ensure the image remains in proportion.

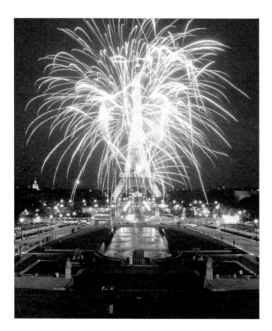

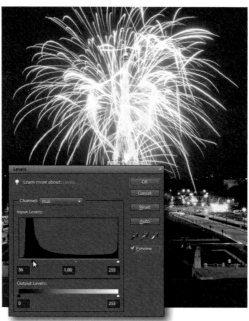

2 The layer's background is almost black so we can use the Screen blend mode to filter it out, leaving just the bright areas of the firework visible. This gives us an almost perfect result with no harsh contrasting edges.

3 We can see the background is still visible against the original photo. Open the Levels dialog *ctrl* *L* *⌘* *L* and drag the Shadows slider in from the left a little; you'll see the light area at the bottom begin to disappear.

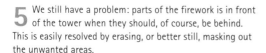

5 We still have a problem: parts of the firework is in front of the tower when they should, of course, be behind. This is easily resolved by erasing, or better still, masking out the unwanted areas.

6 We've placed some additional fireworks to balance the image. Whilst we could have filled more of the sky, in this instance, we want to complement the scene, rather than totally drawing focus from it.

HOT TIP

If you're creating your firework display over a scene with an expanse of water or another shiny surface, you'll need to remember to add a suitable reflection for the fireworks as well. See Chapter 10 for more details.

SHORTCUTS
MAC WIN BOTH

59

Fairy gets her wings

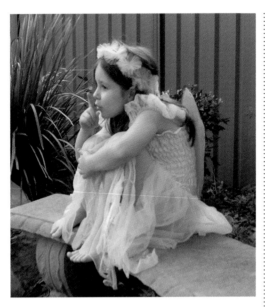

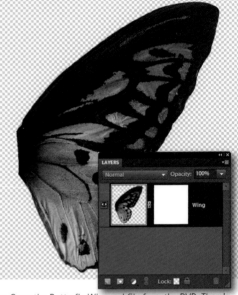

1 Open the Butterfly Wing psd file from the DVD. There's already a layer mask in place. It's important to have the mask as part of the image like this, rather than using the adjustment layer method, as that would make manipulating the image too difficult later on.

CHILDREN LOVE DRESSING UP: either to mimic the latest movie or television characters or just to play a part in their own imagination-fuelled fantasies. With Elements at our disposal, however, we can take things a stage further and turn their fantasy into something more realistic; albeit pictorially, of course.

The following project is split into two sections: in this first part, we'll be concentrating on creating her wings. For this we'll use a layer mask to make the wings transparent. As we'll see, this gives us far more control as we are able to change the opacity selectively, rather than acting on the whole image as we would with layer opacity or blend modes.

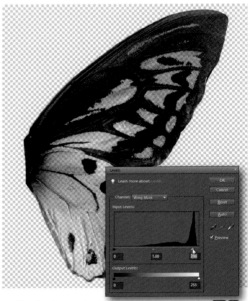

4 Keeping the mask active, open the Levels dialog *ctrl L* ⌘ *L*. We'll begin by dragging the Highlights slider in from the right. This increases the brighter areas of the mask which makes the black of the wings more solid but leaves the colored areas almost unaltered.

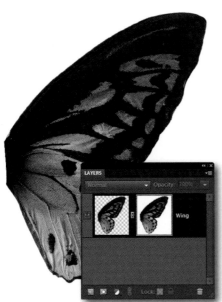

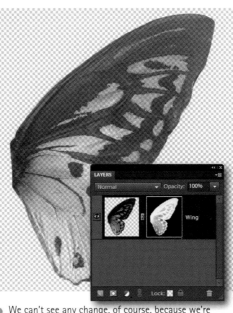

2 Select the entire image using *ctrl A ⌘ A*. Press *ctrl C ⌘ C* to copy the image to the clipboard. Now hold *alt ⌥* and click the mask's thumbnail. We're now working on the mask itself. Press *ctrl V ⌘ V* to paste the image in. Now deselect *ctrl D ⌘ D*.

3 We can't see any change, of course, because we're looking at the mask. Click the image thumbnail again; we can see that most of the image is hidden. Click the mask thumbnail again and press *ctrl I ⌘ I* to invert it. Now most of the mask is lighter and we can see the wing again.

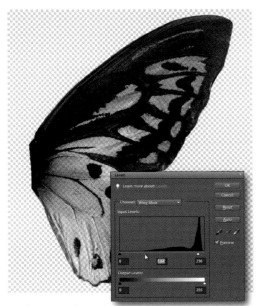

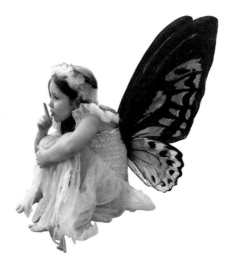

5 To change the opacity of the colored areas, we use the Midtone slider. Dragging to the left makes them more solid, to the right more transparent. We could also affect the whole image using the Output Levels slider: dragging from left to right to make it more solid and vice versa.

6 Now we can add them to our fairy. We've cut her away from the background and added some space so we can fit the wings in. The wing layer has been duplicated then distorted to fit with Free Transform. One layer is in front of the girl with a small part erased to fit her body.

Extending the scene

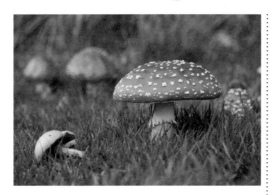

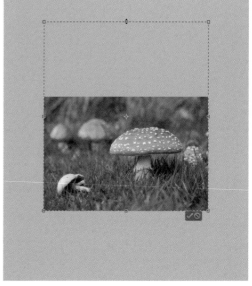

INDING THE PERFECT IMAGE for a montage isn't always easy and you can waste many hours trying. Unless you go out to take your own, specifically with the idea in mind, there will doubtless be something that means it doesn't fit exactly as you intended.

Our project image is a case in point: it's a wonderful image of some toadstools, ideal for our fairy image. The trouble is there isn't enough space to comfortably fit the fairy on the main toadstool. We need to increase the height of the photo – for this we'll use the much overlooked ability of the Crop tool to expand the area of a photo. We will, of course, need to fill in the additional space we have created; we could use the Clone Stamp tool but there is not much to work with in the background and the result would look messy. Instead, we'll bring another photo into the image and blend it in with a layer mask.

1 Grab the Crop tool **C**. Zoom the image out so we have some space around the photo. Click and drag the crop boundary around the entire image. Now drag the top-center handle up to mark out the additional space. Once applied, the area is filled with the background color.

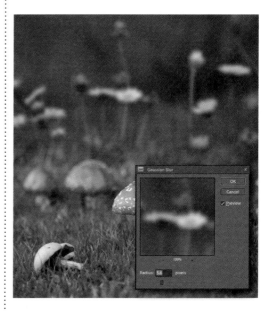

4 We need to match the focus of the original image. Make sure we're working on the image by clicking its layer thumbnail. Open the Gaussian Blur filter, check that Preview is enabled. Now start to move the slider to the right, visually comparing the two photos until it looks realistic.

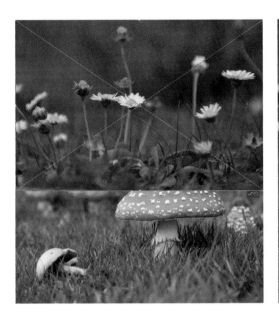

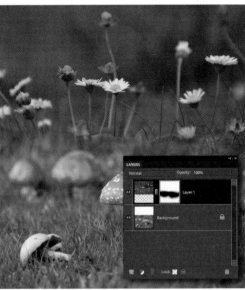

2 From the File menu, select Place and locate the file Daisies.jpg on the DVD. The image is automatically scaled to fit. Click and drag the new image to the top of the document. Press *Enter* to set it down, then select Simplify Layer from the Layers menu to convert it to a regular layer.

3 We obviously need to blend in that harsh edge. Add a layer mask to the new layer by clicking the mask icon. Once it's in place we can start to paint away the area of the mask where the two images overlap. Paint in black using a large soft brush so we get a good, seamless blend.

HOT TIP

It's a good idea to turn off the option of resizing windows when you zoom in and out, as it saves you having to manually drag the window in order to see the space around the image. Press *ctrl* *K* *⌘* *K* to enter the General Preferences then uncheck Zoom Resizes Windows.

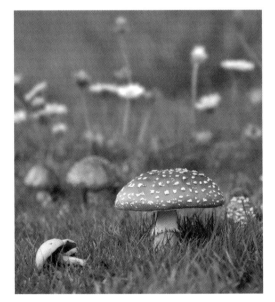

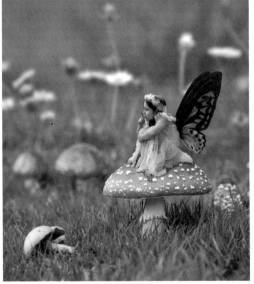

5 The color of the two images doesn't quite match. This was fixed simply by using the Auto Smart Fix command *ctrl* *alt* *M* *⌘* *⌥* *M*. Although these 'magic' options don't always give the best results, it's certainly worth trying them first as they can save a lot of time.

6 All that remains now is to add our fairy. We've imported the saved file from the previous project and scaled it to fit. We've used Levels to adjust her color and contrast slightly, and added a shadow to fix her into the scene. All the techniques for doing this are here in the book, of course.

SHORTCUTS
MAC **WIN** **BOTH**

Reusable images

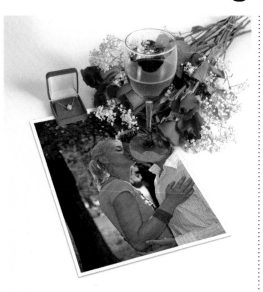

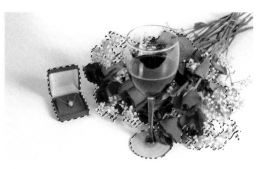

PEOPLE ENJOY GETTING PERSONALIZED items and Elements is a great way of doing this. It can, however, be a very time-consuming job to create an image from scratch each time. This is where working with layers and masks comes into its own. We can create and save image templates that can be used over and over again. These can be used for almost anything: wedding album covers, birthday cards, invitations; the list goes on.

The trick is to make sure the subject image is quick and easy to replace. In this instance we'll add a photograph to our example image so it appears under all the components of the scene. Initially this takes quite a bit time for the selection work, but once this has been done all we ever need to do is change the photo; a task which takes seconds to complete.

1 First we need to make a selection of the box, glass and flowers. A combination of the Quick Selection tool and the Selection Brush works well. We'll ignore the shadows and we only need to include enough in the selection to be able to slot a variety of photo sizes under the objects.

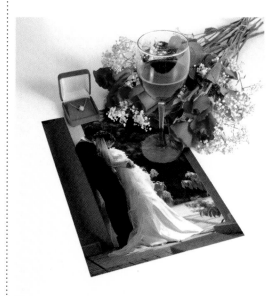

4 Create a layer below the cutaway layer. Set the blend mode to Multiply. Select a soft brush. Set the color to black. Now begin to paint in some shadows around the box, glass and flowers. Lower the opacity to match the existing shadows on the rest of the image.

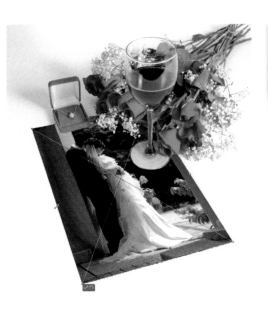

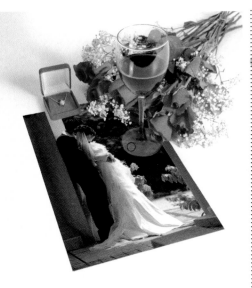

2 Press *ctrl J* *⌘ J* to create a copy on a new layer. Click the background layer's thumbnail in the Layers panel. Go to File > Place and select Wedding.jpg from the DVD. The image will be sandwiched between the the two layers. Hold *ctrl* *⌘* and drag the corners to position the

3 We have a problem with the glass: we should be able to see through it. Make the cutaway layer active and add a layer mask. Grab the Brush tool *B* and select mid-gray for the foreground color. Paint over the base and stem of the glass to make it translucent.

Our example image is fairly complex and selections won't always be as tricky as they are here. It is, however, worth spending the time making the cutout as perfect as possible as it only needs to be done the once. To make the file a little more lean, we can merge the cutout and shadow layers together (*ctrl E* *⌘ E*). The opacity and translucency are retained in the single layer.

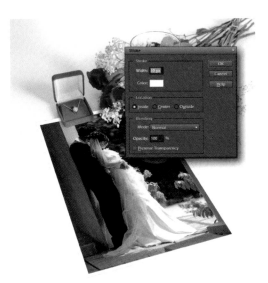

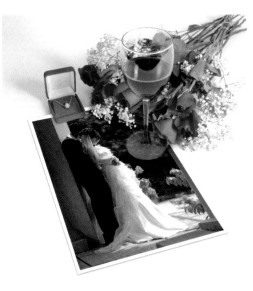

5 To add to the effect, create a new layer above the photo layer. Now hold *ctrl* *⌘* and click the photo layer's thumbnail to load its selection. Select Edit > Stroke (outline) Selection. Set the width to about 10 pixels. Set white as the color. Make sure Location is inside and click OK.

6 Finally, we've added a small drop shadow to the photo to add a little more depth. We can now save the image as a .psd file, which keeps the layers intact. To reuse the template we simply open it and place a new photo using the existing one as a guide, as we have in the intro image.

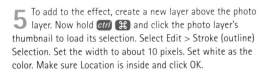
SHORTCUTS
MAC WIN BOTH

3

Panorama power

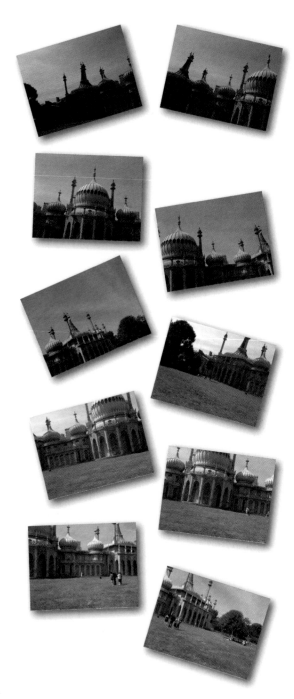

S O MANY OF OUR GADGETS now either come with, or can be fitted with, a digital camera. No matter where we are, we will almost always have a way of taking photos. This is great, of course, but there is a downside. Devices such as cell phones have limited space in which to place the camera lens, so they are generally fairly small and rarely have a zoom facility – some have digital zoom but the less said about that, the better. This makes taking pictures of buildings or other large landmarks difficult because you have to be at a fair distance to capture the whole thing. This is often impractical or if it is possible, the results lack clarity and the resulting prints may not be as detailed as they could have been, even with today's high megapixel camera phones.

There is a solution, of course. Elements has an incredible panoramic stitching feature. All we need do is move closer to our subject and take several photos in overlapping sections. Here we took shots across the top half of the building first, then moved back along the bottom. This way we were able to keep the images fairly level. We feed these into Elements which then goes off and does its magic, producing one complete image at the other end. Fantastic!

The final image has a length of just over 11 inches at 300dpi. This could probably be blown up 2 or 3 times without loss of quality. That's nearly 3 feet long from a 2 megapixel camera phone. Imagine the size you could achieve if you did the same with a high-resolution DSLR!

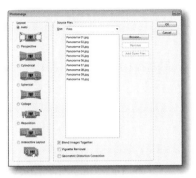

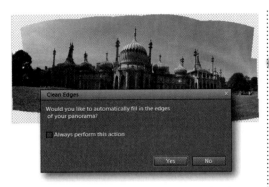

1 We'll begin by opening the panorama dialog: File > New > Photomerge Panorama. Click Browse and find the Panorama Power folder on the DVD. Select all the images by clicking the first file, holding *Shift* while clicking the last file. They'll appear in the dialog window.

2 We'll leave the Layout option set to Auto and make sure that Blend Images Together is checked. Click OK and it will begin to perform its magic. The initial result is a little ragged but Elements has a trick up its sleeve: the Clean Edges dialog will appear. Click yes and wait a while.

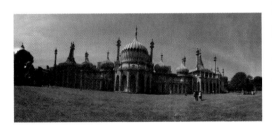

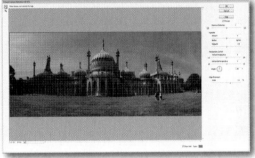

3 Elements has used its new Content Aware Fill technology to analyze the areas around the edge of the image and fill them to blend in. It's made a great job of it, with only a couple of small problems on the left by the tree and at the bottom of the grass.

4 We need to fix the photo's crookedness: select Filter > Correct Camera Distortion. Alter the angle using the central spire as a guide; 2.9 degrees is about right. This does leave gaps, however, so we can increase the Edge Extension a little to compensate.

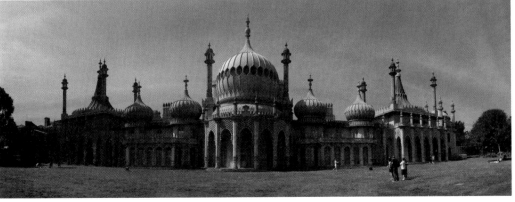

5 Here's our finished image. The minor problem areas from before were removed when we scaled the image up to adjust out the edges. Overall, it's an astonishingly good result with very little effort required and no need for cloning or additional cropping, thanks to the clever new Clean Edges feature in Elements 9.

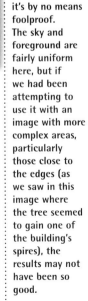

Digital cameras

BEING AN ELEMENTS USER, it's likely that you'll already have a camera of some type, even if it's not digital. You may, however, be looking to buy your first, or upgrade from your current model and, with so many different cameras on the market, choosing the right one can be a difficult decision. There are many factors to take into consideration and they are largely based on how much you intend to use it and for what purpose; you don't really want to be carrying huge amounts of equipment around with you if you're only interested in taking the occasional snapshot and similarly, if you're a keen photographer, you might be disappointed with the lack of features on a smaller model.

There are three main types of digital camera: let's begin with the compact models. Firstly, small is not necessarily a sacrifice in quality or features. Even at entry level, 3 megapixels (Mp) will give you a perfect quality 7" x 5" print and a reasonable one at Letter or A4 size. Some have a fixed lens whilst others offer a moderate amount of optical zoom – don't fall for the digital zoom gimmick, though; the results are often lower quality because the image is enlarged by the software in the camera, and not by the lens. The features vary from set point-and-shoot modes to a reasonable amount of manual control, depending on the model.

Next in line are the mid-range cameras, sometimes referred to as prosumer (from professional-consumer). These are bulkier than the compacts but are generally higher quality having larger image sensors and more manual control of the settings. The lenses are larger with a good zoom factor; again, many still include the digital zoom feature in an attempt to make the package more attractive to the buyer.

Finally, we have the DSLR (Digital Single Lens Reflex) cameras. These are the most expensive, and largest, but do give the best image definition: most producing photos that can be printed at A3 with no degradation. They have the same control features as their film-based brethren and their lenses are interchangeable. Many share the same mounts as their analog predecessors, giving you the option of using your existing ones, if you choose the same manufacturer.

It's worth noting that when it comes to the resolution of a camera, bigger isn't necessarily better, especially on the compact cameras which use a smaller sensor; the receptors need to be more tightly packed and the definition of the image can suffer as a result. For most purposes anything between 5 and 12 megapixels is sufficient. Professional DSLRs tend to start at 6Mp and can go as high as 20Mp or more, but you'll be paying out serious money at that level.

Once you've decided on the type of camera, you then need to choose the specific make and model: this can be another minefield, of course, and it's certainly a good idea to read reviews, both in magazines and online. There are two websites well worth visiting: **www.dpreview.com** and **www.stevesdigicams.com**; both offer highly in-depth information about almost every camera currently available — and sometimes advanced previews of the latest technology, as well as archives of the older models too.

From a photo-montage perspective, having a good camera certainly helps when it comes to sourcing images for your artwork. We'll talk about stock libraries elsewhere in the book and whilst you're almost certain to find the image you need on at least one of the sites, there's still no substitute for taking your own; you are in full control of the pictures and can get just the right angle and distance to suit your needs. You can create your own library of images, especially if you have a camera that you can carry with you easily at all times; that way you'll always be ready to capture those interesting scenes and textures. You can also set up a small home-studio for photographing smaller objects, either by buying a dedicated light box and lamps or, if you're feeling particularly adventurous, you could build your own – there are numerous websites with instructions on how to do this.

You might even consider uploading your own images to one of the many free stock libraries and add to the constantly growing resources. You may think that your contributions will be just a drop in a very large ocean, but you may just provide someone with a picture of something nobody else has. If your pictures are of high enough quality you could subscribe to one of the micro-stock websites such as **www.istockphoto.com** or **www.shutterstock.com**. You never know, you may start earning some extra money from it, especially if you sign up with a lot of different ones. There's always the excitement of seeing one or more of your pictures in use on someone's website or in a book such as this, perhaps.

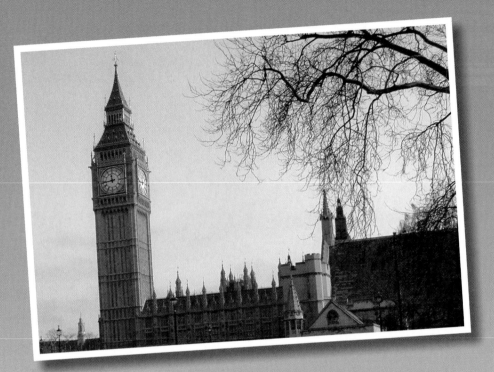

The Palace of Westminster is one of London's best-loved and most-photographed attractions. But the dull gray sky that's almost as much a London landmark makes the whole image look dull. How much better when we substitute a blue sky with fluffy clouds. It isn't hard to do, even though that tree may look fiddly.

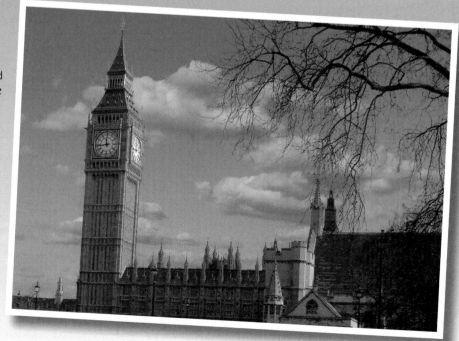

4
Image adjustments

DIGITAL CAMERAS are the best gadget the Elements user can own. But even the best camera can't produce sunny skies on an overcast day, or make snow from thin air, or change the color of a car. Fortunately, we have a solution.

Elements allows us to make any changes we like to an image: literally anything we can imagine can be changed within a single image. We can turn silver into gold, alter the time of day, and give the impression of speed.

But we can also enhance our images without adding anything new. Got a dull, lifeless photograph? We'll see how to liven it up in just a few steps – and how to recover apparently lost information from shadows and burnt-out highlights.

Adjusting images with Levels

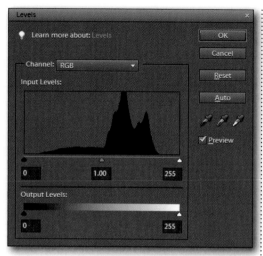

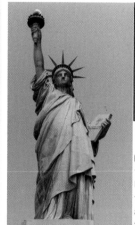

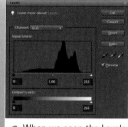

1 When we open the Levels dialog using *ctrl L* ⌘ *L*, all the sliders are in their starting position: the black and white triangles to the extreme left and right, and the gray triangle sits in the middle.

ELEMENTS INCLUDES SEVERAL METHODS for adjusting the brightness, contrast and tonal range in images. By far the most powerful – and the most versatile – is Levels, which gives a large degree of control over your pictures. Getting to grips with Levels will mean you're able to fine-tune your images to get perfect results.

The Levels dialog is in three parts: the histogram, the graph which shows the spread of tones in the image; the Input Levels, which allows you to adjust highlights, shadows and midtones; and the Output Levels, which controls the final brightness and contrast of the finished image.

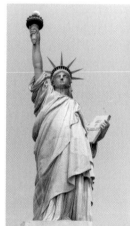

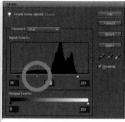

4 Dragging the center gray slider will affect the midtone values. Here, dragging the slider to the left brightens the image, without changing the brightest and darkest areas.

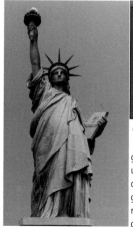

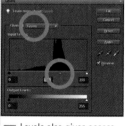

7 Levels also gives access to the individual red, green and blue channels, using the pop-up menu. Here, dragging the midtone on the green channel to the right reduces the total amount of green.

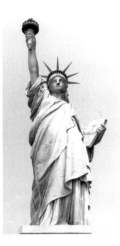

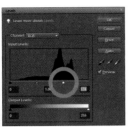

2 Dragging the small white triangle in the Input section to the left will brighten the image overall. Similarly, dragging the black triangle to the right will darken it.

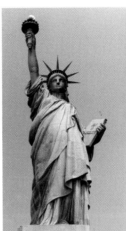

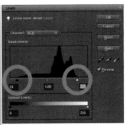

3 A good way to balance an image is to drag the black and white triangles so they touch the extreme edges of the histogram. This gives the image the full tonal range and makes it much crisper.

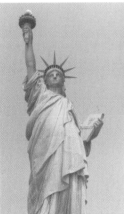

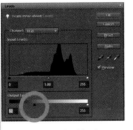

5 Dragging the black Output triangle to the right makes the image brighter; dragging the white triangle to the left would make the whole thing darker. Moving either will reduce image contrast.

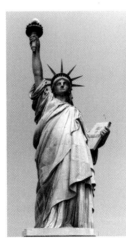

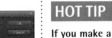

6 Pressing the Auto button will examine the histogram and produce what Elements thinks is the best result. Often, pressing this button can produce a marked improvement at a stroke.

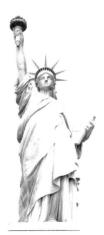

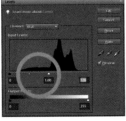

8 When we drag either the black or the white Input triangles, the middle gray triangle moves with it to remain spaced halfway between light and dark.

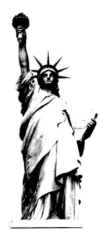

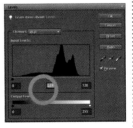

9 By dragging this midtone gray marker towards the light end, we can produce a strong, graphic effect.

SHORTCUTS
MAC WIN BOTH

73

Shadows and highlights

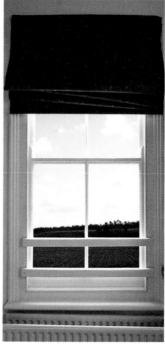

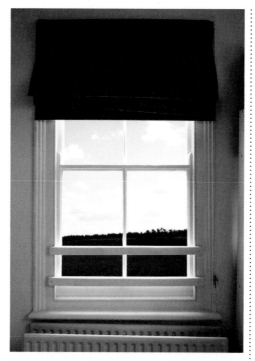

EXPOSURE IS THE ONE factor that photographers worry about more than any other. Professional photographers will always 'bracket' their exposures – that is, they'll take a range of exposures of the same image to make sure they've got the right one.

The real difficulty comes when we're faced with an image like this: a view through a window. In the image captured by the camera, above, we can see that the room itself is too dark (we can barely make out the blind texture among those deep shadows), while the view is so bleached out as to be wholly indistinct.

We can fix both of these problems in one go, with the Shadows/Highlights adjustment. It's a hugely powerful tool, which can rescue even the most poorly exposed photographs.

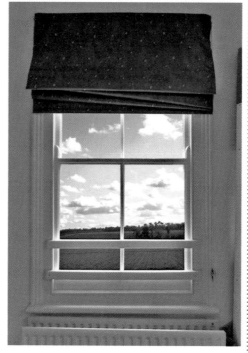

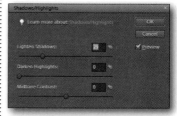

1 After opening the image, go to Enhance > Lighting > Shadows/ Highlights, and the dialog above will appear. As long as the Preview button is checked, any changes you make here will be visible immediately in the image. The default setting for this adjustment is to Lighten Shadows by a value of 25% and, as we can see here, this setting manages to rescue some of the darker areas of the image. We can already see that there's a yellow pattern in the blind, for example.

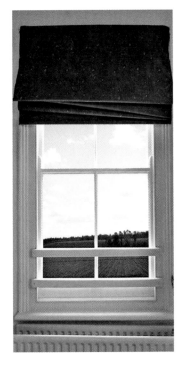

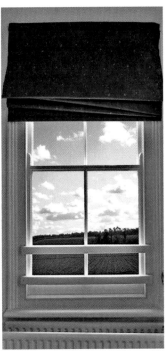

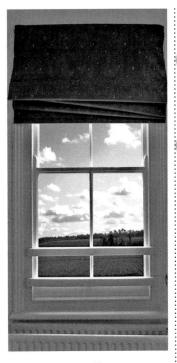

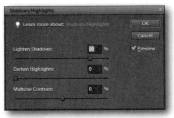

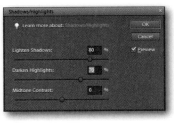

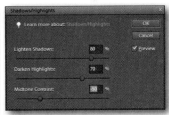

2 That's not enough for our purposes. Let's increase the value significantly – here, we've dragged the slider to raise it to 80%. Now, the pattern and texture in the blind can be clearly seen. In addition, we can see that the dark field outside the window has now acquired some definition: the trees on the hill are now distinct from the plowed field in front of them.

3 Now let's turn our attention to the Highlights. As the image stands, the sky is greatly over-exposed. Dragging the Darken Highlights slider addresses this problem: the further to the right we drag it, the more detail we're able to see in the sky. We've dragged it here to a value of 70%, and this means that the clouds now stand out from the sky behind them.

4 Although we could stop there, it's worth looking at the final slider – Midtone Contrast. Generally, we'd welcome contrast, as it provides definition within the image. Here, though, the result of tweaking both the shadows and the highlights has resulted in a window frame that's so well defined that it overpowers the view through it. By lowering the midtone contrast we take out a little of that over-defined molding, drawing the eye through the window to the view instead.

HOT TIP

Not all cases are as extreme as this one. The adjustment is also useful when a person has been photographed with side lighting: by lightening the shadows and darkening the highlights, we're able to give the impression that the lighting came directly from the front.

75

Bee flat to bee sharp

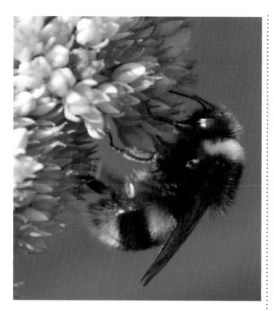

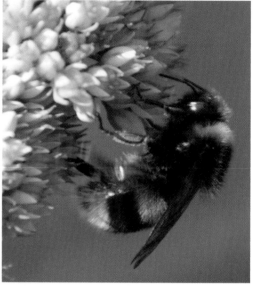

WE ALWAYS STRIVE to get the best possible images but sometimes, even with the best equipment, we can end up with an image that is slightly soft.

In our example the combination of the extreme close-up and the bee's movement has resulted in a less defined photo. There is, of course, no way to get a clearer image once it's been taken but we can enhance it to give the impression of it being a lot sharper. We'll have a look at two different sharpening methods here, each providing a slightly different effect.

Rather than working directly on the image, however, we'll use a grayscale copy and blend it with the original; this way we have far greater control over the final effect.

These effects can, of course, be applied to any image, regardless of its original clarity; by reducing the amount of adjustment we can give a photo some added pop.

1 Here's our slightly soft photo in need of a little attention. We're not going to work on the image directly so the first step is to duplicate the background layer. Both techniques require a grayscale layer so we need to desaturate the layer by pressing ⌃ ctrl Shift U ⌘ Shift U.

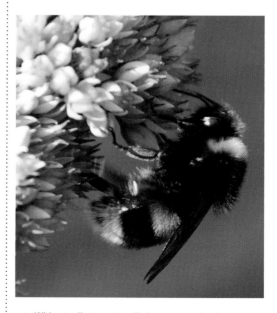

4 Without adjustment applied we can overlay it onto our original image. Set the blend mode to Soft Light. The image is now looking a lot sharper whilst retaining much of its tonal qualities and color balance, something that could be affected if we'd applied the effect directly to the image.

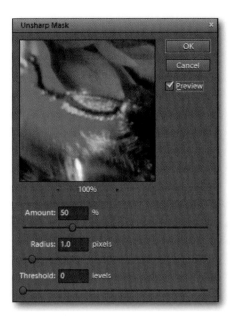

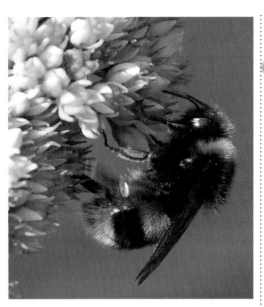

2 For the first technique we'll use the Unsharp Mask adjustment. This can be found at the bottom of the Enhance menu – in previous versions it can be found in the Filter menu under Sharpen. The dialog may look a little daunting but it's surprisingly straightforward.

3 The default settings are fairly tame and have little effect on our image. Drag the Amount slider to the right; don't be afraid to increase it higher than you would normally, it won't look as severe when we blend it with the original. In this case we raised it to 350%.

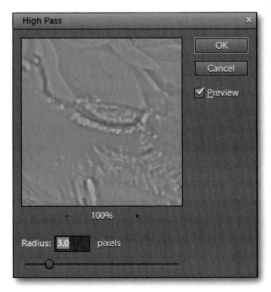

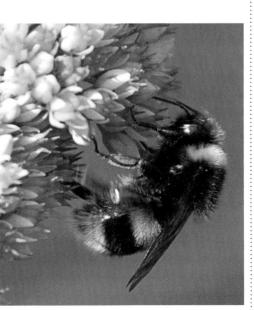

5 The second technique makes use of a little-known filter called High Pass; this resides in the Filter menu under Other. There is only one slider and, unlike Unsharp Mask, we only need to make a small adjustment to achieve good results – we've used a setting of 3 pixels here.

6 As before, we need to change the blend mode; this time, set it to Hard Light. This is a more subtle effect than the Unsharp Mask version, concentrating more on the edges than the entire image, but still gives superb results and leaves the original color almost unchanged.

RAW adjustment

YOU WOULD BE FORGIVEN for thinking that RAW is something that should be left in the realm of the professional photographer. This is not the case, however, as more and more compact and so-called 'prosumer' (the not-quite-DSLR type) cameras are now able to record their images in RAW.

So what is so special about this format? When you take a photo the camera records the data its sensor sees into memory. Normally this would then be converted to a JPEG by the camera and stored on its memory card. Various enhancements are carried out during this process, making sometimes irreversible changes, and being compressed, there is already a slight degradation in quality. RAW images are not processed by the camera. The recorded image is saved unaltered (more or less) to the memory card. The data is instead decoded by the software on the computer. This gives us far more editing power as we can work on the separate color channels to make more precise corrections. The main benefit, however, is RAW's non-destructive editing. Whenever a change is made, the original image remains untouched. The alterations are written to a control file which in turn tells the software how to display it. These changes can be output to a separate version of the image, either by opening it in Elements or saving it as a .dng (Digital Negative) file directly from the Camera Raw dialog.

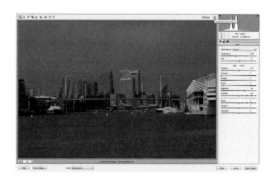

1 Go to the File menu and open RAW adjustment.crw from the DVD. Before we start working on our image, make sure we are working in full screen mode. This can be done by pressing **F** or by clicking the button just to the left of the histogram window.

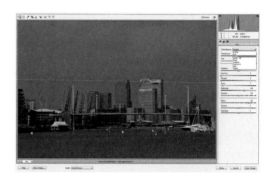

4 Now we can start color correcting and enhancing the image. Firstly we'll set the white balance; this generally defaults to As Shot. The image was taken in sunny conditions so set it to Daylight. This gives us a slight blue hue and brings out the color of the sky and water.

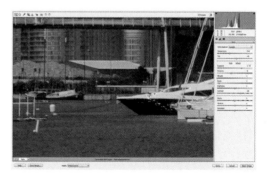

7 Blacks is the opposite to Recovery, dealing with the heavy shadow areas. Again, there aren't too many in this image. Press **U** to display them; they show up in blue. There's a very small area on the hull of the boat. This time drag to the left to tone them down.

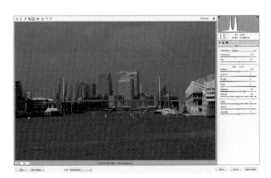

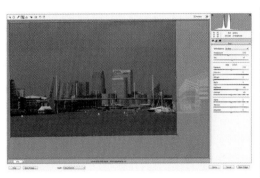

2 One of the first things we notice is the image is crooked. Select the Straighten tool from the toolbar (or by pressing **A**). Find a suitable guideline – the opposite ends of the bridge work well. A boundary appears showing the change in angle. Pressing **Enter** sets the changes.

3 We can also crop the image down a little. Select the Crop tool **C**. The skew-adjusted boundary appears again. We want to keep the same image aspect: hold **Shift** and drag the bottom-right corner in – enough to remove the cut-off ship and its mooring. Press **Enter** again to set it.

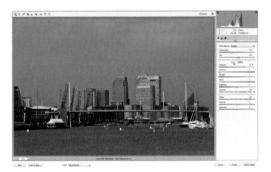

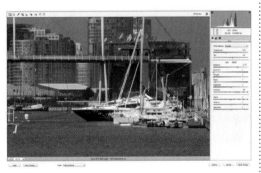

5 It's always worth trying the Auto correction option. Even if it's not perfect, it serves as a good baseline. It's done a pretty good job here. If we weren't happy with the changes, we could select Reset Camera Raw Defaults from the fly-out menu on the tab bar to return it to its initial state.

6 We'll concentrate on the lighting adjustments first. Recovery deals with blown highlights. There are very few in this image. Press **O** to turn on the highlight clipping warning. A small red area appears on the boat on the right. Drag the slider to the right until most of the red area is gone.

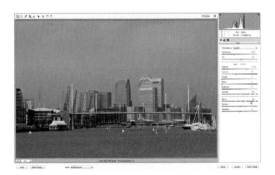

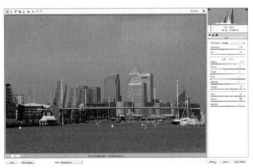

8 The previous adjustments have left the image slightly washed out. Grab the Clarity slider and drag it to the right. This acts as a subtle form of sharpening by boosting the midtones of the image. A value of 60% works well here and takes away the haziness.

9 The last adjustment we'll use is Vibrance. This boosts the less saturated color whilst leaving more saturated ones untouched. It really deepens the sky and the softer colors of the buildings. Finally, we can save all our changes by clicking Done. They will be there next time we open this image.

Photomerge: exposure

ONE OF THE DIFFICULTIES with photography is the inability to capture both bright and dark areas of the scene at the same time. Unlike our eyes, which can create a happy medium between the two extremes, the camera falters, leaving us with horribly blown out highlights when we try to capture shaded areas and disappointingly dreary shadows if we expose for the bright areas.

Fortunately, we have a solution. The Photomerge: Exposure command basically compares the differences between two or more photographs at different exposure levels to blend and output one composite image comprising the best of the batch. The photos can either be shot separately at the time, exposing for light, shadow and midtone – the filter will also realign the images if necessary – or, as we will see here, create them using the Camera Raw dialog where we can save different exposures of the exact same image, so they will be perfectly aligned from the outset.

There are two modes: automatic and manual. The former is the default and will often do the job without any need for alteration. It's not perfect, however, so we can also get our hands dirty and define the regions of the image ourselves to perfect the result.

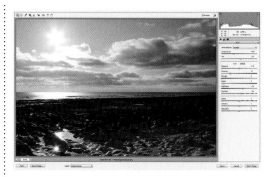

1 Open Photomerge exposure.dng from the DVD. The photo will appear in the Camera Raw dialog. The image has already been straightened and auto-adjusted. We can see that the image has been exposed for the sea; the foreground is dark and the sun and sky are a little too bright.

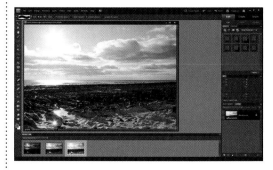

4 Open the original image one last time. Increase the Exposure to brighten up the rocks in the foreground. Save the file, appending the filename with Light. Now make sure the Project Bin is visible; if it's not, you can make it visible by clicking its entry in the Window menu.

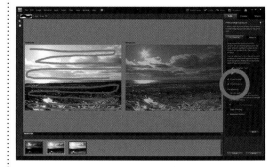

7 Now click the Light image and paint over the rocks in the same way. We now have a much more evenly balanced image. If we click the Show Regions box, we can see where the image has been blended. It's an even split but more complex images would have many blending areas.

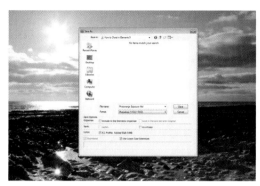

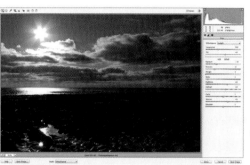

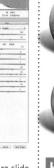

2 We'll use the starting image as our base. Click the Open Image button to open the photo in Elements. We have to save the file as we cannot open more than one version of the same file. We'll add the word Mid to the end of the original filename as it's a midtone equivalent.

3 Open the original dng file again. Drag the Exposure slide to the left. We want to tone down the blown highlights. We can also add a little Vibrance to bring out the blue sky. Open the image in Elements. Save it as before but this time append the filename with Dark.

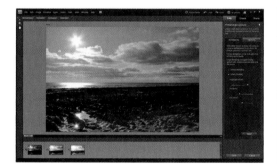

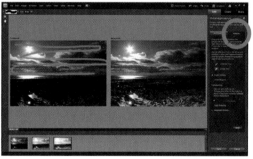

5 Select all three images in the Project Bin. Go to File > New > Photomerge Exposure. When it's finished processing we have our merged photo. It's done a reasonable job but the colors are a little strange. We have a limited adjustment control but not enough to make a difference.

6 Click the Manual tab. Click and drag the Mid file from the Project Bin to the right-hand (background) window. Now click the Dark file's thumbnail to make it the active foreground. Make sure the Selection tool is enabled. Paint a zig-zag line over the sky to replicate it to the background.

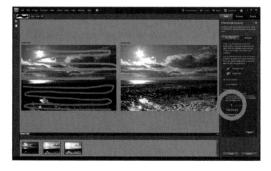

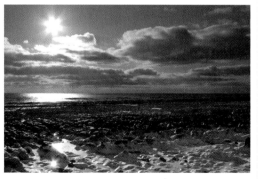

8 The sky is a little too intense. Click the Dark thumbnail to make it active. Now drag the Transparency slider to the right. This works like opacity, allowing the background image to become more visible. It's always best to make the middle exposure image the background for this reason.

9 When we're happy with the effect, we click Done to return to the Editor window. A new document will be created containing both the original mid-exposure image and the merged image as a layer. We can now save it as a Photoshop file to keep the layers or as a single JPEG image.

All that glitters...

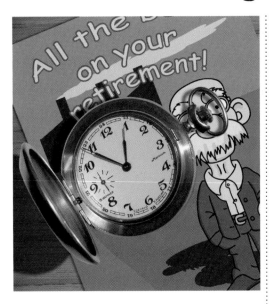

CHANGING A SILVER OBJECT to gold is not a difficult task. The two metals are very similar. They both have the same specular properties: the way light is reflected back from their surfaces (once polished, of course). Silver has a high content of blue, giving it its colder appearance. Gold, on the other hand, is predominantly red and green. It's simply a matter of adjusting the hues to give us the familiar warm color. Although you might be tempted to use a Hue/Saturation adjustment, we'll use the Levels dialog. By working with the color channels individually, we have far greater control.

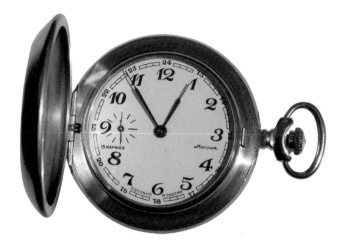

1 Here's our silver watch. The face has been cut away from the rest of the image and placed on a separate layer. We only want to color the body, after all. Because of its slight angle, we used the shape selection technique from Chapter 6.

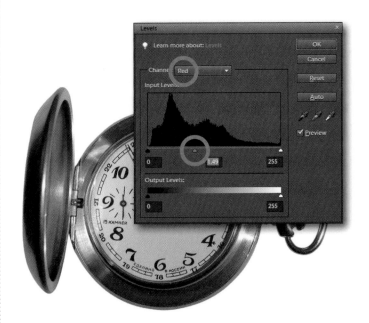

3 Now switch to the red channel. This time increase the amount by moving the midtone slider across to the left. As you can see, our watch is now looking much more valuable. It's still a little dull though.

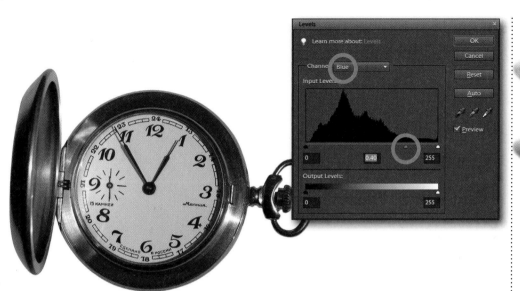

2 Make sure the body layer is active by clicking its thumbnail in the Layers panel. Open the Levels dialog by pressing *ctrl* L *⌘* L. Select the Blue Channel from the drop down menu. Move the midtone slider towards the right. As the blue is subtracted from the image, the color becomes noticeably greener and much closer to gold.

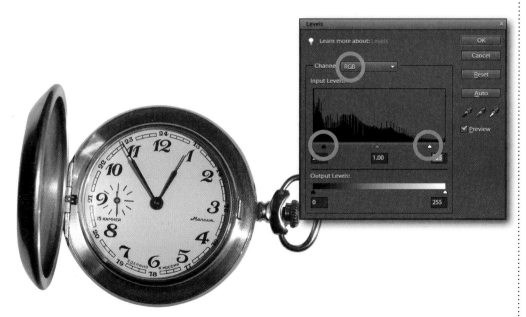

4 Switch back to the composite RGB view. Drag the Highlight and Shadow sliders a little way toward the middle. This gives us a richer tone to the color as well as giving the impression that the metal is much shinier.

HOT TIP

You can also select the individual channel views from the keyboard. Holding *ctrl* *⌘* and **1** **2** or **3** will switch between the red, green and blue channels respectively. Press *ctrl* *⌘* and the ~ (tilde) key to return to the composite RGB view – not the more logical 0, as you might think. This, of course, is the reserved shortcut for the Fit on Screen view mode.

SHORTCUTS
MAC WIN BOTH

The perfect respray

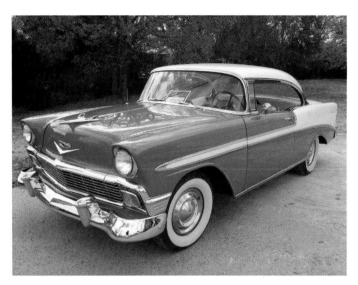

THERE ARE NUMEROUS WAYS to change the color of an object. Most, however, are designed to affect the entire image. We could, of course, use the selection tools to isolate the parts we need to work on. This is a time-consuming practice and often more trouble than it's worth.

For tricky jobs, such as this car with all that complex trim, by far the best method is to use the Replace Color tool. With this we can selectively alter the hue, saturation and lightness of an area without the need to separate it from the rest of the image.

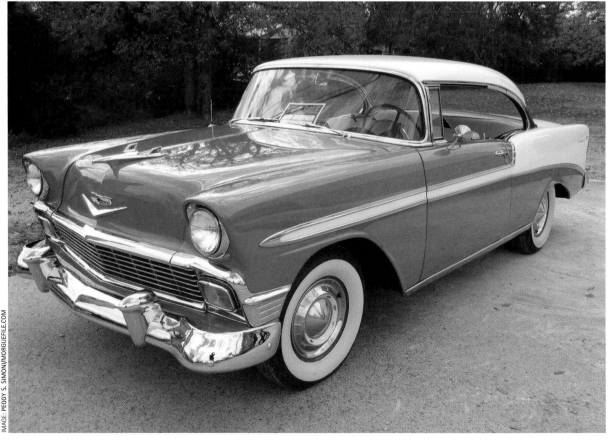

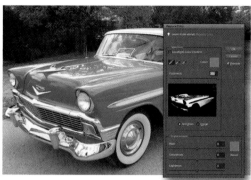

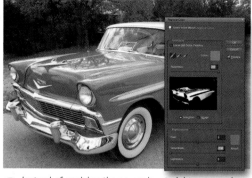

1 Press *ctrl J* *⌘ J* to duplicate the background layer. Open the dialog by going to Enhance > Adjust Color > Replace Color. The white area in the preview shows the selected area after clicking a section of the car's body. We've set the Fuzziness to its maximum, and we'll adjust it later.

2 Instead of applying the new color straight away, we've lowered the saturation completely; this shows up the more subtle shades of red not included initially. We can add these areas to the selection by holding *Shift* and clicking them with the eyedropper.

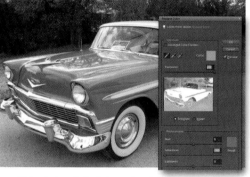

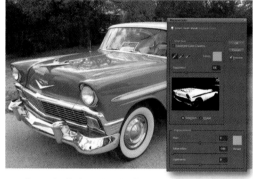

3 We've isolated all of the car's color but we now have a problem: looking at the preview, a large amount of unwanted areas have been included from the rest of the image. This is where we'll use the Fuzziness setting to fine-tune the result.

4 By gradually lowering the Fuzziness value we can see the selection start to tighten up in the preview. Some of the previously selected color will begin to reappear. Zoom in a little and start to add these back in. If necessary, adjust the Fuzziness a little more until you have a good balance.

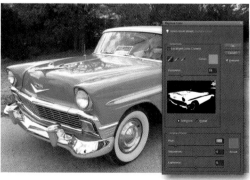

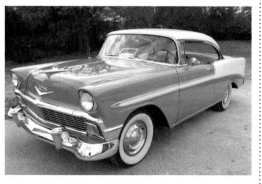

5 Now we can add the new color by raising the Saturation and altering the Hue to the desired shade. As we began by duplicating the image, we can simply erase the unwanted areas, such as the for sale sign in the window and the trees in the background, to let the original show through.

6 You may notice that there are still places where the original hue remains. Often this will be noticeable in the highlights and reflections. As a final touch, grab a soft brush. Set its blend mode to Color. Now you can carefully paint over these areas with the target color.

HOT TIP

The Fuzziness setting of the dialog works in a similar way to the tolerance feature of tools such as the Magic Wand. By increasing the value, Elements will select a greater tonal range of the chosen color. This can be used to avoid harsh lines where two hues meet. It's rarely possible to achieve a perfect result with no excess areas affected. If we keep refining the balance by adjusting the fuzziness and adding in small amounts to the selection, we can keep problems to a minimum.

SHORTCUTS

MAC WIN BOTH

85

Shifting seasons

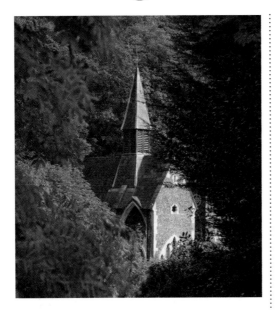

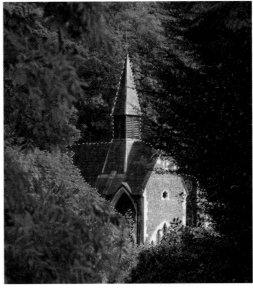

WE CAN'T ALWAYS BE THERE to capture a scene at a particular time of year. Our example image was taken during the summer and whilst it's already a very picturesque scene, it would look particularly beautiful in the fall, with the reds and browns of the leaves framing the chapel nestled within.

There's no need to hang around, of course, we can speed up the seasonal change with Elements. In the previous project we changed the color of the car with Replace Color. We'll use it here as well but we'll need to take a slightly different approach as we want to make the shades of the leaves different. We can't do this in a single action, so we'll change portions of the image individually to build up the effect.

1 Duplicate the background layer `ctrl` `J` `⌘` `J`. Now use the Quick Selection tool to make a selection around the chapel. Soften the selection slightly with Refine Edge or Feather. Press `ctrl` `Shift` `I` `⌘` `Shift` `I` to inverse it. Now only the trees will be affected.

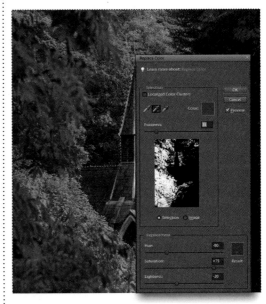

4 We need to add a few more tones in. Click the Add to Sample (middle) icon in the Selection area. Click a few of the areas next to the reds to add them in – not too much as we don't want to include too many shades. Now use the Fuzziness slider to fine-tune the selection. Click OK to apply.

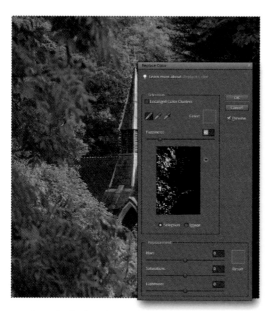

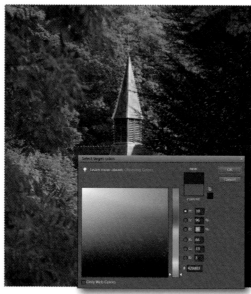

2 Open the Replace Color dialog from the Enhance menu. Click the Selection button so we can see the area of the effect. Choose a suitable starting point such as the large leaves on the left. Click the eye-drop cursor on one of the leaves. The area shows up as white in the preview.

3 Rather than trying to get the right color using the Hue slider, we're going to be a bit bolder. Click the color chip in the Replacement area. Select a fairly deep red/brown hue. We've picked up a little of the green here. Click OK to accept the color change.

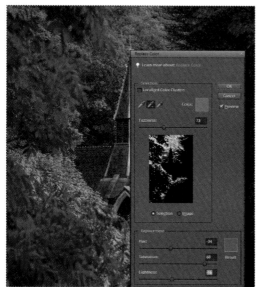

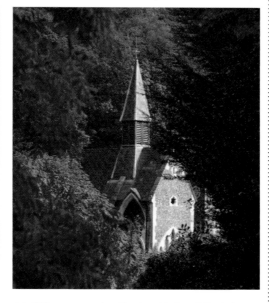

5 Open the Replace Color dialog again. Select a different range of greens and adjust them as before. This time, use a slightly more orange tint in the Color Picker. Try not to make the colors too bold as they can end up looking unrealistic. Repeat the technique for the rest of the image.

6 With our new colors, the chapel looks a little stark. Inverse the selection again. Now create a Photo Filter adjustment layer. The chapel will be masked from the selection. Select the Warming (85) preset and increase the density to give the impression of a warm fall glow.

Photomerge: style match

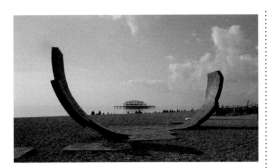

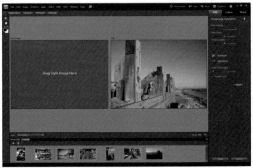

1 The first thing we need to do is open an image. We've chosen a view along the coast with some prominent wooden posts. Now select File > New > Photomerge Style Match. The dialog will open with the photo already placed in the destination slot. We can see the Style Bin at the bottom.

MOST DIGITAL CAMERAS have built-in settings that adjust the image automatically when we take the shot. Some can convert to black and white, or sepia, or add other creative effects. Wouldn't it be great, though, if we could tell our camera to take our pictures in any number of specific styles; an Ansel Adams high-contrast landscape image, for instance, or maybe the gritty HDR style of Dave Hill?

Well, we may not be able to do this in-camera just yet, but in the meantime we have a really superb alternative: Style Match. This is another addition to the Photomerge series in Elements.

We can open one of our own images and tell the program to apply the tones and colors from any photo we choose, either from the supplied presets or one we have sourced ourselves. As

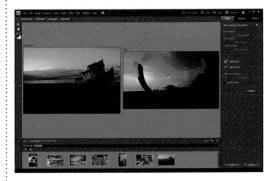

4 We'll try out a different effect now. Using another seascape image, we'll try changing from a sunny daytime scene to a fiery sunset. Here we've placed the Sunset preset in the style box. Without transferring the color tones its effect is not very good at all.

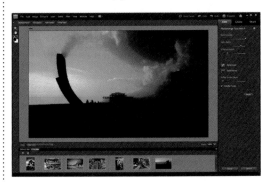

7 We'll use the Enhance Details control to reduce the harsh areas of the image. Lowering it to -3 removes the bright specks from the foreground but because we boosted the Clarity, we still retain much of the definition in the clouds. It's not perfect but it's still a really great image.

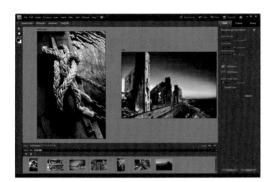

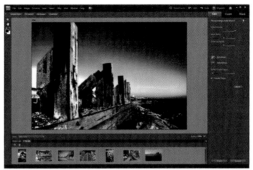

2 Now we'll choose an image from the presets to apply to our photo. This will look great as a heavily contrasted black and white image. We've dragged the Pier Rope image onto the style slot. Initially this only affects the tone of the colors. Not a bad effect in itself but not the effect we want.

3 Go over to the control panel on the right and check the Transfer Tones box. This forces the colors of the style image to be mapped onto the destination photo. We've switched to the After only view here and, as we can see, it's done a superb job without any need for further adjustments.

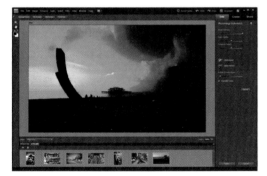

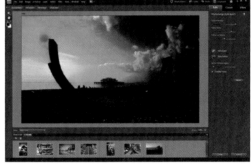

5 Clicking the Transfer Tones box has a much better result but it still has some problems. The definition of the clouds and sky is not great, and there are some harsh areas causing ugly bright spots of orange on the otherwise dark beach in the foreground.

6 We'll go back to the control panel. The Style intensity slider reduces the amount of the overall effect. We'll leave this as it is. We'll increase the Clarity slider to 3. Although it seems we are making the image worse here, it's just the initial step in the process.

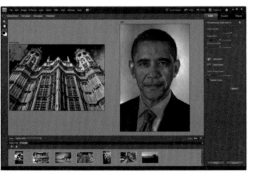

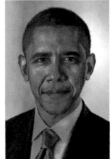

8 So far we've used photos that are similar to the styles we are applying. Let's see what happens if we try something a little unusual. Here we have a picture of President Obama. We'll apply the Silver Hotel preset. Curiously, it's produced an effect not unlike a pastel drawing.

9 If we go one step further and apply the color tones we now have a sketched effect. The initial result is a bit dark. We'll click Done to go back to the Editor. Now we can open the Levels dialog and brighten him up a little. A suprising and rather interesting effect!

HOT TIP

Like many of the automated adjustment filters and tools, the results we get with Style Match are not going to be perfect every time. The effects may not work at all on some photos but on the whole it can produce great images. Often, as is the case with our second image, we can only adjust the problems out to a point. Once we've saved the image, however, we can sort out any major issues – such as the smudge on the tip of the sculpture – in the Editor with the one of the retouching tools.

A splash of color

LEAVING LARGE AREAS of prominent color in an otherwise monotone image to make it leap out at you is by no means a new idea; although it was used to great effect in the movie *Sin City*, which we'll be paying homage to in this project. It has always been possible to create this effect in Elements, of course, but with version 7 came a new tool which makes the whole thing much easier.

The Smart Brush is a combination of the Quick Selection tool and Adjustment Layers: as you click or paint, the selected area dynamically builds a mask, so only that part of the layer's effect is visible. The great thing is that because they are Adjustment Layers, we can change the look of the image in an instant by simply choosing another preset or by altering the opacity or blend mode.

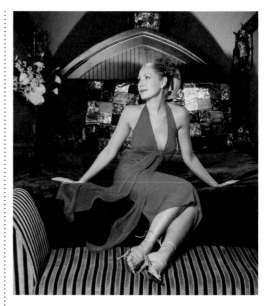

1 Here's our starting image. It's fairly striking to begin with but we can make it really stand out with just a few simple steps. Begin by grabbing the Smart Brush tool **F**; go to the Preset Picker, select Photographic from the drop-down list and choose Natural Tone BW.

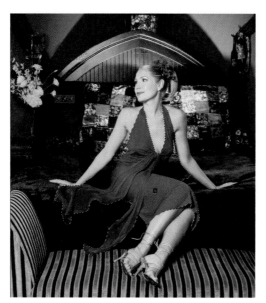

4 Continue clicking around the dress, varying the brush size accordingly. The tool is good but not infallible and some areas have spilled onto the bed and parts of the skin. We can remove these by holding **alt** **⌥** to temporarily switch to subtract mode and click/paint over them.

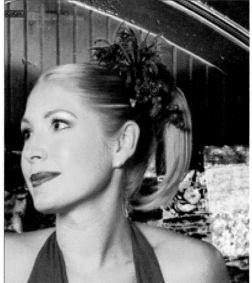

5 We've added as much as is possible with the Smart Brush. Pressing **F** again gives us the Detail Smart Brush. Using this, only the immediate area is affected so we can resize the brush and paint the rest of the areas in. We can also use it to touch up any other areas around the dress.

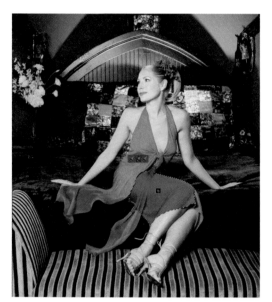

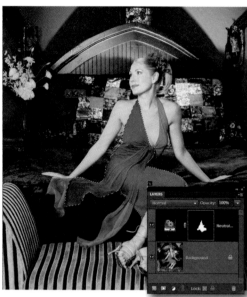

2 It makes more sense to work on the areas we want left intact and switch them later, than to spend time on the background. We'll start with the lower part of the dress. Using a fairly large brush, but making sure it stays within the confines of the dress, click once to begin the selection.

3 The small square that appears marks the starting point of the selection and is color coded for when there is more than one effect layer applied. Add some more areas in by clicking once each time. If we look at the Layers panel we can see how the effect is starting to build up.

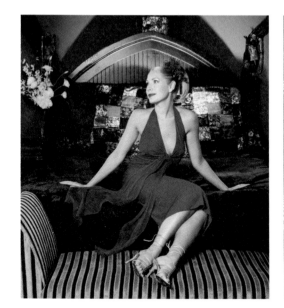

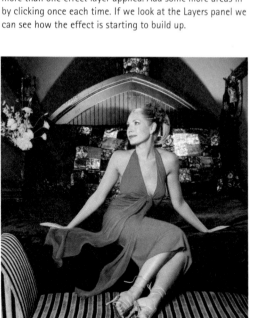

6 Here's our image with all the areas painted in. We're almost ready to reveal the final effect but as a last piece of tidying we can use Refine Edge (see Chapter 1 for more detail) to clean up the fringing that's been left around some of the dress.

7 Clicking Inverse in the Options bar swaps the areas around and gives us a stunning result. We found the black and white to be a little too bright so we've changed the Adjustment Layer's blend mode to Color, as this gives us a slightly even contrast.

SHORTCUTS
MAC WIN BOTH

91

Smart bling

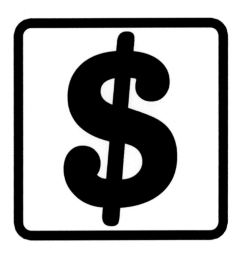

THE PREVIOUS PROJECT introduced us to the power and ease of use of the new Smart Brush. We only used a single layer for the effect but, as we'll see, you can apply as many as you need. Each can be a stand-alone effect or one that enhances the rest of the artwork.

There is a whole host of preset styles available by default and they can also be installed. Because they are standard Adjustment Layers, we have hundreds of possible effects at our disposal: we can even import Photoshop-only layers, which gives us extra scope.

The custom presets and installation instructions can be found in the Goodies folder on the DVD.

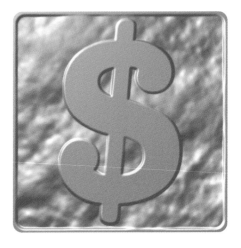

1 Our starting image is just a simple embossed image created using a similar technique to the wax seal in Chapter 7. It's a bit dull and looks like pressed plastic at present – not very exciting at all. This is all about to change, of course: select the Smart Brush **F** and choose the Gold preset from the Style Picker window.

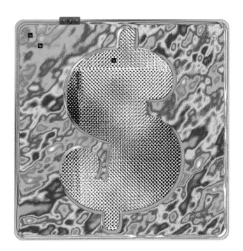

4 Let's really add some value with some diamond encrusting. Deselect again and choose the Diamond preset. Decrease the brush size so it fits comfortably within the dollar emblem and start to paint. We have a bit of a problem, though: because some of its edges are low contrast, the texture has spilled out. We'll deal with this next.

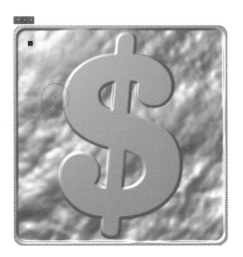

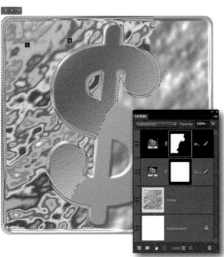

2 Using a large brush, paint across the whole of the artwork; we can quickly select it in just one or two strokes. We're not simply changing the color, however, we're also altering the tones of the image – in essence we're dynamically applying the technique we used in the silver to gold project at the beginning of this chapter.

3 Now to create the impression that the surface is polished. Firstly, deselect *ctrl* D ⌘ D, to force the tool to add a new effect layer. Go back to the Style Picker and select Metallic. As we can see in the inset, painting over the object again applies a new texture on top of the gold layer which, in turn, interacts to create the shiny surface.

HOT TIP

The colored icons that appear on the document are visual links to the individual effect layers. Left-clicking on one takes us straight to the corresponding layer – very useful when we have many different effects. Right-clicking gives the option of editing the settings (unless it's not a native function of Elements). We can also opt to delete the current effect or select another layer by name.

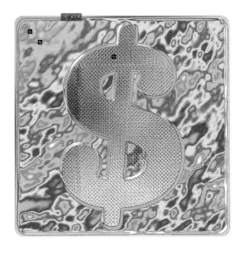

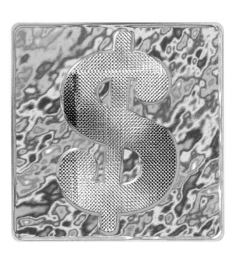

5 We'll use the Detail Smart Brush **F** to clean up the problem areas, as we can work much more accurately. Remember to switch to Subtract mode, either by holding *alt* ⌥ or by clicking the icon in the toolbar. As the texture has covered up the shape, we can lower the opacity of the Adjustment Layer to enable us to see more clearly.

6 Here's our completed artwork: not bad for only a few minutes' work. Once we have our effects in place we can easily alter them too: we could, for example swap the gold for silver and the diamonds for gold. This is done simply by selecting the relevant layer and choosing another style from the picker.

SHORTCUTS
MAC **WIN** **BOTH**

Changing skies

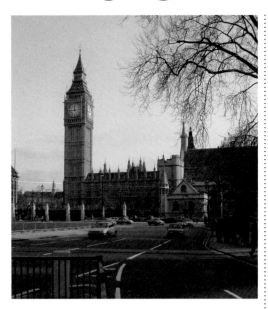

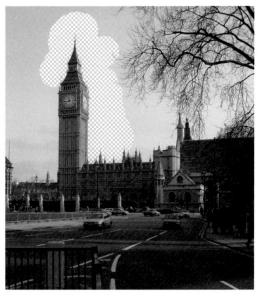

THE BACKGROUND ERASER is a fantastic tool for removing areas of similar color. It's the second of the Eraser tools and it works by sampling the color beneath the crosshair and deleting all the pixels of that color within the radius of the brush. Here, we're going to use it to erase all the sky from this photograph of London's Houses of Parliament and replace it with a more dramatic sky.

Although we could select and delete much of the background using the Magic Wand tool, that won't select inside fiddly areas such as the tree: this is where the Discontiguous setting of the Background Eraser comes in handy, as we'll see in this example.

Before we start with this tool, it's important to duplicate the layer you're going to work on, hiding the original so there's always a copy we can return to later.

1 Select the Background Eraser tool and change its limits from Contiguous to Discontiguous. A Tolerance setting of around 40% works well for this plain sky. Click and drag around the tower to delete the background, but be sure not to let the crosshair stray onto the building.

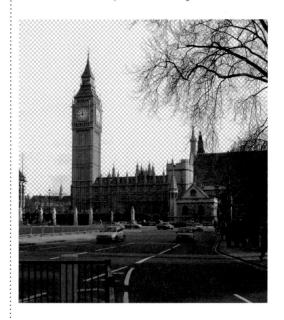

4 Continue erasing all the sky within the image, varying the size of the brush as you need to. Don't worry if some areas of the picture are erased that shouldn't be; we can get those back later. For now, concentrate on getting rid of all that sky.

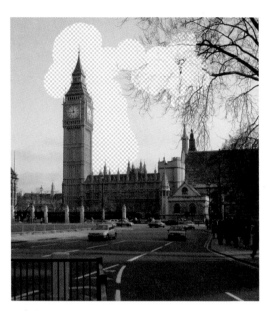

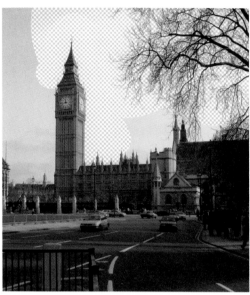

2 When we move into the tree area, we get a problem. Once the crosshair touches the branches, that's the color that's sampled – and so that's the area that is deleted. We need to find another way to remove the sky in there. Undo that step and we'll try again.

3 Make the Eraser brush size much larger – we've used a 175 pixel brush here. Click on a clear area of blue sky within the tree branches and all the sky within the radius of the brush will be deleted. Make sure you don't click on the branches by accident.

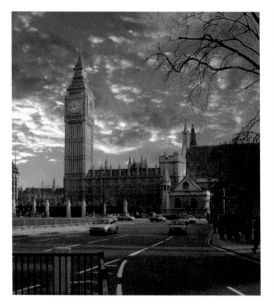

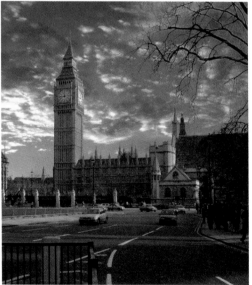

5 When we now bring in a new sky layer behind the buildings, we can see a few mistakes: the clock face has been erased and we can see the new sky through it, and the same applies to one or two parts of the buildings. Just as well we were working on a copy of the layer!

6 Make selections around the missing building parts using the Lasso tool. Now return to the original (hidden) layer and press *ctrl* J ⌘ J to make a new layer from the selection. Move this layer above the clouds layer and the image is complete.

SHORTCUTS
MAC WIN BOTH

Miracle healing

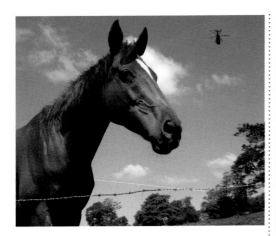

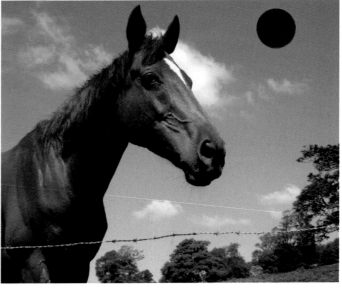

W E'RE NOT ALWAYS IN CONTROL of what appears in our photos when we take the shot; this might be something that moves into the frame just as we press the shutter or an environmental issue. This shouldn't necessarily mean that the photo has to be put in the garbage.

There are many ways of tidying up an image. Here, we're going to look at the Spot Healing Brush. Although this has been around for a while now, there's a new feature that's been added in Elements 9: Content-aware fill. The tool previously only had the Proximity Match option, which samples the area immediately around the brush cursor. This works well but has its failings. Content-aware fill differs greatly as it analyzes the entire image looking for possible areas that match the affected spot. The results can be quite remarkable; it's capable of removing complicated items from an image, often in a single stroke.

1 We'll start by removing the flies from the horse's head. Grab the Spot Healing Brush tool **J**. Set its type to Proximity Match. Choose a fairly small brush. Now we can simply click once on each fly to remove them. We'll set our sights a bit higher now. Increase the brush size to just larger than the helicopter. Click once and release the mouse and the helicopter disappears without a trace.

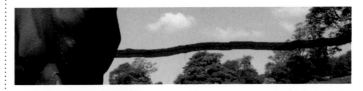

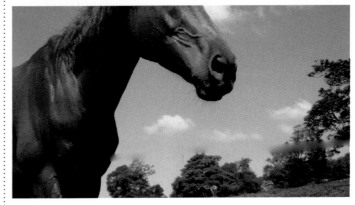

3 Press **ctrl Z ⌘ Z** to undo the last action. Make the brush size just larger than the barbed wire (including the size of the barbs themselves). Now carefully paint along from edge to edge, following the path of the wire. Again, it's not made a good job of it. About the only area that has worked is the plain sky. We're not going to give up, however. It's time to bring out the secret weapon.

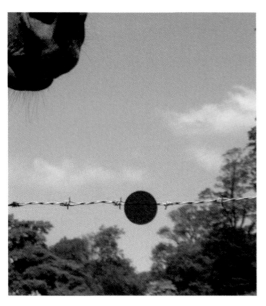

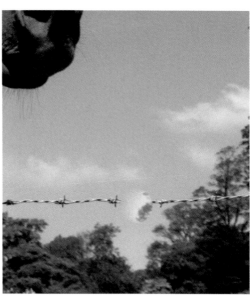

2 Although we were able to remove the flies and helicopter easily with a single dab of the brush, this isn't always the case. If we want to remove the barbed wire we can't use single clicks, as the tool uses the surrounding area to repair the point where you have the brush. The

result, as we can see here, is no good at all; it sees the trees and clouds as different to the pixels directly beneath the brush and assumes it's OK to use those to repair the area. To remove objects like this we need to paint over the whole thing in one go.

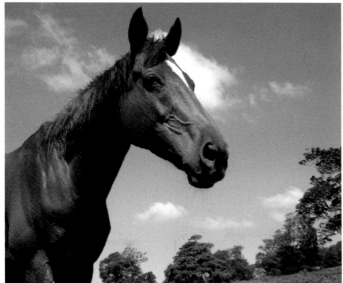

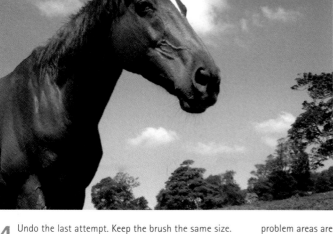

Whilst the Content-aware option of the brush can remove and repair parts of an image with astonishing results, it's not infallible. It works best when there are large areas of a repeating pattern, such as trees or bricks.

Sometimes, however, it's not the tool that's at fault, it's us. We know how the image looked originally and we see problems that other people may not notice. It's often worth walking away for a couple of minutes and looking at the image again.

4 Undo the last attempt. Keep the brush the same size. Go to the Options bar and change the Type to Content-aware. We'll trace along the wire again. This time, however, the result is very different. Aside from some slight blemishes, it's almost impossible to see where the wire was. As the

problem areas are now isolated we will not have much trouble removing them. We can switch between Proximity match and Content-aware in order to tidy up the places that were missed – the strands of hair caught on the barb, for example – or where the tool didn't do such a good job.

Making rainbows

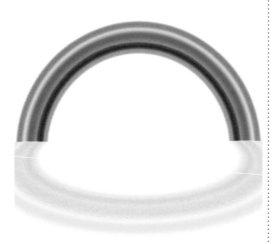

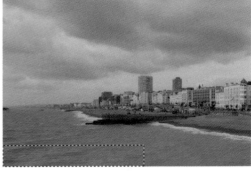

1 Start by creating a new layer. Grab the Rectangular Marquee tool **M** and draw out a selection from the bottom-left corner to around halfway across the document. The height determines the rainbow's width; we don't want it too wide to begin with as we'll be scaling it up later.

WHETHER IT'S THE PROSPECT of finding the fabled pot of gold or simply its beautiful colors, a rainbow can really lift your spirits on an otherwise dreary gray day. The problem is that the conditions have to be just right for us to see one. The sun has to be low and behind us, and it has to be raining, of course. This is not a common combination.

We don't have to rely on science and nature to call the shots, however. We can make our own rainbows in dry comfort. In just a few steps we can not only paint a spectrum across the sky but conjure our own rain as well.

As well as using the technique for photographic effects, we could just as easily use it to create bolder graphic objects to highlight stationery or brighten up collages and album pages.

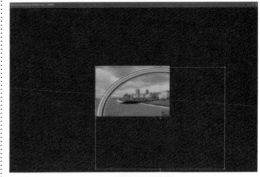

4 Enter Free Transform *ctrl* **T** *⌘* **T** and scale the rainbow up proportionally; it will help to zoom out *ctrl* **−** *⌘* **−** so we can see outside of the image bounds. We can also stretch it horizontally to gain more of an arc. Press **Enter** to commit the changes.

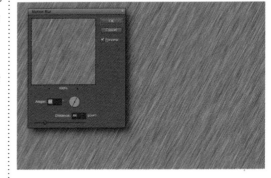

7 Now open the Motion Blur filter. There are no definite settings for this, it's just a case of experimenting with the angle and distance until we get a reasonable rain effect. Click OK to apply the filter. Use Free Transform to scale the layer up slightly to lose the harsh edges the filter left.

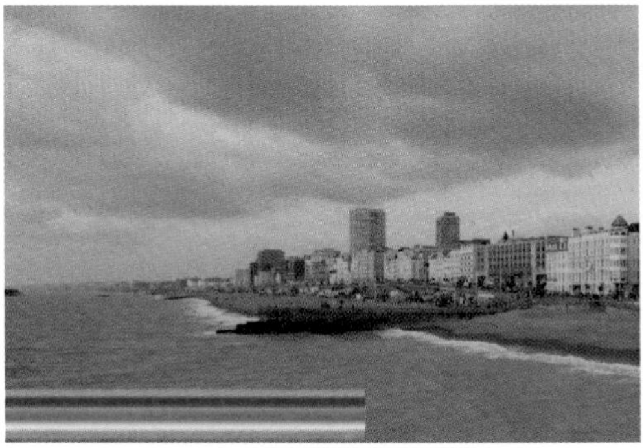

2 Select the Gradient tool G and pick the Transparent Rainbow preset from the Options bar. Make sure Linear Gradient is selected and, holding Shift, click and drag inside the boundaries of the selection from the bottom to the top. Release the mouse and deselect ctrl D ⌘ D.

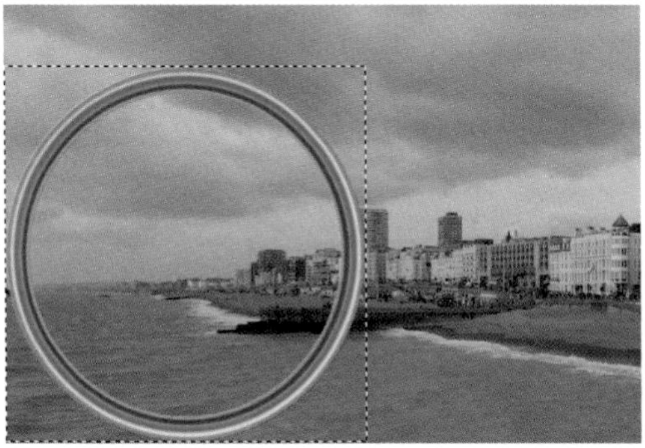

3 Grab the Rectangular Marquee again, hold Shift to keep it square and click and drag from the bottom-left corner of the image to the far right of the gradient. Select the Polar Co-ordinates filter (under Distort) and choose Rectangular to Polar, click OK and deselect.

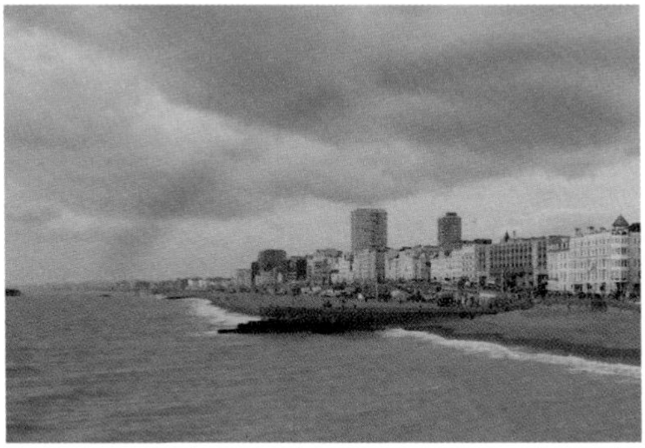

5 We don't want the bottom part of the arc so use a soft-edged Eraser E to remove the excess. Now apply some Gaussian Blur to make it more hazy; the exact amount will vary, depending on the image size. Finally, we'll lower the layer's opacity to fade it out a little.

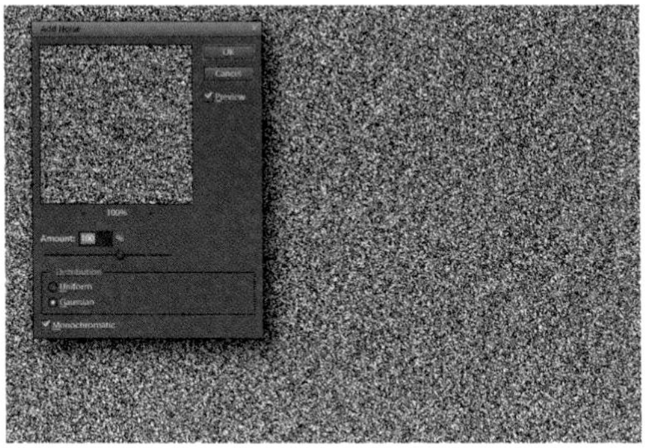

6 We couldn't have our rainbow without rain, of course. Create a new layer above the rainbow, then fill it with 50% gray using the Fill Layer dialog Shift Backspace. Now add some noise: check the Gaussian and Monochromatic boxes and push the amount up to around 100%.

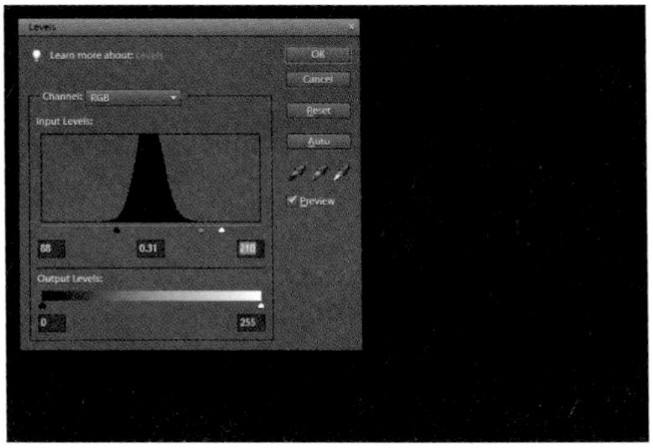

8 Holding alt ⌥, create a Levels Adjustment Layer. Check the Group With Previous Layer and click OK. Now we can adjust the strength of the effect: bring the Shadows up to the edge of the histogram then adjust the midtones and highlights to produce a lighter amount of rain.

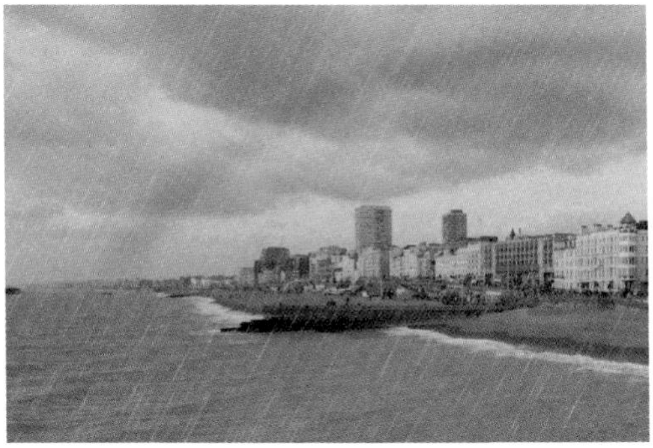

9 Click the rain layer's thumbnail to make it active again and set its blend mode to Screen. This hides the black, leaving us with just the rain. Using an Adjustment Layer means we can go back at any time and edit the settings to increase or decrease the amount as we see fit.

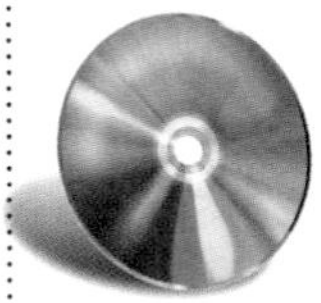

HOT TIP

You may find that when you run the Polar Co-ordinates filter, you get a colored haze around the circle. This is because part of the object gets caught on the edges of the filter. To avoid this, select the Move tool and nudge the gradient up from the bottom by a couple of pixels to leave a gap before making the square selection.

Similarly, if you find you have a gap in the circle, it's because there was a gap between the end of the gradient and the selection.

SHORTCUTS
MAC WIN BOTH

Catching the drops

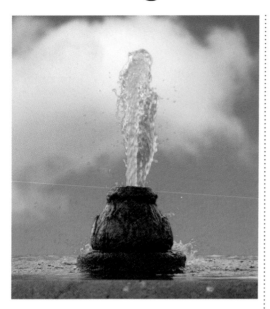

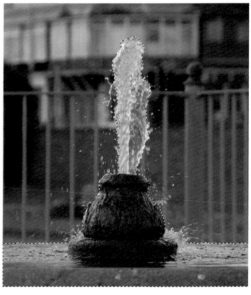

WE CAN'T ALWAYS CHOOSE our backgrounds and whether we just want a better looking photo or need the subject to be placed in a different image entirely, we need to be able to make a good selection and one that comprises all the required details. Our standard tools do a great job in most cases but, as ever, there will always be something that eludes even the most powerful of them.

In our example, the fountain's background is hardly inspiring, so we'd like to cut it away and replace it with something more fitting. The problem we have is all the little splashes of water: we need to keep them because the image would look static and unrealistic without them but it's too much for the Magic Wand to cope with. Zooming in and selecting each one by hand would be far too time-consuming.

As we'll see, by applying a little lateral thought, we can achieve this quickly and very effectively.

1 We'll begin by selecting as much of the fountain and water as possible. The Quick Selection tool is perfect and makes short work of this. For earlier versions of Elements, we could use the Magic Selection Brush or a combination of the Magic Wand and the normal Selection Brush.

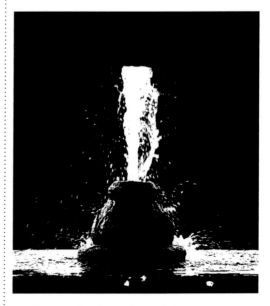

4 There are a lot of areas that we don't want: we can paint these out using a hard-edged black brush. The fountain is saved so we don't have to be too careful around it, as long as we leave the splashes intact. We can erase the area at the top where it meets the windows, for example.

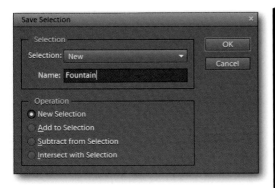

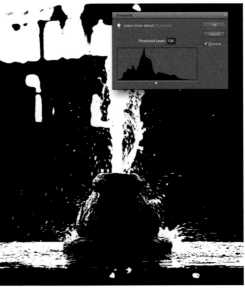

2 With the basis of our selection complete, we'll store it for later: go to the Select menu, choose Save Selection and give it a name and click OK. Now deselect *ctrl* *D* *⌘* *D*. In preparation for the next part of the technique, we'll duplicate the background layer *ctrl* *J* *⌘* *J*.

3 Select the Threshold adjustment from the Filters menu. This converts the light and dark areas to pure black or white. Now we can clearly see where the water drops are. Making slight adjustments to the level gives us some fine-tuning. This is a good balance so we'll apply it.

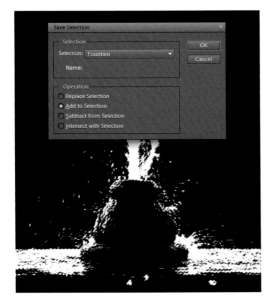

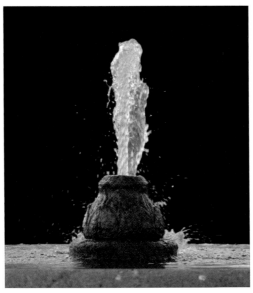

5 Grab the Magic Wand *W* and uncheck Contiguous in the Options bar. Clicking in one area of white will select them all. Open the Save Selection dialog. Choose our previously saved one from the list and click Add to Selection. Finally, click OK. We can hide or discard this layer now.

6 Make the background layer active and load the saved selection. Apply a 1 pixel Feather to soften the edges, then press *ctrl* *J* *⌘* *J* to make a copy. Shown against black, we can see how good the result is. We can add a more suitable background, of course, as our intro image shows.

HOT TIP

As an additional step, we could separate the main water spurt from the rest of the image by selecting with the Rectangular Marquee and cutting it to a new layer *ctrl* *Shift* *J* *⌘* *Shift* *J*. We can desaturate it to remove any unwanted color casts and also lower its opacity a little to make it slightly translucent.

SHORTCUTS
MAC **WIN** **BOTH**

101

0–60 in ten minutes

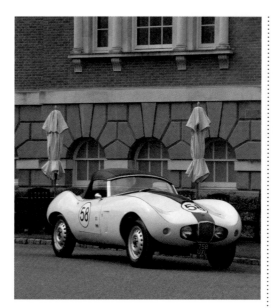

I F YOU'VE EVER TRIED TO PHOTOGRAPH a moving object such as a car, you may have found the results disappointing. When cameras are set to automatic mode they have a nasty habit of removing the action from the image by freezing the motion.

Fortunately for us it's not difficult to put the drama back, or, as we'll be doing with the image above, to create movement from a stationary image. We'll see two different ways of doing this: the first mimics the use of a slow shutter speed by blurring the object in front of a static background. The second method is the opposite effect: the car remains still whilst the background is blurred. This would be the result of panning, i.e. following the subject's movement with the camera whilst taking the shot.

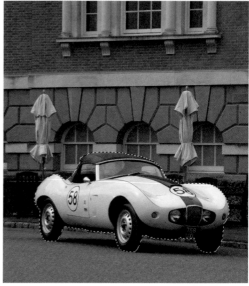

1 The first task is to isolate the car from its background. A combination of the the Quick Selection tool and the Selection Brush is best for doing this, the latter being used to tidy up the tricky areas of low contrast. Copy the car to its own layer by pressing *ctrl* J ⌘ J.

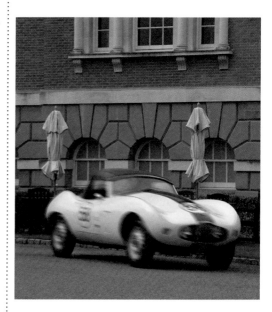

4 You'll notice there's some blurring in front of the car as well as behind, most prominently around the tires and far right of the bodywork. This, of course, wouldn't happen unless it was being vigorously shaken. Select a large, soft eraser. Use the edge to carefully remove the unwanted areas.

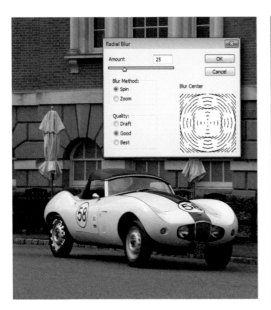

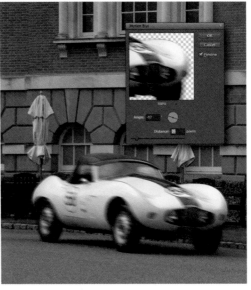

2 One common trait of speed is the wheels. Use the Elliptical Marquee to select one of the wheels (not the tire). Open the Radial Blur filter and set the method to Spin. The amount depends on the required effect; we've used 25 here. Deselect _ctrl_ _D_ _⌘_ _D_ and repeat for the other wheel.

3 First we'll create the effect of the car zooming past. Open the Motion Blur filter – make sure Preview is enabled. Start by setting the distance. Keep this subtle to avoid it looking too much like a cartoon. Now adjust the angle to suit the direction of the car's movement.

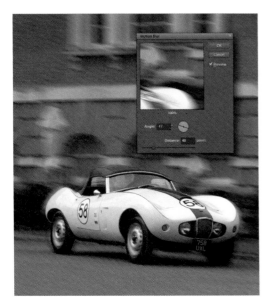

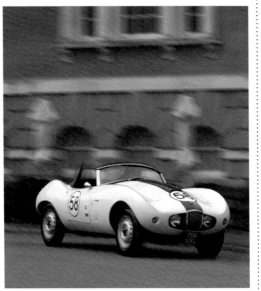

5 Here's a different approach. After completing step 2 above, make the background layer active. Apply the Motion Blur filter; as before, set the distance and angle. You can add a slightly heavier effect this time. Once again there are some unwanted areas. We'll deal with those next.

6 Select the Clone Stamp. Using a small soft tip, go around the car painting over the sections where the overspill is most pronounced. Finally, switch back to the car layer. Use a small eraser to remove the windows to reveal the blurred background of the original image.

HOT TIP

When you're cloning in parts of a blurred image you can often afford to be a little less precise than you would be where the detail is visible. As long as there are no obvious areas where there's a repeating pattern or misalignment, a little artistic license will most likely go unnoticed.

SHORTCUTS
MAC WIN BOTH

Image adjustments

Real world modeling

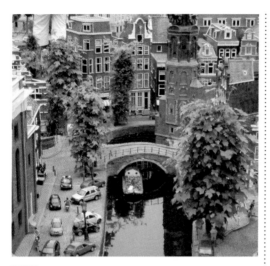

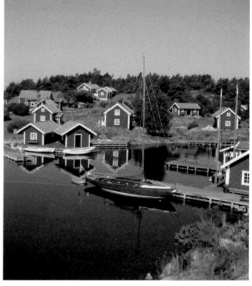

THIS TECHNIQUE IS STYLED AROUND an effect known as Tilt-Shift, which is derived from a specialist camera lens of the same name. Its main purpose is to prevent perspective convergence when photographing subjects such as tall buildings. When using this equipment to capture normal scenes, however, it was discovered that the results could end up looking like scale models, due to the extremely shallow depth of field it produces. We are used to seeing larger areas in full focus and small objects with heavily blurred backgrounds; when this is swapped around our brains can be confused.

The best images to use with this technique are ones that are taken from above the scene – although it can work with different views, such as that shown in our example. It's also good to keep the subject area fairly tight in the frame as we are less likely to be fooled by an image that extends for miles into the distance, as models generally don't have that degree of detail and would take too long to construct.

1 Here we have our starting image: a picturesque fishing village. It almost looks like a model to begin with so our technique is going to work really well. The first thing we need to do is duplicate the background layer `ctrl` `J` `⌘` `J` as we'll be working exclusively with the copy.

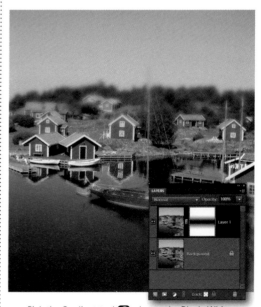

4 Pick the Gradient tool **G**, choose the Black, White preset and set the type to Reflected. Holding *Shift*, click and drag up from the middle of the image to where the trees meet the sky. We now have a narrow area in sharp focus which softly fades to a blur.

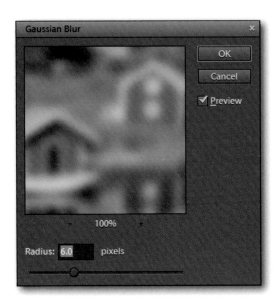

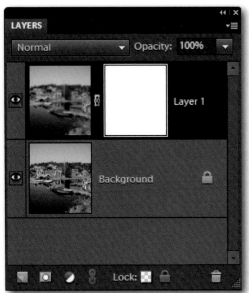

2 Now we'll apply some Gaussian Blur. We don't want to completely obliterate the scene, just knock out the detail. A radius of around 6 pixels works well in the example; the amount will vary for different images, of course, depending on their size.

3 The next stage is to add a mask to the layer. This will allow us to selectively hide parts of the blurred image so the sharp layer below can show through. Click the Add Layer Mask icon at the base of the Layers panel. Nothing happens yet, of course.

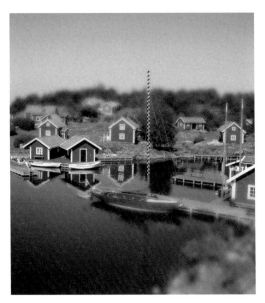

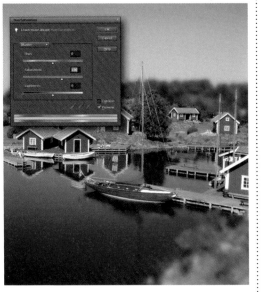

5 It's beginning to look good but there are still a few adjustments to be made. Because we're looking straight at the scene, the masts of the boats should still be in focus. Still working on the mask, use the Polygonal Lasso to outline them and then fill the selection with black to hide the blur.

6 We can use a fairly soft black brush to paint out any additional areas, such as the top of the trees behind the mast, or blur more of the background by painting in white. Finally, we'll add a Hue/Saturation adjustment above the blur layer and raise the saturation to enhance the illusion.

HOT TIP

Remember, we can hide the blur layer to make accurate selections using the original as we're always working on the mask layer. Any changes will show up when we make it visible again. With very fine detail such as we have with the boat's rigging, editing the mask with a brush is much too difficult. Instead, we can use the Polygonal Lasso to follow the lines to the top of the mast and back down the other side then connect them up at the bottom. Now we can use the Stroke command set to black, at around 2 pixels, applied centrally to accurately bring the rigging back into the scene.

SHORTCUTS
MAC WIN BOTH

Sunset silhouette

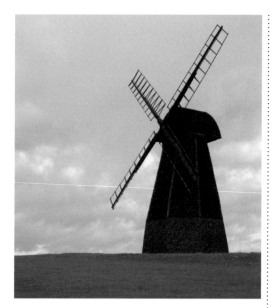

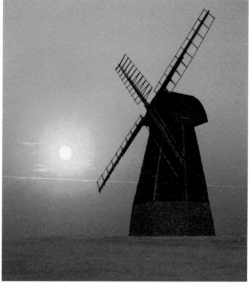

ARLIER IN THIS CHAPTER we looked at replacing a washed out sky with a more impressive one. Simply changing the existing sky isn't always enough, however: depending on the type of scene we want to produce, we will often need to adjust the foreground to match. We'll demonstrate this by transforming our uninspiring photo of a windmill into a lovely evening silhouette.

As the sun sets its light changes, becoming a richer, more orange tone which, in turn, affects the scene's colors. We can mimic this by adjusting the levels of the image; it's important not to darken the subject too far as we still want to be able to see some detail.

Producing images in this way not only lets us rescue dull photos, but also allows us to create difficult to capture or sometimes impossible views: with Elements, the sun will always be just where we want it.

1 Here we've duplicated the background layer and removed the sky: the Magic Wand in discontiguous mode made easy work of the fiddly areas of the sail frames. Our sunset image is then placed on a layer behind. It's not looking particularly convincing at this stage, though.

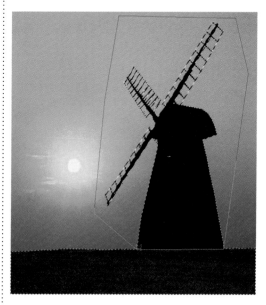

4 We'll add a shadow to complete the scene: load the windmill layer's selection. Only the outline is needed so grab the Polygonal Lasso tool, hold *Shift* *alt* *Shift* ⌥ to switch to intersect mode, and draw across the windmill's base. Follow on with a loose selection around the rest.

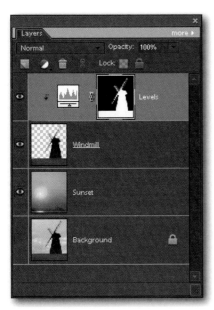

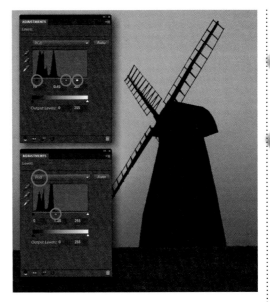

2 Make the windmill layer active and load its selection by holding *ctrl* ⌘ and clicking its thumbnail in the Layers panel. Create a Levels Adjustment Layer; the selected area becomes a mask so the changes we make will only affect the foreground image.

3 Drag the midtone slider across to the right to make the tones richer and darker. Increase the Shadows slightly and bring the Highlights up a little by dragging the slider to the left. Select the red channel *ctrl* *1* ⌘ *1*. Drag the midtones a little to the left to deepen the red hue.

HOT TIP

It's often not possible to remove all traces of the background, particularly in small, intricate areas of the photo. When placed against a darker image these lighter areas can show up as a halo around the isolated object. We could zoom in with a smaller eraser to tidy it up but this is fiddly and we could end up removing parts of the image we meant to keep. Instead, use the Burn tool to darken and blend in the offending areas; this can also be used to paint over any brighter elements in the scene that the Levels adjustment doesn't affect.

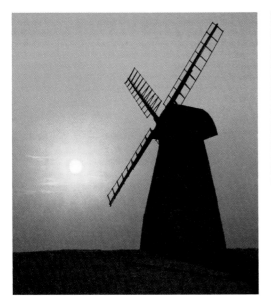

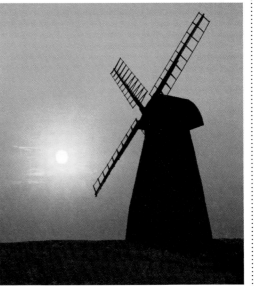

5 Create a new layer above the Adjustment Layer and fill the selection with black. Deselect and enter Free Transform mode *ctrl* *T* ⌘ *T*. Distort the shadow into position by holding *ctrl* ⌘ and dragging the corner handles – you'll need to zoom out to stretch it past the bottom edge.

6 The shadow is too harsh so we'll use a small amount of Gaussian Blur to soften the edges and lower the opacity a little so it's not completely black against the background. As a final step, we've used the Ripple filter to add the effect of the shadow falling across the uneven grass.

SHORTCUTS
MAC WIN BOTH

That's snow business

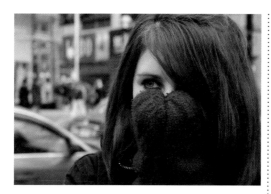

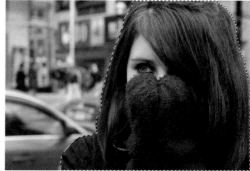

WE DON'T SEEM TO GET THE SAME amount of snow as we did in years gone by; whilst some people would say this is a good thing, it is a shame not to see the stunning white backdrop blanketing the streets and countryside – it does make a particularly great photo opportunity, after all.

This is not a problem for the montage artist, however. With a little effort we can take almost any scene and add a little wintry magic.

This technique can be used to make great seasonal greetings cards or calendars, or just to create a scene you may never see – snow in Egypt, perhaps?

1 First we'll make a selection of the girl using the Quick Selection tool **A**. We don't need to worry too much about the fine detail. Once you've made the selection press *ctrl* **J** **⌘ J** to create a copy on a new layer. This will allow us to add snow both in front of and behind her.

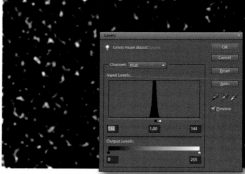

4 Open the Levels adjustment *ctrl* **L** **⌘ L**. Start by dragging the Highlights arrow over to the left so it meets the right edge of the histogram. Now pull the black shadows control over towards the highlight arrow. As we do this the image tightens up, creating snow-like flecks.

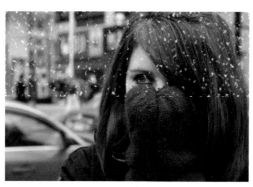

7 Press *ctrl* **J** **⌘ J** to duplicate the layer. Use the Move tool **V** to slide it over next to the original. Now go to Image > Rotate and flip the layer both horizontally and vertically. This gives us a better pattern without obvious repeats. Press *ctrl* **E** **⌘ E** to merge the two layers.

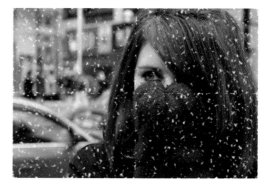

8 Create a duplicate of the merged layers. Move it beneath the copy and flip it both ways as before. Finally, merge the two layers. We have a problem though: there are ugly joins across the image. Grab a soft-edged Eraser and paint them out, being careful not to leave large holes.

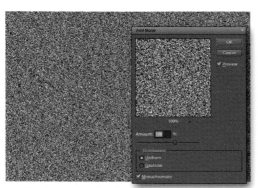

2 Now to start creating the snow. Make a new layer `ctrl` `alt` `Shift` `N` `⌘` `⌥` `Shift` `N` above the girl's layer. Fill this with 50% gray. Now go to Filter > Noise > Add Noise and set the amount to around 100%. Check the Monochromatic box and click OK.

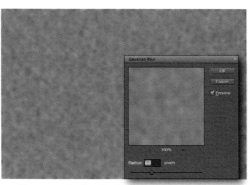

3 Now open the Gaussian Blur filter. We're looking to achieve a soft, mottled effect here. Somewhere around a 6 pixel radius gives us the best result on our example image; any more would not contain enough contrast for the technique to work correctly.

HOT TIP

Remember when using the Move tool or Free Transform, you can hold `Shift` while you drag the layer to keep it constrained to horizontal or vertical movement. This is very useful for techniques such as this, where keeping layers aligned is essential.

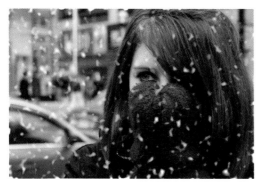

5 Setting the layer's blend mode to Screen removes the black, leaving us just with the snow. This works well as it is but we can take it a step further. Duplicate the snow layer and hide the original for the time being by clicking the eyeball icon next to its thumbnail in the Layers panel.

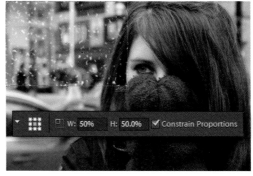

W: 50% H: 50.0% ✔ Constrain Proportions

6 Press `ctrl` `T` `⌘` `T` to enter Free Transform. Make sure Constrain Proportions is checked. Now type 50% into the width field. The layer will shrink to a quarter of its size. Drag it over to the top left of the image and press `Enter` to set the transformation.

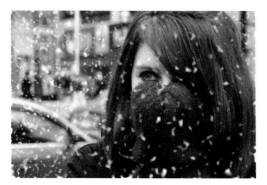

9 Drag the layer down between the girl and the background in the Layers panel. It now looks like the snow is in the distance. Make the original snow layer visible again. The combination of the large foreground flakes and the smaller ones in background makes it much more realistic.

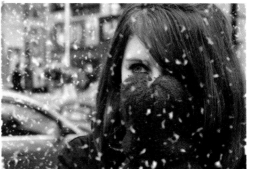

10 Snow tends to mute the colors of a scene, especially in the distance. As a final step add a Hue/Saturation Adjustment Layer between the girl and the background. Lower the saturation slightly to tone down the colors in the background. This also gives more focus to our subject.

SHORTCUTS

MAC WIN BOTH

But is it art?

THE ART WORLD CAN BE A FICKLE and sometimes intimidating place. Whilst the majority of its denizens are more than happy to welcome new concepts such as digital art with open arms, there will doubtless be the old-school stalwarts who balk at the very notion of something as utilitarian as a computer being the medium for any kind of creative expression. This is nothing new, of course: photography also received the same amount of steely renunciation when people started using it as anything other than a functional method of preserving images of people and places. It took the work of the late, great photographer Ansel Adams and others like him to prove that the photograph could have just as much visual impact and provide the same aesthetic pleasure as paintings by the old masters.

Unfortunately, as with many things, there can also be a degree of fighting within the ranks as well. There are those who frown upon certain aspects of digital art, such as photo-montage and 3D imagery, seeing it as compensation for lack of talent because it's not created from scratch and often uses other people's work as a constituent. This is, of course, a ludicrous way of thinking. Nobody thinks to question the validity of art-forms such as decorative floristry, which quite obviously doesn't necessarily require the flowers to be grown by the artist beforehand; it is, after all, the end result that matters and not how it was achieved.

Squabbling aside, one of the main accomplishments of the digital age is its ability to unlock and uncover artistic flair. We may shy away from trying out our ideas, often because we lack confidence in our abilities, believing that we'll make irreversible or costly mistakes. Another reason might be one of space and time, or the lack thereof: a studio requires a fair amount of working space and it's not always practical to set one up permanently; it can take a while to ready the materials and pack them away after a session, all of which does nothing to aid the creative process.

This is where computers come into their own. In general they're fairly self-contained, taking up only a small proportion of space and they can be ready for action in just a few minutes. What really sets them apart, however, is their forgiving nature: make a mistake on canvas and you've got a fair amount of tidying up ahead of you – at worst you'll have to paint over it and start afresh, which is demoralizing to say the least.

Working digitally is a different matter entirely. With technologies such as layers, non-destructive adjustments and styles, and not forgetting the trusty undo function, you can afford to think more freely in the knowledge that you have these safety-nets to catch you, should you falter and lose your artistic balance.

It's not all plain sailing, of course. The standard equipment that comes with a PC, usually a mouse, is great for moving the cursor around the screen to point at links in web pages, menus and highlight passages of text in a word-processor, but not so good for creating a masterpiece. Imagine trying to draw with a pencil shaped like a soap bar: it's not impossible, but it can be awkward and become uncomfortable after a while. If you're considering any kind of digital art as a serious hobby or even as a profession then a graphics tablet is an essential purchase. They can take a while to get used to, however; there's often a period where hand-eye coordination causes problems — we are usually more accustomed to looking directly at what we're drawing, rather than away to a screen. Once you have overcome this, it's unlikely you'll want to stop using it: outlining and selections can be achieved in half the time and you can really see the difference with the painting tools. Using a pressure-sensitive device makes shading an absolute delight, rather than the constant size and opacity changing nightmare it once was. Many tablets have configurable buttons on the stylus which can be set to emulate key-presses; for example, you could set one up as the spacebar, allowing you to pan around the image whilst zoomed in for close-up work. Some also have an eraser function when the stylus is flipped over, which also saves time.

There are, of course, some things that even the most powerful computer technology can't provide you with: imagination and determination. You're on your own there, but without the constraints that may have been holding you back before, you're free to express yourself in whatever way you see fit. There is no rule book to abide by here, just do what seems good at the time.

Who knows, those images you had locked away in your head might be just what the art editor of a magazine is looking for, so get creating!

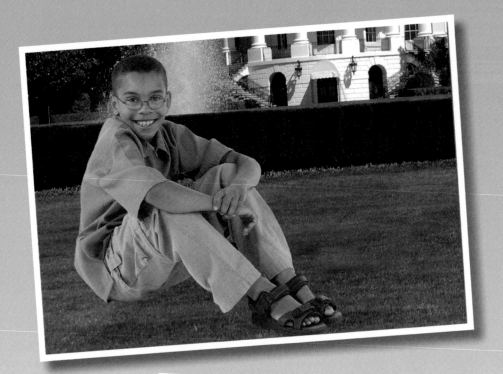

It's not difficult to create a simple montage like this one – a boy sitting on the White House lawn. But while he may be in the correct place, the image above looks unconvincing. By adding shadows, both on the boy and beneath him, we greatly increase the sense of realism, making it appear as if he was really photographed in this location.

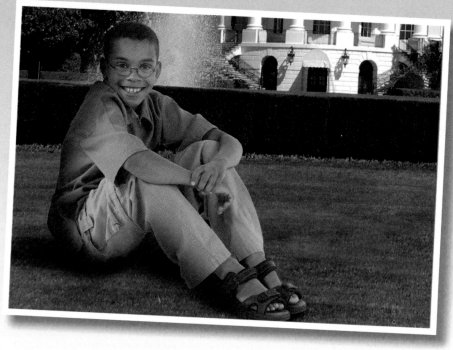

5
Light and shade

WHEN WE COMBINE IMAGES from several different sources, we can scale them, rotate them and distort them to fit the space – but they still won't look quite right. In order to achieve a true, realistic appearance, we need to add shadows. Whether they're cast on the ground, the wall or on other objects, it's shadows that will help your montages to work as complete images and to look less like obvious compositions.

Of course, there's a lot more to light and shade than just adding shadows. In this chapter we'll also look at how to make fire from scratch, how to add a spotlight effect to a stage curtain, and how to turn day into night.

Shadows on ground and wall

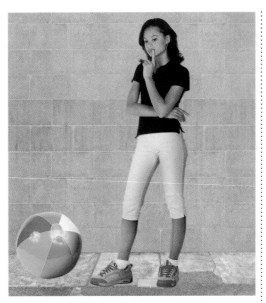

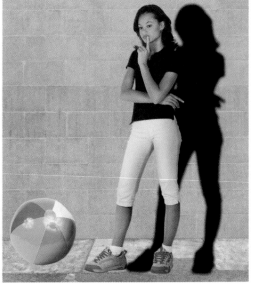

SHADOWS CAN MAKE THE DIFFERENCE between a convincing montage and one that looks like several images placed together. And yet, shadows are often overlooked in the rush to get things done.

It's easy to make shadows on the wall and on the ground – easier still if the base of the wall is at right angles to the viewer, as it is here. The ball, the girl and the background are three separate layers, which makes it easy for us to place shadows between them.

We'll look at two different methods for creating shadows: the girl and the ball require different treatments to produce their effects.

1 Begin by loading up the girl as a selection by holding **ctrl ⌘** and clicking on her thumbnail in the Layers panel. Make a new layer, feather the selection using **ctrl alt D ⌘ ⌥ D**, and fill with black. Deselect, move this layer behind the girl, and drag it out to the side.

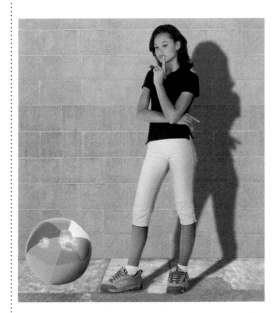

4 All we need to do now is to reduce the strength of this layer so we can see through it. We can change the opacity by dragging the slider at the top of the Layers panel; a simpler way is to use the number keys – **3** for 30%, **4** for 50% and so on. We've used a 50% opacity.

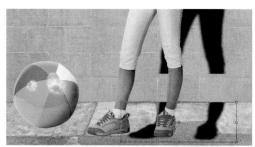

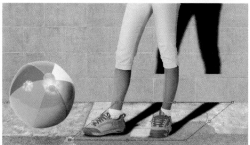

2 Now make a rectangular selection of the shadow at about knee height. Enter Free Transform with `ctrl` `T` `⌘` `T`, and drag the top center handle down to meet the bottom of the wall. Then hold `ctrl` `⌘` as you drag the bottom center handle to meet her feet.

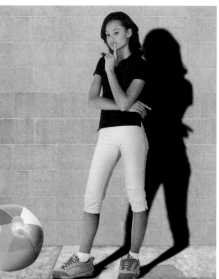

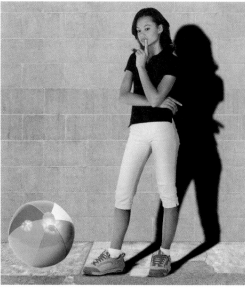

3 With the floor section of the shadow complete, we can move on to the wall part. Select the remaining piece of shadow with the Marquee tool and simply drag it down until it meets the ground. Stretch it vertically slightly if you need to.

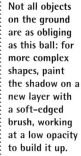

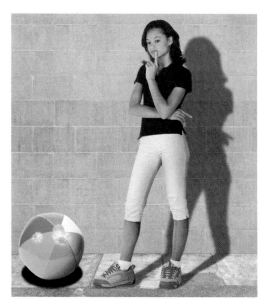

5 The ball's shadow requires a different treatment. As it's a spherical object, it will cast an elliptical shadow, so use the Elliptical Marquee tool, on a new layer, to make a selection. Feather it as before, and fill with black. Make sure it's behind the ball layer.

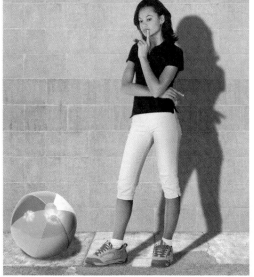

6 Lower the opacity of the ball shadow to match that of the girl, and then move it so that its position corresponds with the angle set by the girl's shadow. As it's a separate layer, it's easy to move and transform it until it looks exactly right.

Painting soft shadows

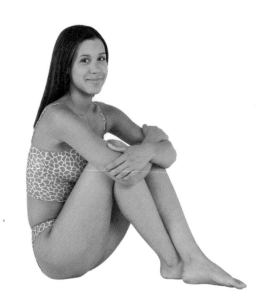

O N THE PREVIOUS PAGES we looked
at how to create shadows cast on a
wall and on the ground, by duplicating the
figure and filling with black. But some kinds
of shadow can't be created this easily: seated
figures, such as this one, need shadows to be
painted by hand.

As well as adding shadows beneath the figure,
we need to add some shading to the figure
itself in order for the effect to work properly.
The technique we'll use here is more efficient
than painting directly onto the figure and gives
us greater flexibility and accuracy.

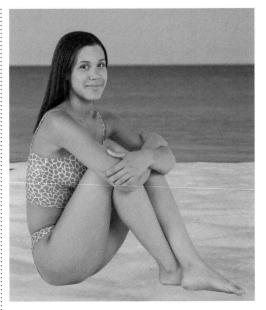

1 When we place our figure of a seated girl onto this
beach background, she looks as if she's hovering above
the surface: we need to add shadows to place her more
firmly on the ground.

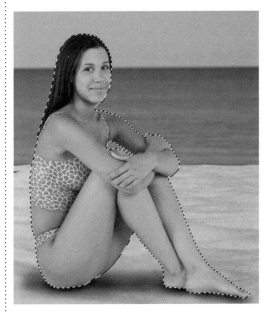

4 We also need shadows on the girl herself, to make sense
of those cast beneath her. Although we could paint
directly onto her layer, here's a better method. First, hold
ctrl ⌘ and click on the thumbnail of the girl's layer in the
Layers panel to load this area up as a selection.

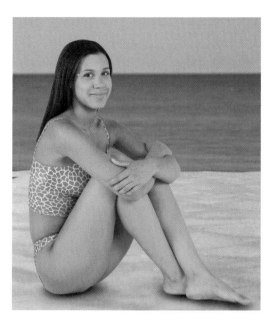

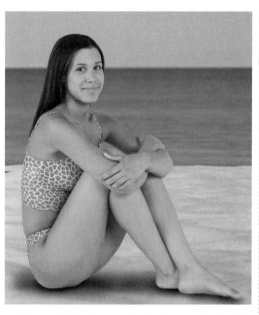

2 Begin by making a new layer between the girl and the background. Using a soft-edged brush set to an opacity of around 40%, paint the shadows beneath the places where she's touching the surface. By working at a low opacity, we can build the shadow up in stages.

3 Now switch to a larger, soft-edged brush and reduce the opacity of the brush still further. We can now paint the shadows cast by her body and her legs: they're fainter than those directly beneath the points of contact and the lower opacity will help us achieve this effect.

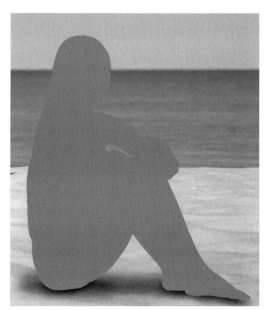

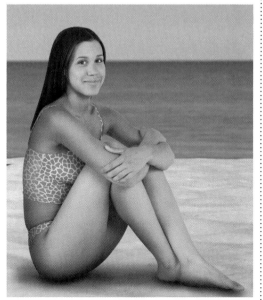

5 Make a new layer and, in the dialog that appears, set the mode to Hard Light and set it to fill with a Hard Light neutral color (mid-gray). Then inverse the selection using *ctrl* *Shift* *I* *⌘* *Shift* *I* and delete the area outside her: here's how the layer would look if it were set to Normal.

6 When set to Hard Light, the gray is invisible. But when we use the Burn tool, set to a soft-edged brush, to paint on this layer, we can darken it up. Add shading to her undersides, beneath her legs and bottom, to link her shadow into the shadows we've already painted beneath her.

SHORTCUTS
MAC WIN BOTH

117

Turning day into night

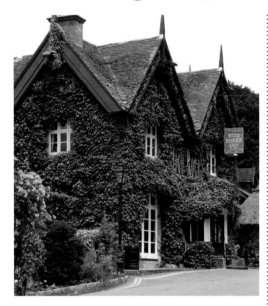

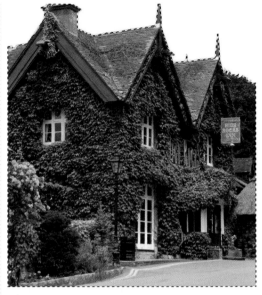

T AKING PHOTOS AT NIGHT generally requires the use of a tripod to avoid shaky or fuzzy images. You won't always have one with you, especially if you're just out for the day and happen to spot a scenic view such as the quaint English pub in the above photo. Whilst it's a great picture in its own right, it probably looks equally as good after dark.

In the following tutorial we'll fast-forward to a night view almost exclusively using Adjustment Layers to create the effect. This way we can have total control over the look and feel of the final image or take it back to daylight whenever we wish.

1 Use the Magic Wand **W** to select the sky; hold **Shift** to add the different sections together. Any stray areas can be tidied with the Selection Brush or Lasso tools. Inverse the selection **ctrl** **Shift** **I** **⌘** **Shift** **I**. Now press **ctrl** **J** **⌘** **J** to create a copy of the foreground.

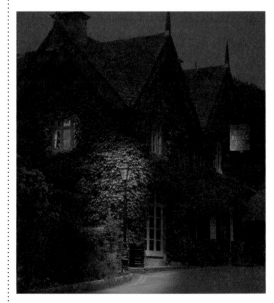

4 Now we'll create the lit areas. Click the Color layer's mask thumbnail. Now select a soft brush set to a low opacity and begin to paint in black over the areas where light would fall: around the lamp and windows. This hides the color layer to reveal the original daylight image beneath.

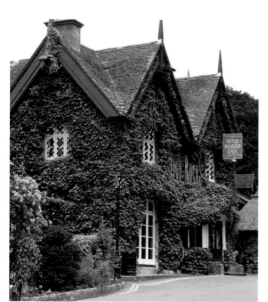

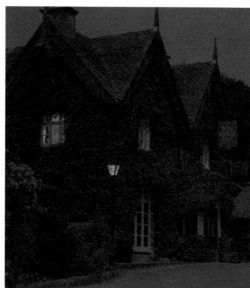

2 The next stage is to isolate the glass of the street lamp and the windows that will be lit. The Polygonal Lasso is best for this job: hold *alt* ⌥ to switch to the Freehand Lasso to select the tricky areas around the leaves. Add a light feather to the selection and copy to a new layer.

3 Create a Levels Adjustment Layer between the building and the layer you just created; accept the defaults for now. Add a Solid Color layer above that. Select a midnight blue color; this will create the night effect. Set its blend mode to Multiply and drop the opacity to around 80%.

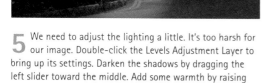

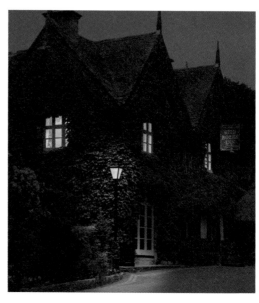

5 We need to adjust the lighting a little. It's too harsh for our image. Double-click the Levels Adjustment Layer to bring up its settings. Darken the shadows by dragging the left slider toward the middle. Add some warmth by raising the red channel's midtones and lowering the blue.

6 Create a new Solid Color layer above the windows. Choose a fairly deep orange hue, set the blend mode to Linear Dodge and drop the opacity to tone the effect down a little. Now press *ctrl* **G** ⌘ **G** to create a clipping group and restrict the color to the light sources.

SHORTCUTS
MAC **WIN** **BOTH**

119

Making fire

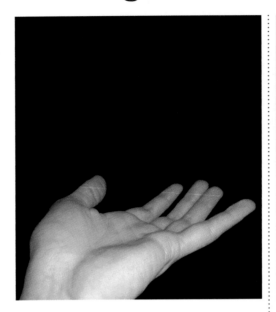

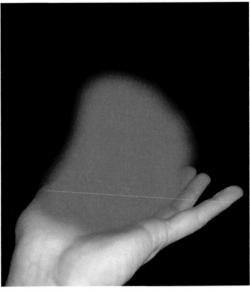

1 Begin by painting a blob, using a soft-edged brush, on a new layer. The shape and size don't matter that much at this stage, as we'll transform both later in the process; this is just the starting point.

ACCORDING TO LEGEND, it was Prometheus who brought fire to mankind – and suffered a particularly grisly fate as reward for his efforts.

Here's a method of creating fire that doesn't end up with us being chained to a rock and having our livers repeatedly pecked out by eagles. (Strange storytellers, the ancient Greeks.)

We'll create our fire from scratch, the only photograph being the hand we choose to place it on. Of course, you could set fire to anything – a house, a car, a landscape; whatever you choose, bear in mind that the effect will work very much better if you start with a black or very dark background. Flames rarely have the same impact on a bright summer's day.

This is the kind of image you can keep working at until the result looks exactly as you want it: there's a lot of fun to be had from continuously tweaking those flames.

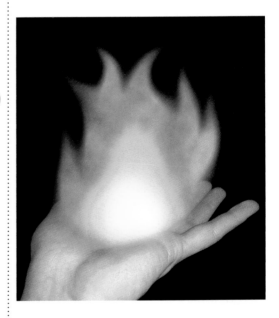

4 We need a bright heart at the center of this flame. Using a soft-edged brush, paint a yellow glow covering about a third of the flame area; then switch to white and paint a much smaller blob of color right at the bottom. It's already starting to look quite flame-like.

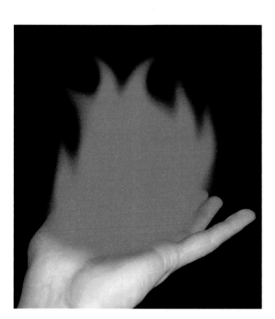

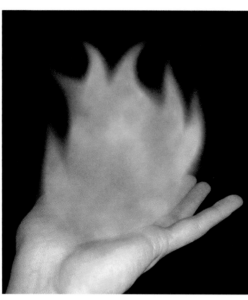

2 Use the Smudge tool, set to a strength of around 70% – 80%, to smudge that red blob into the beginnings of flame-like structures. Make sure the tool is not set to Sample All Layers, or you'll end up smudging the hand as well.

3 To make the basic texture, first lock the layer's transparency by clicking the Lock icon at the top of the Layers panel (or press **/**). Set the foreground and background colors to red and yellow, and apply Filter > Render > Clouds.

HOT TIP

Locking the transparency in step 3 allows us to apply the Clouds filter just to the flame area – otherwise, it would fill the whole canvas. We need to unlock it again in step 6, so that we can distort the flame layer. Getting from step 5 to step 6 took longer than the whole of the rest of the process: it's a slow and painstaking procedure to get this to look right. Don't rush it and you'll be rewarded for your efforts.

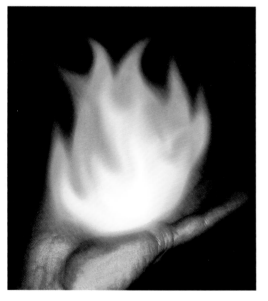

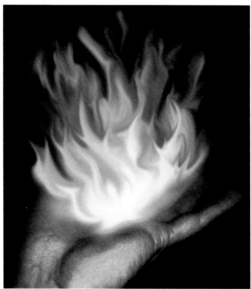

5 Using the Smudge tool once more, tweak up that yellow and white into fire-like shapes, reaching up into the body of the flame. This is also a good time to darken the hand: open the Levels dialog and drag the middle gray triangle to the right, about 80% of the way along.

6 Now unlock the transparency on the layer and work on the flames with the Smudge tool once more. Switch between large and small brush sizes to work on large areas and details; remember, you can smudge down from outside the flame area as well as up from the middle of it.

SHORTCUTS
MAC WIN BOTH

121

Instant candlelight

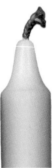

EVEN THOUGH CANDLES have long been obsolete as a source of lighting, we still rely on them for the warm atmosphere they bring and for the sense of occasion they lend to any event.

On the previous pages, we looked at how to create a fireball. Making a single candle flame is a slightly different process, in that it's painted entirely 'by hand', using no filters.

This isn't a difficult procedure, but it can result in a spectacular image: the trick is to paint each stage slowly, building up the effect as we go along.

If you want to take it a step further and add smoke to your flame, you can see how it's done in 'Smoke without fire', in Chapter 6.

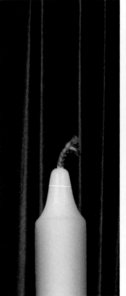

1 Start by placing your candle on a dark background so the flames show up well. We've used a deep red curtain.

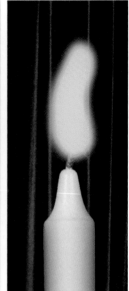

2 On a new layer, paint a rough shape in pale orange, using a soft-edged brush. Don't worry too much about the exact shape yet.

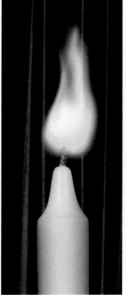

7 Continue smudging the top of the flame, perhaps with a smaller brush, until you're happy with the shape.

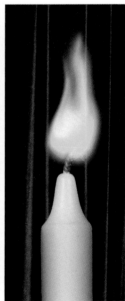

8 Changing the mode of the flame layer from Normal to Hard Light gives it added impact.

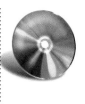

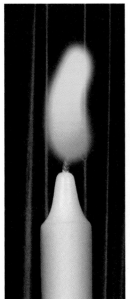
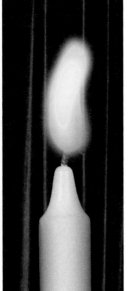
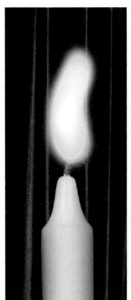
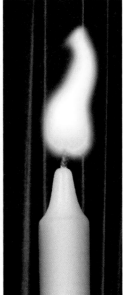

3 Use the Burn tool **O** set to Midtones, and darken the bottom of the flame around the wick to give the flame depth.

4 Switch to the Dodge tool, set to Highlights, and use it to brighten the center of the flame, turning it from orange to yellow.

5 Continue painting the flame in with the Dodge tool until the center is a brilliant, glowing white (but don't overdo it).

6 Now use the Smudge tool **R**, with a large brush size, to twist the candle flame into a more appropriate shape.

HOT TIP

When we started to brighten the flame in step 4, we brought the yellow down into the orange a little way. Continuing with the Dodge tool in step 5 hardens the edge between the yellow and the orange, automatically producing the subtle glow effect we see at the base.

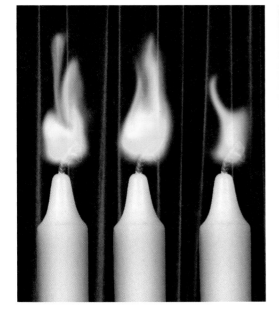

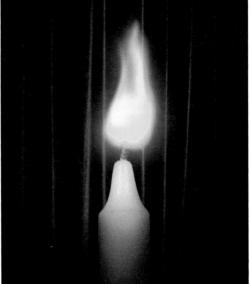

9 It's possible to create a huge variety of flame shapes by distorting the original painting with the Smudge tool – particularly handy when you want to make a row of candles. No need to paint each flame, just duplicate and smudge it.

10 For a stronger result, try painting a soft glow on a new layer behind the flame, using the same orange we started with (but at a low opacity). Darkening the background also draws attention to the flame itself.

SHORTCUTS
MAC WIN BOTH

Stage lighting

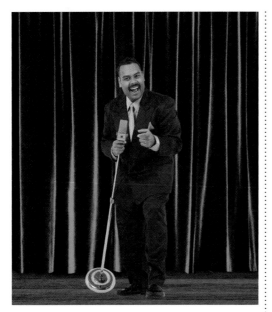

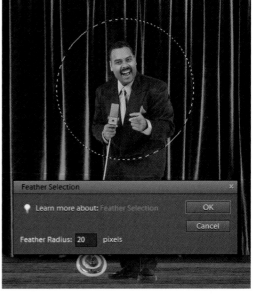

W E ALL WANT TO BE ON THE STAGE. Now, thanks to Elements, we can easily achieve this ambition.

The trick to creating stage lighting is to think in reverse. You might imagine that the way to add a spotlight effect would be to place a bright disk over the affected area, but you'd be wrong. Rather than adding light to the spotlit region, we'll subtract it elsewhere – in the form of a shadow with a circular hole in it.

And just for good measure, let's add a glow from the spotlight just out of shot and a shadow cast on the curtain behind.

1 Begin by making a circular selection: hold **Shift** as you trace with the Elliptical Marquee tool to make a perfect circle. Now use **ctrl** **alt** **F** **⌘** **⌥** **F** to bring up the Feather dialog and add a large feather radius – about 20 pixels is sufficient for this task.

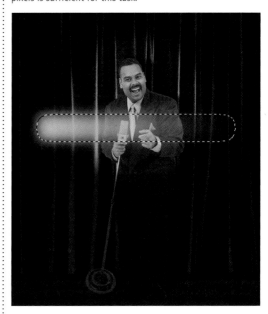

4 Now for the visible light. Make a rectangular selection and feather it as before, with a feather radius of 20 pixels. Choose a very pale yellow color and, on a new layer, use the Gradient tool set to Foreground to Transparent to drag from left to right, making a faded glow.

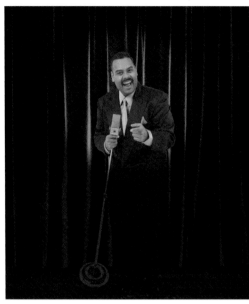

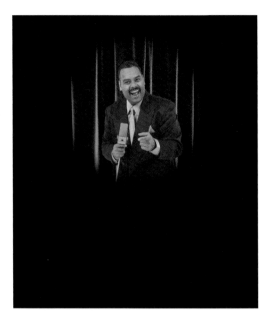

2 Make a new layer and inverse the selection by pressing `ctrl` `Shift` `I` `⌘` `Shift` `I`. Now, everything except the feathered circle is selected. Press `D` to make the foreground color black, then `alt` `Backspace` `⌘` `Backspace` to fill the selection with the foreground color.

3 At the end of the previous step, the shadow was so strong that we were unable to see anything through it. Lower the opacity of the shadow layer, either by dragging the slider at the top of the Layers panel or by pressing a number key: pressing `7` gives an opacity of 70%.

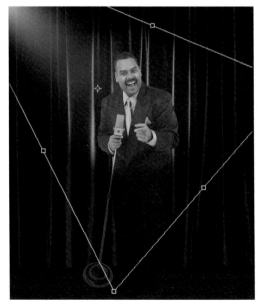

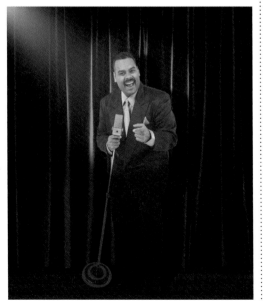

5 Use Free Transform (`ctrl` `T` `⌘` `T`) to rotate and distort the glow so that it comes in from the top left of the picture. Holding `ctrl` `alt` `Shift` `⌘` `⌥` `Shift` while you drag one of the corner points produces a perspective distortion, giving the impression of the beam getting larger.

6 Finally, add the shadow behind the man. Load his selection by holding `ctrl` `⌘` as you click on his thumbnail in the Layers panel. Use the technique described earlier in this chapter to make a shadow that sits on the curtain behind him and runs along the ground to his feet.

HOT TIP

You can add more than one spotlight glow if you like: simply duplicate the glow and flip it to come in from the opposite side of the image. If you do this, be sure to add an additional shadow behind the man, cast by that light.

SHORTCUTS
MAC WIN BOTH

Divine light

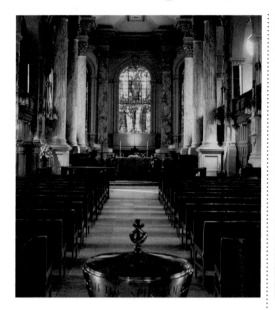

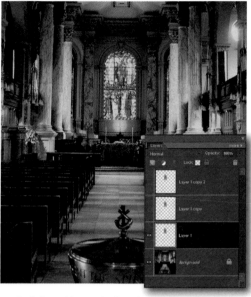

OMETIMES IT'S NECESSARY to exaggerate an effect (for the purpose of illustration, for instance) and as long as we don't overdo it, a little hyper-reality can really make an image stand out.

We'll demonstrate this by creating the impression of light beaming through a stained-glass window and projecting its image on to the floor of the church. Whilst this is not an unnatural occurrence, it's unusual to see it in such bold effect.

We don't have to use stained glass, of course; we could apply the technique to a normal window, for instance, projecting the shadows of the frame instead of the colors of the glass.

1 Begin by making a selection of the window. The Magnetic Lasso or Quick Selection tool work well here. Now press *ctrl J* ⌘ J three times to make as many copies. Turn the last two layers off by clicking their visibility icons in the Layers panel.

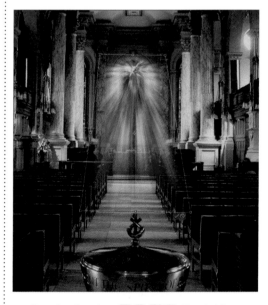

4 Enter Free Transform *ctrl T* ⌘ T. Now, holding *ctrl* ⌘, click and drag the bottom corner points out to distort and elongate the rays down the aisle and extend them a little more at the top. Press *Enter* to commit the changes. Finally, set the layer's blend mode to Screen.

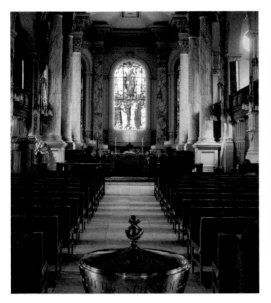

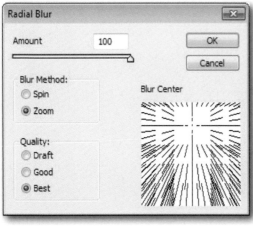

2 We'll start off the effect by brightening up the window as though the sun is behind it. Make the first copy's layer active by clicking its thumbnail in the Layers panel. Add a Simple Outer Glow layer style; we can leave it at its default settings. Now set its blend mode to Color Dodge.

3 Now for the light rays: make the second copy active and visible again. Open the Radial Blur filter, set the Method to Zoom, raise the Amount to maximum and select Best for the Quality. Now click and drag the Blur Center so the majority of the lines are pointing down. Click OK to apply.

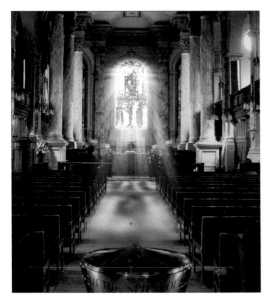

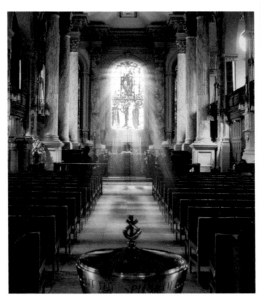

5 Switch to the top layer and make it visible. Open the Gaussian Blur Filter and set a moderate amount of blur: enough to soften the window's detail. Flip the layer vertically via Image > Rotate and now use Free Transform as before to move and distort the layer so it lays along the floor.

6 Change the blend mode to Hard Light – or Vivid Light for a more intense effect – and lower the opacity to fade the colors slightly. Finally, use a small, soft Eraser **E** to tidy up where it overlaps unwanted areas such as the ornament in the foreground and the front edges of the steps.

HOT TIP

The Radial Blur filter works really well here as we are viewing the window head-on. If, however, the picture was taken at an angle, it would be a slightly different technique: we would need to duplicate the blurred layers and flip one horizontally so we could have the rays emanating in different directions.

SHORTCUTS
MAC WIN BOTH

127

Shading using Hard Light

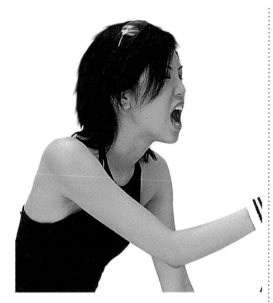

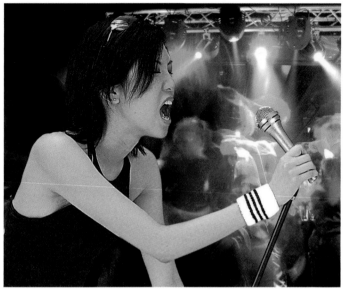

1 When we place the girl on the nightclub background, she looks quite artificially placed in the scene: her coloring in no way matches the tones of the background image. To begin, hold `ctrl` ⌘ and click on the girl's thumbnail in the Layers panel to load it up as a selection. Make a new layer and, in the dialog, set the mode to Hard Light, filled with Hard Light neutral color.

WHEN WE LOOKED AT SHADOWS earlier in this chapter, we were always painting with dark colors. But in this scene, set in a nightclub, we want to add the impression of the singer being lit by multicolored stage lighting from different angles.

Rather than painting directly onto the girl's layer, we'll create a new layer in Hard Light mode. By painting on this, we can add the effects we want without damaging the original layer; we can also edit the effects later, to produce exactly the effect we want.

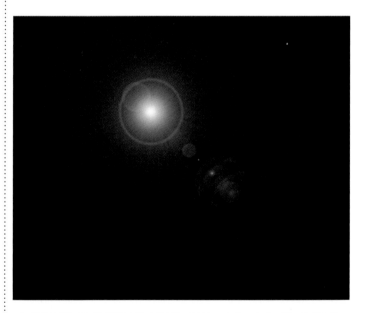

4 Let's add some Lens Flare to make the scene more impressive. We could add this filter directly to the background or to the girl – but we get far more control if we first make a new layer, filled with black. Then choose Fliter > Render > Lens Flare and position the flare in the preview window so that it's pointing down from the left.

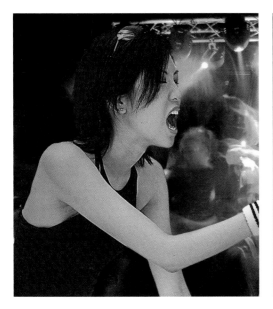

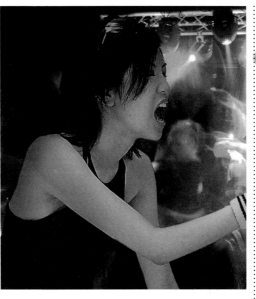

2 Group this new Hard Light layer with the girl's layer, so it only shows up where the two overlap. Using a soft-edged brush, sample some of the pink color from the background and paint it on the girl's shoulder to look like light reflecting off her.

3 Continue sampling colors from the background, painting them on the Hard Light layer as appropriate. You'll need to choose fairly dark colors to paint with: too bright and the effect will look artificial. As it's a separate layer, if we make a mistake we can easily paint over it.

HOT TIP

Although we've used a Hard Light layer to paint in color, we could also use the technique for painting in black to create traditional shadows – or, for a more subtle look, paint them in dark brown or dark blue instead, depending on the lighting of the scene. By painting shadows on a separate layer, we keep the original intact.

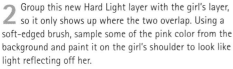

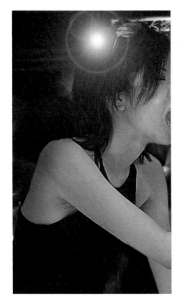

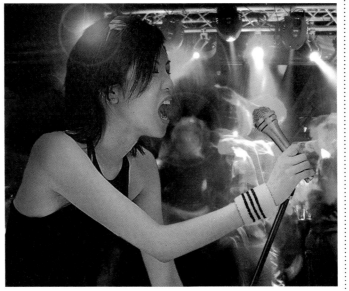

5 When we change the mode of this Lens Flare layer from Normal to Screen, all the black disappears so we can see through it to the scene beneath and move it into place.

6 In the previous step, the Lens Flare layer appeared where we created it – right at the top of the layer stack. But if we move it beneath the Hard Light layer, then it appears to originate from behind the girl's head. We can still see an outline of the ring it created in front of the girl, but the dazzling white center is hidden by the Hard Light layer.

SHORTCUTS
MAC WIN BOTH

Deceiving the eye

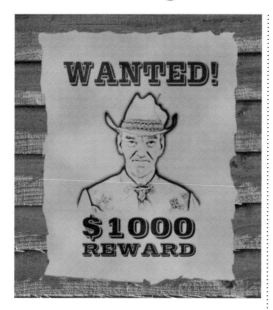

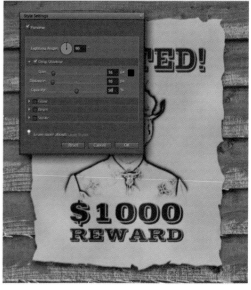

OW WE PERCEIVE THE SURFACE of an object visually is largely due to how light falls across it. Everything from the waves of the ocean to the contours of someone's face are defined by the variance in the tones.

In this project we have a wild-west style wanted poster. This has been created from scratch - using techniques in the book, of course. In its current state, it looks two-dimensional and lifeless, especially when set against a real background.

We can enhance the image immensely simply by adding a shadow but we can take it further still. Folding over a corner instantly portrays depth and by painting in areas of highlight and shadow using the Dodge and Burn tools we can create the impression that the poster has been wrinkled, as though dried in the high-noon sun. An interesting thing to notice here is how the artwork appears to be distorted, even though we don't actually alter it. Clever stuff!

1 We'll start by adding a drop shadow layer style to the poster layer using the Low preset. It needs adjusting slightly so select Layer > Layer Style > Style Settings. Set the angle to 90° to match the background's shadows. Drop the opacity to 50% and lower the Size and Distance a little.

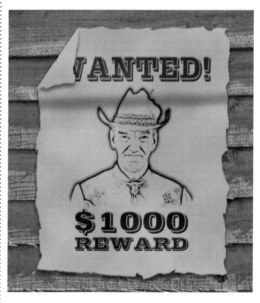

4 Set the shading layer's blend mode to Hard Light. Grab the Burn tool ⬤. Choose a medium-sized soft brush. Set the Mode to Highlights in the Options toolbar. Set the Exposure to around 40-50%. We'll begin by following one of the edges of the fence to make a crease.

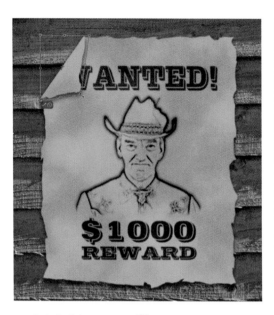

2 Grab the Polygonal Lasso **L**. Mark out one of the corners of the poster. Press *ctrl* *alt* *J* ⌘ ⌥ *J* to cut the area to a new layer. The shadow style will be applied to the new layer. Now use Free Transform *ctrl* *T* ⌘ *T* to rotate and distort the folded corner into position.

3 Press *ctrl* *E* ⌘ *E* to merge the fold and the poster layers. Create another new layer above the poster layer. Load the poster's selection again. Now press *ctrl* *Delete* ⌘ *Delete* to open the fill dialog and set the content to 50% gray. This will be our shading layer.

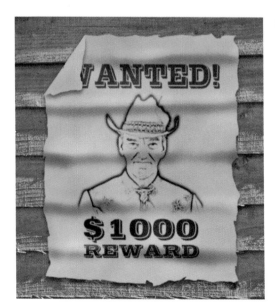

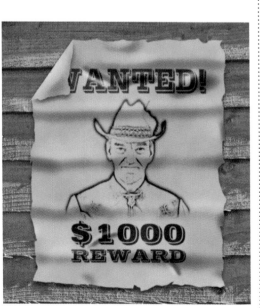

5 Hold *alt* ⌥ to temporarily switch to the Dodge tool. Now add a highlight just above the shadow you just painted. Continue to add horizontal creases – remembering not to go over the top of the corner fold, of course. Try to vary the tones to give a more uneven effect.

6 Add some random wrinkles at different angles and sizes across the poster to break up the linearity. If we swap the highlights and shadows, we get a dent, rather than a bulge. We can also add some shading to the folded corner to give the impression it's slightly rounded.

HOT TIP

Drawing the creases is made much easier if you're using a pressure-sensitive tablet, as you can control the amount of effect as you paint. If you don't have one, you may want to lower the exposure setting a little more and make several sweeps for each crease to build up the effect. If the final result seems too strong, we can always lower the opacity of the shading layer.

SHORTCUTS
MAC WIN BOTH

131

Flashlight illumination

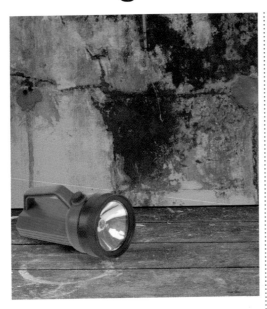

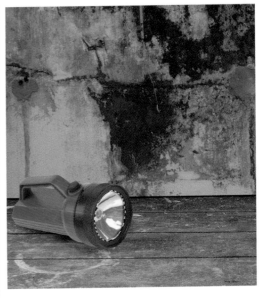

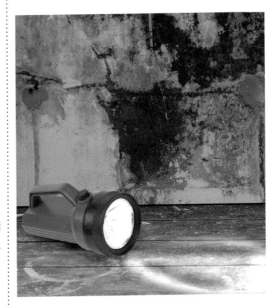

DARKNESS CAN PROVIDE AN IMAGE
with a much needed change in mood; a
technique frequently used in horror or thriller
movies – the lurking terror is very rarely in a
well lit, designer basement, after all.

Our starting image is a bit dull and lacks
any sense of purpose: it's just a flashlight in a
light room that may just be in the process of
being renovated. Its owner's probably gone off
to find his sandwich. By turning out the lights
and switching on the flashlight, however, we
instantly add an air of mystery to the scene:
where is this place, and why has the flashlight
been left lying on the ground in what appears
to be a derelict house? Suddenly thoughts of
jolly decorators on their lunchbreak are replaced
by those of deserted buldings and lurking fiends
in hockey masks – or perhaps not.

1 Make sure the flashlight layer is active by clicking its
thumbnail. Now make a selection around the lens. This
is quite tricky because of the angle; see the sidebar for a tip
on how best to achieve this. Once done press `ctrl` `J` `⌘` `J`
twice to create two new copies.

4 It's beginning to shape up but something's not right: the
flashlight needs to be switched on to cast its light, of
course. Make the second lens copy active and set its blend
mode to Linear Dodge. This has the effect of making the
already light areas much brighter.

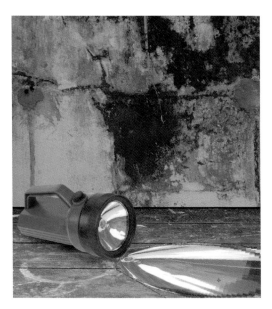

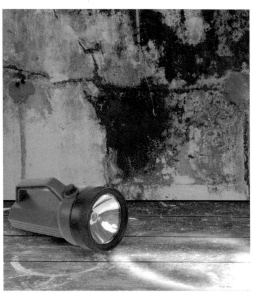

HOT TIP

We can't use the Elliptical Marquee to select the lens of the torch because of its odd angle. Instead, we can use the Shape tool method of selecting irregular areas, which is described in the next chapter.

2 Press *ctrl* *T* *⌘* *T* to enter Free Transform. Now stretch out one of the lens copies to create the shape of the beam area on the floor in front of the flashlight. You'll need to zoom out to see the handles as they will be outside of the canvas area. Press *Enter* to apply the transformation.

3 Press *ctrl* *I* *⌘* *I* to invert the colors of the layer. Now apply some Gaussian blur; we can use a large amount as we don't want too much of the original detail showing. Finally, set the blend mode to Linear Dodge. Most of it will disappear, creating the effect of the beam pattern.

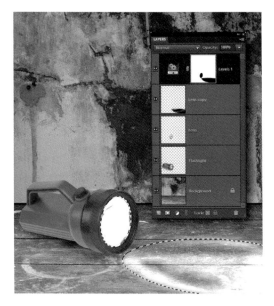

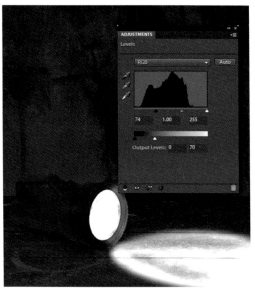

5 Load up both the light beam and lens layers' selections by holding *ctrl* *Shift* *⌘* *Shift* and clicking their thumbnails in turn. Now create a Levels Adjustment Layer at the top of the stack. We need to invert the mask *ctrl* *I* *⌘* *I* so all but the light areas will be affected.

6 Drag the right-hand Output levels slider across to the left to lower the overall brightness. Now push the Shadows value to the right to give a richer effect. Finally, load up the flashlight's selection and use a soft black brush to paint out the mask inside the bezel to lighten it up.

Cooking up a storm

LIGHTNING IS NOT THE EASIEST OF
phenomena to photograph. Firstly,
electrical storms are not as common in some
parts of the world as they are in others and
secondly, there's the problem of braving the
weather – not the best of environments for
a camera. There's the issue of getting a good
image as well; the best we can hope for is one
or two lucky shots, let alone getting a picture of
lightning striking just where we need it! Even if
it does, the chance of being ready to capture it
is not very likely, and lightning never strikes the
same place twice, of course.

In this project we'll find out that it's not at all
difficult to create a stormy scene and place a
realistic lightning strike just where we want it.

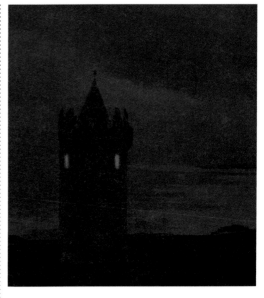

1 This picture of an isolated castle on the coast will make
an ideal starting image. We have everything here: it's
dark, mysterious and we already have some menacing-
looking clouds as a backdrop. All we need now is to add
some raging, untamed weather.

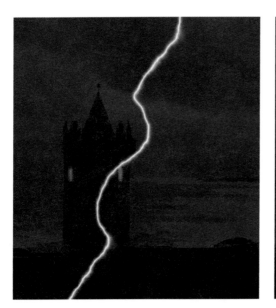

4 Change the layer's blend mode to Screen to filter out
the black areas. Now open the Levels dialog and drag
the shadows and midtones sliders to the right until most of
the cloud texture has disappeared. The rest can be removed
with the Eraser tool **E**.

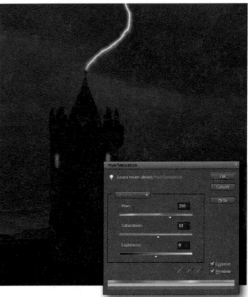

5 Instead of scaling the lightning, we can just choose a
suitable portion and erase the rest, then move it into
position. Open Hue/Saturation **ctrl U** **⌘ U**, check the
Colorize box and drag the Hue slider to the right to add a
tinge of blue; we can also increase the saturation if needed.

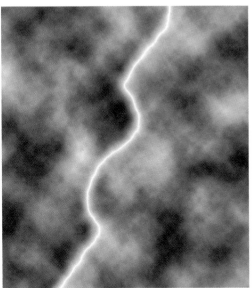

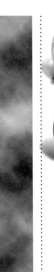

2 Create a new layer *ctrl Shift N* / *⌘ Shift N* and fill it with white. Now take a soft black brush and paint a slightly jagged line down from the top of the document to the bottom. This will become our bolt of lightning. Finally, use a larger brush to fill one side of the canvas with black.

3 Make sure the default colors are set by pressing *D*. Now apply the Difference Clouds filter. This gives us a narrow and more defined line. Press *ctrl I* / *⌘ I* to inverse the image and we can see our lightning bolt beginning to take shape.

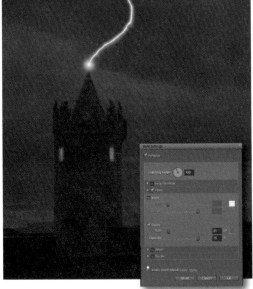

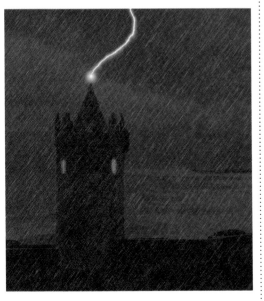

6 Create a new layer above the lightning. Use a soft, low-opacity brush to build up a small glow where the lightning hits the tower. Now add a Simple Outer Glow layer style; double-click the style icon in the Layers panel to change its color to the same kind of hue as the bolt.

7 Finally, our image wouldn't be complete without a heavy downpour. We've used the technique from the rainbow project in the previous chapter and used much stronger settings to give the impression that our tower is in the midst of a truly ferocious storm.

HOT TIP

We've created a simple example of the effect here but we could just as easily add more layers to build up a really tropical or magical storm. We could also use a very low opacity brush to paint in brighter areas on the clouds to give the effect of them being lit up by the lightning as they extend off into the distance.

SHORTCUTS

MAC WIN BOTH

Can I get a job doing this?

THE SHORT ANSWER IS: YES. The longer answer is: Well, yes – if you have the skill, determination and free time available, and if you happen to bump into the right people.

The question of whether it's possible to make a career out of doing photomontage work occurs, at some stage, to just about everyone who's ever dabbled in Photoshop or Elements. It's an appealing proposition: the idea of spending one's days tinkering with images for profit sounds like a great way of occupying oneself.

The trouble is, the world just isn't crying out for more photomontage artists. It's not like studying to become a dentist or a plumber. There's no standard course, no regular qualification, and absolutely no guarantee of a career of any sort at the end of the line. This, coupled with the fact that you're not alone in wanting to pursue this path, means that there are far more people out there capable of manipulating images than there is demand for such services.

But if you're really determined, then there are several steps you could take to make the dream a possibility. It all depends on whether you have the free time to develop your skills without being paid to do so.

The first, and most important step, is to get your work published. Art editors are notoriously busy and preoccupied people, who are driven by deadlines and the need to fill the space between the text and the advertisements in their publications. What matters to them are four main factors: Can you interpret a brief? Do you have the skill needed to turn in a good job? Do you have an interesting or unique style? And, above all: Can you be sure to meet a deadline? For ultimately, it doesn't matter how good or inspired your work is if you're unable to turn it in on time. If you don't meet the deadline, you'll never hear from them again.

Art editors are far more likely to take a chance on commissioning work from an unknown artist (yourself) if you can demonstrate that others have already placed their faith in you. Of course, it's something of a catch-22 situation: you can't get the work unless you've already had work published, and you can't get work published unless someone gives you the work.

One solution is to begin by offering your services, for free, to publications or websites who couldn't afford to pay for them. This might include local newspapers, community and sports magazines, charity websites, church and workplace newsletters, and so on. Get as much work in print or on websites as you can, to show that you're capable of sustained effort.

Only when you have a fair body of work to show should you then approach magazine and newspaper art directors. But start small: writing to *The New Yorker* offering to draw their covers is unlikely to produce a positive response, at least in the early days.

Self-promotion is a key part of bringing your skills to the attention of those who matter. These days, it's easy to set up and maintain your own website, and you should take the opportunity to show off as much published work as you can in this way. Feel free, as well, to show 'personal' work done for your own entertainment – but be aware that this won't carry as much weight with potential employers as work you've been commissioned to do.

Another way of getting started is to get a job in a publishing office, doing menial tasks such as scanning and filing photographs. Before long you'll come across an image that needs tweaking; show what you can do, and if you're any good your skills will be recognized.

You can, of course, set up a website offering your services directly to the public. Many people offer photo restoration, custom greetings cards, and photo caricature services; a few make a reasonable living out of it.

Decide where your strengths lie. You may be proficient at restoring photographs, removing ex-spouses from family shots, or caricaturing politicians. Develop your area of expertise and find new ways of performing the task. People are far more likely to use you if you can offer a service that no-one else can.

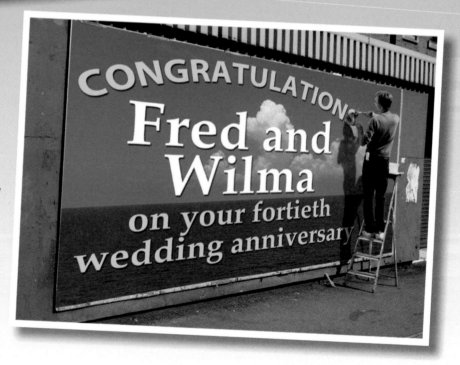

Making cards, notices and invitations is an enjoyable hobby in Elements. But why settle for a standard, head-on view of the text when we could show it on a billboard? It's easy to distort any text or images so they appear to be viewed in perspective, giving the design far more impact.

Transformation and distortion

COMPOSING MULTIPLE IMAGES into a single montage almost always involves scaling, rotating and moving the elements around. In this chapter, we'll look at the basics of using that most powerful tool, Free Transform: with its multiple keyboard modifiers, it's capable of producing good results.

There's more to distortion than simply scaling and rotation, though. In this chapter we'll explore how to make an image fit a flag, a mug and a computer screen, as well as several other surfaces, showing how to use Elements' tools and filters to match an image to just about any surface.

The science of transformation

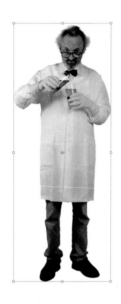

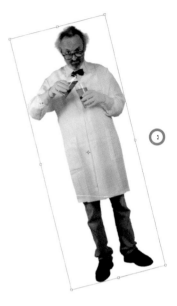

WHEN PUTTING A MONTAGE TOGETHER, it's almost certain that you'll need to resize one or more of its components to fit the scene. You may also want to distort an image for a particular effect: to give it a 3D appearance such as photos scattered on a surface or placed on a virtual gallery wall, for example.

Free Transform allows you to move, rotate, scale and distort your image in real time so you can compare and position in place to match the rest of the artwork. You can perform this on an individual layer or, if you have grouped multiple layers together, alter them in unison.

1 Press **ctrl** **T** **⌘** **T** to enter Free Transform mode. Its bounding box will appear, surrounding the layer content. The **Enter** key applies the transformation, **esc** cancels it.

2 Click and drag within the box to move the layer around the document. Placing the cursor outside the boundary and dragging will rotate the layer around the center point.

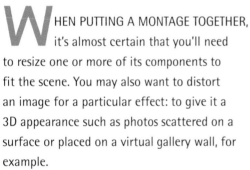

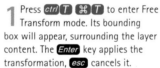

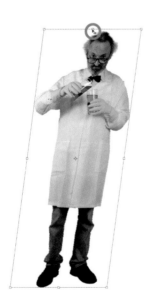

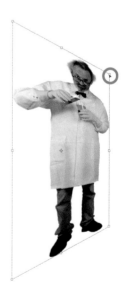

6 Hold **ctrl** **⌘** while dragging a center handle to skew the image. Additionally, if the **Shift** key is also held, the skew is constrained to horizontal or vertical movement.

7 Press **ctrl** **alt** **Shift** **⌘** **⌥** **Shift** when dragging a corner to distort the image in perspective. This can be both horizontal and vertical, depending on the direction you move the cursor.

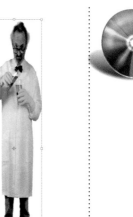

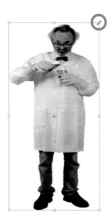
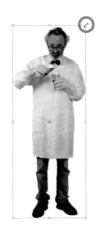
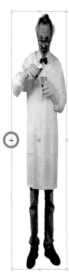

3 By grabbing and dragging a corner handle you can scale the layer up or down freely. This, by default, is relative to the opposite corner, which remains anchored in place.

4 By holding the **Shift** key whilst dragging a corner, the layer will be scaled in proportion to its original size. This option can be used when you need to ensure the shape remains constant.

5 Use the left or right center handles to adjust the width of the image. The top and bottom handles, as you might expect, scale it vertically.

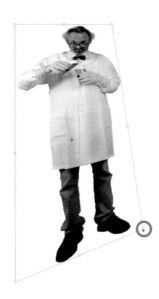
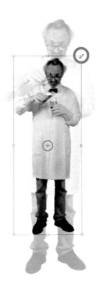
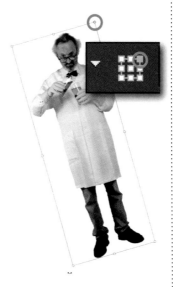

8 You can distort the image freely by holding **ctrl** ⌘ when dragging a corner handle. This can be used to accurately match an existing part of the artwork: a billboard, for example.

9 Use the **alt** ⌘ key to force the image to scale around the center point, rather than the opposite corner. This works with most of the transformation modes.

10 You can change the reference point to one of nine positions from the Options toolbar. This allows you to rotate the image using a different pivotal point.

Distorted field of vision

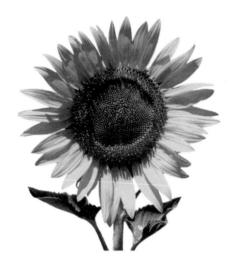

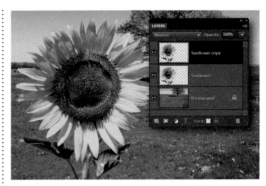

1 Here's our field with a single sunflower. We'll start by duplicating the flower. Make sure it's the active layer. Press *ctrl* *J* *⌘* *J*. This is normally used to create a layer from a selection; as there isn't one defined here, it simply copies the entire image.

B Y MIMICKING PHOTOGRAPHIC EFFECTS we can fool the viewer into believing an image is real, if only temporarily. This technique has been used frequently in the movies, television and other media – especially before digital technology was accessible. Indoor sets would have lavishly painted backdrops to give the impression they were shot on location. The scenery would be out of focus and not instantly recognized as fake.

We'll use this trick here to create a field of sunflowers using just a single object duplicated and scaled down many times. One larger flower is kept in the foreground, drawing focus away from the rest. The copies are all partially covered by one another; this prevents the viewer making an instant comparison. By blurring the rear rows and background, we are fooled into believing they extend far into the distance; we are accustomed to seeing photographs taken with a shallow depth of field so we don't question it.

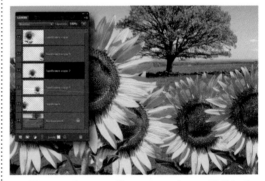

4 We can make some adjustments to the row. We'll begin by swapping some of the layers around. This gives us a more uneven appearance. To do this, click and drag the thumbnails above or below one another in the Layers panel. Keep them behind the original flower, of course.

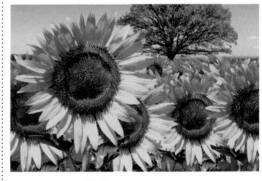

7 Press *ctrl* *J* *⌘* *J* to duplicate the current layer. Select the layer behind. Scale it down quite a way. Now duplicate it. Move them both to create a long row. Press *ctrl* *E* *⌘* *E* to merge them. Repeat this a couple more times until the foreground is more or less hidden.

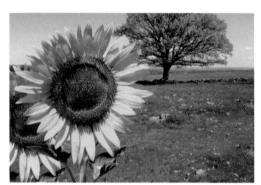

2 Click the original flower layer's thumbnail. Press `ctrl` `T` `⌘` `T`. Make sure Constrain Proportions is checked. Click and drag the top-right handle to scale the flower down. Click and drag inside the box to offset it from the original. Keep it a little lower than the foreground flower.

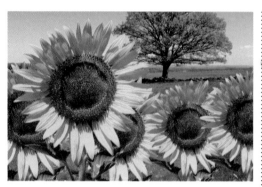

3 Now we'll complete the initial row. Repeat the first two steps to create three or four new flowers. Adjust the size and position slightly each time. Make sure you keep them fairly evenly spaced; they wouldn't be growing too close together in real life.

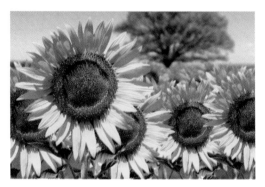

5 Now we'll start adding the rows behind. Group all four flower layers by multi-selecting them in the Layers panel. Press `ctrl` `alt` `E` `⌘` `⌥` `E` to stamp them onto a new layer. This will be created above the group so drag it down the stack so it sits behind the others.

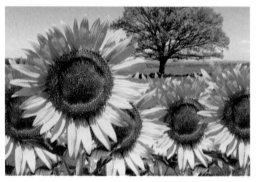

6 We'll fill that empty ground space behind the front row. Flip the layer horizontally via the Image > Rotate menu. Use Free Transform to scale and position the layer so its stalks are staggered behind the front row. Because they're hidden we can distort them a little more than before.

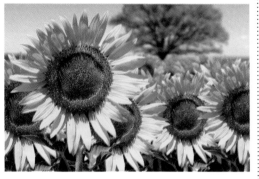

8 To create the impression of depth we'll add some Gaussian Blur. Start with the first merged group. Add a small amount of blur, enough to knock the focus out. Move to the next adding a little more. When you've finished with the flowers you can blur the background to match.

9 The ground beneath the flowers is still visible and noticeably blurred. Grab the Burn Tool `O`. Set the mode to Highlights. Now use a large soft brush to paint in shadow over the grass. Finally, select the foremost flower rows. Add some shadow to their stems to complete the effect.

HOT TIP

If you're using a version of Elements which doesn't support layer grouping, you'll need to create the merged layers in a slightly different way. Start by creating a new layer above the layers you want to merge. Link the images together by clicking the empty box to the left of their thumbnails in the Layers panel. Using the keyboard shortcut `ctrl` `alt` `E` `⌘` `⌥` `E` will duplicate and stamp the layers down to the new

SHORTCUTS
MAC WIN BOTH

143

Simple perspective distortion

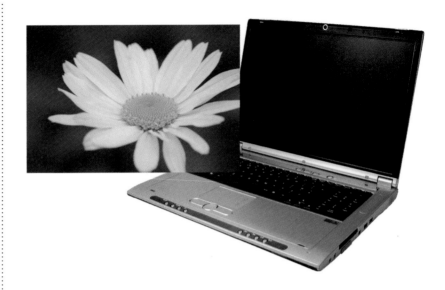

ONE OF THE MOST USED distortion techniques in photomontage is to add or replace an image where it will be viewed in perspective. This could be anything from a photo lying on a table to a billboard in a street scene.

As we'll discover in the following tutorial, this effect can be achieved quickly and simply using the Free Transform tool. The task is made easier still if we already have a basis for our distortion: the laptop's screen in our example. We'll also see how the effect can be made more realistic by blending the images to retain the original highlights of the screen.

1 Here we have our laptop along with the image we want placed on its screen. We'll use the screen's existing perspective as our guideline. Firstly, make sure the flower is the currently active layer by clicking its thumbnail in the Layers panel. Now enter Free Transform mode by pressing ctrl T ⌘ T. We'll begin by moving the image roughly into position. Click and hold within the bounding box. Now drag the photo across so it's covering the laptop's screen.

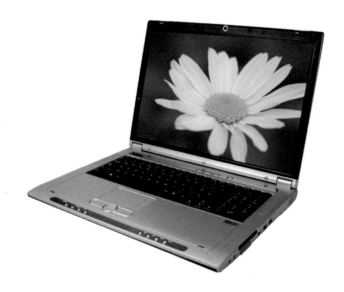

3 The image is now more or less in place. Check to see if any fine tuning is needed. It's best to do this before you commit the transformation. This is mainly to avoid further quality loss but also because subsequent editing will result in the Transform tool's bounding box being squared off to the document, rather than conforming to the image as it is now, making it very awkward to align the image. Simply grab and adjust any of the point(s) as before.

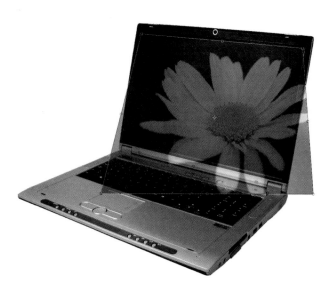

2 Press and hold <kbd>ctrl</kbd> <kbd>⌘</kbd>. This puts us into Distort mode, allowing the individual control points to be freely manipulated. Start by clicking and dragging one of the corners to the corresponding corner of the laptop's screen. Try

to leave a little space between the new image and the bezel of the laptop. This adds a bit more realism as displays generally don't extend right up to the edges. Repeat the process for the remaining three corners.

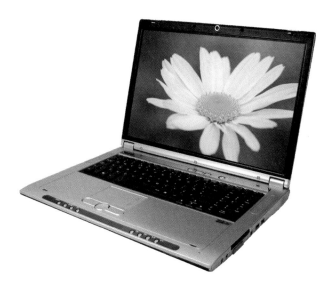

4 With the distortion applied, the photo of the flower looks much more a part of the whole image. It's still not completely convincing, though. Adding the new layer has hidden the reflection and shading on the original screen. This

has made the display seem a little flat. We'll fix this by changing the photo layer's blend mode, in this instance using the aptly named Screen. As the base layer is black, the two images blend, allowing the highlights to appear over the photo.

Tricky selections

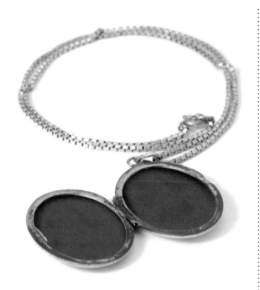

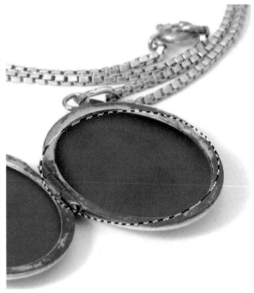

E VEN WITH A WELL-STOCKED ARSENAL of selection tools at our disposal, there will be times when it seems we have been defeated. Take our example image, for instance: we want to select the inside of a silver locket so we can place our own images inside – easy enough, you'd think?

Given its shape, we'd instinctively reach for the Elliptical Marquee tool but there's a problem: the angle at which it was photographed means it's not a perfect oval; the marquee can only be scaled horizontally and vertically so try as we might, we'd never get it to match. We need to be able to distort its shape, and that's the key word: using the Ellipse Shape tool, we have the ability to fine-tune it to fit the most stubborn areas of our images and create the perfect selection.

1 As we can see here, because the Elliptical Marquee can only be scaled horizontally and vertically, we simply cannot match the perspective. As soon as we get one part of the selection to match, the rest falls out of line. Wrestling with it is just an exercise in futility.

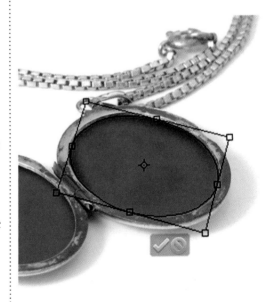

4 Staying in Free Transform, hold *ctrl* ⌘ to switch to Distort mode. Now we can manipulate each of the handles individually to get a precise match with the locket's edge. It can be a little fiddly getting it just right but the result will definitely be worth the additional time spent.

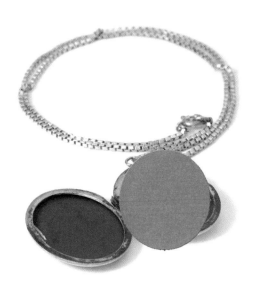

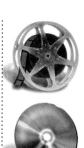

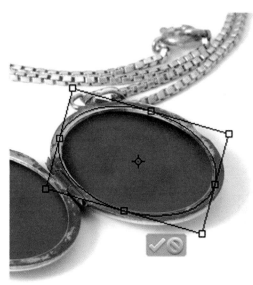

2 Select the Ellipse Shape tool **U**. We don't need to be too precise to begin with so draw out a shape roughly the same size as the aperture of the locket. It will be filled with color initially but that's not important as we only want to use its outline, which we'll deal with next.

3 Lower the shape layer's opacity to 0%. This removes the color fill, leaving us with an unobtrusive outline to work with. Enter Free Transform **ctrl T** **⌘ T**, now rotate and scale the shape; we can get a better match than with Marquee tool but it will need adjusting slightly.

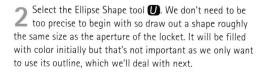

Make Selection

Rendering

Feather Radius: 0 pixels

OK

Cancel

☑ Anti-aliased

Operation

◉ New Selection
○ Add to Selection
○ Subtract from Selection
○ Intersect with Selection

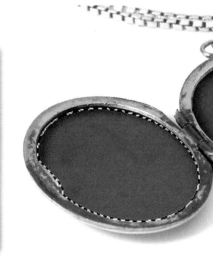

5 With our shape in position we can create the selection. Right-click on the document and choose Make Selection from the Context menu. This gives us more control over its attributes. Click Anti-aliased and hit OK. If we didn't set this, the selection would be too jagged.

6 The left-hand part of the locket is a little different as the clasp breaks up part of the oval. The technique is still the same but after we've created the selection we just need to remove the area around the clasp using the Polygonal Lasso, remembering to hold **alt** **⌥**, of course.

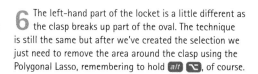

SHORTCUTS
MAC WIN BOTH

Locket and load

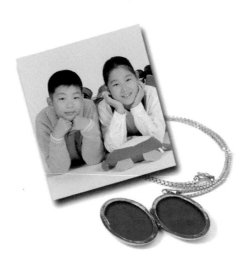

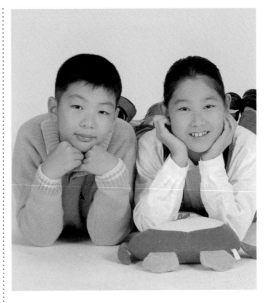

FOLLOWING STRAIGHT ON from the previous technique, we'll be putting the selections we made to use. We'll add photos into the windows of the locket with a little-used function called Paste into selection. This is very similar in concept to clipping layers together, which we covered in the 'Hiding and showing' chapter. We can still scale, rotate and distort the image to get it looking the way we want. The main difference is that only one layer is used.

This makes for a tidier document but with one important caveat: once the images have been positioned they are set permanently on the layer. This might sound a little counter-productive when we are so keen to keep things editable, but there are times when we just need to make one-off changes and would most likely flatten the layers anyway; this saves us the bother of doing so.

1 First we need to open our source image. For ease, we've saved it as a layer on the psd file on the DVD. Make it visible and active then select the whole document *ctrl* **A** **⌘ A**. Now press *ctrl* **C** **⌘ C** to copy the image to the clipboard. Once done, we can hide the layer again.

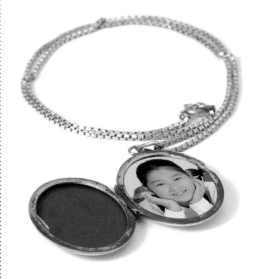

4 Now hold *ctrl* **⌘** and drag the control handles to distort the image so it follows the perspective of the locket. Press *Enter* to commit the changes. At this stage we can still move the selection or go back into Free Transform if needs be. Finally, deselect to fix it in place permanently.

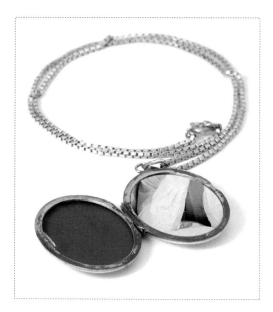

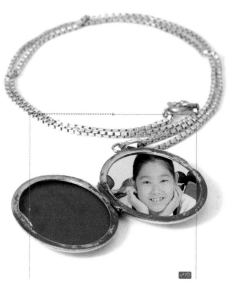

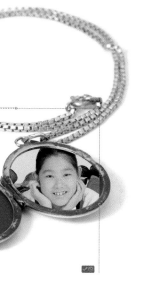

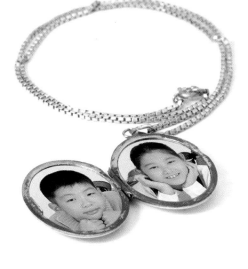

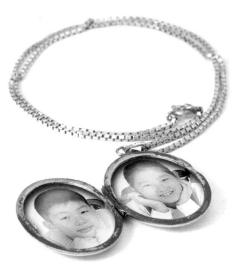

2 The selections have also been saved with the file so we can go straight to Select > Load Selection and choose Right Window. Make sure you're on the background layer then press *Shift* *ctrl* *V* *Shift* *⌘* *V* to paste the clipboard image into the selection.

3 It doesn't look like much at the moment because it's been pasted in at full size and we can only see a small portion. Enter Free Transform *ctrl* *T* *⌘* *T* and scale the photo down so we can see the girl's face. We'll stay in Free Transform so we can adjust the perspective.

5 To add the image into the left window we can load up the other saved selection and simply use the Paste into command again, as it will still be retained in memory. Then it's just a matter of scaling it down and distorting to show the boy.

6 We've created a new layer above the locket and loaded up both window selections. These have been filled with 50% gray and the blend mode changed to Hard Light. We've used a soft white brush to add some highlights and an Inner Shadow layer style to give the impression of glass inserts.

149

Wrapping around surfaces

ADDING ARTWORK TO CURVED SURFACES can present the montage artist with all manner of problems to overcome. The most awkward are objects such as cylinders. When they are viewed at an angle the perspective effect causes not only the width to recede as it moves further from the camera, but the depth of the curves become considerably different between the top and the base.

In these situations, applying a uniform distortion to the artwork simply won't do the trick. The result will be confusing and look unrealistic. There is, of course, a solution, demonstrated here by placing a graphic around the surface of a plain coffee mug.

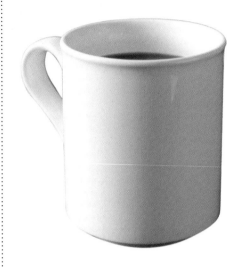

1 Although it's not obvious at this stage, as a result of the perspective effect, the slight angle at which this mug has been photographed causes the depth of the curves at the top and bottom to be different depths. This will be far more noticeable when the artwork is applied and initially distorted.

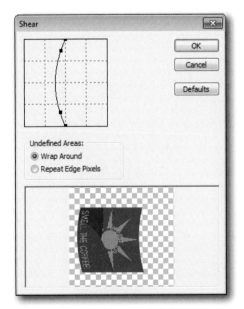

4 Open the Shear filter dialog. By default, there is no distortion. Control points can be added by clicking and dragging on the line. It's better to create these towards the edge, rather than a single point in the center. This gives a smoother curve. You can see the effect in the preview.

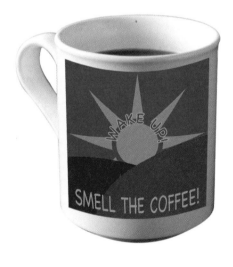

5 The artwork has been rotated back to the correct orientation. As you can see, the top is true to the curve of the mug but the bottom is far too shallow. Firstly, enter Free Transform mode. Holding *ctrl* ⌘, drag the bottom corners in to match the perspective of the mug's edges.

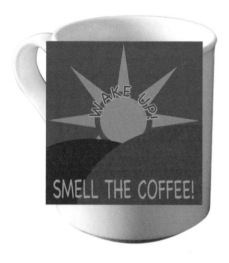

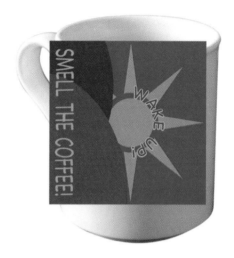

2 The artwork has been imported from a separate file. Press *ctrl* **T** **⌘T** to enter Free Transform. Make sure Constrain Proportions is checked. Now hold *alt* **⌐** and scale the artwork down to the appropriate size. Using the modifier key ensures it's scaled around the center.

3 Before we can apply the distortion, the artwork must be rotated by 90°. The Shear filter only operates on the horizontal axis. This can be achieved with Free Transform (hold *Shift* to constrain to 45° increments) or from the menu: Image > Rotate > Layer 90° Right.

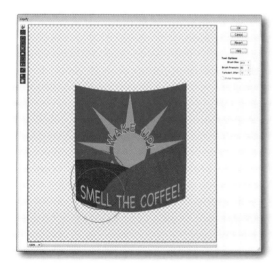

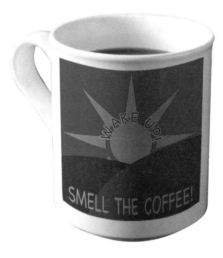

6 Open up the Liquify filter (under Distort in the Filters menu). Select the Warp tool. Using a large brush, drag out the lower part of the artwork to increase the curve's depth. Try to use as few strokes as possible to avoid the edge becoming uneven.

7 Our artwork now fits the shape perfectly. It still looks a little out of place, though. The problem is that the mug has shadows and reflections whereas the artwork appears flat. This is easily solved. Set the layer's blend mode to Multiply. Finally, lower the opacity a little.

HOT TIP

The display in the Liquify dialog only shows the active layer. This makes it difficult to match up with the existing image. Before you open the filter, move the document window over to one side. You can then resize the filter's window and place it next to the original for reference.

SHORTCUTS
MAC WIN BOTH

151

Making curls and folds

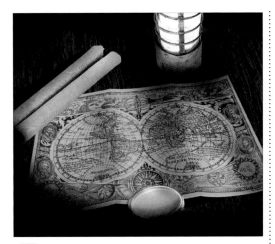

P**APER TENDS TO HOLD ITS SHAPE** after being folded or rolled up for any length of time. This can be an annoyance in everyday life, as anyone who has experience of hanging wallpaper will testify. In the controllable world of digital montage, however, we can use these traits to our advantage.

In this tutorial, we'll see how distortion and shading can transform a piece of flat artwork into a convincing three-dimensional map; one that has been rolled and folded many times. Of course, the technique can be customized for many other situations.

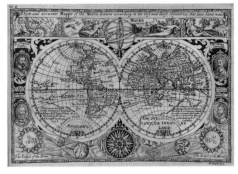

1 We first need to add some extra blank space to accommodate the distortion. We'll do this by increasing the canvas, rather than shrinking the artwork. Press `ctrl` `alt` `C` `⌘` `⌥` `C` to open the Canvas Size dialog. Check the Relative box. Increase the size by around 30%.

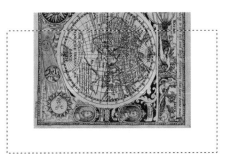

4 Rotate the canvas 90° right. With the Marquee tool still selected, position the cursor in the center of the right panel. Click and hold to start a selection. Hold the `alt` `⌥` key. Drag out the bounding box to the edge of the canvas. This ensures the distortion will be centered on the layer.

7 Create a new layer at the top of the stack. Hold `ctrl` `⌘` and click the left panel's layer thumbnail. Now add and hold the `Shift` key. Click the other two layers in turn to add their selections. Fill this with 50% gray. Press `ctrl` `D` `⌘` `D` to deselect. Set the layer's blend mode to Hard Light.

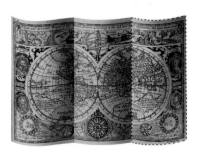

8 Load up the selection for one of the panels. Add some highlight and shadow using Dodge and Burn (see the chapter 'Light and shade' for more on this technique). Because we've restricted the area, we get a nice solid crease line. Repeat for each of the other panels.

152

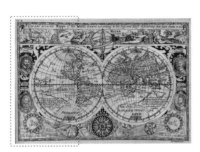

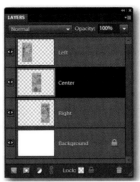

2 We need to separate the artwork into sections. We'll use the map's original fold lines as a guide. Grab the Rectangular Marquee **M**. Line the cursor up with the left fold line. Now drag out the selection to enclose that panel. Press *ctrl* *Shift* *J* ⌘ *Shift* *J* to cut it to a new layer.

3 Press *alt* *[* ⌥ *[* to re-enable the previous layer. Now select the right side of the map. Again, cut this to a new layer. You'll now have three individual pieces. Should you wish, you can press *ctrl* *[* ⌘ *[* to move the layer down the stack, thus placing the layers in the correct order.

Always use Canvas Size to create additional area to your document. As long as the background is separate from the rest of the image, you can adjust it as much as you like without losing quality; as would be the case with scaling down the artwork. Also, if like the map example, you do not need to stick to specific dimensions, use the Relative option and increase the size by percentage. You'll find it much easier to visualize than measurement units.

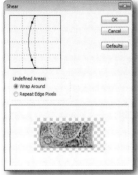

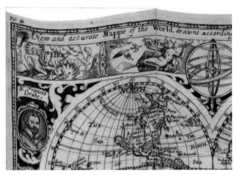

5 Open the Shear filter. We want our edges to be curling upwards so the bend needs to go to the left. Click on the grid to add two new control points. Drag them out to form a shallow curve. Repeat this for the other two layers; vary the curves a little on each.

6 Rotate the canvas back. Make the left panel layer active. Press *ctrl* *T* ⌘ *T* to enter Free Transform. Position the cursor over the right-middle handle. Hold *ctrl* *Shift* ⌘ *Shift*. Click and drag to match it up to the adjacent layer. You may also want to raise its opposite edge as well.

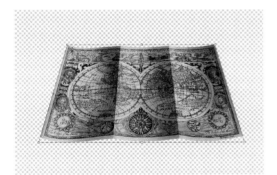

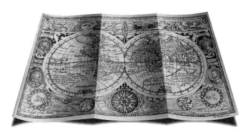

9 Hide the background layer by clicking its eyeball icon. Press *ctrl* *Shift* *E* ⌘ *Shift* *E* to merge the visible layers. Press *ctrl* *T* ⌘ *T*. Hold *ctrl* *alt* *Shift* ⌘ ⌥ *Shift*. Click and drag a top corner in towards the center. Reduce the height with the top-center handle.

10 Load up the map's selection. Hold *alt* ⌥. Use the cursor keys to nudge up by one pixel. This gives the impression that the map has thickness. All that remains is to add a shadow. This is simply a copy of the map layer flipped and distorted. Finally, it's blurred and the opacity lowered.

The ripple effect

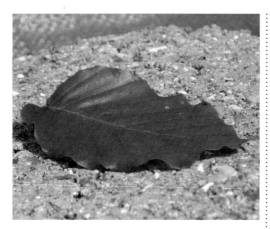

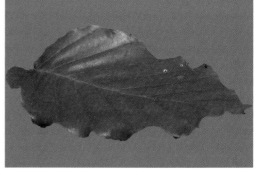

1 Open the leaf image from the DVD, it's already been placed on a new layer and the background has been filled with 50% gray. This will allow us to fine-tune the effect once everything is in place. We'll hide the leaf's layer for the time being whilst we create the water texture.

RESPECT WHERE IT'S DUE to the photographers with the skill and, more importantly, the patience to capture the ubiquitous image of a leaf or other such object causing delicate ripples as it lands on water. As pretty and serene as this all is, many of us simply don't have the time to wait for that perfect moment. We don't need to, of course. The effect can be recreated quickly with neither a tree or a lake to be seen.

We photographed the leaf at a suitable angle to avoid the need to make excessive changes to fit in with the rest of the scene. We'll use a few different distortion techniques here. The main effect is creating the ripples; we'll use the rather misleadingly named ZigZag filter to create this.

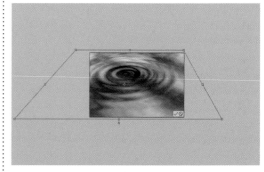

4 Enter Free Transform *ctrl* *T* *⌘* *T*. Holding *ctrl* *alt* *Shift* *⌘* *⌥* *Shift*, drag one of the bottom corner handles out to alter the perspective. Release the keys. Hold *Shift* to constrain the dimensions and drag a corner point again to scale the image up to the required size.

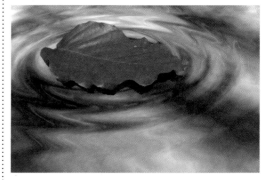

7 The leaf looks too flat on the surface as it has no reflection. Duplicate the layer *ctrl* *J* *⌘* *J*. Switch back to the original by clicking its thumbnail. Set the blend mode to Multiply. Now use Free Transform to distort the copy and give the leaf some depth.

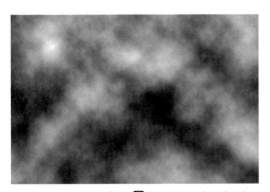

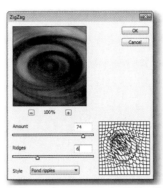

2 Create a new layer. Press **D** to ensure you're using the default black and white palette. Fill the layer with the Clouds filter. We want a good spread of tones here. You can rerun the filter a few times by pressing **ctrl F** **⌘ F** until you're happy with the result.

3 Now to make the ripples. Select the ZigZag filter from the Distort sub-menu. Select Pond Ripples as the style. We're creating a close-up image so we only need a small amount of ridges but a large amount of distortion. The exact settings will vary from image to image, of course.

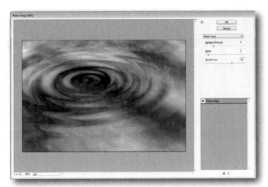

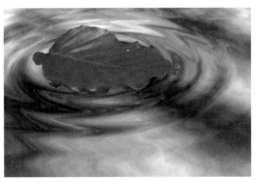

5 We'll add some highlights using the Plastic Wrap filter (found under the Artistic sub-menu). Keep the effect subtle: overdoing it will leave us with syrup rather than water. Apply the filter. Lastly, press **ctrl Shift L** **⌘ Shift L** to boost the contrast with Auto Levels.

6 With the ripples in place we can make the leaf layer visible again. Make sure it's the top-most layer. Drag it to the top of the stack in the Layers panel if necessary. We'll use Free Transform to alter its size and adjust the perspective slightly.

It can be difficult to use Free Transform when the area takes up the entire size of the document, especially if you need to expand it. Press **ctrl –** **⌘ –** a couple of times to zoom out. You'll now be able to see the whole image and have space to use the control handles. If you are not using the maximized view mode, you'll need to drag the window out as well. This can be changed in the program's preferences by unchecking Zoom Resizes Windows.

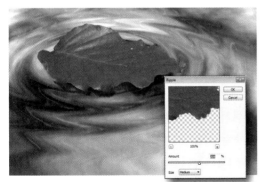

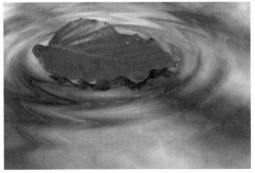

8 We'll add a sense of movement by distorting the reflection. Open the Ripple filter. Set the size to medium. Increase the amount gradually to give it a slight distortion. Soften it down by applying a small amount of Gaussian Blur. Lastly, lower the opacity a little.

9 Set the water layer's blend mode to Overlay. Switch to the Background layer. Open the Hue/Saturation dialog **ctrl U** **⌘ U**. Check the Colorize box. Now adjust the hue and saturation to suit the image. Finally, drop the water layer's opacity to soften the effect.

155

A flag for all nations

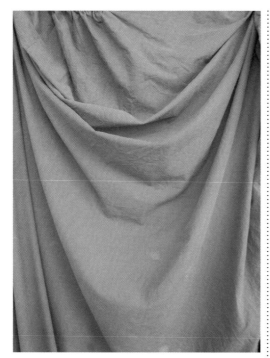

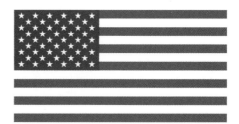

1 Here's our flag artwork. This is a rasterized vector image. Graphic objects such as this work really well in this format. They can be rendered at any size and will never lose their quality. We've added some space around the image to allow for the distortion effects.

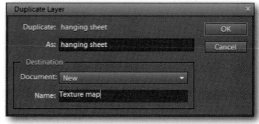

COMPONENTS OF A MONTAGE OR EFFECT are often created from the most unlikely of sources. The above image for instance: just a photo of an old bedsheet hanging up? Well yes, it is, but for the resourceful and imaginative artist, it can be a whole lot more!

We'll be using the image with the Displace filter to transform a two-dimensional graphic of the Stars and Stripes into a realistic flag blowing in the breeze. The technique is versatile too. As well as fabrics, it can be used with many other types of texture; almost anything which has a raised pattern such as rock, tiles or even the bark of a tree. In our example, the image can be saved as a template which can be reused with different nationality images or patterns.

4 The Displace filter uses a separate texture map document to apply its distortion effect. Select Duplicate Layer from the Layer menu. Choose New for the destination. You'll need to give it a name. This will create a new copy of our grayscale sheet.

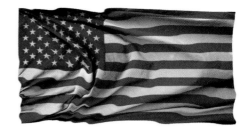

7 Turn the sheet layer back on. Set its blend mode to Multiply. The effect is taking shape but there's a bit of a problem: the two layers no longer match; as yet only the flag has been distorted. Press *ctrl* **F** ⌘ **F** to reapply the filter using the same settings, without opening the dialog again.

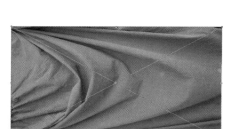

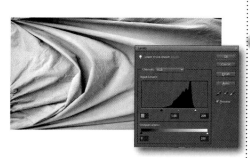

2 Open the sheet image from the DVD with the Place command. Rotate and scale it to match the flag graphic. Remember to uncheck Constrain Proportions in the Options bar. Press *Enter* to fix it down. It's still a Smart Object so right-click on the layer's thumbnail and click Simplify Layer.

3 Press *ctrl* *Shift* *U* *⌘* *Shift* *U* to desaturate the new layer. We don't need the color, just the tones of the folds. Add some more contrast by tightening up the highlights and shadows using Levels. This will give a much stronger effect on the texture map and overlay.

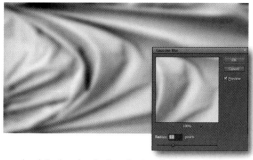

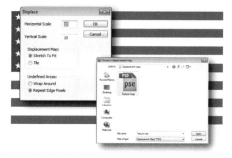

There will be occasions where you find the filter has caused areas of unwanted distortion, as with some of the stars on the flag. This is largely unavoidable as the image has been stretched too far over an area of strong contrast. You can often disguise the problem with a carefully placed foreground object or perhaps, as with our final image, some blur, if the context allows. You could, of course, use the Liquify filter to reposition the stars, too.

5 Load the layer's selection. Apply a Crop from the Image menu to remove the excess areas. Press *ctrl* *D* *⌘* *D* to deselect. Now apply some Gaussian Blur to soften the harsher edges. Finally, save the image as a new file on the hard-drive in Photoshop format.

6 Go back to the flag document. Turn off the sheet layer for now and make the flag layer active. Open the Displace filter dialog. Use the default settings and click OK. A file dialog will appear. Browse to where you saved the texture map. Double-click the file to apply the filter.

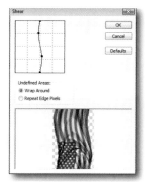

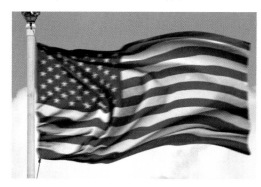

8 We'll add a shallow wave to the flag. Group the two layers. Press *ctrl* *alt* *E* *⌘* *⌥* *E* to create a merged copy. Hide the original layers. Now rotate the image 90° left. Open the Shear filter. Apply a very slight S curve. Click OK and rotate the layer back to its correct angle.

9 Here's our final image. A small amount of Motion Blur has been added to give a greater sense of movement. The addition of the flagpole and background boosts the realism of the scene. Save as a Photoshop document; you can always return to the image to change the nationality.

Not so extreme close-up

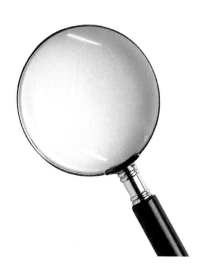

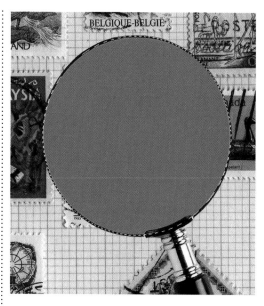

FILTERS OFTEN SUFFER FROM ABUSE
and consequently can quickly achieve
cliché status. Even though their effects can
be gradually increased, there is too much of a
temptation to take it straight to the extreme.
Spherize is one such casualty. Because of its
potential for caricature, it rarely sees anything
between -100% and 100%. It can, however, be
used for much more subtle duties.

The following example uses the filter in
moderation to create the illusion of an image
being enlarged through a magnifying glass, in
this instance on a collection of postage stamps.
You'll also see how glass can be replaced using
layer styles and blend modes. This is a great
effect for drawing attention to something in
your artwork or simply as a realistic component.

1 To save time, we've already cut away the original glass
from the frame. Make a selection around the inside edge
of the frame with the Elliptical Marquee **M**. Create a new
layer between the magnifier frame and the background layer.
We'll call it Glass. Fill the selection with 50% gray.

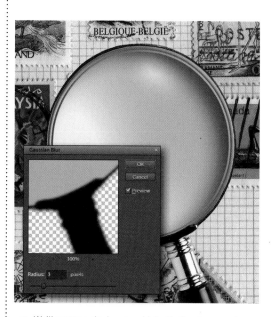

4 We'll create a shadow to add depth. Create a new layer
above the background layer. Load the magnifier frame's
selection and fill it with black. Now load the glass layer's
selection; this time fill it with a light gray. Press *ctrl* **D**
⌘ **D** to deselect. Apply some Gaussian Blur to soften it.

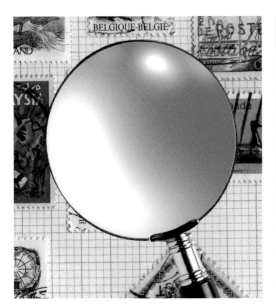

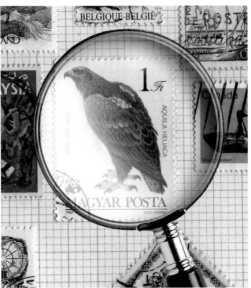

2 Deselect *ctrl* **D** **⌘ D**. Select the Dodge tool and set the Mode to Highlights. Use a large soft brush to paint in a large area of highlight. Use a low exposure, building the effect up with several strokes. Reduce the brush size and add a couple of random spot effects for good measure.

3 We'll use layer styles to give our glass some substance. Begin by applying the Scalloped Edge Bevel preset. Now add a High Inner Shadow. Set the layer's blend mode to Hard Light. The gray becomes invisible, leaving us with just our highlights and styles showing. Lower the opacity slightly.

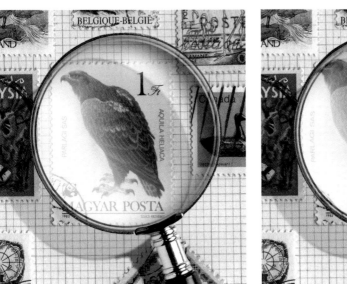

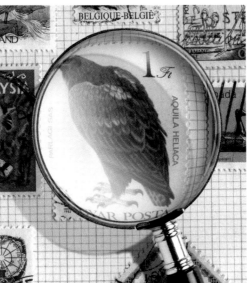

5 Press *ctrl* **T** **⌘ T** for Free Transform. Scale, rotate and reposition the shadow layer to give the impression the magnifying glass is a distance above the background. Set the blend mode to Multiply. Finally, lower the opacity. The lighter gray fill now looks like diffusion through the glass.

6 Duplicate the background layer. Load up the glass layer's selection. Open the Spherize filter. Apply the desired amount of distortion to the copy of the background; 80% in the example. Click the shadow layer's thumbnail to make it active. Press *ctrl* **F** **⌘ F** to reapply the filter.

HOT TIP

Using selections to constrain filters is not only used for localizing the affected area. If you also feather the selection first, the effect of the filter will be blended in or its strength lessened as it reaches the edge of the selected area.

SHORTCUTS

Smoke without fire

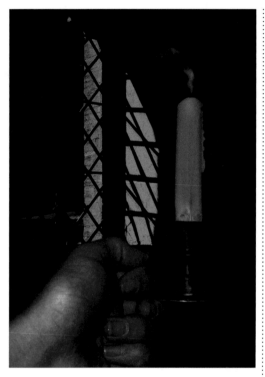

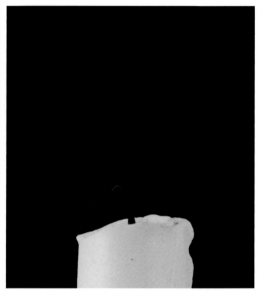

1 Here's our candle. It's been placed on a black background to make the effect easier to see whilst we're putting it together. This can always be replaced with a more fitting backdrop once it's finished. We'll begin by adding a new layer `ctrl` `alt` `Shift` `N` `⌘` `⌥` `Shift` `N`.

PHOTOGRAPHING SMOKE CAN BE TRICKY. You need to get the lighting correct and capture the picture at just the right moment or you'll have to start again from the beginning. Even when you do have an image you're happy with, using it in a montage involves a lot of fiddly selections and masking. Creating the effect from scratch is not as difficult as you might think.

In the following tutorial we'll see how smoke can be conjured up quickly and easily using the Liquify filter. Its range of tools lets you manipulate an image as though it were oil on water; this can produce natural looking free-form effects.

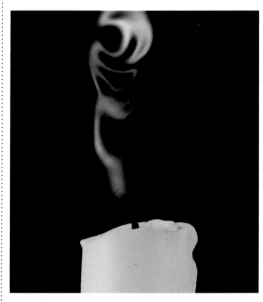

4 Add another new layer. Create a clipping group with the smoke layer `ctrl` `G` `⌘` `G`. Press `D` to restore the palette to its default. Fill the layer with the Clouds filter, which gives us a more random texture. Merge the two layers together by pressing `ctrl` `E` `⌘` `E`.

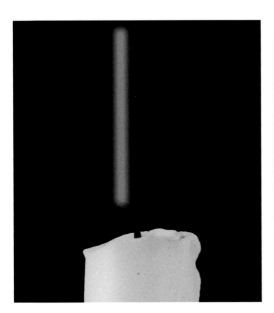

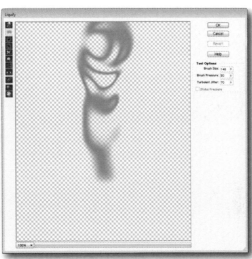

HOT TIP

The Liquify filter can be a little hit and miss. If you make a mistake, pressing ctrl alt Z ⌘ ⌥ Z steps backwards progressively. You also have the ability to restore areas selectively with the Reconstruct tool **E**. Simply paint over the required area to undo the changes. Varying the brush pressure controls the speed at which the image is rebuilt. If you decide to start afresh, click the Revert button. This will return the image to its initial state without having to exit from the dialog first.

2 Select the Rectangular Marquee **M**. Draw out a long thin box from the wick to the top of the image. Fill the selection with a strong color, red in this instance; it needs to show up well in the Liquify dialog. Press ctrl D ⌘ D to deselect. Lastly, add some Gaussian Blur to create a soft

3 Now for the fun part. Open the Liquify filter from the Distort sub-menu. Experiment using a combination of the tools to spread and distort the line. Vary the brush size and pressure to create a more random effect. If you're using a pressure-sensitive tablet, check the Stylus Pressure box.

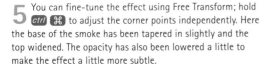

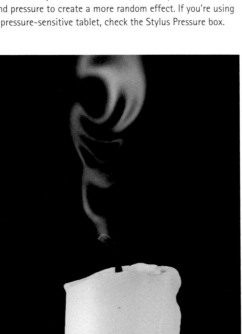

5 You can fine-tune the effect using Free Transform; hold ctrl ⌘ to adjust the corner points independently. Here the base of the smoke has been tapered in slightly and the top widened. The opacity has also been lowered a little to make the effect a little more subtle.

6 Create a layer above the candle itself and change its blend mode to Color Dodge. Set the foreground color to orange. Now use a soft, low opacity brush to paint in a small glow on the end of the wick. A hint of blue has been added to the smoke using a cooling Photo Filter Adjustment Layer.

SHORTCUTS
MAC **WIN** **BOTH**

161

Troublesome perspective

ONE OF THE PROBLEMS WE FACE when we are creating montages from different photos is the angle at which they were taken. Unless they were specifically shot for purpose, the different elements of the scene may not fit together properly because their perspective does not match.

Our example illustrates this perfectly. We have a young wizard casting a spell and a castle turret for his background. The boy's angle does not match the floor of the castle room, which was shot at a mid-level angle with a wider lens, so he looks out of place. We could try and distort his feet to match the perspective, of course, but that would be difficult and could end up looking unnatural. Instead, we'll adjust the angle of the floor. This, as we'll discover, is much easier than it sounds!

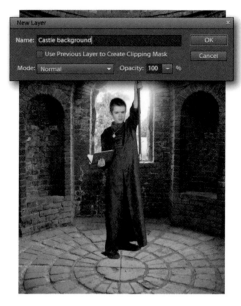

1 The image comprises two layers: the background layer and our young wizard. We won't duplicate the background this time as that will be confusing when we start distorting it. Instead, we'll convert it to a regular layer by double-clicking its thumbnail in the Layers panel.

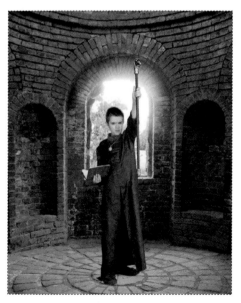

4 That's looking much better but we now have a gap at the bottom that we need to get rid of. Instead of selecting the Crop tool, hold *ctrl* ⌘ and click the castle layer's thumbnail to load its selection. Now go to Image > Crop. The image will be trimmed down. Now deselect.

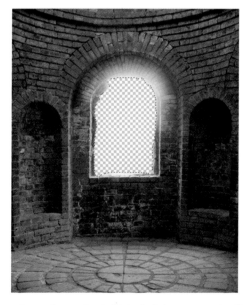

5 Our castle was shot in bright daylight, not very wizardly. First, hide the boy's layer. Now, make a selection around the inside of the window. The Quick Selection tool is perfect. Soften the edge slightly with Refine Edge or Feather. Press *Backspace* to delete the area then deselect.

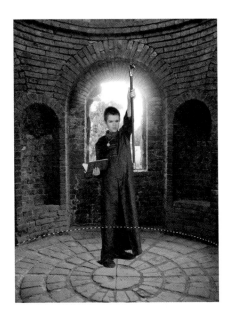

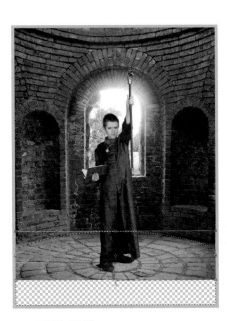

2 We don't want to distort the whole image, of course. Grab the Elliptical Marquee tool **M**. Place the cursor in the middle of the floor. Press and hold *alt* ⌥ while dragging out the selection to keep it centered. We want it to surround the whole floor area up to the edge of the walls.

3 Press *ctrl* *T* ⌘ *T* to enter Free Transform. Now drag the bottom-middle handle upwards. We can use the boy's feet to gauge the correct perspective. When it looks about right, press *Enter* to commit the changes. Lastly, deselect by pressing *ctrl* *D* ⌘ *D*.

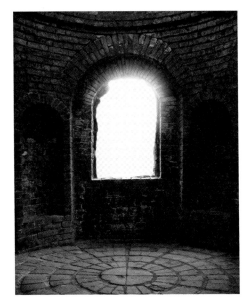

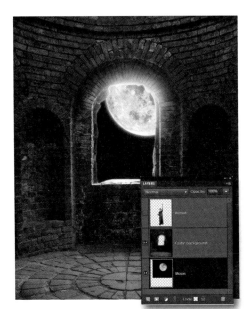

6 Press *ctrl* *J* ⌘ *J* to duplicate the background. Set the layer's blend mode to Multiply. This tones down the glare from the window and darkens the interior of the room, giving it a much stronger texture. Press *ctrl* *E* ⌘ *E* to merge the two layers together.

7 To finish this part of the project, go to File > Place and load Moon.jpg from the DVD. Press *Enter* to set it in place. Press *Shift* *ctrl* *[* *Shift* ⌘ *[* to send it to the back of the layer stack. Use the Move tool **V** to reposition it so it matches the bright spot of the window where the sun was.

HOT TIP

This technique is not without its problems: the brickwork of the walls has been distorted where we've brought the floor up. Being an old building we can just about get away with it. If it were more prominent, however, we would need to patch it with the Clone Stamp tool or by pasting in a selection from another part of the image.

SHORTCUTS
MAC **WIN** **BOTH**

163

It's a kind of magic

CONTINUING ON WITH OUR WIZARDLY project, we're going to conjure up a magical vortex from the boy's staff. Before we do this, however, we need to make a couple of final adjustments to the scene.

Both photos were taken in daylight but our scene is now lit by the moon. This casts a blueish hue and is much cooler. We'll simulate this by adding an Adjustment Layer which affects the whole image. We also need to add a shadow of the boy to fix him into the room properly. Having done this we can go on to create our magical effect; using the ever-versatile Clouds filter to produce the power-waves emanating from his staff.

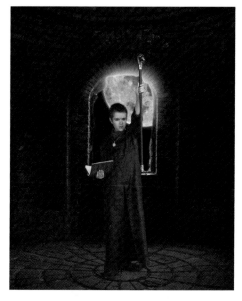

1 Select the boy's layer and make it visible again. Add a Hue/Saturation Adjustment Layer. Check the Colorize box. Drag the hue slider into the blue range, around 220. Increase the saturation, around 50 here. Set the layer's blend mode to Multiply and lower the opacity to around 70%.

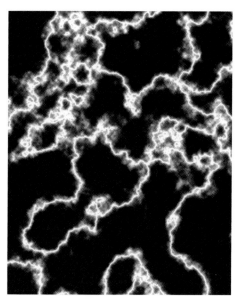

4 Press *ctrl* I ⌘ I to invert the colors. Open the Levels dialog *ctrl* L ⌘ L. Drag the Shadows slider across to the right; the white areas will start to disappear leaving only the brighter areas. Now use the Midtone slider to fine-tune and give us this whispy lightning effect.

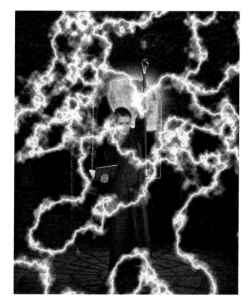

5 Press *ctrl* U ⌘ U to open the Hue/Saturation dialog. Check Colorize. Drag the Hue slider into the purples and increase the saturation a little. Set the layer's blend mode to Screen. The black areas of the layer disappear leaving us with just the lightning.

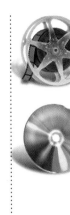

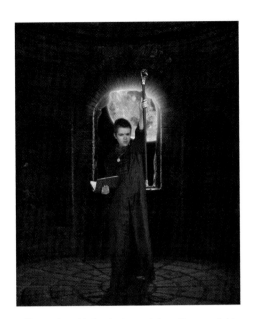

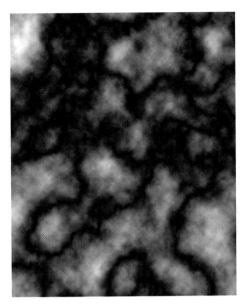

2 Next we've added a shadow cast from the moonlight coming in through the window in front of the boy. Rather than explaining it again here, the techniques for doing this and also adding the shading on the boy's feet can both be found in the previous chapter.

3 Create a new layer at the top of the stack. Press **D** to select the default palette. Hold *alt* ⌥ and select Filter > Render > Clouds for more contrast. Now apply Difference Clouds. We want the strong 'veiny' appearance. We can undo and reapply both filters until we get the best effect.

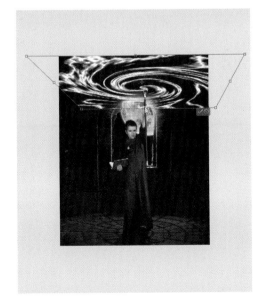

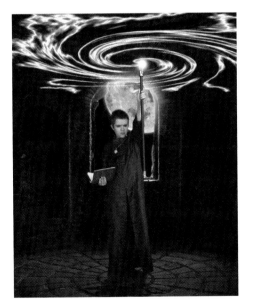

6 Open the Twirl filter (Distort). Drag the slider to around ±340°. This gives us a good effect without being overdone. Click OK to apply. Enter Free Transform *ctrl* *T* ⌘ *T*. Now hold *ctrl* ⌘ and drag the handles to distort and position the vortex over the boy's head in perspective.

7 Load the boy's selection. Now grab the Eraser tool and erase the areas that fall behind the staff to make it more three-dimensional. Deselect and erase the stray parts of the effect around the edges. Finally, grab the Brush tool and use a soft tip to dab a white glow at the top of the staff.

HOT TIP

For an extra-powerful effect, we could duplicate the lightning layer in step 5 before running the Twirl filter. The raw lightning could be edited to leave a few arcs jumping off the staff down to the floor and across the room.

SHORTCUTS

MAC WIN BOTH

165

Keep your composure

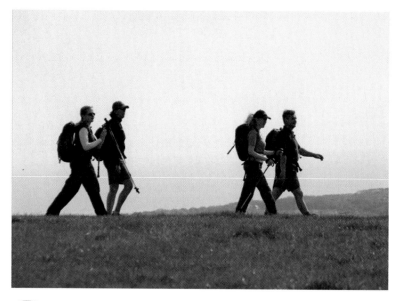 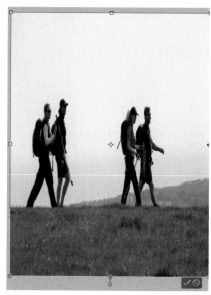

SOMETIMES, WE HAVE the perfect image but it's been shot at the wrong aspect. Our example would be great for a promotional flyer or magazine cover but it's a landscape image and we would need it in portrait. We'd want to keep the four people in the image too so cropping isn't possible.

Elements now has a secret weapon: the Recompose tool. This behaves very much like Transform but with one important difference: it analyzes the image on the fly, working out what it thinks is important detail and what's not. In our case this is the grass and hills. The people remain untouched.

1 Opening our example image we can see that it's a landscape image but has a lot of space that could be reclaimed to make it narrower. If, however, we try to scale down disproportionately using Transform *ctrl T* ⌘ *T* the end result is

not a pretty sight. Just by scaling it down to half the orginal width the people are horribly squashed up, making the image unusable. Press the Escape key to cancel the transformation and it will snap back to its original state.

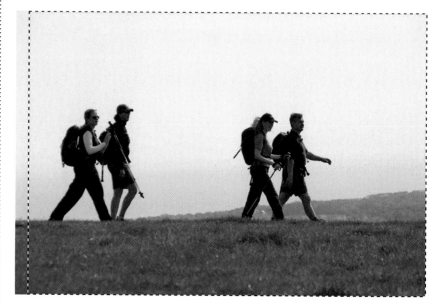

3 Because the tool looks for less detailed areas of the image first, it took away the left edge of the photo. We can prevent this happening by using a selection to protect that part of the image. Press Escape to cancel again – or Undo

ctrl Z ⌘ *Z* if you committed the changes previously. Grab the Rectangular Marquee tool *M*. Now drag the boundary across the image but leave a vertical section on the left-hand side of the image clear.

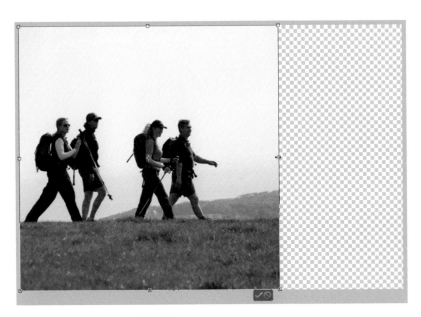

2 Select the Recompose tool *ctrl* *alt* *R* ⌘⌥*R* or choose it from the toolbox; it's found as part of the Crop tool group. We immediately get a bounding box around the whole image. If we grab the middle-right handle and start to drag across to the left we see that instead of the whole image compressing down, the wider expanse of the ground starts to disappear and the people are moved closer together but remain at their proper size.

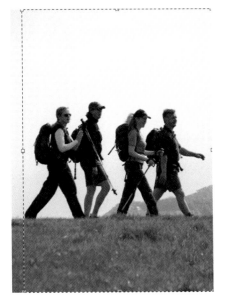

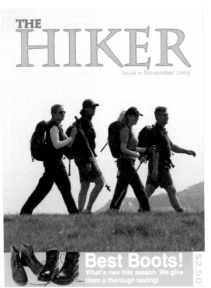

4 When we select the Recompose tool again and scale across from the right, it only affects the area within the selection, leaving us with a border which looks less cramped. Press *Enter* to apply the changes. On larger images this may take some time as the image is rendered. All that remains is to crop out the empty section of the image and we have our portrait shot ready to be used as a flyer or magazine cover. This definitely is a simple and highly effective tool!

THE HIKER
Issue 1. November 2009

Best Boots!
What's new this season. We give them a thorough testing!
$2.50

HOT TIP

If we want the image to be constrained to a particular size, we can select one of the presets from the Options bar. This contains many standard photographic sizes. When one is selected the image is automatically sized to those proportions. The results aren't always perfect but it can save a lot of time.

SHORTCUTS
MAC WIN BOTH

Drawing comparisons

ONE OF THE QUESTIONS MOST FREQUENTLY ASKED by newcomers to digital imaging is which program should they choose: Photoshop Elements or the full Photoshop product. There is no definitive answer; each has its merits. The basis for the decision should be one of individual requirements.

A common misconception is that Elements is Photoshop's poor relation, only suitable for photography hobbyists who need a simple program to catalog their images and perform quick fixes such as removing red-eye from portraits or correcting color casts. Although there is a definite leaning toward the amateur market, Elements is more than capable of producing the same standard of artwork as its big brother. Elements still has around 90% of the features found in Photoshop; it merely lacks some of the more high-end functionality associated with professional pre-press. You'll find all the same filters and the majority of adjustments are present. Some are cut-down versions offering less in the way of fine tuning, though not at the expense of their usefulness. There is also a degree of symbiosis between the two programs. Look under the hood of Elements and you'll find technologies from recent Photoshop releases packaged to perform a specific purpose. Similarly there are parts of Elements that have traversed the other way.

There is, of course, one distinct difference: the price. Presently, Photoshop will happily relieve your bank account of $600 upwards, depending on the version you choose. Elements, on the other hand, will cost you around $100 for the full product (less for an upgrade from previous versions). This makes it an ideal solution if you have a limited budget.

So, with all that said, what exactly are the differences between the two programs and can you survive without whatever it is that's missing? As we mentioned before, Elements does not feature some of the tools required for press-quality printing such as comprehensive color management and the CMYK color space. This, however, does not mean it cannot be used professionally; the images in this book were all produced using it, after all. Most designers' applications such as Adobe's InDesign will convert the images and to an extent, allow you to adjust the color. There are also many third-party utilities which perform the same function; Apple's OS X has Graphic Converter, for example.

The differences become less of an issue when you start comparing the tools and commands. Many of Elements' shortfalls can be overcome with a little lateral thinking. Here are the main 'extras' found in Photoshop, with workarounds:

Photoshop tool	What it does	Elements workaround
Pen tool	Draws Bézier paths	Use selections instead, and save as Alpha channels; save as .psd or TIFF file
Curves adjustment	Adjusts color and brightness	Use Levels instead
Vanishing Point filter	Places images in scene in perspective	Use Free Transform to distort layer
Black & White adjustment	Changes color image to monochrome	Use Gradient Map Adjustment Layer with default colors
Layer styles	More control over layer styles	Be creative with built-in styles or import styles from Photoshop
CMYK mode	Prepares artwork for commercial printing	Use third-party software to convert to CMYK mode
Smart Filters	Allows editable filters with selective masking	Duplicate target layer and lower opacity, use a mask to hide the effect
Image Warp	Allows free distortion of layers	Use Shear or Liquify filters for similar effect

There are some features in the full Photoshop that have no Elements equivalent – such as Smart Objects, Video and 3D Layers (Photoshop Extended edition only), and support for specialist video modes. But in the main, Elements is capable of satisfying 99% of every montage artist and photographer's requirements.

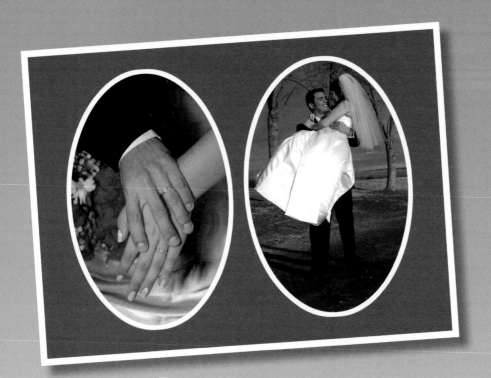

Textures can make all the difference to a piece of artwork. Here are two versions of a wedding album layout. The first is flat and uninspiring; everything is clean and squared off. The second, with its satin background and gold-framed images, sets the mood and adds that all important interest factor.

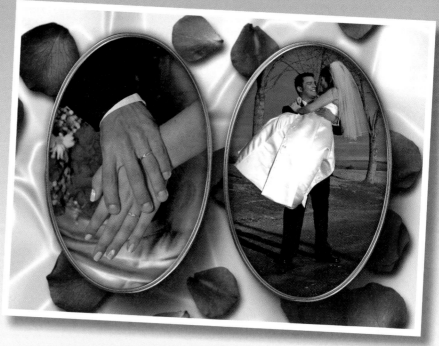

7

Materials and textures

OUR SURROUNDINGS ARE DEFINED BY TEXTURES. We can, for example, see at a glance that something is made of wood simply because of its familiar grainy appearance. We recognize certain materials such as silk by the way the light catches its folds and creases.

In this chapter, we'll look at ways of creating textures such as wood and cloth from scratch. This gives you more freedom as you are not constrained to the size of your source images.

We'll also see how existing images can be manipulated to match your theme: torn edges for newspaper clippings or ticket stubs, or ageing an object by covering it in dust.

Conjuring curtains

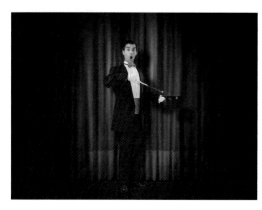

ALL THE WORLD'S A STAGE, as William Shakespeare would have us believe, and what stage would be complete without the familiar heavy red and gold drape curtains?

The following tutorial demonstrates a quick and easy way of creating an undulating texture resembling the folds of heavy hanging material. This has many potential uses: you may want to mock up some decor for a room in the house. You could also use the effect to create a template or intro for a home movie DVD. Why not create a montage and give a family member the stardom they deserve?

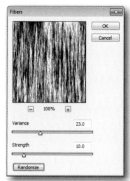

1 We'll begin by creating a new document *ctrl* N ⌘ N. Make a new layer and fill it with 50% gray. Press **D** to set the default palette colors of black and white. Go to Filter > Render > Fibers. We want a nice mix of lights and darks for this technique. Click OK to apply the filter.

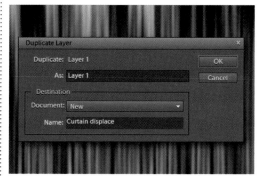

4 We'll be using the Displace filter later on so this is a good place to stop and create the displacement map. Go to Layer > Duplicate Layer. Set the destination to New. Give it a name and click OK. This will create a new document. Save this to disk and close the document's window.

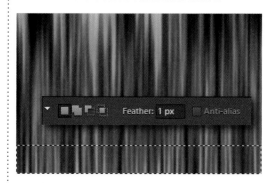

7 We'll apply the distortion to a separate layer. Grab the Rectangular Marquee tool **M**. Set the Feather radius to 1 pixel – this ensures we won't have a hard edge. Now make a fairly wide selection along the bottom of the curtain. Press *ctrl* J ⌘ J to copy it to a new layer.

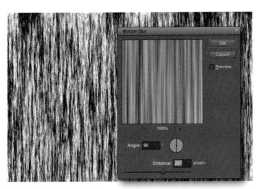

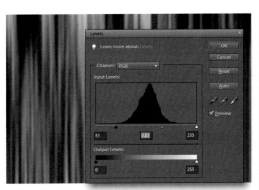

2 Although this gives us a rough material style texture it's not quite right for this purpose. Go to Filter > Blur > Motion Blur. Set the angle to 90° so the effect is vertical. Now drag the distance up until we have a smooth set of lines but still with a slight variance here and there.

3 Apply a small amount of Gaussian blur to smooth out the texture; we used a 3 pixel radius here. Open the Levels dialog *ctrl* L / ⌘ L. Add some more contrast by increasing the shadows and midtones. This gives the impression of the folds being deeper in some places.

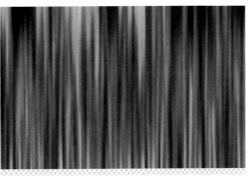

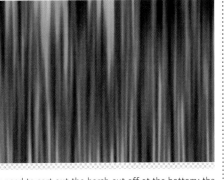

5 Make sure the curtain layer is active. Open the Hue/Saturation dialog *ctrl* U / ⌘ U. We're going to make the curtains a rich red. Check the Colorize box. Drag the Hue slider over to the far left. Now bring the Saturation slider up to around 60. We don't want it to be too overpowering.

6 We need to sort out the harsh cut off at the bottom; the pleats should follow on to give an uneven edge. Grab the Move tool **V**. Hold *Shift* and tap ⬆ on the keyboard twice to nudge the layer up. This will give us enough space to work with.

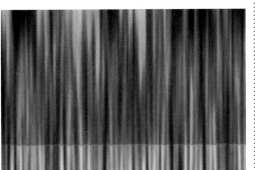

8 Go to Filter > Distort > Displace. We only want the effect to be vertical, so set the the Horizontal Scale to 0. We also want the effect to go down, so set the Vertical Scale to -10. Click OK. Choose the displacement map you saved earlier from the file selection dialog and click Open.

9 Nudge the layer down a little with the Move tool so it's visible below the curtain. Open Hue/Saturation again. Click Colorize. This time set the hue to a rich yellow color and increase the saturation. Finally, merge the two layers together by pressing *ctrl* E / ⌘ E.

HOT TIP

The Displace filter has many uses but it is difficult to get to grips with. Unlike most filters, it does not have a live preview, which makes it impossible to know what the outcome will be. Getting the correct effect is really a question of trial and error. It's an idea to spend some time fiddling with the options and values to see how they behave.

SHORTCUTS
MAC WIN BOTH

173

Quick and easy wood grain

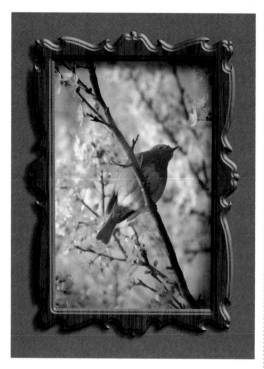

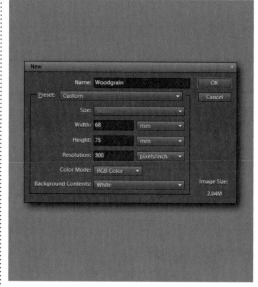

1 Create a new document `ctrl` `N` `⌘` `N`. Add a blank layer `ctrl` `alt` `Shift` `N` `⌘` `⌥` `Shift` `N`. Press `D` to ensure the default palette is set. Fill the layer with 50% gray; the Fibers filter won't work on an unfilled layer. Now duplicate the layer by pressing `ctrl` `J` `⌘` `J`.

PHOTOS OF WOOD TEXTURES can be found in almost any stock library. You can, of course, take your own. As abundant as they may be, sometimes you may not be able to find just the right style to use in your artwork. Here's where filters come to the rescue.

On the previous page, we saw how the Fibers filter can be used to create the effect of plush material. Here, we'll use it to generate the effect of wood grain – it's very versatile. To further the realism, various inconsistencies such as knots and twists are added. Just like the real thing; once made, you can use it to apply to all sorts of objects: an ornate picture frame (as the inset shows), some polished flooring, or simply as a backdrop for your images.

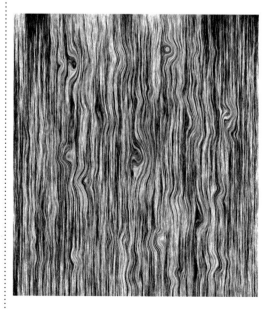

4 Add a few more knots and distortions; experiment with the different tools like Bloat and Twirl. When you're happy with the effect, click OK. Set the layer's blend mode to Overlay. Although you won't notice any difference just yet, we're setting the layer up to allow color to be added.

174

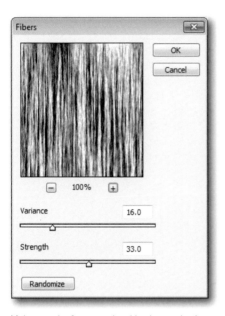

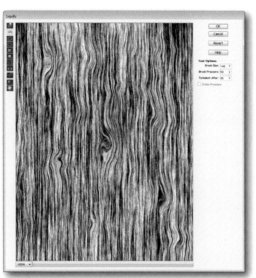

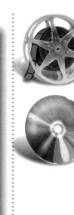

2 Make sure the foreground and background colors are set to the default black and white by pressing **D**. Open the Fibers filter dialog. Adjust the settings until you have a fairly reasonable looking grain. Variance gives more randomness; Strength gives more contrast to the effect.

3 We'll add some bends and knot holes. Open the Liquify filter. Grab the Turbulence tool. Choose a medium brush size. Set a fairly low Turbulence: we don't want the effect to be too wild. Now click and drag the cursor down in short strokes randomly around the document.

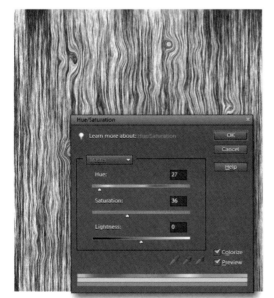

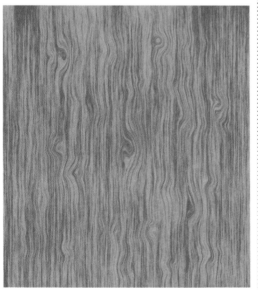

5 Click the plain gray layer's thumbnail to make it active. Open up the Hue/Saturation dialog **ctrl U** **⌘ U**. Check the Colorize box. You'll see the effect immediately. Use the Hue, Saturation and Lightness sliders to create the shade you want your wood to be.

6 You may decide the grain layer is too dark or coarse. Try experimenting with different blend modes. You could also use the Levels dialog to change the contrast, making it lighter or darker. Here, we've changed the blend mode to Soft Light and lowered the opacity a little.

HOT TIP

Just like many of the other tools in Elements, holding down the **alt** **⌥** key (referred to as the modifier key) when you're using a tool in Liquify temporarily changes its behaviour. For example, if you have the Twirl Clockwise tool, selected, holding the modifier key will switch it to the Counter-clockwise tool.

SHORTCUTS
MAC **WIN** **BOTH**

Pattern forming

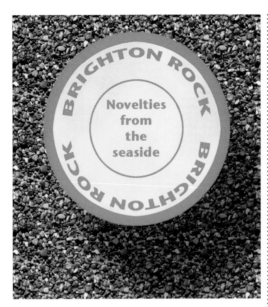

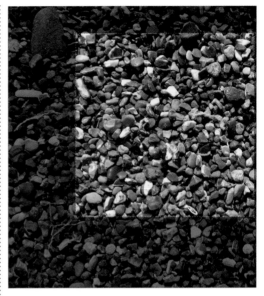

PATTERNS ARE EVERYWHERE around us: grass, brickwork, ocean waves, wood grain – the list is endless. When we want to use them in our designs, we often need to have a repeating pattern; a background for a website or collage, for example. This is where we run into problems: attempting to create a tiled pattern straight from the camera or scanned image with no alterations will most likely result in ugly seams where each instance butts up against the next; this is especially noticeable with complex patterns. We need to be able to make them seamless to enable them to fill any required space with almost no visible flaws.

1 Here's an image of some pebbles. Grab the Crop tool **C**, hold **Shift** to constrain to a square and drag out a suitably sized boundary. We've chosen an area with a good random element but made sure there weren't too many obvious repeats such as large stones or other debris.

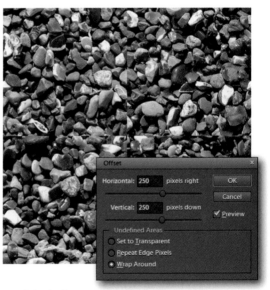

4 Going back to our original cropped image, select the Offset filter (under Other). Set the horizontal and vertical pixels to half the size of the document; our example is 500 pixels so we'll set it to 250 for each. Make sure the Undefined areas are set to Wrap Around and click OK.

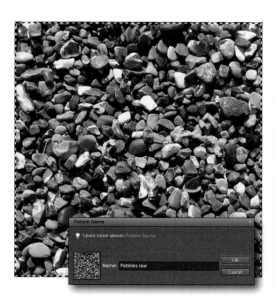

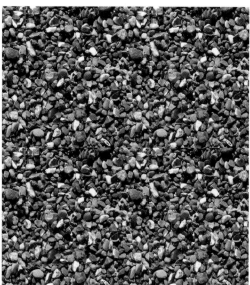

2 Firstly, we'll create our pattern straight from the cropped image. Press _ctrl_ _A_ _⌘_ _A_ to select the whole document. Now, select Define Pattern from the Edit menu; we get a thumbnail of our pattern and a space to give it a name. We'll call this one Pebbles raw.

3 To demonstrate the problem, we've created a larger blank document. Using the Fill dialog _ctrl_ _Backspace_ _⌘_ _Backspace_ with the contents set to Pattern, we've selected our custom pattern and filled the area. Viewing at 100% we can clearly see the tile borders: not very attractive.

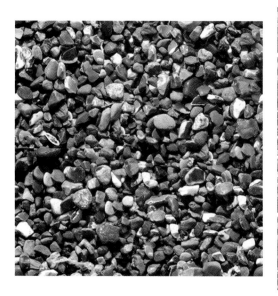

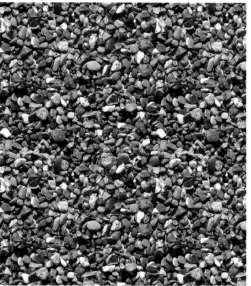

5 We want to hide the tile borders so grab the Clone Stamp _S_, choose an area away from the center, hold _alt_ _⍐_ and click to set it as the source. Now begin painting over the border lines. Continue this, choosing random areas until you are left with a continuous pattern.

6 Now, when we define a pattern as before and fill our large document, there are no harsh edges; much nicer. On close inspection we can still see a repeating pattern of course, but this is much more easily disguised with the other elements of the design.

HOT TIP

It's tricky avoiding the obvious repeats in the pattern. We can lessen the effect by using different scales of image, depending on the size of the background we're filling. We could also take more time and analyze the tones in the image when we are cloning out the lines, making sure there are no prominent areas of particularly strong highlight or shadow which might become more noticeable when we have a background built up with many instances of the tiles. If we were using a pattern with larger, more defined detail, such as leaves, it may be better to copy and paste certain parts, rather than clone them.

SHORTCUTS

MAC **WIN** **BOTH**

177

Lying on a bed of satin

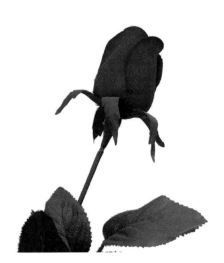

CREATING COMPLEX TEXTURES from scratch is not necessarily as difficult as it may at first seem. Here we are going to combine gradients and blend modes to create a random and fluid effect resembling the intricate folds and wrinkles of finer fabrics such as silk or satin.

The major advantage of generating your own materials in this way is you are never tied to the size of a stock image. You can create the pattern to suit the dimensions of your artwork, without the fear of repetition letting the effect down.

1 Hide the rose layer. Click the backgound layer's thumbnail to make it active. Select the Gradient tool **G**. Choose a Linear Black, White gradient. Set the mode to Difference, then click and drag the guide from corner to corner. This creates a good base for the effect.

4 Go to the Stylize filters sub-menu and select Find Edges. This produces a smoother version of our pattern and leaves the ridges well defined. It's looking good so far but we need to bring back some of the contrast. This is easily done by applying Auto Levels `ctrl` `Shift` `L` `⌘` `Shift` `L`.

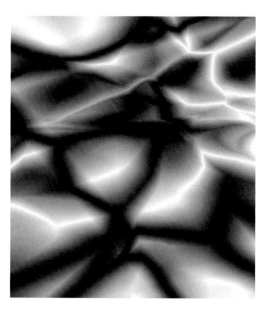

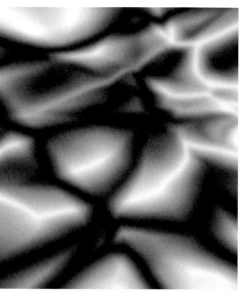

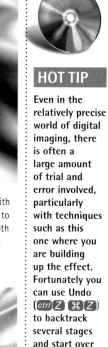

2 Pick a random starting point. Click and drag out another gradient. Make it shorter than before and repeat this several times. Change the position, length and angle on each. Try to create a good balance of small, intricate areas and larger smooth sections.

3 The initial result is a little harsh, so we'll soften it with a little Gaussian Blur. Set a fairly low value: enough to remove the sharpness from the lines and produce a smooth transition between the tones. The amount will, of course, vary depending on the size of the document.

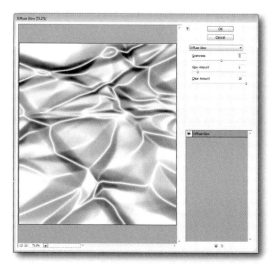

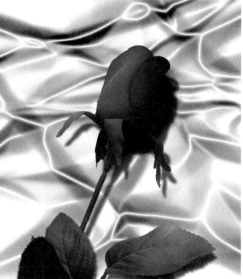

5 Open up the Diffuse Glow filter from the Distort sub-menu. We'll use this to add some texture and spread out the highlights. Push the Graininess up: around half way is sufficient. Add a small amount of Glow; be careful not to wash the image out. Set the clear amount to its maximum.

6 As a final step we'll add some color. The Hue/Saturation adjustment is perfect for this. Remember to check the Colorize box. Some shading has been added to the rose along with a shadow to gel the scene together. More on this can be found in the 'Light and shade' chapter.

SHORTCUTS
MAC WIN BOTH

Making notepaper

USING PAPER IN A DESIGN can add that all-important handmade feel to it. This might be a piece of rich parchment declaring a special occasion or just a simple Post-it note to draw attention to a particular area of the artwork.

In this tutorial we'll create a piece of ruled notepaper using layers and selections. A key point to consider when creating objects from scratch is to give them some texture, in this case by adding some Gaussian noise. This helps them to blend into a montage more convincingly – real life is never as pure as a digitally produced image.

1 Start by creating a new layer. Use the Rectangular Marquee to mark out the shape of your paper. Fill this with white. You can't see any difference, of course, as it is displaying against white. You can either hide the background layer or fill it to make it easier to work on the image.

4 We need to remove the excess part of the box. Hold **ctrl** **⌘**. Click the paper layer's thumbnail to load its selection. Inverse the selection **ctrl** **Shift** **I** **⌘** **Shift** **I**. Now remove the unwanted area by pressing **Backspace**. This leaves us with a single line trimmed to fit.

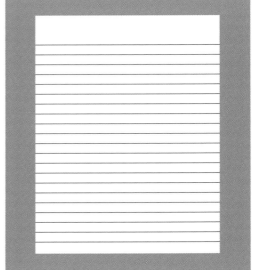

5 Load the line's selection. Select the Move tool **V**. Press and hold **alt** **Shift** **⌥** **Shift**. Tap the down arrow key once. This duplicates the line. Hold **Shift** on its own. Nudge the line down a couple more times to create the spacing. Now repeat the process to fill the page.

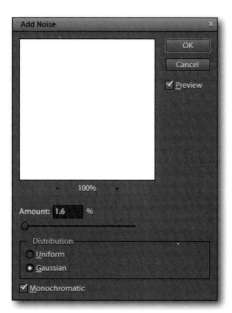

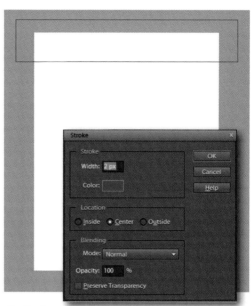

2 Lock the paper layer's pixels with the icon in the Layers panel or by pressing **/**. This prevents the transparent areas from being affected. Select Add Noise from the Filter menu. Check the Monochromatic and Gaussian options. You don't need much, just enough to give a little texture.

3 Create another new layer. Draw a new rectangular selection positioning the bottom edge where the first line on the page will be. The rest of the box needs to extend outside the area of the paper. Select Stroke from the Edit menu. Set the width and color for the desired effect.

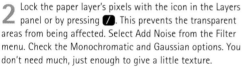

HOT TIP

Creating a selection before using the Move tool to duplicate parts of your artwork results in the copied area staying on the same layer. This is particularly useful when creating repeating patterns as we have here. Without doing so, we would end up with too many unnecessary layers.

6 Create the vertical margin using the same method as the horizontal line. I've chosen a different color here. By lowering the opacity we can control the faintness of the lines. When you're happy with the result press *ctrl* *E* *⌘* *E* to merge the ruled layer with the page.

7 To create the punched holes, draw a small circle using the Elliptical Marquee. Press *Backspace* to clear the pixels. Click and hold inside the selection. Hold *Shift* to constrain the movement. Drag the selection down into position. Delete the pixels again.

SHORTCUTS
MAC WIN BOTH

The art of paper tearing

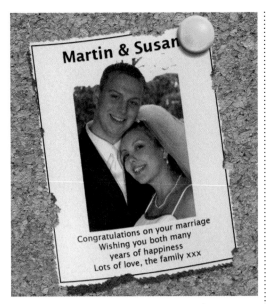

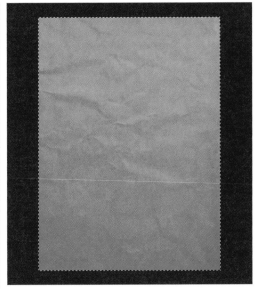

COMPONENTS OF YOUR ARTWORK often need a more handmade appearance, rather than the clean, precise lines of a selection or crop. Images such as the newspaper clipping above look far more realistic with a roughly torn edge.

As you'll see in the following workthrough, it only takes a few quick steps to achieve the desired effect. The technique is also highly versatile and is easily adapted to suit a variety of styles. You might, for example, want to create an old treasure map or a background of notepaper for a web page.

1 Here we have a scan of some crumpled paper. It's already been placed on its own layer. We've changed the background to a more contrasting color, as this makes it easier to see how the effect is progressing than if it was against the default white.

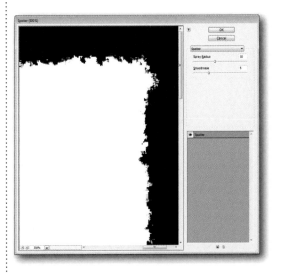

4 Go to Filter > Brush Strokes > Spatter. Zoom in to an area to make it easier to see the effect. We can use the Radius and Smoothness controls to fine-tune the appearance of the rough edge. Don't click OK yet as we are going to add another filter effect on top.

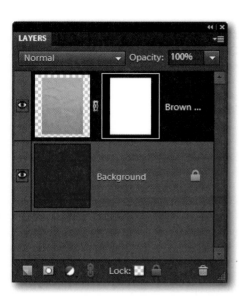

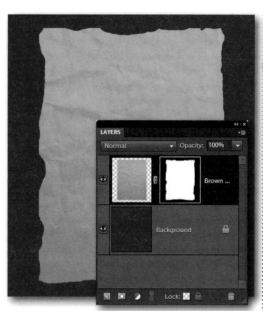

2 We'll be creating the effect using a mask. Begin by loading the paper layer's selection by holding *ctrl* ⌘ and clicking its thumbnail. Now click the Add Layer Mask icon. The mask's shape is automatically defined from the layer's selection.

3 Let's begin by making the edges of the paper a little less straight, as though it has been torn from a larger piece. Grab a hard-edged brush. Set the color to black. Now paint out random areas around the edges. This is only affecting the mask, of course. The paper image remains intact.

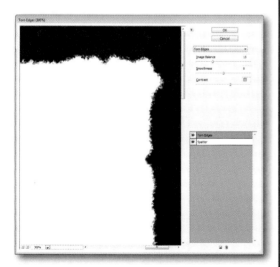

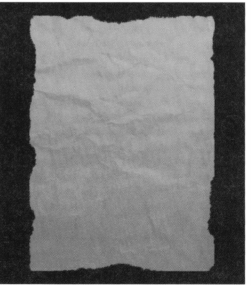

5 Click the New Effect Layer icon at the bottom of the dialog. Initially this duplicates the current effect so go back to the menu and choose Torn Edges. Again, we can finesse the effect using the slider controls. Once we're happy with the result, we can click OK.

6 Here's the final image. The mask has hidden the areas of the paper giving us a great rough torn edge. Because the image itself is not directly affected, we can always go back and edit the mask. We now have the basis for many different effects, such as the newspaper clipping in the intro.

Creating old paper

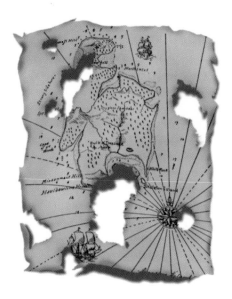

S O FAR WE'VE SEEN HOW TO MAKE
crisp notepad paper and produce the
appearance of fairly carefully torn edges. We're
going to turn the clock back a little farther
now and create the effect of old, battered
parchment.

This simple yet very effective technique is
quick to use and can easily be incorporated into
your artwork. It is, of course, particularly useful
for making old maps – as with the above image
– medieval style letters, and anything else that
needs to appear to have withstood the ravages
of time.

1 Begin by creating a new layer. Use the Freehand Lasso to
draw a ragged outline to mark out the edge of the paper.
Apply a small amount of Feather to the selection; 1 pixel
should be OK. Press **Shift Backspace** to open the Fill dialog,
select Color as the content and choose a light, sandy color.

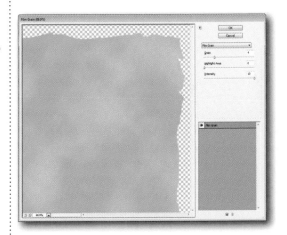

4 We have our mottled effect but it still looks too clean.
We need to give it an earthier appearance: open the
Film Grain filter located under the Artistic menu. Use very
low settings to create a subtle, gritty effect across the
surface of the paper.

2 Press *ctrl* *J* *⌘* *J* to duplicate the layer. Choose the Difference Clouds filter from the Render sub-menu; although we haven't constrained the effect, it only affects the area of the previous layer's pixels. The colors look a little strange but this is only temporary.

3 Set the layer's blend mode to Soft Light; this gives us a nice spread of tones. Depending on the effect you require, you can lower the opacity to make it less harsh. When you're happy with the result, press *ctrl* *G* *⌘* *G* to group the layers, then *ctrl* *E* *⌘* *E* to merge them.

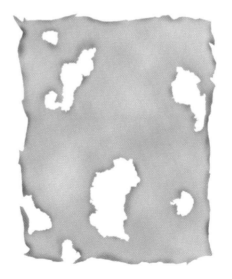

5 To complete the effect we'll add some dark patches around the edge: select the Burn tool *O*, set its mode to midtones, and paint over random areas all around the perimeter. This gives the effect of the paper having been handled and battered over time.

6 As an optional step you can create some holes in the paper to enhance the effect even more. Use the Magic Wand *W* to select the darker patches of the paper, feather the selection then hit *Backspace* to delete the areas. You can also darken the edges as in the last step.

HOT TIP

In step 3 we took the unusual action of creating a clipping group before merging the layers together. If we hadn't, it would have resulted in a thin dark edge appearing around our paper; this is due to combining layers which have been feathered. This can, of course, work in our favour if we wanted to have a slightly heavier border.

Once finished, you can add artwork such as maps or line-art using the Multiply blend mode. These can then be grouped so the missing areas are hidden on the image overlay as well.

SHORTCUTS
MAC WIN BOTH

Ageing a photo in minutes

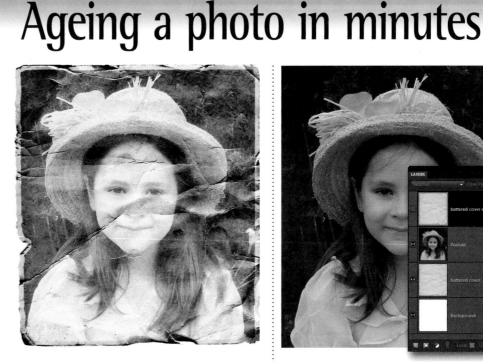

THERE ARE MANY WAYS to restore old, damaged photographs. You'll find one in almost every digital imaging how-to book. In this tutorial, however, we're going to do the exact opposite. By taking a perfectly good picture and applying a variety of effects we'll create the impression that it has been less than well cared for.

Although this might seem a little perverse, it serves as an extreme example of what can be achieved by combining and blending existing textures with a photo. In this case, we'll use the reverse side of an old, battered book cover. The dents, folds and creases provide an excellent basis for the effect.

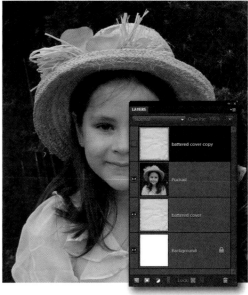

1 Open the image from the DVD. We've placed the battered book cover image beneath the girl's layer. Click the cover's thumbnail. Press *ctrl J* ⌘ *J* to duplicate it. Drag the copy layer above the girl's and hide it for now by clicking its visibility (eyeball) icon.

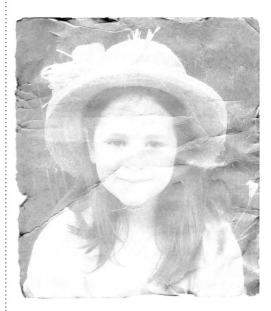

4 Make the copy of the cover visible and click its thumbnail to make it the active layer. Press *ctrl Shift U* ⌘ *Shift U* to desaturate it. Set the layer's blend mode to Hard Light. Combined with the base layer, this really helps to bring out the crumpled texture.

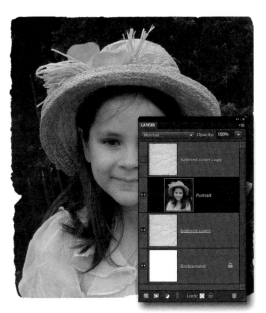

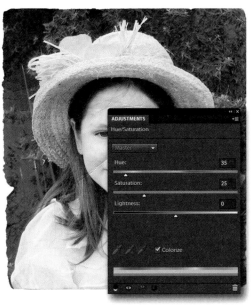

2 Click the girl's layer in the Layers panel. Now press *ctrl* G ⌘ G to group it with the book layer. Only the areas that correspond to the layer beneath are visible, so the edges of the photo now follow the rough outline of the crumpled cover.

3 Set the girl's layer blend mode to Hard Light. This allows the texture beneath to show through. Create a Hue/Saturation Adjustment Layer above the girl. Make sure Colorize is checked. Drag the Hue slider across to create a sepia-like coloring.

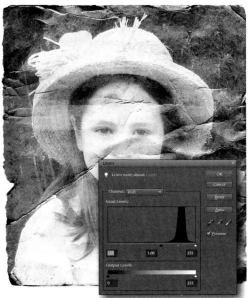

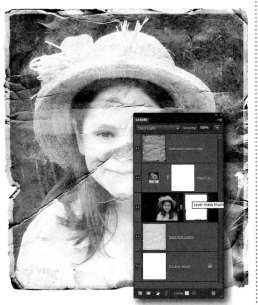

5 The image has become a little washed out due to the white of the book layer. Press *ctrl* L ⌘ L to open the Levels dialog. Drag the Shadows slider across to the right to increase the contrast. This also brings out grainy areas, which really adds to the aged effect.

6 Click the photo layer's thumbnail to make it active. Load up either of the texture layers' selections. Go to Select > Modify > Contract. A value of 15 pixels works well. Click OK. Now add a mask by clicking the icon at the base of the Layers panel. This hides part of the photo, creating a border.

A quick repair job

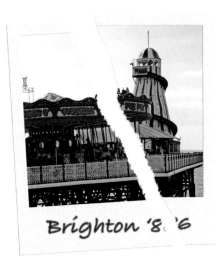

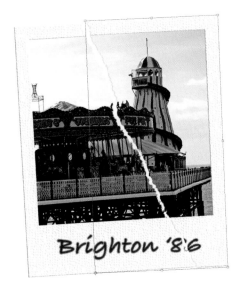

WHILST WE'RE ON THE SUBJECT of damaged photos, it appears that this seaside Polaroid has seen better days (actually, it was torn using the technique from earlier in the chapter). We could spend hours retouching and seamlessly blending the image to a state where nobody would ever know it had been in two parts. We're not going to, though. Instead, after crudely placing the pieces together, we'll create some strips of old, worn Scotch tape to make it look as good as new, almost.

This is a slightly over the top example to illustrate the technique. You could, of course, use the effect in your scrapbook projects or to stick virtual photos up in your web gallery. With a bit of customizing, it could easily become solid electrical tape or even sticking-plasters.

1 We'll begin by putting the two halves together. They're on separate layers so we can use Free Transform to place them together. If it were a single layer, you could use the Lasso tools to select the pieces first. We want it to look botched so you'll want to leave some overlapping areas.

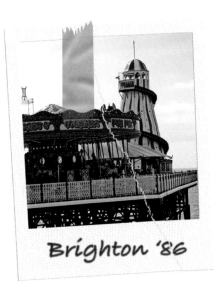

4 Select either the Dodge or Burn tool **O**. Choose a soft brush set to Highlights. Create some light and dark shading to give the appearance of the tape lifting. You can switch between Dodge and Burn modes by holding **alt** **⌥** whilst painting. Keep the effect subtle for the best results.

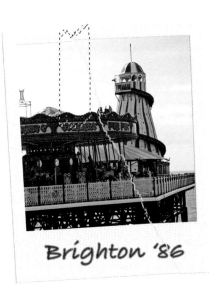

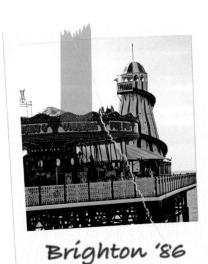

2 Add a new layer above the photo. Grab the Lasso tool **L** and draw a jagged selection. Press **alt** **⌥** and release the mouse to switch to Polygonal mode. Drag out a side. Click and hold to switch back to freehand. Add the other ragged end. Join it up with another straight line.

3 Press **Shift** **Backspace** to open the fill dialog. Select 50% gray as the Content. The hue of a neutral color can always be altered. Scotch tape is semi-opaque (even when aged) so set the Opacity to 50%. Finally, press **ctrl** **D** **⌘** **D** to deselect.

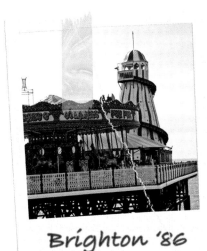

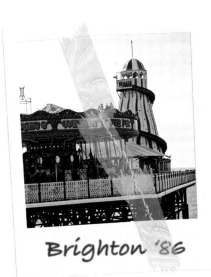

5 To give our tape a really authentic appearance we've used the Plastic Wrap filter (from the Artistic sub-menu). This is supposed to be old tape: we need to add some discoloration. A Hue/Saturation adjustment is good. You can control the effect from one dialog.

6 Press **ctrl** **T** **⌘** **T**. Reposition the tape. Rotate it to follow the tear. You could draw additional pieces from scratch. A quicker way is to press **⌘** **⌥** **T** **⌘** **⌥** **T**. This creates a new copy on the same layer. You can flip and distort them enough to appear sufficiently different.

Letting the dust settle

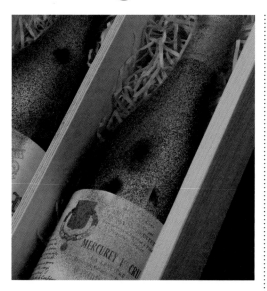

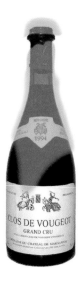

DUST IS USUALLY SOMETHING we don't like seeing. As with many things, there are exceptions, wine being one. Cellars often have bottles which have rested undisturbed for many years as they reach maturity and, as a result, have accumulated a thick layer of dust.

If, however, you're not a connoisseur and need a picture in a hurry, you can create the desired effect in a few easy steps. We'll be using a bottle for the workthrough but the technique could just as easily be applied to many different subjects: items in an attic, perhaps. You could even use it in promotional material for a cleaning company – a before and after shot, for example.

1 Here's our bottle. It's been isolated and placed on its own layer. Begin by grabbing the Selection Brush **A**. Set the Mode to Mask. Now use a soft tip to paint in the areas where you want the dust to be. Don't worry too much about spilling over the edges; they'll be tidied up.

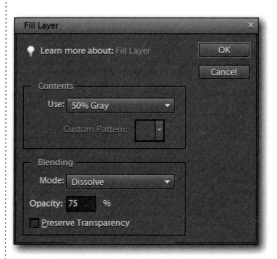

4 Create a new layer above the bottle. Open the Fill dialog (*Shift Backspace*). Set the contents to 50% gray. Choose Dissolve for the blend mode. Now lower the opacity a little; in this case to 75%. Dissolve uses the opacity value to determine the visibility of the layer's pixels.

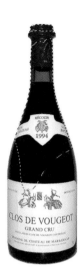

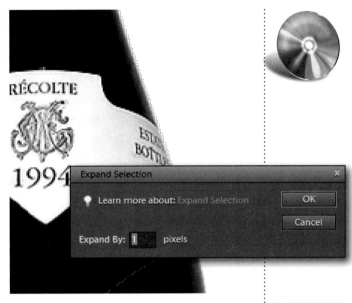

2 Switch back to Selection mode. Press `ctrl` `Shift` `I` `⌘` `Shift` `I` to inverse the selected areas. Hold `ctrl` `alt` `Shift` `⌘` `⏴` `Shift`. Click the bottle layer's thumbnail; the keypress forces the selection to Intersect mode. Anything outside of the bottle's edge is discarded.

3 Even a thin layer of dust has depth. We need to create some extra space for the effect to sit outside of the bottle's edge. Choose Modify > Expand from the Select menu. I've used a value of 1 pixel here. You could, of course, use different values to produce thicker layers.

HOT TIP

For extra realism, you may want to create some areas where the dust has been disturbed. This can be achieved by using a soft Eraser set to a low opacity. Parts of the layer can be progressively thinned out; great for creating fingermarks where the object has been handled.

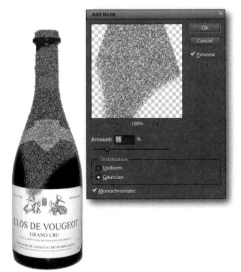

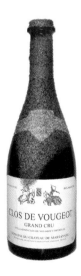

5 The result is not too bad; it's a little uniform, though. Press `ctrl` `D` `⌘` `D` to deselect. Add some Noise to give a more random texture. Follow this with a very small amount of Gaussian Blur; you just need to take the harshness away from the effect.

6 Almost done. Select the Burn tool `O`. Set the Range to Highlights. Using the edge of a large, soft brush, darken down the sides of the dust layer. Use the shape of the bottle as a guide. Now hold `alt` `⏴` to temporarily switch to Dodge mode. Lighten up the front area a little.

SHORTCUTS

MAC WIN BOTH

You spin me round

FOLLOWING ON CLOSELY from the previous theme, we're going to use noise to create a different kind of dusty texture: this time, it will form the worn groove of a much-played vinyl record.

We'll create the whole thing from scratch – if you'll pardon the pun – using just layers, noise and blurs. The result is exceptionally realistic and can be used as the basis for musically styled collages or perhaps a novelty greetings card for an aspiring rock star in the family.

1 Create a blank document and add a new layer. Select the Elliptical Marquee **M** and holding **Shift** to constrain the proportions, create a large circle by clicking and dragging out from the top-left corner. Press **D** to select the default colors and fill the layer with black **alt** **Backspace** **⌥** **Backspace**.

4 Copy the layer **ctrl** **J** **⌘** **J**. Press **alt** **Shift** **Backspace** **⌥** **Shift** **Backspace** to fill only the visible pixels with black. Enter Free Transform **ctrl** **T** **⌘** **T** and holding **alt** **Shift** **⌥** **Shift** to scale proportionally around the center point, drag it to the size of the inner circle of the record.

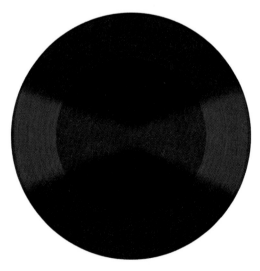

5 Press **ctrl** **E** **⌘** **E** to merge the layers. On a new layer, use the Polygonal Lasso **L** to draw a bow-tie shape across the record. Fill this with white. Deselect and add a strong Gaussian blur, and drop the opacity to around 20%. Press **ctrl** **G** **⌘** **G** to clip the layer with the record.

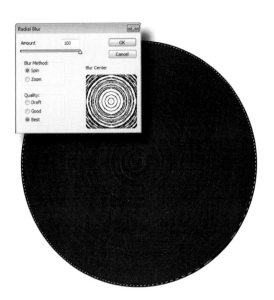

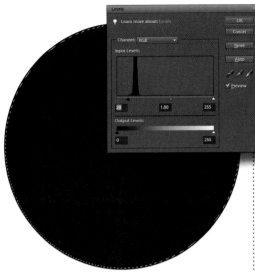

2 Use Select > Modify > Contract to reduce the size of the selection by around 5 pixels to leave a smooth edge. Add some monochromatic Gaussian Noise: around 50% is adequate. Now select the Radial Blur filter: set the Amount to 100, the Method to Spin and set the Quality to Best.

3 The result is good but a little light so open the Levels dialog *ctrl* **L** **⌘** **L**. Begin by dragging the Shadows slider to the right so it meets the left edge of the histogram; this darkens the overall surface. Now drag the Highlight slider to the left until the texture becomes more defined.

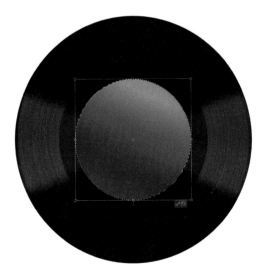

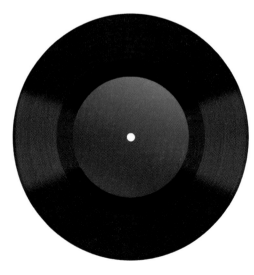

6 Create a new layer. Now load up the record's selection and select the Gradient tool **G**. Choose a suitable preset: we've used Red, Green. Now drag right across the surface of the record. Finally, scale it down a little smaller than the center circle with Free Transform to make the label.

7 To create the center hole: press *ctrl* **J** **⌘** **J**. Now scale the layer down to the correct size and load up its selection. Hide the background layer and press *ctrl* *Shift* **E** **⌘** *Shift* **E** to merge the visible layers. Finally, press *Backspace* to remove the pixels.

HOT TIP

We used a gradient here to create a quick effect for the record's label. We could just as easily import some proper artwork, however, by loading the label layer's selection and using the Paste Into command that we covered in Chapter 6; or by using a clipping mask to hide the unwanted parts that extend outside of the label's boundary.

To add a more three-dimensional effect, we could also apply an inner-bevel layer style. If we do this after flattening the layers it will apply to both the outer-edge and the center hole.

SHORTCUTS
MAC WIN BOTH

193

A little light relief

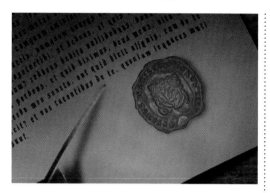

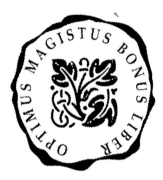

PREVIOUSLY, WE SAW how the use of subtle shading can create the illusion of depth, changing a simple flat object into a three-dimensional one. The same is true for creating raised surfaces.

In this example, we'll create a traditional wax seal using a black and white logo as the basis for the effect. The edge of the artwork has been created purposely uneven to enhance the effect, giving the appearance of the hot wax spreading as the template stamp is pressed into it.

1 Here's our black and white artwork on its own layer. Grab the Magic Wand. Uncheck the Contiguous option. This tells the tool to select every instance of the specified color in the image. Click anywhere in the black area. Now press *ctrl* C ⌘ C to copy the selection to the clipboard.

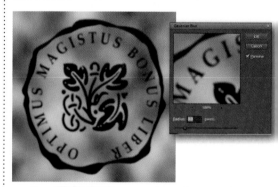

4 Press *ctrl* V ⌘ V to paste the previously saved selection then deselect. Press *ctrl* *alt* F ⌘ ⌥ F to open up the Gaussian Blur dialog again. This time, set a much lower value. We need to soften the edges but keep the detail visible. A value of around 3 pixels is used here.

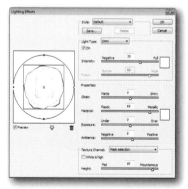

7 Go to Filter > Render > Lighting Effects. Begin by loading the selection we saved earlier from the Texture Channel menu at the bottom of the dialog. Uncheck White is high. Increase the height to 90. Choose the Omni light type. Drag its circle out to the edges of the artwork.

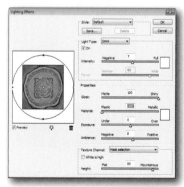

8 The default settings are not good at all; we can hardly see the artwork. Lower the Intensity to around 7; this gives us a nice even lighting. We can also alter the properties. Increase the Gloss setting to 100. Set the Material to -100. This will give us a good result so click OK.

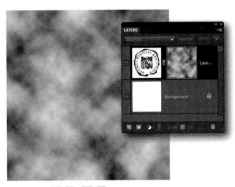

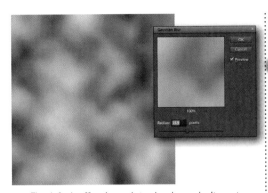

2 Press *ctrl* D ⌘ D to deselect. Create a mask by clicking the icon at the base of the Layers panel. Hold *alt* ⌥ and click the mask thumbnail. Press D to restore the default colors. Now apply the Clouds filter. The reason for using the mask will become evident later.

3 The default effect is much too harsh; we don't want any hard edges. We'll soften it down with Gaussian Blur. Set it to a fairly high pixel radius: around 15 worked well here. We want to achieve a smooth tonal blend similar to the above image.

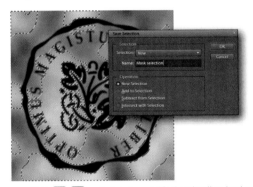

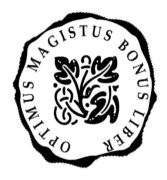

5 Hold *ctrl* ⌘ and click the mask's thumbnail to load up the selection. Only a few small areas will appear; this is OK. The boundary only shows on areas that have more than 50% opacity. Choose Save Selection from the Select menu. Give it a name and click OK. Press *ctrl* D ⌘ D to deselect.

6 Hold *Shift* and click on the mask to hide it. Now click the artwork's thumbnail to exit Mask Edit mode. Re-enable the Magic Wand's Contiguous option. Select the area outside the artwork. Press *ctrl* *Shift* I ⌘ *Shift* I to inverse the selection. Create a new layer. Fill this with white.

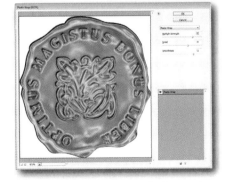

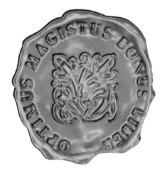

9 The result is OK but a little matt. Sealing wax has a mixture of flat areas and shiny highlights. The Plastic Wrap Filter is perfect for this. It can be found under the Artistic section of the Filter menu. Use the sliders to bring out the detail and give it a more moulded appearance.

10 Finally, deselect then open the Hue/Saturation adjustment dialog. Click the Colorize box. Now adjust the sliders to add some color. We decided on the archetypal deep red. We finished up by adjusting the contrast with Levels to give a richer effect.

Stamp duty

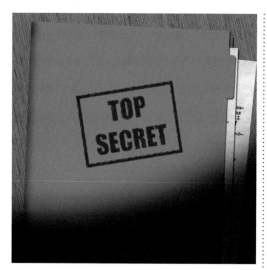

THERE WILL BE OCCASIONS where we want to use a piece of artwork or effect again in our projects. We obviously wouldn't want to keep recreating it each time. We could, of course, save it in the conventional way then import it into a document when it's needed, but there is a better way – creating our own brush preset. This has several benefits: we can save them, either individually or as sets to create libraries; they are non-destructively scaleable and can be resized far more quickly than the usual transformation method; they also take up relatively little disk space and because they are self-contained files, they can easily be shared between other Elements and Photoshop users.

When creating a brush, it's important to know how they work. In essence, they are very similar to a mask, using grayscale to determine their opacity. Pure black appears 100% solid, becoming more transparent the closer it gets to white, where it disappears completely. We'll see this in action here by creating a simple rubber stamp effect. We could create a brush from any piece of artwork, of course, even photographs.

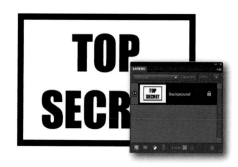

1 Let's start with a new blank document. Select the Type tool **T**. We want a bold font for this project: Impact is a good one. Set the text alignment to Center. Click the document to start a new text layer and type Top Secret, with a carriage return (*Enter*) in between the two words.

4 We could create our brush at this point. Rubber stamps wear down after a while and stop transferring the ink completely. We can give our artwork a worn look but we'll need it to be on a single layer so we can apply the filter. Press *ctrl* *Shift* **E** *⌘* *Shift* **E** to merge the layers together.

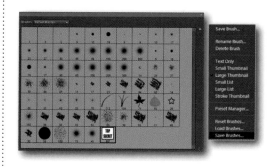

7 Select the Brush tool **B** if it's not already. Our brush will appear as the last entry in the currently selected brush presets. Although it will be stored automatically, we'll save it, as a precaution. Click the brush, then open the fly-out menu and click Save Brushes. Name the file and click OK.

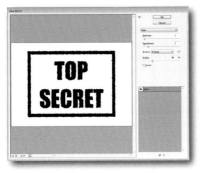

2 Create a new layer. Select the Rectangular Marquee **M**. Holding **alt** 🔲 click and drag the boundary out from the center of the document – remember to leave enough space around the text for our border. We can reposition the selection by additonally holding the spacebar.

3 Select Stroke (Outline) Selection from the Edit Menu. We need a strong border so a width of 20 pixels is good for this size image. Set the color to black and the location to Inside – this gives us sharp-edged corners. If we'd used Center or Outside, the corners would be more rounded.

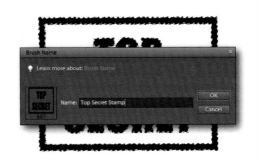

5 Press **D** to reset to the default color palette. Go to Filter > Distort > Glass. Choose the Frosted texture. Experiment with the Distortion and Smoothness settings to roughen the edges a little; it only needs to be a subtle effect. Click OK to apply.

6 Now we can go ahead and create our brush. Use the Magic Wand to select the artwork; hold **Shift** to add the individual parts. Go to Edit > Define Brush from Selection. It's important to give it a meaningful name as this will make it easier to find amongst the other presets.

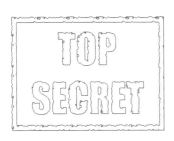

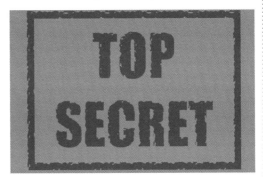

8 Save or discard the original artwork document and create a new blank one. Here we can see the outline of the brush. Just like a mask, the original white areas are hidden, leaving only the slightly uneven black areas where we applied the filter.

9 We've filled the background with color to demonstrate the effect. Being a brush, we can quickly scale it up or down using the left and right square bracket keys **[ ]**. We can also change its color simply by setting a new foreground color – we've chosen red, of course!

HOT TIP

Although flattening the layers in step 4 goes against our principles of always keeping the original artwork layers, in this instance it's a very simple image and easy to recreate. If we were working on something more complex, we could merge it to a new layer using **ctrl alt Shift E** **⌘ ⌥ Shift E** then hide the original layers to avoid confusion.

SHORTCUTS
MAC **WIN** **BOTH**

Finger-friendly stained glass

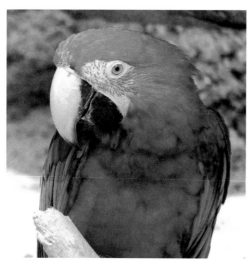

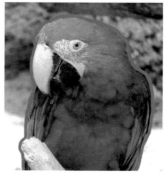

1 Begin by creating a new layer. Set the foreground to mid-gray. Use a small, hard-tipped brush to trace the outline of the bird. It needn't be perfect as long as you capture the shape.

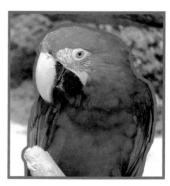

2 Select the entire document by pressing *ctrl* *A* *⌘* *A*. Choose Stroke Selection from the Edit menu. Set the same color and width as the brush. Use Inside as the location.

STAINED GLASS HAS BEEN AN ARTFORM for centuries. From the huge ornate windows of churches and cathedrals to the understated adornment of an urban door, people love its radiance and color.

You may have discovered the Stained Glass filter in Elements; its results are passable but tend to resemble a mosaic more than the traditional effect. In this tutorial, we'll go back to basics and create some of our effect by hand, using a photo as a template for tracing the outline, then applying filters and layer styles to achieve our result.

This technique can be used for all kinds of project. On its own it's a great effect for greetings cards. It could also be used as an ornate border for framing a photo. You could, of course, use this technique as a basis for designing the real thing.

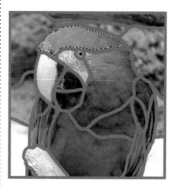

6 Reselect the outline layer by clicking its thumbnail. Grab the Magic Wand **W**. Click an area of the bird to select that section. The top of the head is a good place to start.

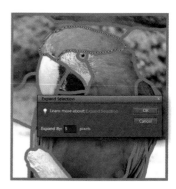

7 We need to ensure there will be no gaps between the leading and the glass. Expand the selection (Select > Modify). A value half the width of the leading is fine.

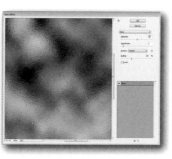

11 Open the Glass filter (under Distort). Set the texture to Frosted. A smoothness value of around 2–3 gives a good stipple effect. Raise the distortion level to blur the texture.

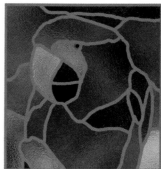

12 Change the layer's blend mode to Multiply. This filters out the lighter areas of the glass, allowing the color to show through, but still retains the effect.

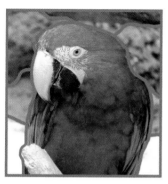

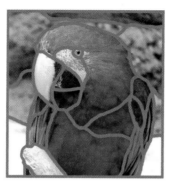

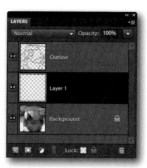

3 The background needs to be divided up into panels. Draw a few lines between the border and the bird's outline. Use some of the contrasting areas of detail as a guide.

4 Now divide up the bird itself. Again, use the prominent details to make up the panels. Remember that each section must be completely enclosed and connected by the leading.

5 We need a separate layer for the individual colors. Press and hold *ctrl* ⌘. Click the New Layer icon in the Layers panel. This creates a new layer beneath the current one.

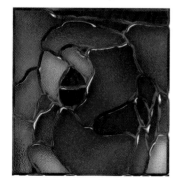

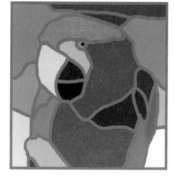

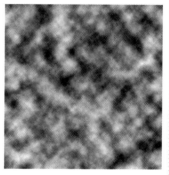

8 Click the layer you created in step 5. Open the Fill dialog *Shift Backspace*. Set the contents to color. Use the eye-dropper to pick a suitable shade from the photo.

9 Press *ctrl D* ⌘ *D* to deselect. Color the rest of the panels by repeating the process from step 6 onwards. I've also painted the center of the eye with a small black brush.

10 Add a new layer between the color and the outline. Press *D* to restore the default foreground and background colors. Fill the layer with the Clouds filter.

HOT TIP

As well as the four presets, you can also load custom textures into the glass filter to use as a basis for its distortion effect. Click the fly-out menu to the right of the Textures menu to access the file dialog. You can use any image saved in Photoshop (psd) format.

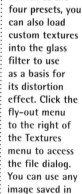

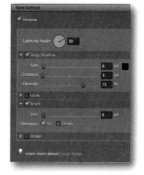

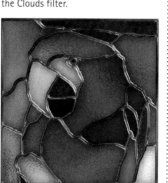

13 Make the outline layer active. Select the Wow Chrome layer styles set from the Artwork and Effects panel. Apply the Beveled Edge setting. It may look a little odd at this stage.

14 Double-click the style icon to the right of the layer's thumbnail. Lower the drop shadow's distance. Adjust the bevel size. Around 6 pixels works for this size of image.

15 Here's our completed image. Adjusting the layer style has made all the difference. You may want to make the glass layer a little lighter using Levels or Brightness/Contrast.

SHORTCUTS
MAC WIN BOTH

Blueprint for design

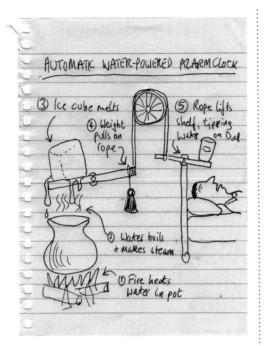

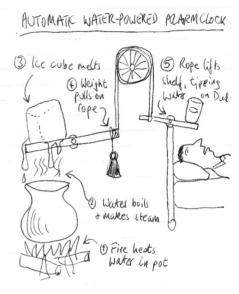

KIDS HAVE WONDERFUL IMAGINATIONS and can come up with all kinds of fantastic inventions – such as this idea for a failsafe alarm clock involving boiling water, melting ice cubes and a tipping glass at the end of the process.

The trouble is, these designs are always sketched on whatever materials come to hand – in this case, a page torn from a spiral-bound notebook. We're going to see how to turn this sketch into an official-looking blueprint, but first, we need to find a way to get rid of the lines in the background of this ruled paper.

1 Begin by opening the Brightness/Contrast adjustment. Drag both sliders all the way to the right to set both Brightness and Contrast at their maximum values. This will make the rules fainter, but won't get rid of them altogether (unless your rules are gray, rather than black).

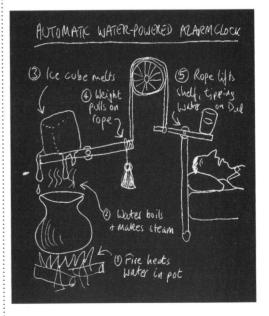

4 Now for the blue background. If the original artwork is still your background layer, double-click its thumbnail to turn it into a regular layer, then set the mode of this layer to Screen. You won't see any difference until you make a new layer behind it, filled with blue.

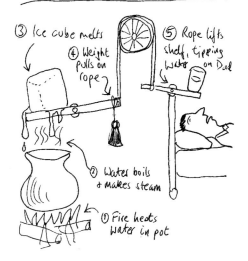

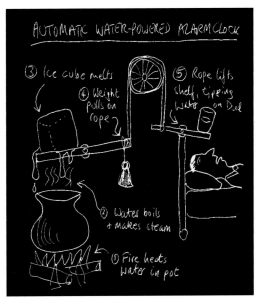

2 Now desaturate the image ⟨*ctrl*⟩⟨*Shift*⟩⟨U⟩ ⟨⌘⟩⟨*Shift*⟩⟨U⟩. This will knock out all the extra colors that crept in during the previous step. Use the Threshold adjustment to turn it to pure black and white. You may need to erase a few stray pieces of line; paint them out with a white brush.

3 With the image fully cleaned up, we're ready to start turning it into a blueprint. Choose Invert to turn the image from black on white to white on black. If any of the ruled lines still show up, paint over them in black to hide them.

HOT TIP

The hardest part of this job is cleaning up the original drawing. It would be better, of course, if kids could be persuaded to use clean, unlined paper – but when inspiration strikes, we use whatever's to hand. This is an extreme example, with solid, dark rules; most clean-up processes won't be as complex as this one. But the combination of Brightness/Contrast and the Threshold adjustment usually does the trick.

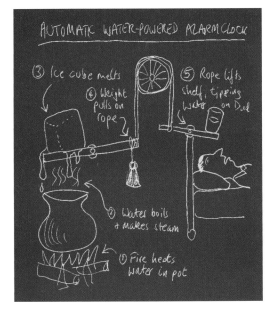

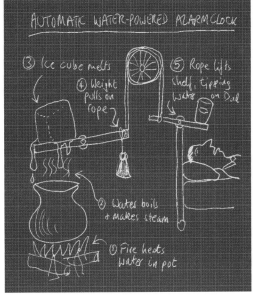

5 The white of the original layer is a little stark, so let's give it a touch of blue. Open the Hue/Saturation dialog and press Colorize. Reduce the Lightness slightly and change the Hue slider to get a pale blue; you may want to increase the Saturation a little as well.

6 Finally, let's place a graph paper grid behind the image. This grid is white on black, and we've set the opacity to just 20% to make a faint background. It's a bit of a fiddle to draw graph paper from scratch, so we've provided this for you on the DVD.

SHORTCUTS
MAC WIN **BOTH**

Unfinished illustration

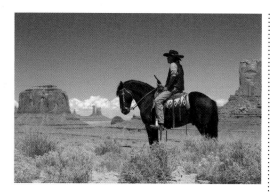

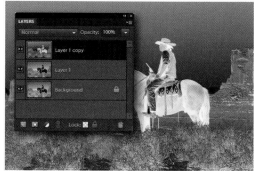

YOU'VE PROBABLY SEEN THIS STYLE of illustration many times, where only parts of the image, generally the main detail, are in color and the rest is left as a sketch or given a lighter wash of paint. It's used a lot in children's books and architectural projects but is also an artform in its own right.

We're going to explore a variety of techniques here in order to create our illustrative style image. Starting with a photo, we'll first convert it to a sketch, then use filters to create a painterly effect, then combine the two, and finally use a layer mask to add or remove portions of the image. The use of layers and masks makes the technique very versatile, allowing us to decide how much of the color we show. We could, of course, simply leave it as a line drawing or decide to go for the full color picture instead.

1 The first stage of the process is creating our ink outline. Duplicate the background layer by pressing *ctrl* *J* *⌘* *J*. Now press *ctrl* *Shift* *U* *⌘* *Shift* *U* to desaturate (remove the color from) the image. Make a copy of this layer. Press *ctrl* *I* *⌘* *I* to invert it.

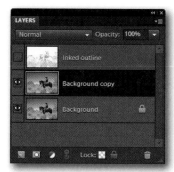

4 We're finished with the outline for now so hide the layer by clicking its eyeball icon. The next step in the process is to create the painted on canvas effect. Select the background layer again by clicking its layer thumbnail and create another duplicate.

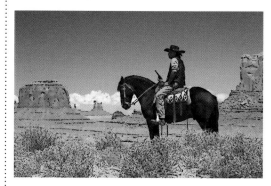

7 The image looks a little blotchy and formless at the moment. Make the outline layer visible again. Now set its blend mode to Multiply. This hides the white area of the layer, leaving just the outline so it overlays our painted effect. This really brings the image to life. We're almost done.

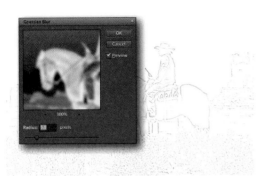

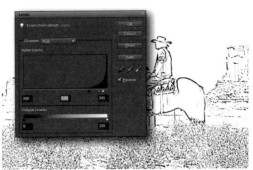

2 Change the blend mode to Linear Dodge. The document will go white; this is normal. Open the Gaussian Blur filter. Set the Radius to 0. Now drag to the right; we'll see the effect emerge. Stop when there is a visible outline – around a 2-3 pixel radius works well for this image.

3 Now we'll make the outline bolder. Merge the layers together *ctrl* *E* *⌘* *E*. Open the Levels dialog *ctrl* *L* *⌘* *L*. Drag the Shadows slider to the right so it meets the left edge of the histogram. Now adjust the midtones and highlights to fade out the grayer areas of the image.

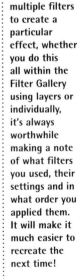

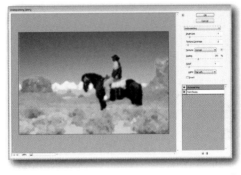

5 Open the Filter Gallery from the Filter menu. Select Paint Daubs from the drop-down menu. We used a Brush Size of 7 and a Sharpness of 4 with a Wide Blurry brush type. This gives us a great painterly effect. Don't click OK yet as we're going to add another filter.

6 Click the New Effect Layer icon at the bottom right of the window. Now select Underpainting from the drop-down. Here we've used a Brush size of 4, Texture Coverage of 2 with the Texture set to Canvas, and a Relief of 4. Finally, set the Light Direction to Top Left and click OK to apply.

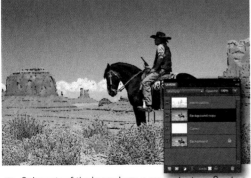

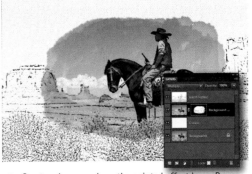

8 Only parts of the image have a canvas texture. Create a new layer beneath the painted layer. Fill this with white. Select Filter > Texture > Texturizer. Set the attributes to match those we used in the underpainting filter and apply it. Finally, set the painted layer's blend mode to Multiply.

9 Create a layer mask on the painted effect layer. Press *ctrl* *I* *⌘* *I* to invert the mask. This hides the content. Now, using a white brush – some of the wet media brush presets work really well – we can start to paint over the mask, bringing back those parts of the image.

Finding images for free

MOST OF THE TIME, you'll be using your own images for the project you're working on – you won't find a more inexpensive source than that. There will be situations, however, when you'll need a photo of an object you don't have the time or resources to take. It may be completely impractical because it's not something you normally find in your home town or even the country you live in; a famous building or indigenous animal, for example. Whilst you could improvise by altering the project or modifying an image of something similar, there is a much better way of tracking down that elusive picture: the World Wide Web.

In recent years, as more people have switched to digital cameras and fast internet connections become more commonplace, huge online stock photography sites have sprung up, containing hundreds of thousands of images. Sites such as **stock.xchng** (www.sxc.hu) and the curiously named **Morguefile.com** (traditionally a publishing term given to reference libraries of old images and cuttings) provide categorized and searchable libraries of people, places and objects from all around the world. Because they are submitted by the public for the public, the quality is not always superb; it does mean, however, that you have a good chance of finding something bizarre which would not make it past the strict scrutiny of the commercial libraries. The biggest benefit, of course, is that they are completely free. The sites are kept running solely on advertising and the good will of public donations. This, of course, is great news for the montage artist on a tight or nonexistent budget.

The exact terms of use vary from site to site. Most, however, allow unlimited use for both private and commercial projects, providing it's not detrimental to either the photographer, their subject or the site itself. When you download an image, it's usually anonymously; the photographer may like to know how their photo has been used but it's rarely mandatory. Stock.Xchng allow the contributors to set their own requirements: some require you to apply for explicit permission, depending on the content – generally, and understandably, when there are recognizable faces. It's one thing to allow someone to post photos of you but quite another to find yourself placed in an image of questionable content.

In addition to the dedicated libraries, there are also community sites such as **Flickr.com** and more recently, **Wikipedia Commons** (commons.wikipedia.org). These operate under the new Creative Commons license – a system devised for intellectual rights management on the internet. Under this license, photographers can determine what can and can't be done with their images. This ranges from complete free rein to total copyright protection; the latter is very often negotiable through polite communication with the person concerned.

It's also worth noting the governmental public domain libraries. These offer more specific images: military, political figures and, of course, there is **NASA.gov** which holds a wealth of scientific, aeronautical and astronomical photos. Again, these images are all free to use for private projects but commercial use carries some regulations; these can be found in the site's terms and conditions.

If all else fails, you can always try a search through **Google** or **Yahoo**. Both have offshoots of their sites devoted to images. Great care must be taken here. Grabbing images from web searches puts you right in the middle of the copyright minefield. If you're using the pictures at a purely personal level, making backgrounds for your computer desktop and so on, you'll be OK – surveillance techniques haven't infringed the home, just yet. If, however, you intend to publish these images as part of your website or as a printed design, make sure you obtain permission from the owner of the site or photo. There's usually an address to write to. If you are in any doubt as to the copyright status, don't risk it; at the very least, you'll receive an irate email asking for removal of the image, and at worst, you may find yourself in court.

As long as you respect the rules and guidelines, there is a wealth of useful content to be found. It can also be a good source of inspiration; you never know what you may come across whilst performing a search. It can often spark a whole new project idea.

A list of free sites along with links to their web addresses can be found on the book's accompanying website: **www.howtocheatinphotoshopelements.com**.

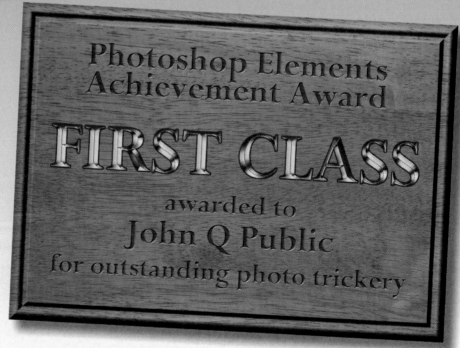

The text above fits neatly enough onto its plaque, but it looks rather painted on. How much more impressive if the wording appears to have been carved into the wood. The words 'First Class' in this example use a metal style not detailed in this chapter, but it's on the DVD for you to import into Elements and use in your own work.

8
Working with text

WE USE TEXT FREQUENTLY IN ELEMENTS. Although you may not think of it as being an essential component of most images, there are often times when adding a caption can lift an image.

But there's more to text than mere captions. Think how good it would look if you could engrave an invitation on stone, or carve it into a piece of wood. How good your holiday slideshow could appear if the first frame showed the title written in a sandy beach. Or imagine customizing a photo of a classic car so that its owner's name was written in gleaming chrome along the side.

We'll look at all these techniques and more in this chapter.

Carving in stone

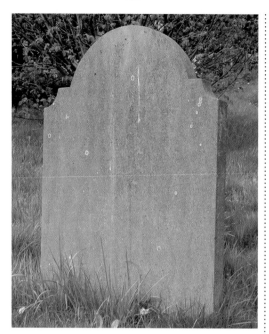

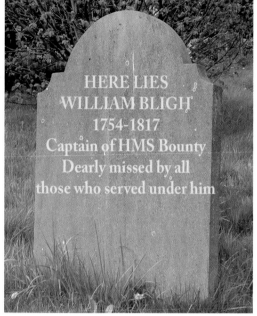

STONEMASONS TAKE YEARS to learn their craft: after all, the one thing that's certain about carving lettering into stone is that there's no Undo key. Make a mistake and it will cost you dearly.

Fortunately, Elements is rather more forgiving when it comes to carving. All we have to concern ourselves with is arranging the text to its best advantage; we can leave it to Elements to add the bevel effect automatically.

As we'll see here, we don't even need to choose a color for the text. This, too, is added directly by Elements, building on the texture already in the stone for added effect.

We'll demonstrate this technique by adding an inscription to this blank gravestone, in memory of the unfortunate captain of the mutinous ship *Bounty*.

1 Begin by typing your text – centered, for a gravestone. Choose a serif font, such as Caslon Bold, for authenticity. No need to worry about the text color at this stage.

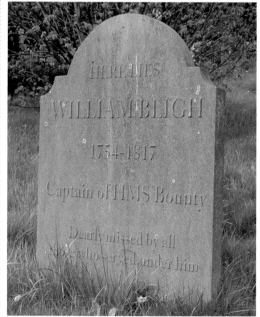

4 Hold *ctrl* ⌘ and click on the text layer's thumbnail to load up the selection. Then hide the text layer, switch to the background layer, and press *ctrl* *J* ⌘ *J* to make a new layer from it. Choose Simple Sharp Inner from the Layer Styles panel to make the basic bevel.

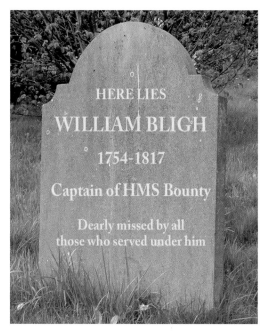

2 Now lay out the text for emphasis. Hold `ctrl` `Shift` `⌘` `Shift` and press the `>` and `<` keys to make selected text bigger and smaller.

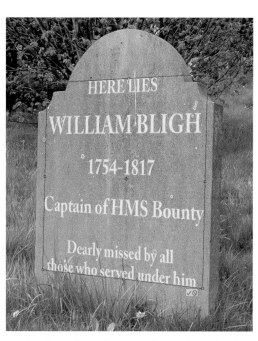

3 In order to distort the text, we first need to make it into a regular layer: choose Layer > Simplify Layer. Now use Free Transform to distort the corner handles in perspective.

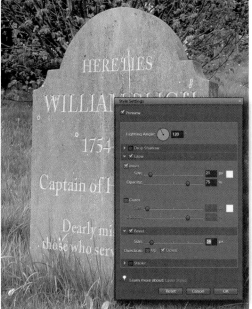

5 We now need to modify that bevel, so open Layer > Layer Style > Style Settings. Change the bevel type from Up to Down to make it carved rather than raised. Adding an Inner Glow, using the default settings, brightens the carved lettering as well.

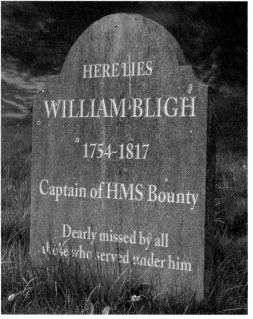

6 To make the carving more realistic, carefully erase the layer with a small Eraser where the grass goes over it. Here, we've also darkened the background layer using the Levels adjustment, and added a new somber sky to complete the spooky graveyard effect.

SHORTCUTS
MAC WIN BOTH

Neon signs with layer styles

ELEMENTS COMES WITH A BUILT-IN selection of neon styles – called Wow Neon. But they're brash, too bright, and look unconvincing on the screen; they're also set to colors that will look dull and muddy when printed out.

For this reason, we've created a set of custom neon layer styles. They can be found on the DVD in the Goodies folder, along with installation instructions. Be sure to load them in before you start the project!

As a first step, though, we'll look at how to round off our basic sign design to give it the sort of smooth corners required for the neon to work properly.

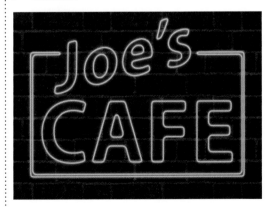

1 We'll begin with a standard piece of black and white artwork. We've created a simple text-based sign here. The design could be more complex, of course, incorporating graphic objects. This has been flattened to a single layer.

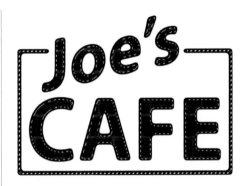

4 Grab the Magic Wand tool **W**. Uncheck the Contiguous option. Click one of the letters. Go to Select > Modify > Contract. Set a value of around 6 pixels and click OK. Now press **Backspace** to delete the selected areas.

7 Now we can add our neon layer style. Go to the Effects palette, click the Layer Styles icon and select the Cheat Styles (which you remembered to install beforehand, of course!). Here we've applied the Neon Pink preset.

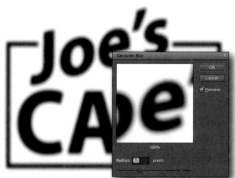

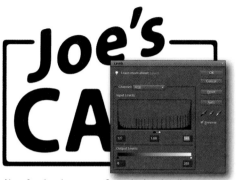

2 We need to soften the edges as they are far too angular for a neon sign. We'll begin by applying a Gaussian Blur. We've used a 6 pixel radius blur, which applies quite a high degree of smoothing.

3 Now for the clever part. Open the Levels adjustment and drag the white and black sliders together so that they almost touch the gray slider. This tightens up the blur, producing a round-cornered version of the artwork.

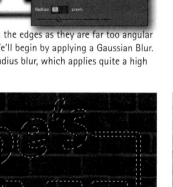

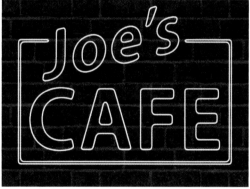

5 Now click the Magic Wand in the area outside of the letters to select the background. Go to Select> Modify > Expand. Set a value of 1 pixel. Hit *Backspace* to delete the pixels and we're left with just the outline of the lettering.

6 Press *ctrl D* *⌘ D* to deselect as we no longer need the selection active. The lettering is currently a little difficult to see. Press *ctrl I* *⌘ I* to invert the image. The artwork is now white instead of black.

HOT TIP

The Gaussian Blur/Levels technique used in steps 2 and 3 can be used to smooth out any artwork, adding rounded corners to just about anything. The more you blur, the more rounded the corners will be. Drag the white, gray and black sliders to the left or right to change the thickness of the lettering after blurring it: experiment to see what works best for your design.

Note: you can't change the color of the inner glow in layer styles in Elements before version 5.

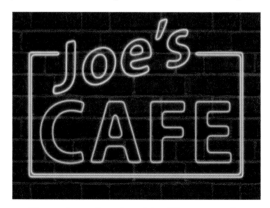

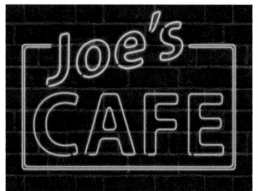

8 We can change the colors of the different parts of the sign. Here we've made a rough selection around the word 'cafe'. We've cut it to its own layer by pressing *ctrl Shift J* *⌘ Shift J* and applied the Neon Green style.

9 The components of neon signs are not made from one continuous tube. We can simulate the breaks by selecting a hard-edged eraser and erasing a small section on each of the parts. The layer style fills around the gaps.

SHORTCUTS

MAC WIN BOTH

211

Instant chrome

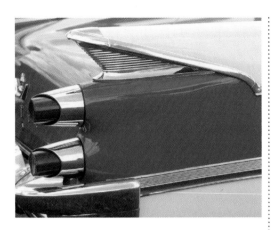

ELEMENTS OFFERS A WIDE VARIETY of ready-made layer styles you can apply to your artwork – among them is a selection of good-looking chrome effects.

As with most layer styles, though, some adjustment is needed before they fit the artwork perfectly. You'll almost always need to adjust the bevel size and the rather over-enthusiastic drop shadow in order to make the style work with your image.

Here, we'll go a step further and make the chrome reflect its background to match the chrome detail already present on this car.

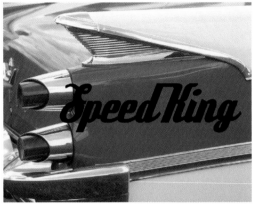

1 Here's our initial lettering: it's set in the freeware font Deftone Stylus, which is easy to find online. After typing the text, turn it into a regular layer using Layer > Simplify Layer, so we can distort it more easily.

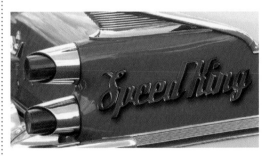

4 That's far too big a bevel for our purposes. Double-click the Layer Styles icon in the Layers panel and change the Bevel size to around 8 pixels. Make a note of this number, as we'll need to use it later.

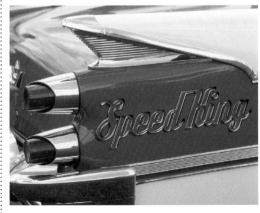

7 Make a new layer and fill with any color. This is a red sampled from the car body. It looks fairly convincing as it stands, as the inner color matches the car well, but we can make it better still.

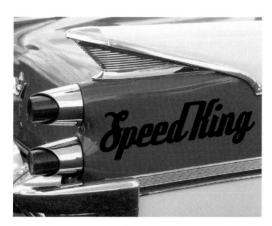

2 Use Free Transform to shear the text so that it fits the side of the car. Hold `ctrl` `⌘` as you drag a corner handle to add a little perspective to it: the lettering gets slightly smaller towards the right-hand side.

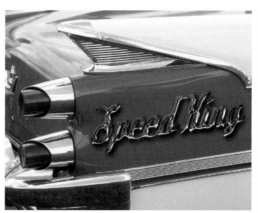

3 Now open the Layer Styles panel and go to the Wow Chrome section. Drag the first style, named Wow Chrome Beveled Edge, onto the layer to apply the effect to the text.

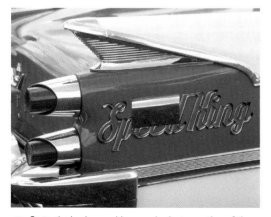

5 We need to reduce the drop shadow amount, too: a far smaller shadow with a smaller offset is needed. By dragging the Lighting slider clockwise, we can also get a better chrome effect.

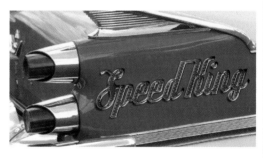

6 Now for the inner part of the lettering. Hold `ctrl` `⌘` as you click on the layer's thumbnail in the Layers panel to load it up; then choose Select > Modify > Contract and reduce the size of the selection by 8 pixels.

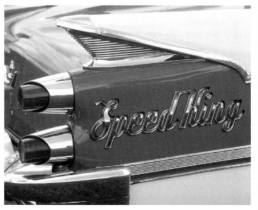

8 Go to the background layer and select a portion of the reflection in the fender with the Lasso tool. Make a new layer from the selection and drag it above the inner color text layer as shown here.

9 Now press `ctrl` `G` `⌘` `G` to group the reflection with the inner color layer. Enter Free Transform and scale the reflection so that it fills the whole of the lettering. The chrome's now a perfect match to the original car.

HOT TIP

In step 9, you may have some difficulty making the reflection fit the full extent of the inner part of the text. Don't worry if it doesn't quite reach the edges: you can always use the Clone tool to copy any of the texture out to the sides, and any missing portions of the top can easily be painted in by sampling and then painting with a soft-edged brush.

SHORTCUTS
MAC WIN BOTH

213

No mess pumpkin carving

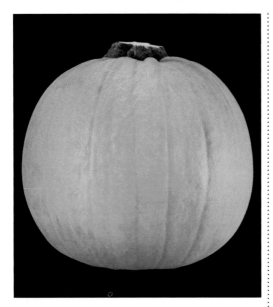

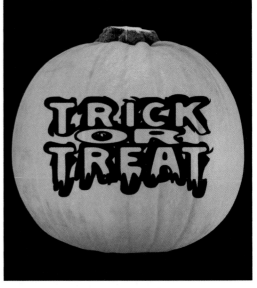

A TRADITIONAL PART OF HALLOWEEN is the scooping out of pumpkins to make Jack-o'-lanterns. Gone are the days of crudely cut out toothy grins, however, it's now an artform with people spending hours carving intricate images of witches and ghosts in order to out-do their neighbors. This is all very messy and time-consuming, of course.

We can achieve a similar image effect to use in our design, without going near the pumpkin's innards. We'll be using a dingbat style font which, instead of having the standard individual letter characters, has entire words or images. This allows our artwork to be completely re-editable; we can change the motif at any time without having to redo the whole image.

It is an impossible image, of course; there are areas where the text is floating, which couldn't really be achieved, but we can afford ourselves a little artistic license here as it makes a great party invitation or poster.

1 Here's our pumpkin with the text layer. We've used a dingbat font: the aptly named Trick or Treat, which gives us the whole artwork in one go by typing one character, in this case the letter A. At present it's looking somewhat flat and not at all like it's been carved.

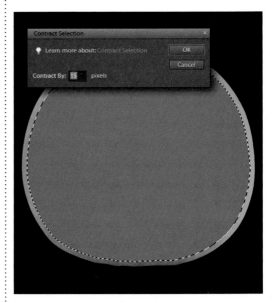

4 Create a new layer above the text layer and load the pumpkin's selection. Go to Select > Modify > Contract. Enter a value of around 15 pixels and fill it with 50% gray. This creates a smaller copy that we can use for the texture inside the pumpkin.

FONT: JESS LATHAM/BLUE VINYL DESIGNS

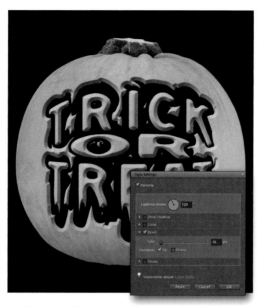

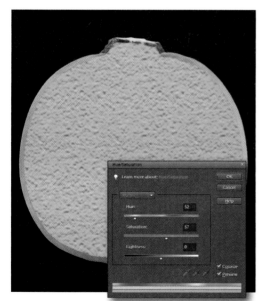

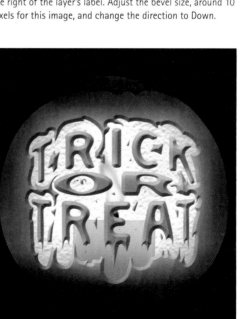

2 Make sure the text layer is active and the Type tool is selected. Go to the Options bar and click the Warped Text button; select Bulge from the menu and choose horizontal as the direction. Now drag the Bend value to the right to try and match the curve of the pumpkin.

3 Choose the Bevels presets from the Layer styles; choose Simple Sharp Outer and apply it to the text layer. The effect needs adjusting so double-click the style indicator to the right of the layer's label. Adjust the bevel size, around 10 pixels for this image, and change the direction to Down.

5 Select the Texturizer filter; set the texture to sandstone and the scaling to 200%. Apply a small amount of Gaussian Blur to soften the effect. Now use Hue/Saturation *ctrl* U *⌘* U set to Colorize and change the color to a warm yellow hue. Press *ctrl* D *⌘* D to deselect.

6 Grab the Dodge tool *O*, set the mode to Highlights and use a large, soft brush to create the impression of a glow radiating from the center. Create a clipping group *ctrl* G *⌘* G with the text layer to hide the excess. Finally, we've added a candle and shading to complete the effect.

HOT TIP

In order to follow the technique, the font must first be installed from the DVD. Browse to the Goodies folder: the font file is named TRICTB__. TTF. Use the following instructions to install it: In Windows: Open the Fonts setting from the Control Panel, go to File > Install New Font and browse to the place you unzipped it to; select the name and make sure Copy fonts to Fonts folder is checked and click OK. For Mac OS X: Double-click the zip file to extract the folder; double-click the font file to open Font Book and click Install Font. You may need to relaunch Elements to get the font to show up in the list.

SHORTCUTS
MAC WIN BOTH

215

Write on the button

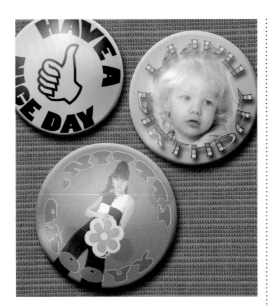

BUTTONS, OR BADGES, as they are also known, are often placed on the front of greetings cards bearing a slogan or message for the recipient to wear on their special day (begrudgingly or otherwise). Why not, then, create them virtually to add an extra element of interest to your own designs.

The text on buttons is often written around the edge in a ring. Although there is no built-in function to do this in Elements, it's by no means impossible; as with many things, it's simply a matter of improvisation. The Text Warp function allows us to bend the words to fit. Best of all, being a type layer means it stays editable. You can go back and change the wording at any time whilst still retaining the quality.

1 Begin by creating a new layer. Use the Elliptical Marquee **M** to draw the outline of your button. Remember to hold **Shift** to make it a perfect circle. Fill this with 50% gray for the moment; we can give it a proper color at a later stage. Press **ctrl D** **⌘ D** to deselect.

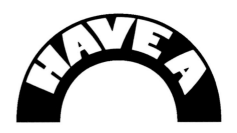

4 The arc doesn't fit because the text is too short. The answer is simply to pad it out using spaces. We can add these before and after the words because we set centered justification. I've hidden the circle and selected the text so the result is visible. The spacing gives us a perfect arc.

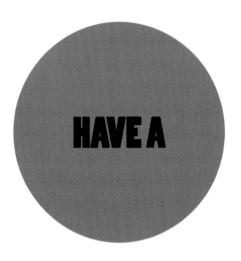

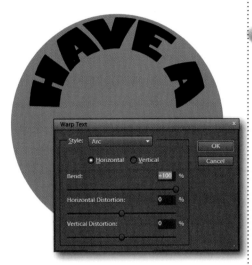

2 Select the Type tool **T**, set the Alignment to center and click to create a new text layer. We need to split our slogan in two halves as we can only bend the text to a maximum of 180° in one go. Don't worry about the size at this stage, we can adjust that in due course.

3 Select text warp by selecting its icon from the options toolbar. Choose Arc from the style menu; make sure the mode is horizontal and increase the bend to 100%. You can also reposition the text without leaving the dialog. It's looking good but we still need to adjust it slightly.

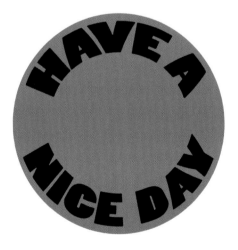

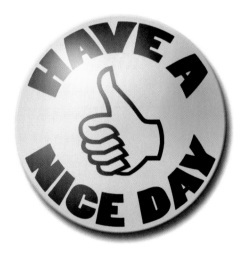

5 We can now add the second part of our text. This time, we need to bend it in the opposite direction. Open the Warp dialog again and pull the Bend slider all the way to the left. Add some extra spacing as we did before. You can also make adjustments with Free Transform if required.

6 We can add some color to the button itself. This can be done with a Hue/Saturation adjustment or the Paint Bucket. I've also added some highlights using the Dodge tool along with a layer style to round off the edge and add a drop shadow. A thumbs-up in the center completes our effect.

HOT TIP

Not all fonts work well with this technique; because of the effect of the warp tool, wider lettering may become too distorted and give an undesirable result. Try to use a condensed font wherever possible. There are many different styles available from sites on the internet so you will generally be able to find one which fits in with the theme of your design.

SHORTCUTS
MAC WIN BOTH

Three-dimensional text

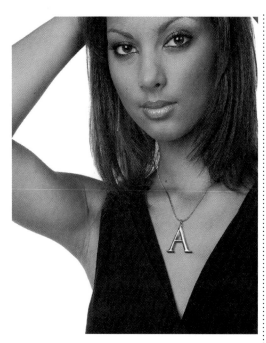

W HEN WE WANT TEXT TO STAND OUT
we tend to use a bold font, often in a
different typeface to the rest of the document.
To really draw attention to it we can take it a
little further and give it a three-dimensional
effect so it jumps off the page at the viewer.

Three-dimensional text is usually generated
by dedicated programs or by using plug-ins;
but, as we'll see in the following tutorial, we
can create the effect in a few simple steps using
the standard Type tool and a crafty trick with
selections, layers and the Move tool.

The technique can, of course, be used to add
emphasis to your artwork as a heading; you
could also use it as part of a montage, creating
a sign to place over a store, for example,
or as the image above shows, adding some
personalized jewelry to a photo.

GOLD

1 We'll begin by creating a new text layer: grab the Type
tool **T**, set the Alignment to center and click in the
middle of the document to place the cursor. Select a suitable
font: larger, rounded styles work especially well. Type out
your text, remembering to leave some space around it.

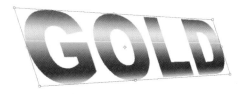

4 Turn the original text layer off to avoid confusion.
Enter Free Transform *ctrl* **T** *⌘* **T**, hold *ctrl* *alt* *Shift*
⌘ *⌥* *Shift* and drag the top-left corner handle up a little
to add some perspective. Keeping the keys held, drag the
top-middle handle to the left to tilt the text back.

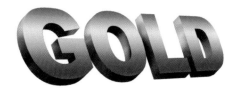

7 Make the rear text layer active again. Grab the Burn tool
O, set a fairly low exposure and choose a large, soft
tip. Using a combination of Midtone and Highlight modes,
darken the areas that would be in shadow. Hold *alt* *⌥* to
switch to the Dodge tool to add in some extra highlights.

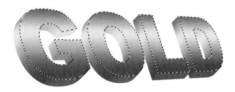

2 Create a new layer and load up the text's selection. Grab the Gradient tool, choose the copper gradient from the Presets panel and set the mode to Reflected. Holding *Shift*, click and drag from the top of the text to the bottom to give a varied range in tones. Press *ctrl* *D* *⌘* *D* to deselect.

3 Unsurprisingly, our text does not look very golden at all. We chose the copper gradient because it gives us a good contrast with strong highlights. A Levels adjustment can be used to alter the hues. The technique for this can be found in Chapter 4.

The addition of shading really helps to bring an image to life. A traditional artist might use different shades of the same color to produce highlight and shadow in their picture; we can brighten or darken the exisiting color using Dodge and Burn – in effect, painting with light. By switching between the Midtone and Highlight modes, areas can be put into shadow, the color made richer and hotspots added; this is especially good for metal effects. It is, however, worth noting that the results can be fierce if overdone so it's good practice to use a low exposure and build the effect up gradually.

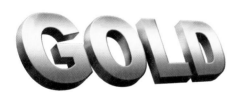

5 Press *ctrl* *A* *⌘* *A* to select the canvas. Grab the Move tool *V*, hold down *alt* and, using the cursor keys, nudge once to the right and once upward to copy the pixels. We'll repeat this rhythmic sequence until the letters have the desired thickness.

6 Press *ctrl* *J* *⌘* *J* to create a new layer from the current selection. This will become the face of our text; we can alter this separately from the rest of the effect. This also serves as a mask so we can add shading to the edges of the lettering without affecting the front.

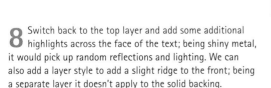

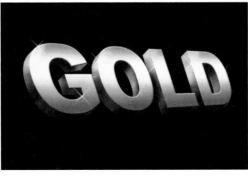

8 Switch back to the top layer and add some additional highlights across the face of the text; being shiny metal, it would pick up random reflections and lighting. We can also add a layer style to add a slight ridge to the front; being a separate layer it doesn't apply to the solid backing.

9 To finish off we've filled the background with black to set the gold off. A new layer has been created above the text and we've added some small sparkles on the brighter points: these are made with the Crosshatch brush under the Assorted tip presets in the brush panel.

Writing in the sand

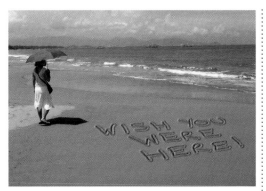

THERE'S SOMETHING ABOUT AN EXPANSE of smooth, untouched sand that begs us to carve something into it; this could be a message of adoration to a loved one or simply a declaration to prove you were there.

We're going to recreate the effect here using distortion and layer styles in a similar way to the stone carving we made earlier in the chapter, except that we'll create the excess sand around the letters where it would have been scraped out.

This quick but effective technique lets us write whatever we want, all without getting a single grain of sand between our toes; it won't get washed away, either.

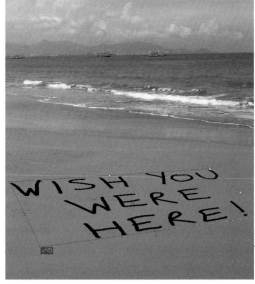

1 Make sure you're working on the text layer by clicking its entry in the Layers panel. Press *ctrl* *T* *⌘* *T* to enter Free Transform; hold *ctrl* *⌘* and drag the corner points to position the text in perspective on the sand. Press *Enter* to accept the changes.

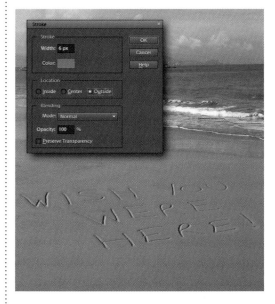

4 Add a new layer and reload the text's selection. Select Stroke from the Edit menu and set a suitable value for the width; use the color picker to select a suitable color from the sand, set the Location to Outside and apply to create an outline around the text. Press *ctrl* *D* *⌘* *D* to deselect.

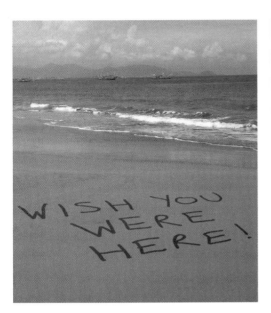

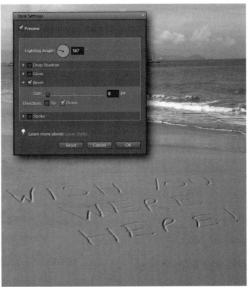

2 Load up the layer's selection. We can hide the layer now by clicking its eyeball icon. Make the background layer active. Press *ctrl* *J* *⌘* *J* to copy the selection to a new layer. Change the layer's blend mode to Multiply to make it darker against the background whilst retaining its texture.

3 Apply the Simple Sharp Inner bevel preset from the Effects panel. Double-click the layer's style icon in the Layers panel to open the control dialog. Lower the bevel value, adjust the lighting angle and set the direction to Down to create a carved appearance.

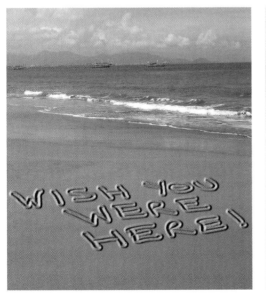

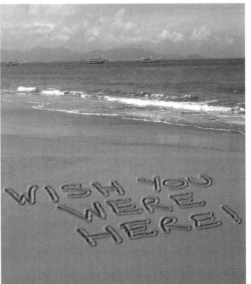

5 Apply a small amount of Noise to add some texture; we used the Uniform, Monochromatic setting with an amount of around 12% here. Add a Simple Inner bevel and decrease its width a little; this time keep the direction set to Up to give it a raised appearance.

6 Set the blend mode to Dissolve and lower the opacity to give the outline a broken-up, grainy effect. We've also lowered the base text's opacity and darkened the two layers a little using Levels, giving the impression of the wet underlying sand showing through.

HOT TIP

The Dissolve blend mode is great for creating grainy effects or for eroding parts of the image. Unfortunately, because it uses the opacity of the layer to determine the intensity, you cannot soften the pixels by applying a blur. To get around the problem, first create a new layer beneath the target layer then merge them together. The resulting layer preserves the effect which will no longer be affected by blurring or further changes to the opacity.

SHORTCUTS

MAC **WIN** **BOTH**

221

Chop and change

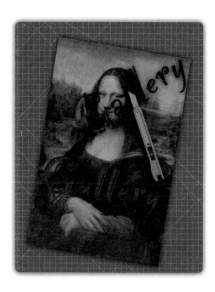

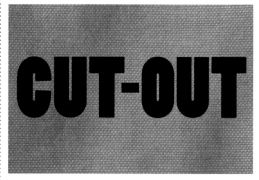

1 We'll start by creating the cut-away effect to show the background beneath the fabric. Grab the Type tool **T** and place some text above the background layer. We've used Poplar Std here as it's a nice clear font; the color is not important as we'll only be using it as a template.

I T'S FAIRLY SAFE TO ASSUME that you wouldn't consider mercilessly plunging a scalpel into a priceless painting solely to advertise your upcoming art exhibition; unless, of course, it was one of those avant-garde affairs, in which case it would be positively frowned upon if you didn't. That aside, it's surprising how often we start hacking into our images without a moment's thought and, whilst we do have the safety of the Undo command, there are far better ways to take chunks out of our artwork.

By using a combination of text layers, clipping masks and layer styles, we can create the effect of words being cut out of a piece of material (or almost any other substance) to reveal a surface beneath. What's more, this technique is completely editable as we never actually cut into the image; we simply create the illusion of doing so.

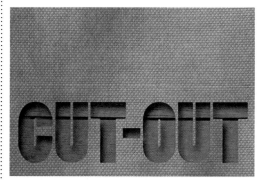

4 That's looking a lot better. Before we add the cut-out text itself we'll make some space for it on the artwork. Grab the Move tool **V** and drag the text down towards the bottom. Because the style is applied to the text layer the effect also moves, so we can position it wherever we want.

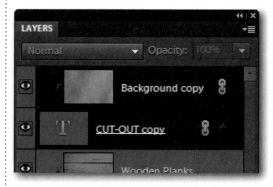

7 We need to reposition the new text but this time we want the pattern to move with it. Click the text layer's label (not the thumbnail), hold *ctrl* ⌘ and click the texture layer's label to form a group. Click the chain icon at the bottom of the Layers panel to make the group permanent.

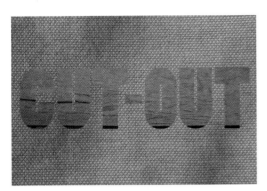

2 Click the planks layer in the Layers panel and make it visible by clicking its eyeball icon. This will be the texture that shows through the fabric. Press *ctrl* *G* ⌘ *G* to group it with the text. This hides everything apart from the area taken up by the text.

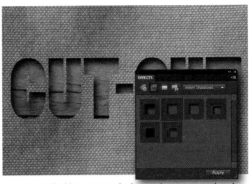

3 It's not looking too convincing at the moment; there's no sense of depth. Make the text layer active and go to the Effects panel; select Layer Styles and from there choose the Inner Shadows from the menu. Select the Low preset by pressing Apply or by double-clicking its icon.

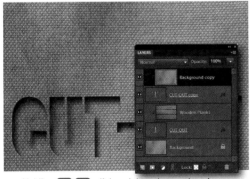

5 Holding *alt* ⌥, click and drag the text layer's thumbnail to the top of the layer stack. This creates a copy without having to relink the original's clipping mask. Duplicate the background layer and drag it above the new text. Finally, create a clipping group with the two new layers.

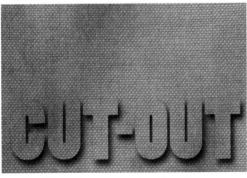

6 We still have the previous style set from the copy. Right-click the style indicator icon and select Clear Layer Style. Now go back to the Effects panel and select Drop Shadows from the drop-down list. The Low preset works well here.

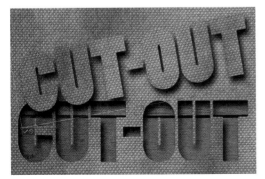

8 Press *ctrl* *T* ⌘ *T* to enter Free Transform; we can now move and rotate the text and its overlay into position in unison. The bounding box seems far too large compared to the text but remember, we are transforming the entire texture layer. Press *Enter* to apply the changes.

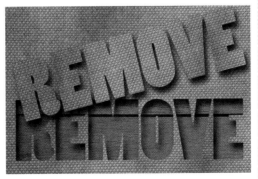

9 With everything in place we can change the text without having to reapply the effects and textures. Double-click the type layer to edit it. This works both ways, of course: you could just as easily change the styles or replace the backgrounds, leaving the text intact.

223

Elements of design

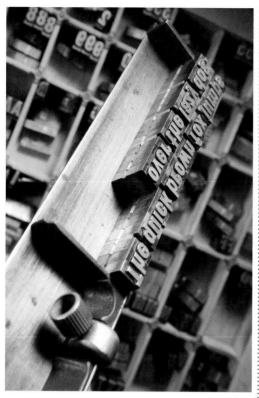

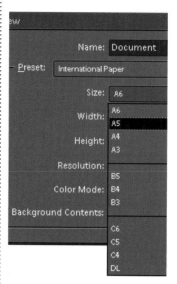

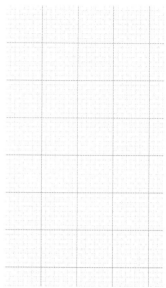

1 When we start a new document we have a host of different presets to choose from or we can create our own custom size, of course. We need to take care when doing this as it may cause problems when we go to print it.

2 One of the most important parts of the design process is the grid. This can be found under the View menu and can be toggled on and off. We can also adjust its size and color from the program Preferences *ctrl* **K** ⌘ **K**.

YOU MAY NOT REALIZE THIS but with Elements we have at our disposal a highly competent layout tool for both text and graphic-based design such as newsletters, posters and flyers. Many functions are already built-in and others can easily be emulated. With rulers, grids, paragraphs, layers and much more to work with, we can produce professional-looking documents with relative ease.

In the following project we'll be looking at some of these features and building a simple column-based layout as we might find in a newspaper or magazine article. The principles for creating a full page are the same, we'd just need to add more columns and arrange them across the page.

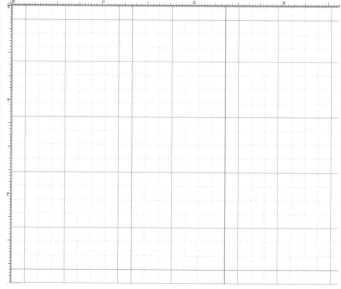

6 Let's put this into practice: we've set up a blank document on which we've created a typical layout comprising a border and three columns spaced with gutters (separation areas for the text and graphics). We can enable the Snap to Grid and Snap to Guides options from the View menu. This makes positioning the design elements much quicker.

This is a paragraph text box. We can move it around, resize it, and even skew it. The text inside will automatically resize to fit the new size and shape.

If there is not enough space to contain the whole paragraph, a small cross will appear in the bottom-right corner handle. We can choose to resize the box, or alter the size of the font.

3 We have rulers `ctrl` `Shift` `R` `⌘` `Shift` `R` for creating designs to a specific size. We can set the measurement units in Preferences. We can also change their origin by clicking and dragging from the top-left.

4 We can add horizontal and vertical guides by clicking on the ruler and dragging down or across onto the document. We can reposition them using the Move tool. Drag them back to the ruler to remove them.

5 Normally, when we add text, we click the cursor at the point we want it to start and type. If we click and drag, however, we create a text-box which can hold individual paragraphs.

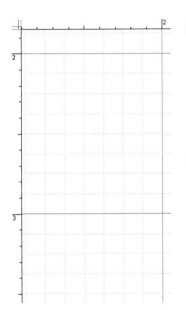

Sweet success!

Congratulations go to Margaret Jones for winning the Horti-cultural Society's home-produced jelly contest for the second year running. There seems to be no stop-ping her when it comes to preserves; and we're not about to try, they're delicious!

She attributes her success to the home-grown fruit and a secret extra ingredient

which goes into each and every jar.

"And my patience and dedication, of course." She adds, smiling broadly.

We look forward to seeing (and tasting) more of her produce; long may she reign as the queen of the fruity spreads.   **A.J.**

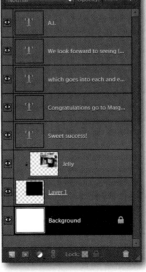

7 Here's the completed article demonstrating how the paragraphs are laid out around the image. Unfortunately, Elements doesn't automatically hyphenate or flow text from one column to another, but it's not too much effort to do this manually. To the right we have the Layers panel showing the structure of the document.

Image size

UNDERSTANDING IMAGE SIZE is a conundrum that puzzles many Elements users. Just what is 'dots per inch' and how do they relate to the megapixel sizes quoted by the manufacturers of digital cameras? What resolution is required for printing, or saving files for the web?

Image size is traditionally measured in dots per inch (dpi), even if you're accustomed to working in centimeters. You can, of course, work in centimeters per inch, but we'll stick to dpi here to be in tune with the convention.

Computer monitors typically display images at 72 dpi. This means 72 pixels across and 72 down, which amounts to 5,184 physical pixels in each square inch of screen space. This is the resolution you should work at when designing for the web. In Elements, when you view an image at '100%', you're seeing it at 72 dpi: in other words, each pixel in the image precisely matches one pixel on the screen. Viewing images at a smaller size – say, 50% – means that each pixel on the screen displays an average of the colour of four pixels in the original document. If you zoom in further, to say 800%, you can see each pixel with much greater clarity; they'll clearly appear as squares.

Commercial printing uses only four basic colors: cyan, magenta, yellow and black. All other colours are simulated by overprinting these four. The bigger the printed dot, the more of that colour is seen, so if in one region there are equally sized cyan and yellow dots, you'll see green. If the cyan dots are twice the size of the yellow, the result will be turquoise. Clearly, these dots need to be tiny if we're not going to notice them, and the smoother the paper, the smaller the dots can be. Newspapers print at around 100 dpi and glossy magazines at around 250 dpi, occasionally more.

When printing on an inkjet printer, however, the color is made up from arrays of tiny dots of equal size. The more dots that are clustered together, the stronger the density of that color. Inkjet printers typically print at 1200 dpi, which produces a smooth tonal range with a dot that's barely perceptible. That doesn't mean you need to work at 1200 dpi in Elements: a size of 150 dpi is more than adequate for getting excellent color prints from most inkjet printers.

Digital cameras capture pixels on a CCD chip: the better the camera, the more pixels on the chip, and so the higher the resolution at which the image can be

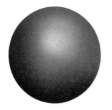
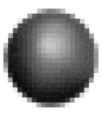
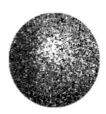
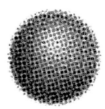

| Original image, composed of smooth colors | Image converted to square pixels on computer monitor | Image printed using dot clusters on inkjet printer | Image printed using different sized dots in magazine |

recorded. If a camera is quoted as having an image size of 3.2 megapixels, it will produce images that measure 2048 pixels wide by 1536 pixels high. Multiplying these values together – the total number of pixels in the image – produces 3,145,728 pixels overall, or rather over three million pixels, and that's what the 3.2 megapixel name refers to.

If its images were printed in a newspaper, a 3.2 megapixel camera could produce a high quality image at up to about 10 x 8 inches. The same image in a glossy magazine could be used at up to around half an A4 page; if printed any larger than this, the pixels in the image would be larger than the printed dot size, and we'd start to see ungainly pixelation in the finished result. When shown on a web page, however, the same image would easily fill the entire area of a huge 30 inch monitor.

The software that comes with most flatbed scanners tends, confusingly, to offer the ability to adjust both the size and the resolution of scans. In fact, these both amount to the same thing; it's the number of pixels captured in total that counts, not the relative dimensions. The easy solution is to scan an image at the size you're going to want to use it, at a resolution appropriate for the medium on which it's going to end up – printed out or on the screen. Err on the high side: you can always reduce an image's size in Elements, but you can't easily increase it without loss of quality. Bear in mind, though, that the larger the file, the slower it will be to work on in Elements.

The Image Size dialog in Elements has the ability to resample images to any size and resolution you choose. But if you uncheck the Resample Image button, it will adjust the size and resolution together. This is a useful method for turning, say, digital camera captures – which typically have a resolution of 180 dpi – into screen-ready files with a resolution of 72 dpi.

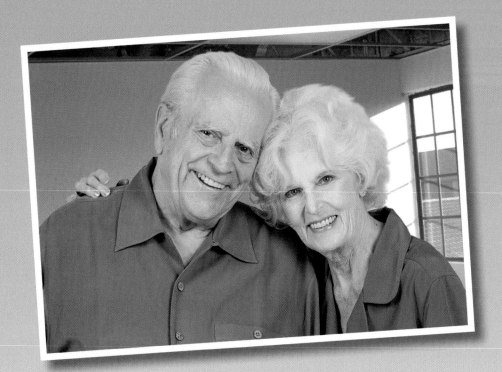

The camera never lies, we're told. But sometimes we wish it would be less scrupulously honest. The photo above is a charming shot of two people who love each other, but how much nicer it would be for them if some of the ravages of time were washed away. And perhaps they could be in a better location, as well.

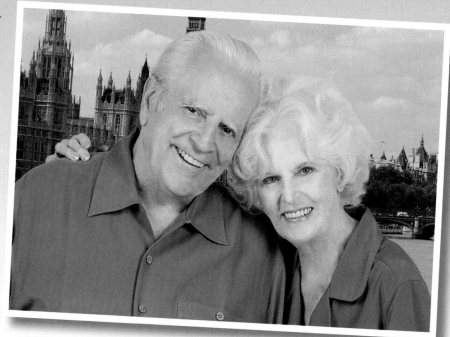

9

People and animals

THE LATE, GREAT W. C. FIELDS told us never to work
with children or animals. Sound advice, for sure. But we
photograph people and pets more than just about any
other subject, so we need to know how to work with them
in Elements.

In this chapter we'll look at how to fix blemishes, how to
reverse the ageing process, and how to make people look
slimmer. We'll also explore several other everyday tasks
to enhance our images – as well as some tasks, such as
swapping heads, that are far from commonplace. Whether
you're making a birthday card for a friend, or simply
enhancing a family photo, we've got the solutions to
make the job easier.

Heads on bodies

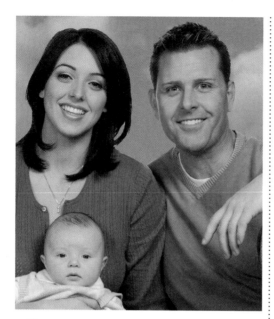

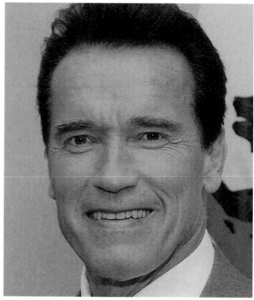

ONE OF THE MOST IMPRESSIVE tricks we can play in Elements is to place a celebrity's head on the body of a family member. It's easy enough to come across suitable celebrities on the internet: one of the best places is Wikipedia, which includes thousands of images of celebrities that are free to use in its Wikimedia Commons department.

The trick to making this technique work lies in choosing a head shot at the right angle to work with your image. Don't worry about the size and the color, as we can easily fix that later; all that matters for now is that the orientation is as close as you can find to the head in the original photograph.

1 We found this picture of Arnold Schwarzenegger on the Wikipedia website. It's just the right angle to fit on the body of the dad in our family shot. The first step is to cut it out from its background, using any of the techniques described in Chapter 1.

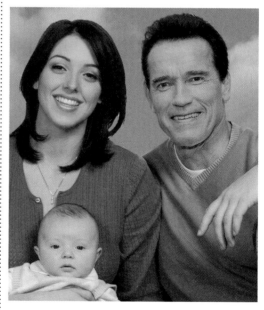

4 Although we got the size and angle right in the previous step, Arnie's coloring didn't match the rest of the photograph. The best way to adjust the color of the new head is to use the Levels adjustment, which also allows us to correct the contrast.

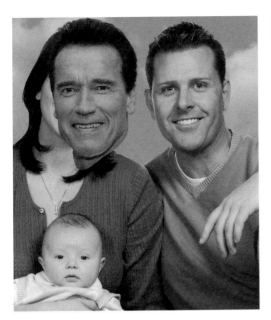

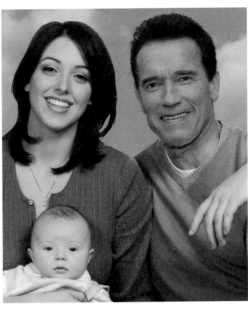

2 Drag the cutout head into the image where you want it to appear. To make it roughly the right size, it helps if you position it next to the target head, rather than on top: by being able to see both at the same time, we can be sure to get the size right.

3 Rotate and further scale the head as necessary using Free Transform, and place it on top of the original head. Take your time with this step, as it's the key to making the montage work. Here, we've rotated the head anticlockwise slightly for a more appealing look.

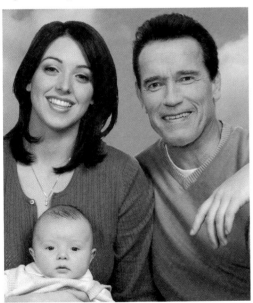

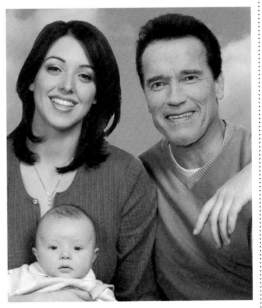

5 There's a hard line under Arnie's chin that needs to be dealt with. The simplest way of removing this is to use a small, soft-edged eraser to smooth out the join; for more control, however, use a layer mask – see Chapter 3 for more details on how to do this.

6 Finally, we need to remove the pieces of the original head that are still visible behind Arnie. On the background layer, use the Clone tool to sample pieces of the background and paint them in to cover up the original ear and other features that stick out.

231

Photomerge: faces

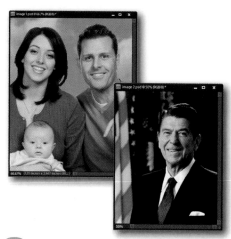

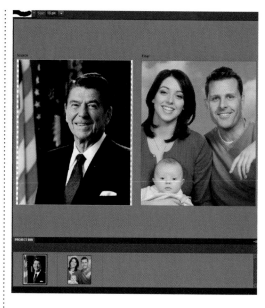

ON THE PREVIOUS PAGES we looked at how to place a head on a different body. Elements 6 brought us a new technology, Photomerge, which automates the process.

Unlike the previous method, Photomerge doesn't require us to cut out the original head first: it can recognize a head shape within an image, even against a background as complicated as the one behind Ronald Reagan in this example.

The technology isn't perfect and it can be a little tricky to control: but it's a quick way of moving heads between images and can be a lot of fun to play around with.

1 To begin, make sure the head you want to copy into the mix is on the left in the Panel Bin – drag it there if it isn't in place already. Now choose New > Photomerge Faces. You'll be prompted to drag the final image into the space on the right.

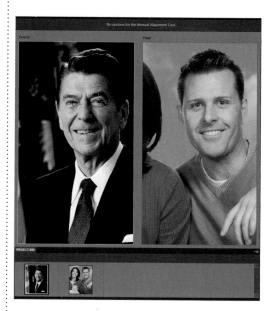

4 Move the markers on either image and press Align Photos again to correct the distortion. It can take a few tries to get it right: you need to move the markers in the opposite direction to what you'd expect in order to undistort the face.

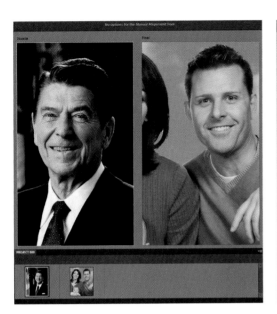

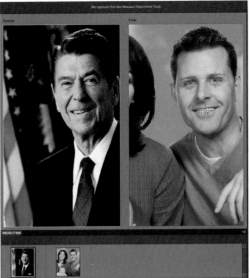

2 Now click on the Alignment tool within the Photomerge dialog and three numbered crosshairs will appear. Drag these onto the first image – one for each of the eyes and one for the mouth. Accurate placement of these markers is essential to making this technique work, so zoom in first.

3 Now place the markers on the second face in corresponding positions and click the Align Photos button. As we can see, this has produced a rather distorted shot of Reagan in the first frame; we need to adjust the positions of the markers to correct this.

HOT TIP

If you find that too much of the image has been copied into the picture, use the Eraser tool within the Photomerge dialog to remove some of the drawn pencil line. Experiment with erasing and redrawing pencil lines until you get a result that works well.

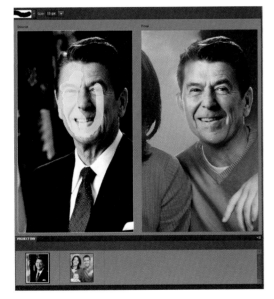

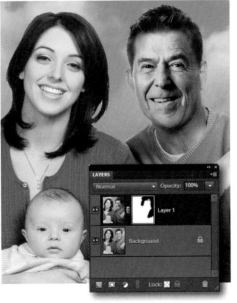

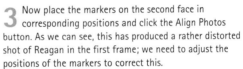

5 Now for the fun part. Grab the Pencil tool and draw over Reagan's face. In a couple of seconds, the face will appear superimposed over the family photograph. As we can see, though, it's also darkened up the sky behind the figure and Reagan's ear overlaps the original ear.

6 We can't do much more editing here, but pressing Done will produce a new document with two layers – the original family shot and the family with Reagan placed over the top. Erase parts of this layer or use a layer mask to make a better fit.

233

Cosmetic surgery: healing

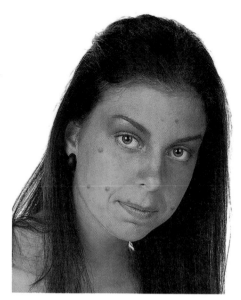

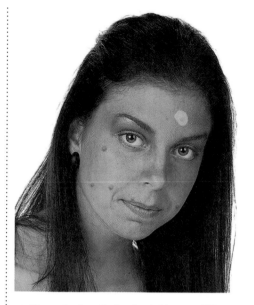

HERE'S A GRUMPY TEENAGER. So what else is new? Well, this teenager has a reason to be grumpy: she's about to go on a hot date and her face is covered in acne spots. (To be fair to the original model, we should point out that we added these blemishes ourselves.)

A two-week course of antibiotics could clear this up – but we have a quicker method. Using the Healing Brush and the Spot Healing Brush – how appropriate – we can lose those ugly spots with just a few clicks.

Using this innovative tool isn't always plain sailing, however, as we'll see here: when the blemishes are close to an edge, unwanted effects can occur. This tutorial explains the best way to prevent those errors.

1 Choose the Spot Healing Brush (shortcut: **J**) and make sure it's set to use a hard-edged brush. This seems contradictory: you'd expect a soft brush to blend in better. But that's not how this one works. Paint roughly over the spot on the forehead and you'll see where you've painted.

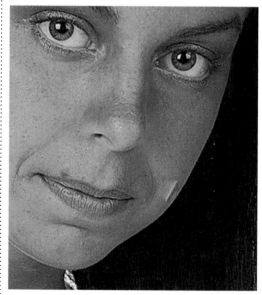

4 When we paint over the spot on her left cheek, however, something goes wrong. The tool has inadvertently sampled the edge of her face, producing what looks like an ugly scar. There are occasions when the Spot Healing Brush doesn't have a clear enough region from which to sample.

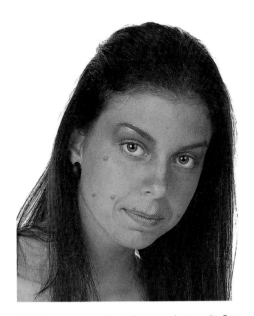

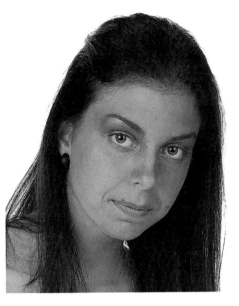

2 As soon as you release the mouse button, the Spot Healing Brush does something extraordinary: it samples the texture around the place you painted and blends that texture in perfectly with the surroundings. Our first spot disappears instantly.

3 We can carry on in the same manner, painting over each spot in turn on the girl's right cheek. Paint just enough area to cover the spot, and no more, for the tool to perform at its best.

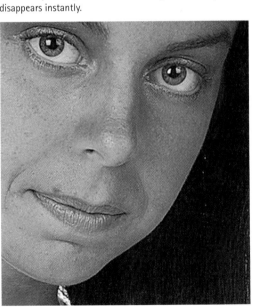

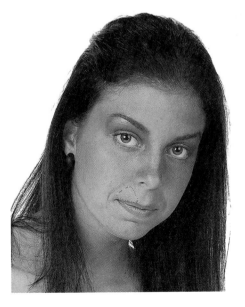

5 Undo that last step and, instead, switch to the regular Healing Brush. This works in a slightly different way: first, we hold *alt* ⌥ and click a point from which to sample the texture – the forehead works well – and then paint over the spot. Now, it disappears as we wish it to.

6 The spot above the lip presents a different problem. The spot is just too close to the mouth. Before healing, make a selection that includes the spot, but which stops at the top of the mouth. Now, when we use the tool, it won't act outside that area – and so the mouth is left intact.

HOT TIP

The Healing Brush is a hugely powerful tool. Use it to remove birds from the sky, beetles from a rock, or even commonly unwanted picture elements such as telegraph wires and signposts. The really clever thing about it is that you don't need to match the lighting or even the color: only the texture is sampled and is blended in perfectly with the background.

SHORTCUTS

MAC WIN BOTH

Cosmetic surgery: weight loss

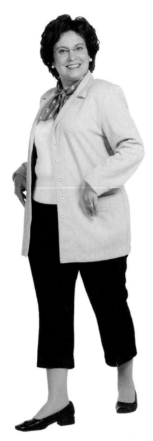

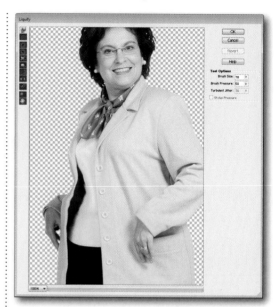

1 Use Filter > Distort > Liquify to enter the Liquify dialog. The default tool is Warp: use this to push the waist in, as we start to slim our model. Use a large brush size: small brushes will simply create additional wrinkles and that's the very thing we want to get rid of.

THIS IS THE WEIGHT LOSS PROGRAM the world's been waiting for: no diets, no exercise, just a ten-minute workout with the Liquify filter.

In order to make this procedure work properly, you'll need to cut out your image from its background. Otherwise, the existing background will be too distorted to look realistic.

We'll use this image of a woman who, while not obese, would perhaps value the opportunity to shed a few pounds.

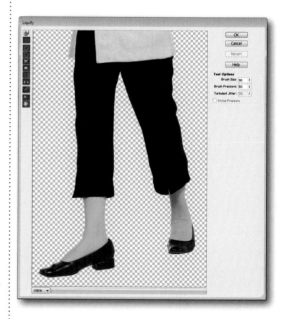

4 Don't forget such details as slimming the ankles – again, by pushing in from either side. It's details like this that make all the difference between a convincing montage and one that looks fake. But be careful not to get carried away if you want a realistic result.

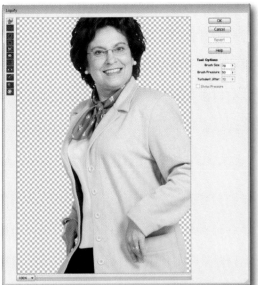

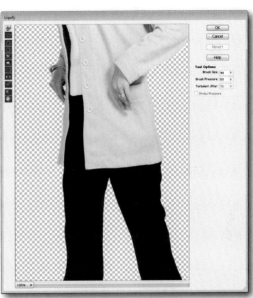

2 It's easy to distort the hands by accident when smearing them with Liquify. The solution is to stick with a large brush size and to click and drag directly on the hand. With luck, the entire hand should move as one; switch to a smaller brush to clean up if necessary.

3 Push the bottom and the tops of the legs into the center to make them appear slimmer. Again, be careful not to distort the hands.

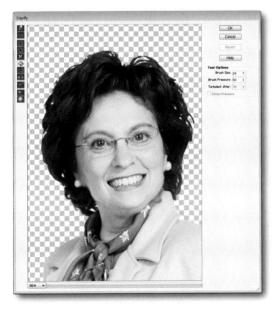

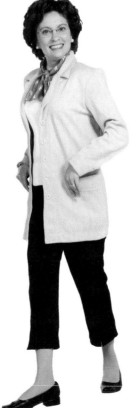

5 The face is trickier. With a smaller brush size, push the chin and neck inwards. Switch to the Bloat tool and press on the eyes to make them slightly larger: this accentuates the features and makes the whole face look less chubby.

HOT TIP

Use the square bracket keys (**[** and **]**) to make the brush size smaller and larger. The size changes very slowly when you do this; to speed it up, hold the **Shift** key as you press the bracket keys.

Although we've looked at making realistic changes here, there's no limit to what you can do with the Liquify filter. Try changing expressions or growing devil's horns out of someone's head.

SHORTCUTS

MAC WIN BOTH

Age and youth

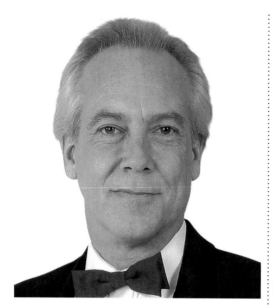

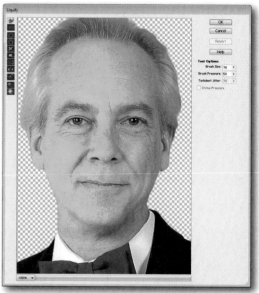

1 The first thing to do is to tighten that sagging chin. Go to Filter > Distort > Liquify and use the default tool to push the chin up and in. Start with a large brush: you can use the **[** and **]** keys to make the brush size smaller and larger.

HOW OFTEN HAVE YOU TAKEN a photograph of an elderly relative, only for them to complain that they look much older than they expected? We all have an idea of how we appear to others, and the image in our minds is often several years younger than we really are.

If only there were a way to take the years off without resorting to expensive and painful surgery. Well, there is: we can harness the power of Elements to darken hair, remove wrinkles, tighten that sagging chin and present an altogether more youthful appearance.

We've taken the approach to extremes in this tutorial; generally, you'd only want to remove a few lines and creases. And perhaps fix that chin. Oh, and you may as well darken the hair a little while you're at it...

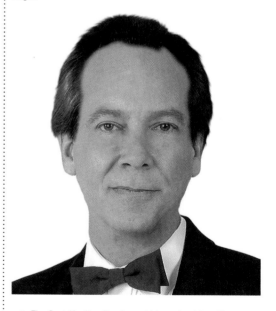

4 The Spot Healing Brush would have trouble with wrinkles close to facial features. Instead, switch to the regular Healing Brush and *alt* ⌥ click on the center of the forehead to set the source point. Now when you paint over the wrinkles they'll heal perfectly. Remember the bags under the eyes and the wrinkles beneath the chin.

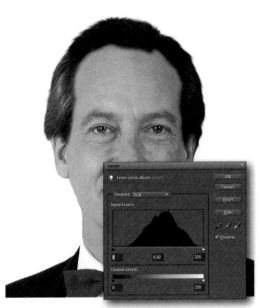

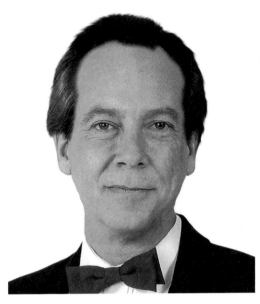

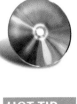

HOT TIP

If there's no color left in your figure's hair, then use the Hue/ Saturation adjustment, checking the Colorize button, to add some artificial coloring. You may need to color the eyebrows as well: select them when you select the hair and apply the same treatment to them.

2 Select the hair with the Lasso tool and apply a 5 pixel feather to it (*ctrl* *alt* **D** ⌘ ⌥ **D**) to soften the edge. Make this into a new layer with *ctrl* **J** ⌘ **J** and open the Levels dialog. Drag the middle gray triangle to the right to darken the hair.

3 Use the Spot Healing Brush **J** to paint out the lines on the forehead. It will sample texture from around the area you paint, patching the lines perfectly. Because there's so much clear forehead texture around the wrinkles, the tool works well here.

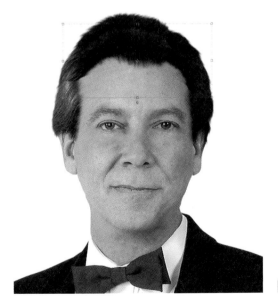

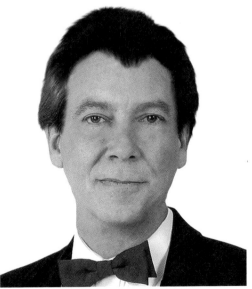

5 Let's address the hair loss that our unfortunate senior citizen has suffered. Rebuilding hair is tricky, but here's a simple solution. Select the top half of the hair and use *ctrl* **J** ⌘ **J** to make a new layer from it. Drag it down using the Move tool or Free Transform so it covers more of the forehead.

6 Switch to the Smudge tool **R** and choose a soft-edged brush – or one of the star-shaped custom brushes. With a pressure of around 70%, smudge the new hair both up into the original and down onto the forehead. This tool makes it easy to blend the new hair in with the old. Our rejuvenated favorite uncle is now complete.

SHORTCUTS

MAC WIN BOTH

Adding people to the scene

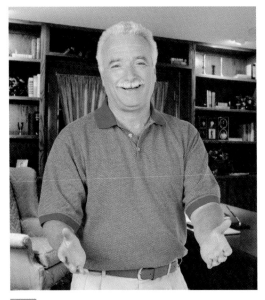

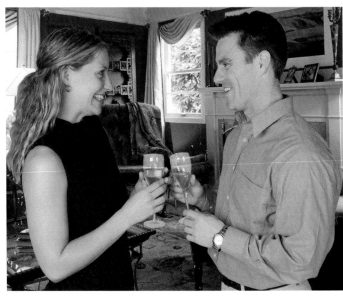

T HE SCENE IS AN ENGAGEMENT PARTY: the blushing bride-to-be shares a glass of champagne with her future husband. Such a shame her father couldn't be there to enjoy the occasion... but, thanks to Elements, he can be. Adding people to a scene is just one of the techniques every Elements montage artist should be familiar with.

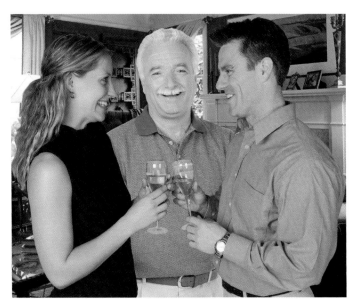

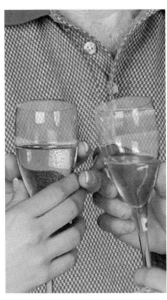

2 After a lot of painting in and out, pressing **X** to swap between foreground and background colors, we're able to tuck Dad firmly behind the couple. Since they're both holding glasses, though, we need to make them slightly transparent: and this is how it's done. Still working on the layer mask, set the foreground color to white (to paint the figure back in) and set the opacity to just 20%. Now, when we paint over the glasses area with a hard-edged brush, we reveal a hint of Dad's shirt pattern as seen through the champagne glasses.

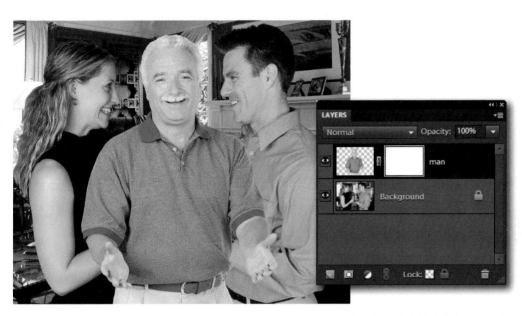

1 We'll start by cutting the bride's father out from his original background (we've already done this for you in the version included on the DVD). Once he's been moved into the engagement photo, the first step is to use Free Transform to make him the right size. Again, we've done this for

you. Next, we need to place him behind the happy couple. Although we could do this with the Eraser tool, it's far easier, not to mention less destructive, using a layer mask – once we have added the mask we can paint on that layer to hide him behind the couple.

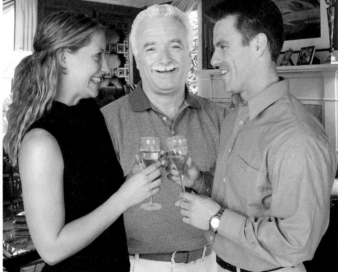

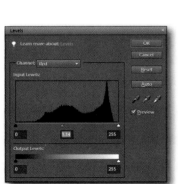

3 The final problem is one of coloring. The photo of Dad was too blue in comparison with the bride and groom photo. So switch to Dad's layer and open the Levels adjustment dialog. Begin with the Blue channel (*ctrl* 3 ⌘ 3), dragging the middle gray slider to the right to

reduce the amount of blue in the image. Then switch to the composite RGB channel and drag the same slider to the right to reduce the brightness overall. Finally, switch to the Red channel (*ctrl* 1 ⌘ 1) and this time drag the slider slightly to the left to increase the amount of red a little.

HOT TIP

Using the layer mask technique makes it far easier to slot a figure into a scene. But be sure to pay attention to the colors: it's rare that the skin-tones from two different photographs will match, and it's here that most montage artists fall down badly. It can help to think backwards: if an image is too green, try adding blue and red rather than simply taking out the green.

SHORTCUTS
MAC WIN BOTH

Cleaning up the scene

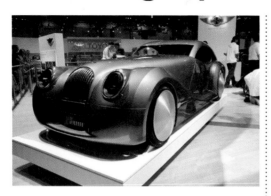

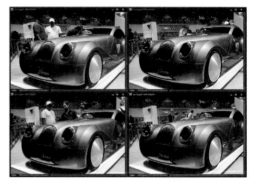

1 Opening all four images, we can see the people are in different positions in each one but none of the images are good enough individually. Select the New > Photomerge > Scene Cleaner. A dialog will appear asking you to choose the images. Click Open All.

IT SEEMS FITTING TO FOLLOW the previous technique of adding people to an image with one for removing them; and, thanks to an impressive feature in Elements, what would have been a laborious and highly time-consuming task has been made as simple as making a few strokes of the pen.

The aptly named Scene Cleaner is one of the Photomerge set of commands in the Guided Edit section; its function is to remove unwanted people or objects from around the subject of the photograph. This might be a popular scenic view with a steady flow of visitors or, as with our example, a particularly popular attraction at a show. In situations like this, it's not always possible to stop people moving into the frame but what we can do is take several shots in roughly the same position but with enough time in between for different areas to be populated. When we open the images in the cleaner, they are automatically aligned so we can blend different areas from each together and hopefully finish up with a largely uninterrupted scene.

All the project images can be found on the DVD in the Tutorial Images folder.

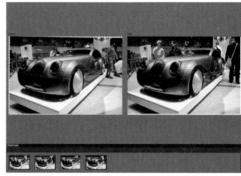

4 Grab the Pencil tool and set its size; it doesn't need to be large, around 20 pixels is sufficient. Now paint over the man in white; start from his head and loop around his body – the color reflects the source photo you are currently working on. When we release the mouse, he disappears!

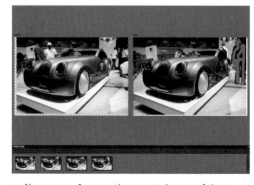

7 Now we can focus on the area at the rear of the car. Looking at our image set, Car 1 looks like the ideal candidate. We'll concentrate on the man in the suit: draw across him so all areas are marked. When we release, we see that the man behind the car is also removed; clever stuff!

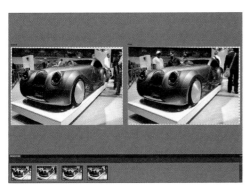

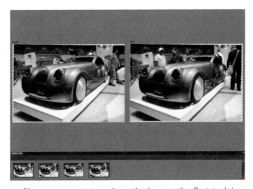

2 Once we're in the Scene Cleaner's dialog, we need to select our base photo: we've chosen Car 2 by dragging its thumbnail from the Project Bin over to the final image frame. We can see the images have been cropped slightly; this is due to the automatic alignment process.

3 Now we can start work on the image: the first task is to remove the three men standing behind the car. To do this we need to choose a suitable source image from our set. Clicking through each of the photos, Car 3 has the least obtrusive background, so we'll use that.

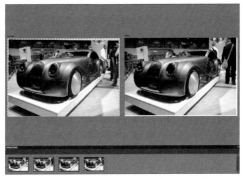

5 Painting over the man in blue results in both being removed, well almost. There is still a part of a red shirt visible through the window of the car. If we try to remove it, however, we bring in the man in blue from the source image. Fortunately, we can undo this: *ctrl* Z ⌘ Z.

6 We'll switch to a different source photo now. Car 4 seems the best choice. We only need to click once to remove the remnant of the red shirt; this is replaced by the man's head in the distance, which is much less distracting. That's all we need this image for at present.

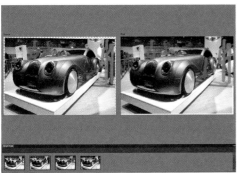

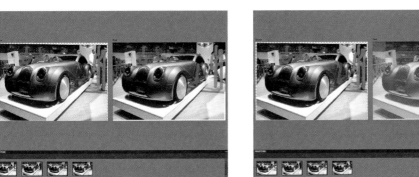

8 Although the man in the suit has been removed, his reflection in the body of the car remains. We can remove that just as easily, of course. We could replace it with the man in the white shirt, as it should be, but that's too noticeable; instead, we'll use the reflection area from Car 4.

9 Our scene is just about complete now. It's worth pointing out some of the additional options: if we check Show Regions, we get a color overlay showing where areas have been replaced and blended. We can also fine-tune by using the Eraser to remove sections we don't want.

HOT TIP

If you've taken time to select the right images to use with the Scene Cleaner, or any other tool which uses a lot of files, you don't want to keep going back and opening them each time. If you need to stop working on the project at any time, there is a little-known option in the Project Bin under the Bin Actions menu called Save bin as an album. Using this we are asked for an album name; the image locations are stored so we can then open them all by selecting the album name from the drop-down list.

SHORTCUTS

243

Eyes wide shut

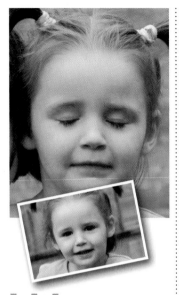

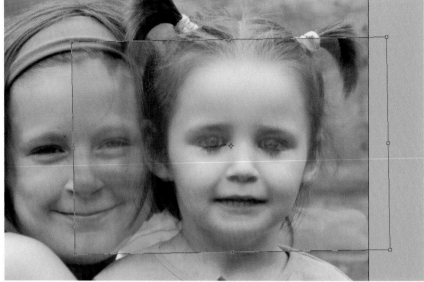

W E MAY HAVE the ability to take as many pictures as we want with our digital cameras, but unfortunately we still can't guarantee they'll be great shots every time, as is the case with our example. While the kids obliged us with a lovely pose for the portrait, one of them blinked at precisely the wrong moment.

All is not lost, however: using another picture (shown in the inset) of the girl in which her eyes are open, we can copy them from one image to the other and blend them in seamlessly, rescuing our photo from the delete pile.

1 The second image has been brought into the document as a new layer, and we've lowered the opacity to enable us to see the original image below. The girl is facing slightly to the right in the first photo but to the left in the second, so we need to flip the layer horizontally. We can now use Free Transform to scale, position and rotate the layer, matching it as closely as possible. Don't spend too much time trying to get it perfect first time; we can make finer adjustments later.

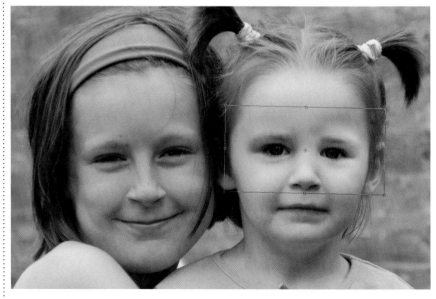

3 With just the eyes overlaid on our original photo we can see that, whilst it's a very close match, we still need to do a little fine-tuning. Enter Free Transform mode again; because we're now working on a smaller area, we can make more accurate adjustments. In this case all that's needed is a very slight rotation and a nudge upward. These changes can make all the difference. Our brains are trained to read faces and any anomalies can be glaringly obvious.

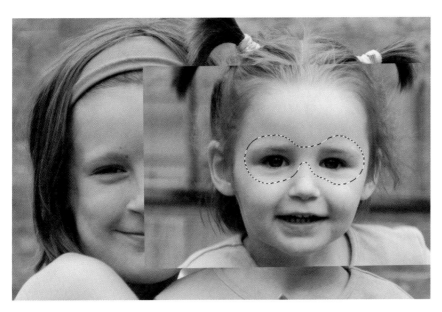

2 Now we have the layer in place we can bring its opacity back up to 100%. At this point we could use the eraser to remove the excess from the image; there is a far better way, however. Grab the Selection Brush **A** and choose a large,

soft tip. Paint in a loose, mask-like selection over and around the eyes; now press *ctrl* J ⌘ J to create a copy of the eyes on a new layer. We can hide or discard the previous image as it's no longer needed.

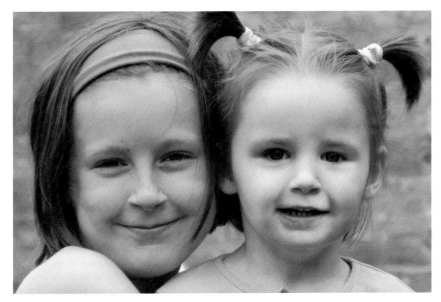

4 We're almost done – there's just a bit of tidying up to be carried out. Because the second image has slightly different lighting, some areas are too bright for the original photo. Select a medium size, soft eraser **E**, lower its opacity

and use its edge to feather out the area around the periphery of the eyes to bring back some of the original shadowing. As she has such a nice smile in the other photo, we've added that in the same way to finish the image off.

Warhol-style pop-art

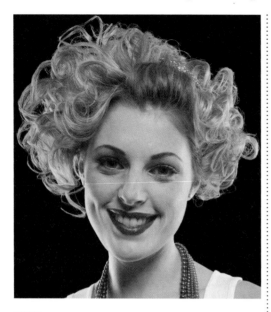

THE ICONIC IMAGE OF MARILYN MONROE is one of Andy Warhol's most famous works. He used the screen-printing process to transfer photographs to canvas which were then overlaid with blocks of heavy, garish color, giving them the now familiar impressionistic style. The aim was to streamline the process to enable the images to be mass-produced whilst each would be slightly different to the last.

We can recreate the effect surprisingly easily: by simplifying the photo to purely black and white we can then build up the image using individual layers of color – a digital version of screen-printing, as it were. Because we're using Adjustment Layers we can, of course, edit the image time after time, changing its colors or altering the level of detail.

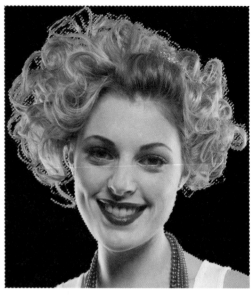

1 Start by isolating the woman from the background; the best choice for this image is the Magic Wand **W**. Disable the Contiguous option to select all the black areas at once; tidy any stray areas on the face with the Selection Brush **A**. Inverse the selection and copy to a new layer.

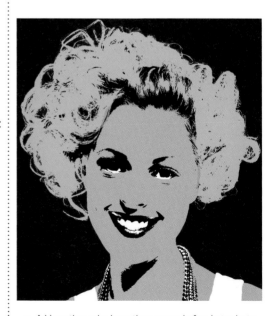

4 Add another color layer the same as before but select a yellow for the hair. Again, paint over the mask to reveal the color. Now add a white layer for the eyes and teeth: this time set the mode to Overlay. The order of the layers can be important as the blend modes affect surrounding layers too.

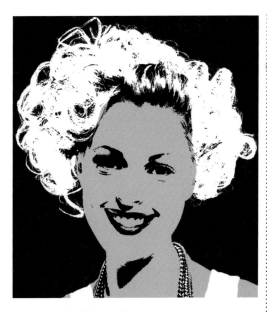

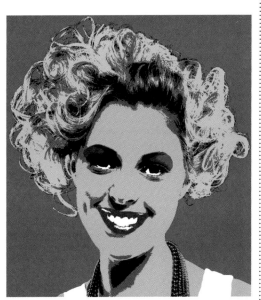

2 Add a Threshold Adjustment Layer above the new layer. The initial result is too strong and we've lost a lot of the detail. Slowly drag the slider to the left until all but the main features are visible – make sure the eyes are fairly well defined. Press _ctrl_ _G_ _⌘_ _G_ to create a clipping group.

3 Create a Solid Color Adjustment Layer above the Threshold layer. Select a suitable color for the skin-tone and set the blend mode to Darken. Now click the layer's mask thumbnail and fill it with black to hide the effect. Using a hard brush, paint in white to reveal the areas of color.

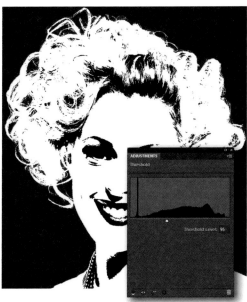

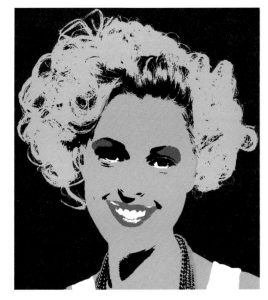

5 Create a red layer for the lips; this will need to be set to Lighten. Paint in the eye-shadow and the necklace. If you're finding it tricky to see which parts should be a certain color, hold _alt_ _⌥_ and click the original photo's visibility icon; this toggles the effect on and off by hiding the layers.

6 Duplicate the head layer and place it at the top of the stack. Set its blend mode to Color Burn and lower the opacity to 50%. Create a new Threshold adjustment and this time drag the slider to the right to increase the black detail. Add a plain, colored background to complete the effect.

HOT TIP

Holding _alt_ _⌥_ whilst selecting an Adjustment Layer from the menu in the Layers panel forces its option dialog to appear. From here you can rename it, choose to create it as a clipping mask, and set the blend mode during the creation process.

SHORTCUTS
MAC WIN BOTH

Hollywood glamor

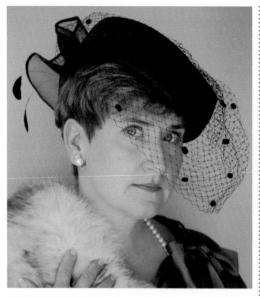

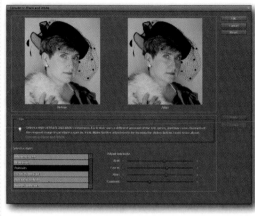

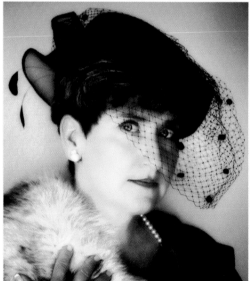

CONTINUING ON THE THEME of iconic portraiture, we're going to take a look at the photographic style of the 1940s and 50s; in particular, images of the film stars of the day. These were often shot in high contrast black and white but with a selective soft focus effect. This smoothed out the skin, giving the subject a glowing, dreamlike appearance.

1 We'll start, as ever, by duplicating our background layer by pressing `ctrl J` `⌘ J`. From the Enhance menu, select Convert to Black and White. This opens a dialog showing the before and after image along with presets and fine tuning controls. We'll use the Portrait preset.

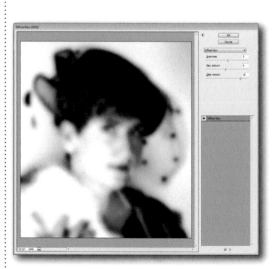

4 Create a duplicate of the blurred layer. Go to Filters > Distort > Diffuse Glow. Set a moderate amount of Graininess. The Glow should enhance the highlights but not overpower the image. Finally, set a high Clear amount. This controls the amount of diffusion, similar to opacity.

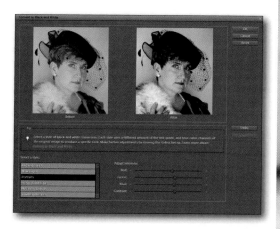

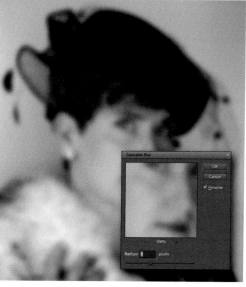

2 This preset levels out the tones of the image, which looks OK, but we want a more high-contrast style. Drag the Contrast slider to the right – a value of around +40 works well. For other images it may be necessary to try different presets or alter the individual color settings.

3 We'll blur the image to smooth out the model's skin. Duplicate the black and white layer. Now open the Gaussian Blur filter. We'll need a fairly heavy effect so set a radius of around 8 pixels. Change the layer's blend mode to Overlay. This enhances the contrast and softens the skin.

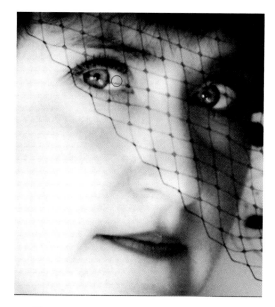

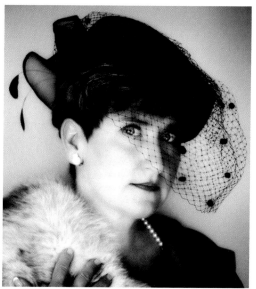

5 We can see the effect is far too strong. Set the blend mode to Hard Light. Now lower the opacity – around 45% here. Merge the two layers *ctrl* **E** **⌘ E**. Now grab the Eraser **E** and using a small, soft brush, go over the eyes, lips and eyebrows to reveal the lighter, sharper image below.

6 Use a larger brush size to bring back the detail in her hair and the fur she's wearing; be careful not to go over her hand. Finally, open the Correct Camera Distortion Filter dialog. Drag the Vignette slider all the way to the left. Now lower the midpoint a little to finish off the effect.

SHORTCUTS

249

Bobblehead caricature

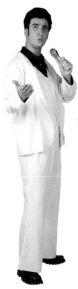

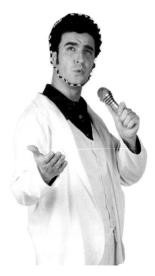

T YPICALLY, CARICATURES FOCUS on one or more of the subject's features which are then drawn greatly exaggerated. Bobbleheads, on the other hand, have huge versions of the person's head atop a ludicrously small body. The head and body are usually connected by a spring, which, when tapped, causes the head to bob about – hence the name. These collectable models generally depict sporting personalities but some movie stars also have their own jittering counterparts.

As we'll see in the following example, we can, of course, create our own digital versions. This simple yet effective technique can be used to make great humorous greetings cards or gifts for friends and relatives.

1 Our singer is already on a separate layer so begin by loading up his selection. Select the Freehand Lasso tool, holding *alt* *Shift* ⌥ *Shift* and carefully draw a line starting from his ear and down around his jawline. Close this off with a loosely drawn area around the rest of his head.

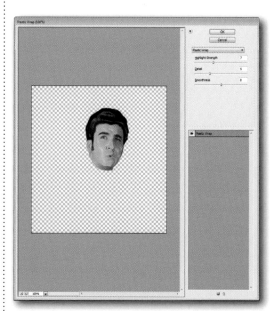

4 Now we've toned down his features we can give him a real plastic appearance with the Plastic Wrap filter. Experiment with the slider adjustments until you have the desired effect; we want to keep it fairly subtle. As before, apply this to the body layer as well.

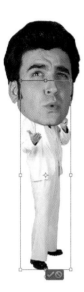

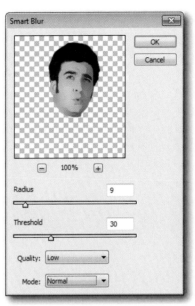

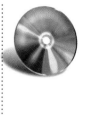

Smart Blur

OK

Cancel

100%

Radius 9

Threshold 30

Quality: Low

Mode: Normal

2 Copy the head to a new layer with `ctrl` `J` `⌘` `J`. Click the original body layer's thumbnail and use Free Transform to scale it down to a suitably comical size; we want to emphasize the face whilst retaining the body detail. You may also want to tilt the head slightly to the left.

3 We need to make him look more like a a model: open the Smart Blur filter and leave the quality set to low. Adjust the Radius and Threshold to smooth out the detail but retain a suitable amount of clarity to the features. Switch to the body and reapply the effect by pressing `ctrl` `F` `⌘` `F`.

HOT TIP

The results from the Plastic Wrap filter can vary immensely depending on the lighting and quality of the source image. If you are having difficulty producing a balanced effect, try duplicating the layer(s) before applying the filter. Doing this enables you to fine-tune the result by altering the opacity and blend mode to produce a more subtle effect.

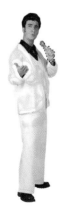

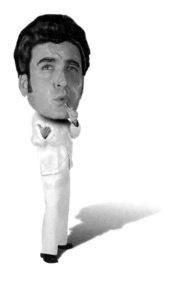

5 We need to have the hand with the microphone in front of his head. Hide the head layer for now and make sure the body layer is active. Draw a selection around the hand using the Lasso, copy it to a new layer and move it above the head in the Layers panel by dragging its thumbnail.

6 Here's our finished image. We've increased the saturation a little and added some shading under his head with the Burn tool; this helps to bond the image together. We've also given him a shadow to place him properly – see Chapter 5 for more on how to do this.

SHORTCUTS
MAC WIN BOTH

All in the mind

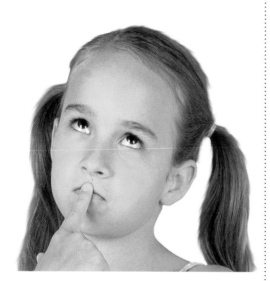

WHAT'S ON A YOUNG GIRL'S MIND?
Hard to say with any certainty – but
we can make a safe bet that it would include
teddy bears, ponies and candy. We're going to
show these interests graphically, by lifting the
top of her head and placing all these items
inside.

The only thing we have to concern ourselves
with here is the correct order of the layers in
the stack. In order to place everything inside the
head, we need to position the objects between
the face and the interior – which means
splitting that rim into two, so the front half will
remain in front.

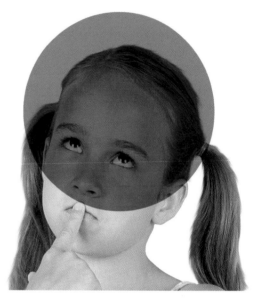

1 The first step is to draw the inside of the head, as an
ellipse. But Elements has no tools for drawing an ellipse
at an angle; we'll make it easy for ourselves by first drawing
a circle, on a new layer. Here, we've filled it with blue and set
it to Multiply so we can see through it.

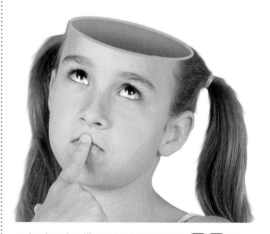

4 Load up the ellipse selection by holding **ctrl** ⌘ and
clicking on its thumbnail in the Layers panel. Use Select
> Modify > Contract to make the selection around 8 pixels
smaller; then, using the Burn tool, darken the interior so that
it looks hollow.

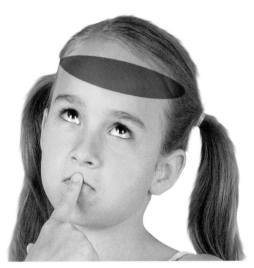

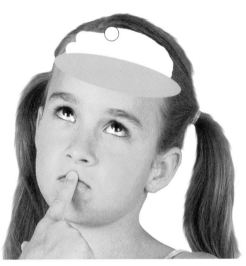

2 Use *ctrl* *T* *⌘* *T* to enter Free Transform, and rotate and squeeze the circle so it becomes an ellipse at the right angle. Don't stretch it all the way out to the right: remember, her head is actually some distance inside all that hair.

3 Fill the ellipse with a flesh color sampled from her skin and change its mode back to Normal. With the ellipse selected, move to the girl's layer and press *Backspace* to delete her head from this area; then deselect. Use the Eraser *E* to remove the top part of the head above the ellipse.

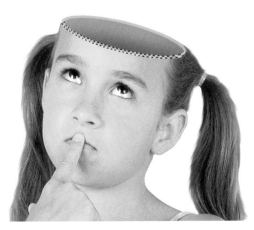

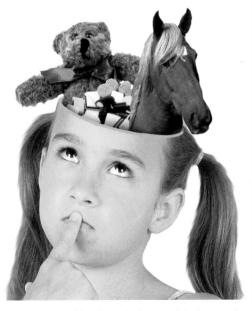

5 Don't deselect. Instead, inverse the selection using *ctrl* *Shift* *I* *⌘* *Shift* *I*, so that just the pink rim is selected. Hold *alt* *Shift* *⌥* *Shift* as you trace a loop around the front half of the rim; press *ctrl* *J* *⌘* *J* to make a new layer from this section and bring it to the front.

6 Send the head interior to the bottom of the layer stack, so that it's placed behind the head. We can now add all our objects as we like, behind the head layer, and they'll appear to be inside it. Add a little shading, on a new layer, to complete the effect.

HOT TIP

All the elements inside this head are behind the head layer. If we wanted the horse's nose, for instance, to poke in front of the head, then we'd need to select the nose and use *ctrl* *J* *⌘* *J* to make a new layer from it. When we bring this to the top of the layer stack, we can move the horse and its nose together, and position them as we wish.

SHORTCUTS
MAC WIN BOTH

Dog in a basket

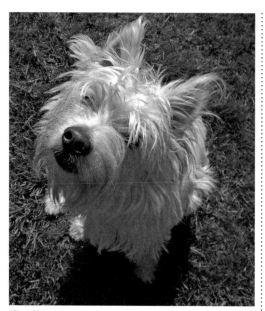

HAIR AND FUR are among the trickiest materials to cut out in Elements. Take this photograph of a dog, for instance: we can see its wispy, shaggy fur well enough, but how on earth are we supposed to cut it away from all that grass?

The solution, as ever, is to cheat. Rather than even attempting to use one of the many selection methods to trace around the fur, we'll do a smooth cutout and then redraw the fur using the Smudge tool.

We're going to practice our technique with a dog's fur here, but we can use the same method on people: it's far easier to recreate the effect of flyaway hair using the Smudge tool than it is to try to cut it from a complex background.

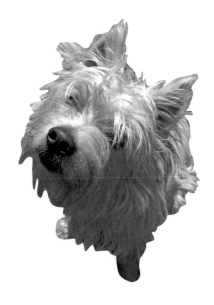

1 Begin by cutting out the dog from the background, using the Lasso or Selection Brush, or any of the selection tools described in Chapter 1. No need to be too accurate here – you don't need to trace over every strand of hair; but cut inside the hair rather than outside it, so that no grass is included in the selection.

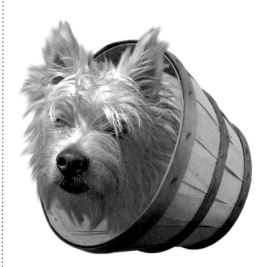

4 Continue all the way around the dog, pulling out clumps of fur with the Smudge tool. Refer to the original photo if you like, but it's just as easy (and just as convincing) to guess at what the fur will look like. If you find 80% pressure is too great, reduce it for a smaller effect.

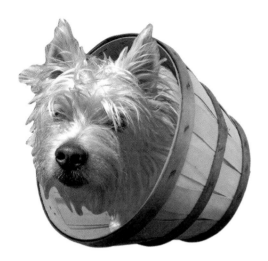

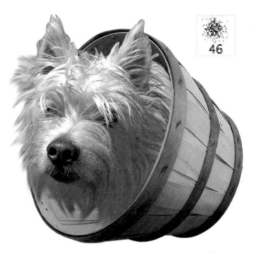

2 We've decided to place our dog in this basket, for no reason other than it looks cute there. To make this work, we've first copied the front half of the basket to a new layer: with this section in front of the dog and the original behind, it's easy to manipulate the two so that it looks as if the dog's sitting inside.

3 Switch to the Smudge tool, set to a pressure of around 80%. The key to making this easier lies in choosing the correct brush for this tool: a Spatter brush, which is one of the default Elements brushes, is perfect. Drag out clumps of fur around the edge of the dog, following the direction in which it would naturally grow.

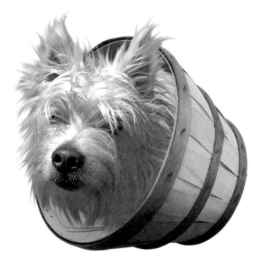

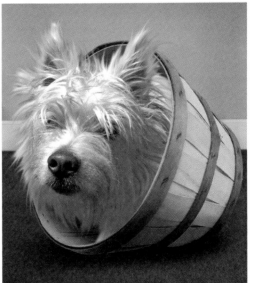

5 We now need to tweak out a few individual strands of fur for added realism. Still using the Smudge tool, choose a small, soft brush – around 3 pixels in diameter – and pull out the strands one at a time. This greatly increases the realism of the fur.

6 The technique works well enough against a white background, but it really comes into its own when we place the entire assembly into a real room. Paint in shadows beneath the basket and inside it, under the dog, for a more realistic appearance.

HOT TIP

This technique works best if you have a pressure-sensitive graphics tablet: it's far easier to tweak out the fur if you can vary the pressure, rather than relying on the uniform pressure provided by a mouse alone.

TIFFs, JPEGs and the rest

ONE OF THE MOST BAFFLING issues facing the Elements user is the Save As dialog. It should be straightforward: after all, all you want to do is save your file. So why are there so many options? Here are all the main file types you'll see listed, with an explanation of what they're used for.

The formats you'll need

Photoshop (.psd) is the full file you're working on, containing all the layers, styles, effects, Adjustment Layers, and so on. Save in this format when you want to carry on working on your image.

JPEG (.jpg) stands for Joint Photographic Experts Group, and is a highly compressed format that's good for delivering images over the internet. There's a trade-off between high quality and small file sizes: the higher the JPEG value, the more faithful the image will be to the original, but the bigger the file.

TIFF (.tif) stands for Tagged Image File Format, and this was the file format of choice before JPEGs came along. It's not lossy, as JPEGs are, and the resulting files are much bigger; unlike JPEGs, it can contain both layers and selection channels, so is good for exporting images for use in other applications.

JPEG 2000 (.jpf, .jp2) is a newer version of JPEGs that offers better quality and also supports selection channels. Most web browsers can't read this format, though, so it's no good for internet delivery. Sadly, Adobe dropped support for this format in Elements 8 and files in this format will no longer open by default. All is not lost, however: a fully-functional third-party plugin is available from the following website: http://www.fnordware.com/j2k/. With this installed you will be able to use the dedicated JPEG2000 sites: http://www.thefullmontage. com and http://www.absolutvision.com.

Compuserve GIF (.gif) stands for Graphics Interchange Format, and is a format introduced in 1987 and used primarily for web delivery. It includes only a very limited range of colors, so images will look very rough; on the plus side, it can contain multiple frames of an animation.

PNG (.png) stands for Portable Network Graphics, and is a more recent format intended for internet delivery. It's not that commonly used, although it does support transparency and so is useful for web designers.

Photoshop Raw (.raw) is the high-end, high bandwidth version of images captured by professional-quality digital cameras. Many professional photographers prefer this format for its extended tonal range.

Photoshop PDF (.pdf) stands for Portable Document Format, which was developed so that one complex file including text and graphics could be viewed identically on multiple computer platforms. The Photoshop Elements version is there to provide compatability.

The formats you won't need, but may as well know about

BMP, or 'Bitmap' (.bmp) is a format designed for use internally by MS-DOS and, later, Windows. It's hugely wasteful, resulting in enormous file sizes.

Photoshop EPS (.eps) stands for Encapsulated PostScript, and is the format images used to be converted into for color printing. It's now rarely used, except for jobs in unusual color spaces – such as those to be printed in CMYK plus a special Pantone color.

Scitex CT (.sct) was a high-end reprographic format in the early days of desktop publishing. CT stands for 'continuous tone'.

Targa (.tga) was a graphics format used on graphics cards for IBM compatible PCs. Many games still create screenshots in Targa format; the online game 'Second Life' accepts textures in this format, which supports transparency.

The formats you don't even need to know about

PICT (.pct) and **PCX (.pcx)** were internal formats used by early Mac and DOS computers respectively. Along with Photo Creation Format and Pixar, they're only provided as options in case you want to open graphics files created many years ago on ancient computer systems.

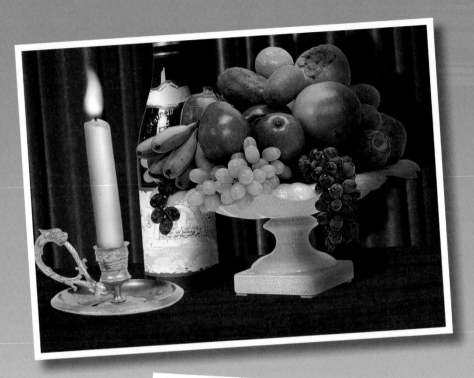

A simple still life, above: the fruit bowl, candlestick, and bottle are all on separate layers, as are the table and the curtain behind. Adding the shadows was straightforward enough, but the scene is dull and looks unrealistic. Adding reflections to that wood surface really brings this picture to life, giving it an extra dimension.

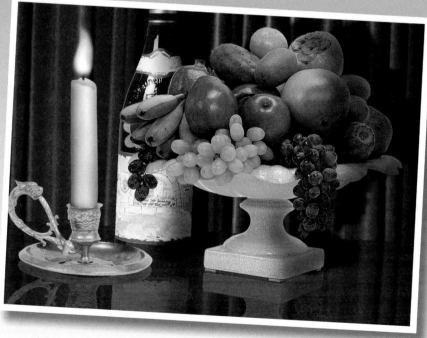

10

Shiny surfaces

GLASS, METAL AND WATER all have one thing in common: they're shiny. Which means that any objects placed on these surfaces will have reflections.

Making reflections can be as easy as simply flipping an object vertically and lowering the opacity. But it can also be much more complex, if the object in question is photographed from an angle. We'll show how to split an object into its constituent planes in order to reflect each one individually.

We'll also look at making rippled reflections in water, show how to place people and things inside bottles, and look at that most easy and powerful tool for making instant liquid – Plastic Wrap.

10 Shiny surfaces

Upon reflection

ADDING A REFLECTION TO A SURFACE converts it from being flat and matt to bright and glossy. The more vivid the reflection is, the shinier the surface appears. Different materials produce varying levels of reflectivity depending on how much light they absorb or let through. A piece of glass on its own will let most of the light through. This results in a sharp but faint reflection. Add a backing to it, such as silver, and you have a mirror. This bounces most of the light back, giving a perfect copy of the person or object.

In the following tutorial we'll create a soft reflection by fading it out as it extends further away from the original object. This gives us a similar appearance to the acrylic surfaces used in product photography. This can easily be adjusted to suit your requirements by altering the depth and intensity of the effect.

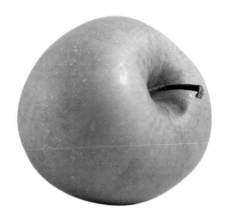

1 Here's our subject. It's already on its own layer. We'll need to duplicate this to use as our reflection. Press *ctrl* J ⌘ J. We'll be using the lower layer for the reflection. This will allow us to place it behind the original, giving the impression of depth and substance.

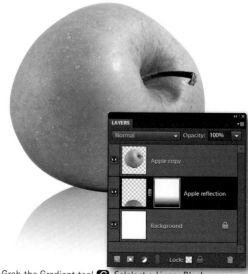

4 Grab the Gradient tool **G**. Selelect a Linear Black, White gradient. Click the layer mask's thumbnail to make it active. Position the cursor at the bottom of the document. Holding **Shift**, click and drag the cursor up. I took it to around a third of the way up the original apple here.

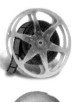

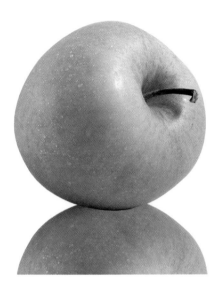

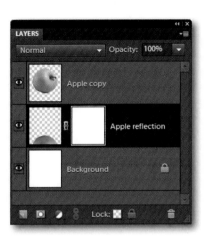

2 Flip the layer vertically via Image > Rotate > Flip layer vertical. Use the Move tool **V** to drag the layer down. Hold *Shift* to constrain the movement vertically. This ensures the two images remain aligned. Leave an overlap so the reflection layer remains slightly behind.

3 We have a mirror image of the apple but it's too perfect, we want the effect of a shiny plastic surface where the reflection would gradually fade out. We'll begin by adding a mask. Make sure the reflection layer is active. Now click the Add Layer Mask icon at the bottom of the Layers panel.

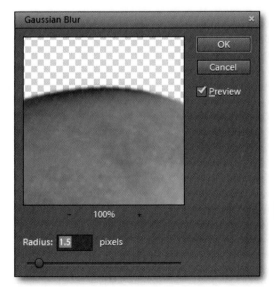

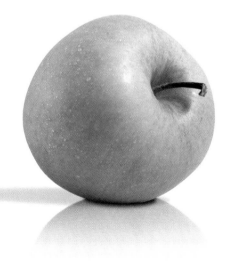

5 We'll add some blur to the reflection to give it slightly more softness. Click the reflection layer's thumbnail to make it active again. Open the Gaussian Blur filter. You won't need to use a lot for this effect; just enough to knock it out of focus a little.

6 To finish off we'll add a shadow. This is created with another copy of the apple filled with black. See the chapter 'Light and shade' for more on the technique. For reflective surfaces such as this the shadow needs to be much lighter than if it were cast on a matt surface.

Complex reflections

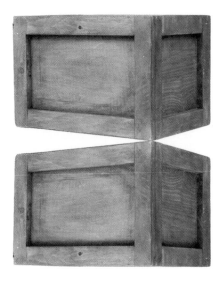

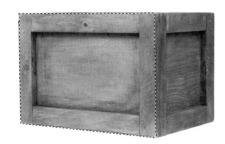

1 The first step is to divide the object into separate layers: grab the Polygonal Lasso and make an outline around one side of the box. Press *ctrl* *J* ⌘ *J* to copy it to a new layer. Now repeat this for the other side remembering to make the original box layer active again, of course.

O N THE PREVIOUS PAGE we created a reflection for an object that had been photographed head-on; a simple task of flipping the image vertically and placing it beneath the original. Problems start, however, when the photo is taken from an angle, as we can see from the image above. Elements can only work in two dimensions so inverting the image gives undesirable results.

For tricky jobs such as this we need to break the object down into separate layers; these can be distorted individually to produce the correct effect.

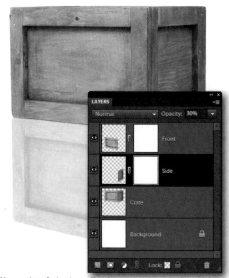

4 We need to fade the reflections out but we cannot do this in one hit because the angles on the front and side are different. Add a layer mask to both the front and side layers by clicking the Add Layer Mask icon at the base of the Layers panel.

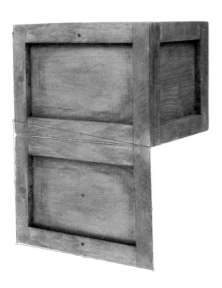

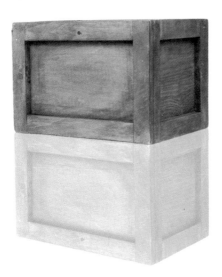

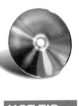

2 Go back to the front panel layer and flip it vertically, then press *ctrl* **T** **⌘** **T**. Drag it down and match one of the corresponding corners on the base of the original box. Hold *ctrl* *Shift* **⌘** *Shift* and drag the opposite center handle up to skew the panel into position.

3 Repeat the last step to add the side panel. At present we have two boxes on top of each other; a good effect in itself but we need to make it more like a reflection. The first thing to do is drop the opacity: around 30% works well here – do this for both layers.

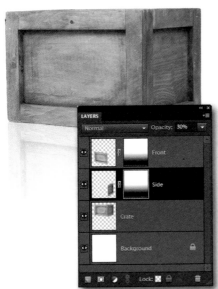

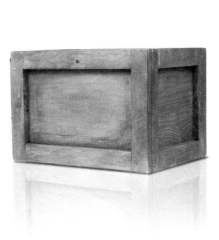

5 Select the Gradient tool **G** and choose a Linear Black, White gradient. Click one of the mask's thumbnails to make it active. Now click halfway along the bottom edge of the panel, then drag straight up to the top of the reflection. Repeat this for the other panel.

6 Finally, we'll add a shadow to place the crate firmly on the ground. Create a new layer above the background; use the Polygonal Lasso to draw a selection around the bottom of the crate. Fill this with black, blur it slightly and lower the opacity a little.

263

Window reflections

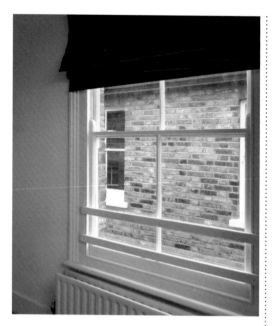

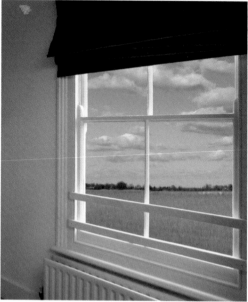

1 We can easily select the window area using the Lasso tool. By making a new layer, filled with a solid color, we create a mask for the window; any view placed on top of this layer, and grouped with it, will be seen 'through' the window.

T HE VIEW THROUGH THIS WINDOW is far from inspiring: the side of the house next door adds little life to the scene. We'll replace this view with a new one to improve our outlook.

The complications arise when we begin to place figures in the scene. A person in the room will look convincing enough just standing in front of the window, as long as he appears at the right scale for the room; but, if we leave it at that, we're ignoring the fact that there should be glass in the window, which should create a reflection.

Adding a reflection certainly makes the glass itself exist as a medium. But how do we make the glass cope with multiple reflections? The answer is to subtract one reflection from the other, to create a wholly convincing effect.

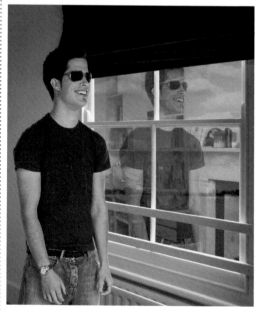

4 The man is reflecting in the window, and we should be able to see a reflection of the rest of the room as well. Almost any suitable interior will do, as long as its horizontals match that of the window perspective: it doesn't need to be a view of the same room.

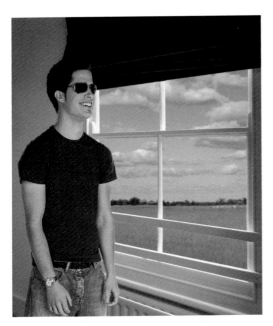

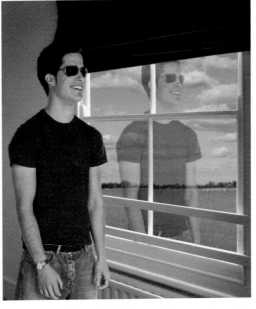

2 Placing our figure in the scene, looking obliquely down the field, adds that human element that brings the image to life. But the window itself looks distinctly empty and we need to add glass to it.

3 Because of the angle of view – and the symmetry – of our figure, we can simply duplicate him and position a slightly reduced copy (to allow for perspective), grouped with the view, at a low opacity – here, around 50%.

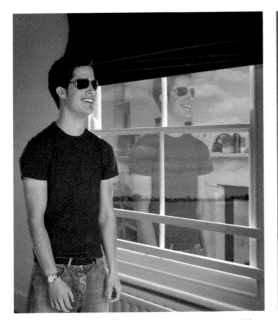

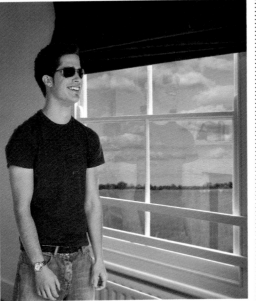

5 The trouble with the previous step was that we could see through the man to the room behind. Of course, his reflection should obscure the room. So hold *ctrl* ⌘ and click on his thumbnail to load his selection; then switch to the room reflection layer and delete from there.

6 We made the reflection of both the room and the man strong enough to see what we were doing in the previous few steps. In reality, we'd expect a much less visible reflection. Here, we've reduced the opacity of both layers to just 20% for a more convincing result.

HOT TIP

Our man happened to be at exactly the right angle to allow us to 'translate' him through the window. In most cases, you'd need to flip your figure horizontally in order for the reflection to work properly. It's a lot easier if the window isn't at an angle as extreme as the one in our example.

SHORTCUTS

MAC **WIN** **BOTH**

From railway to waterway

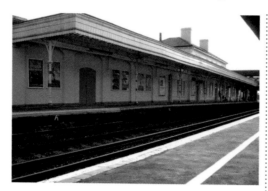

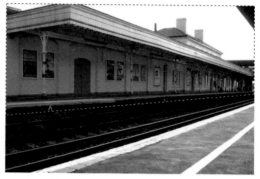

CREATING REFLECTIONS IN WATER requires a slightly different approach to those of solid surfaces such as metal or wood. Being a liquid, it has different properties to take into account such as turbulence and refraction. We need to distort the reflection to match the state of the water. This could be anything from the subtle ripples on a pond to the hazy elongated lights of cars on a rain-soaked road.

In the following example we'll convert this railway platform into a canal. By using a combination of layers, filters, and distortion techniques, we can quickly create a realistic water effect which can be tailored to suit many different images, for example: beautiful lakeside scenes, rock pools for a sea life project, or simply puddles on the ground.

1 First we'll create the reflection: draw a selection using the Polygonal Lasso following the perspective of the platform; I've used the yellow letters as a guide. Create the rest of the selection around the top of the image. Now save the selection via the Select menu.

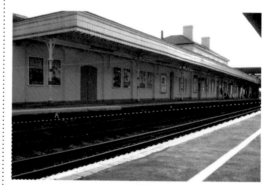

4 Inverse the selection `ctrl` `Shift` `I` `⌘` `Shift` `J`. Go to the Select menu and load the selection we saved earlier. Make sure Subtract from Selection is checked and click OK. Now grab the Polygonal Lasso, hold `alt` `⌥` and remove the area of the platform from the foreground.

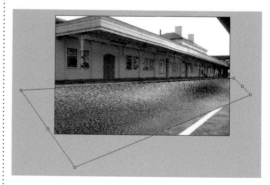

7 Use Free Transform to distort the water into place. This doesn't need to be a perfect fit; the texture can become too pixelated if it's stretched too much. We need to adjust enough to stop it looking too flat. Once you've done this, press `ctrl` `G` `⌘` `G` to group it with the base layer.

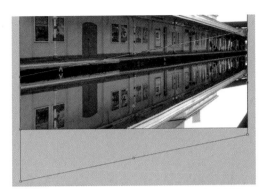

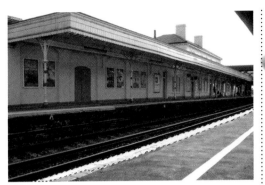

2 Copy the selected area to a new layer **ctrl J** **⌘ J**. Flip the layer vertically to make a mirror image. Select Image > Transform > Skew. Hold **Shift** and drag the layer down to line the layers up, then pull the right-middle handle up to correct the perspective.

3 Hide the reflection layer for now and click the background layer's thumbnail to make it active. Select the line at the edge of the platform with the Magic Wand; hold **Shift** to add any missing areas. Add a small amount of feathering; 1 pixel will be fine here.

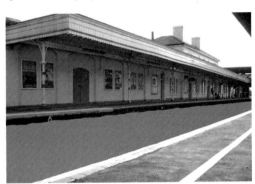

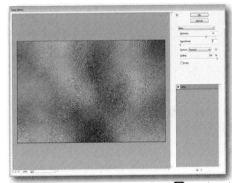

5 Create a new layer between the platform and the reflection. Fill the selection with 50% gray and deselect. Paint in a slight unevenness to the back edge using a hard brush; remember to make it less pronounced as it moves further into the distance.

6 Add another layer above the last. Press **D** to select the default palette, now fill the layer with the Clouds filter to generate a random pattern. Choose the Glass filter from the Distort menu. Set the texture to Frosted, now use the sliders to create a fine-rippled effect.

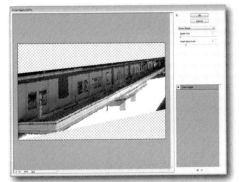

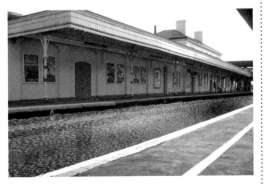

8 Make the reflection layer visible again. Set its blend mode to Soft Light and group it with the water layer. We need to add some ripple to the reflection itself as it would be distorted by the water's surface. This is easily done with the Ocean Ripple filter.

9 Select a large, soft eraser; using the edge, erase some of the lower area of the reflection to fade it out. We'll also add a little tint to the water. We've used a Photo Filter Adjustment Layer set to Cooling at a very low density. You could use a Hue/Saturation adjustment set to Colorize.

HOT TIP

Although it's generally good practice to avoid using the Eraser, there are times when it's quicker and more practical to do so. If you're worried about making a mistake, duplicate the layer as a precaution.

SHORTCUTS

MAC WIN BOTH

10

Goo, slime... and molasses

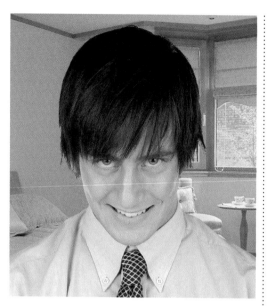

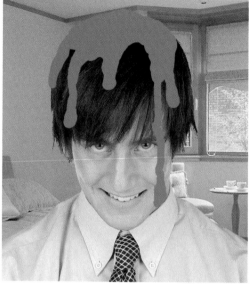

ELEMENTS IS AWASH WITH FILTERS for performing special effects – everything from knocking up a quick pointillist Seurat painting to making an image look like it's reflected in rippling glass.

Sometimes, though, filters can have surprising results. One of our favorites is Plastic Wrap, which – surprise, surprise – makes objects look as if they're wrapped in plastic. This isn't a job it does very well, but what it can do is to make glistening, slimy liquids from the most basic of ingredients.

Here, we'll show how to use the Plastic Wrap filter to add a few spoons of molasses to the top of this man's head. Why? Well, why not?

1 Begin by making a new layer. Select a mid-gray and, using a hard-edged brush, paint in the area to be taken up by the goo. If you're having trouble painting convincing drips down the face, try using the Smudge tool to smear the color where you want it to go.

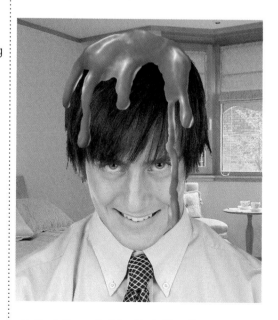

4 Here's the result of that Plastic Wrap filter: a glistening dollop of – well, something gray. We can fix that in the next step. If you find you don't get the effect you want, undo the filter, add a little more shading, and use `ctrl` `F` `⌘` `F` to apply it again without having to open the dialog.

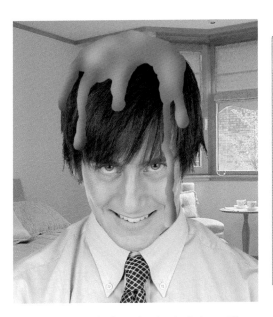

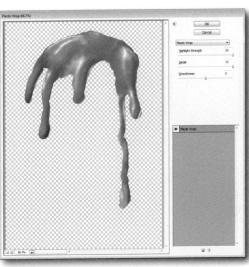

2 Now add some shading to it using the Dodge and Burn tools, set to Highlights. Remember, if you hold *alt* ⌥ when using either tool, you'll get the other one temporarily. All we're aiming for here is a random lumpy texture, to give Plastic Wrap something to work on.

3 Choose Filter > Artistic > Plastic Wrap. (Why is it in the Artistic section? No idea.) Push the Highlight Strength and Detail settings up to their maximum – no half measures here – but leave the Smoothness round about the mid point to add some texture to the stuff.

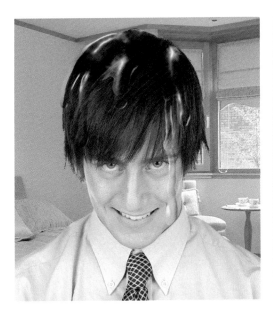

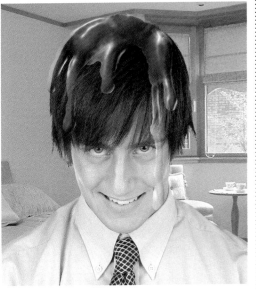

5 When we change the mode of this layer from Normal to Hard Light, using the pop-up menu at the top of the Layers panel, all the gray disappears, leaving us with just the highlights and shadows. As it stands, this looks more like water than molasses.

6 We can add color using the Hue/Saturation dialog, checking the Colorize button and dragging the Hue slider until we get the color we want. If we left this slider at the far right, we'd get a convincing impression of a bottle of red wine poured over his head. Your choice!

Plastic Wrap can be used to create all kinds of liquid effects – spilt wine, dripping water, vinegar, coffee, and oil – just by changing the hue and the brightness. It's also good for creating icicles and all kinds of shiny, lumpy surfaces.

The real effectiveness of this filter depends on getting the shading right in step 2: keep applying the filter, using Undo if it isn't right, then adding more shading and reapplying the filter until it works. Subtlety is the key here: don't go for deep shading, but paint in the shadows and highlights with a very light touch.

269

Preserving the occasion

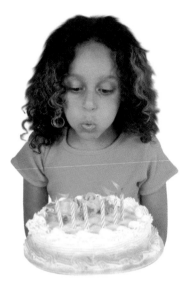

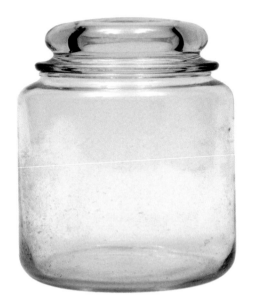

E VER BEEN AT A SPECIAL OCCASION – a
birthday, perhaps, or a family event –
and wished you could keep it forever? Taking
a series of photographs is one method, but
here's another that will preserve your favorite
memories for all time in a unique way.

The technique we use here will help us to
place this girl in a preserving jar. But it could
also be used to place snorkeling kids into a fish
tank or to position people and objects in just
about any glass container.

We'll begin with the cutout photograph of
our girl blowing the candles out on her cake
and then we'll go on to make her look as if she's
really inside the glass jar.

1 Here's our bottle. If you want to photograph your
own container, make sure it's against a plain white
background: a white sheet of paper behind it will work well.
And try not to use the flash on your camera or you'll get an
ugly glare off the glass surface.

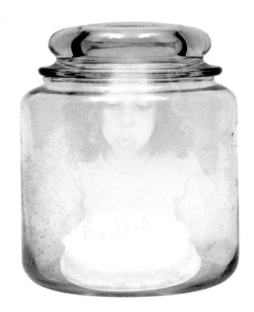

4 Press ctrl G ⌘ G to group the new jar layer with
the girl's layer, so it only shows up where it overlaps
her layer. The rest of the jar is now returned to its original
appearance. But the effect is now too strong: the girl has
almost disappeared inside that container.

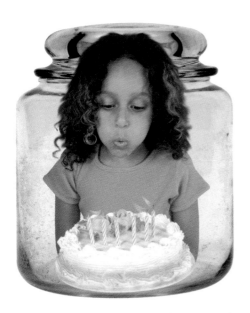

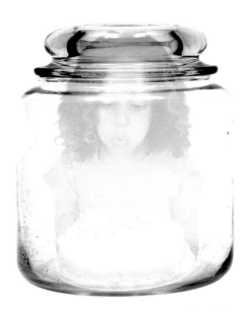

2 When we place the girl on top of the jar, we can resize her to fit the shape using Free Transform (*ctrl* T / ⌘ T). She may now fit the jar, but the effect is far from convincing: we need to add a couple of treatments to make it look as if she's really inside.

3 Duplicate the jar layer and move it above the girl's layer; then change the mode of the jar to Hard Light, using the pop-up menu at the top of the Layers panel. The effect is to make the whole jar too bright; we can correct this in the next step.

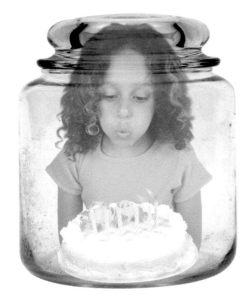

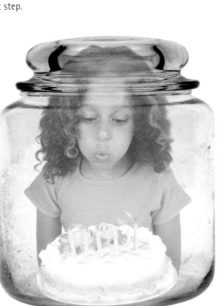

5 We can reduce the strength of the effect by lowering the opacity of the duplicated jar layer. Experiment with different settings to see what looks best: here, an opacity of 40% gives a good balance. The value you end up with will depend very much on the glass container you photograph.

6 Finally, we need to pay attention to the thick glass at the top of the jar, where it meets the lid. Use a small, soft-edged Eraser to remove those parts of the girl's head behind these thicker glass areas and we'll get a much more convincing result.

Keeping it real

POSSIBLY THE GREATEST COMPLIMENT you can receive for one of your montages is when the viewer does not realize it is one in the first place. This need not be as time-consuming and laborious as you may think: a large part of producing a convincing image, after all, is creating an illusion to fool the viewer. It may not survive close scrutiny, but unless we're trying to conclusively prove to NASA that we had reached the Moon long before Neil Armstrong, we can afford a little artistic license.

Creating a realistic image depends on a number of factors: most importantly the individual components of the artwork need to fit together as seamlessly as possible. The direction at which the people and objects are lit needs to be the same – there's no point having someone caught in a spotlight, for instance, if their face still appears to be in shadow. We also need to make sure the shadows themselves are correct and, more importantly, present to begin with; everything casts a shadow of some sort, even if they are too faint to notice initially — they help to define depth, placing their associated object within its surroundings. Getting the color right also plays an essential role: be careful not to use garish hues as this could result in an unnatural looking image.

So, with all that said, how do we go about translating it into our artwork? The answer is often staring right back at us: a lot of the time we'll be adding to an existing photo so we can take our cues from there, adjusting the new elements accordingly and sampling the colors and tones, comparing them as we go. Things become trickier when it comes to building a picture from the ground up where our clues aren't there to guide us — we're far from helpless though.

Just as a traditional artist studies their subject and surroundings to set it to canvas, we can do the same. It's by no means a crime to use reference material to make sure we achieve the correct effect and it's certainly preferential to trying to use guesswork alone. A good starting point is, of course, the internet and image search engines such as Google or Yahoo are superb resources; it's highly probable that we'll find what we're looking for and, because we're not actually including the image within our artwork, copyright is not an issue; also, we need not be too concerned with the image's dimensions as long as it's possible to see the detail. We can, of course, take our own reference shots as well: again, these don't need to be award-winning photographs, they just need to be of a good enough quality to see the effect, so even quick snaps from a cell phone should be sufficient.

There will be occasions when we need to see different versions of the same effect and also have the ability to view it from different angles; something that a still image cannot offer. In these situations improvising with props is often a great solution as they don't necessarily need to be the exact objects and only need to be crudely put together; as long as the outcome is a good representation, we can transpose it to our design. It's surprising how many things we can find within immediate reach with which we can improvise: we might, for example, want to see how a shadow falls across an uneven surface such as a staircase; so instead of grabbing the nearest family member and have them stand in different positions, we can quickly put together an impromptu mock-up by folding a sheet of paper and positioning a suitably illustrative object; then use a flashlight or similar maneuverable light source to create the desired effect.

We're not always going to be producing images depicting plain old reality, of course; we'll often be creating montages that are highly stylized or in a fantasy theme: there will always be a demand for fairy princesses and other such magical pictures, after all. This often demands more attention to detail than with their more sublime counterparts; people tend to scrutinize them far more closely, even though they know they cannot be real. It's highly unlikely we'll stumble across a real photo in a search but we can still apply the same principles from the real world to our artwork: reflections, shadows, and color still play their part in creating a convincing scene. We do have the advantage that nobody can really say how a picture of this ilk really should look, so we can be a little more lenient with the rules.

Finally, remember that there will always be flaws and unexpected elements in a real scene: try not to make your images too clinical. Try adding some random areas of light and shadow — it's often the smallest details that have the most impact.

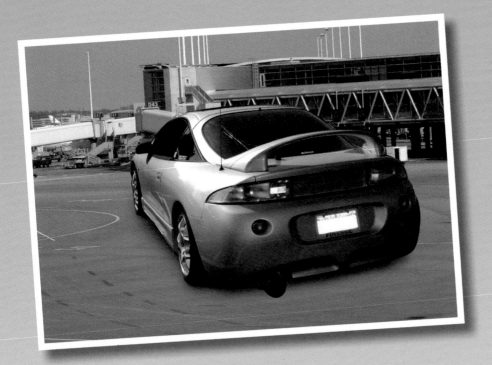

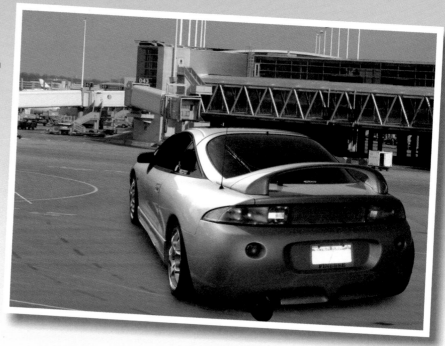

Two images of a car on an airport runway. It's the identical car in both photographs, but in the top image it looks false and out of place, whereas in the bottom one it belongs in the scene. The difference is that in the top picture the car is too high for the perspective of the scene; in the bottom one, the perspective is correct.

11

The third dimension

ALMOST EVERY PHOTOGRAPH WE TAKE captures a scene
in three dimensions. When we want to add, edit, or adjust
objects in the scene, we need to pay close attention to the
perspective in the original scene if we're going to achieve
anything like a convincing montage.

There are complex rules governing how perspective works,
and these have been refined ever since they were first
formulated by the Persian philosopher Alhazen in the
11th century. Since we're dealing with photographed
images, rather than a blank canvas, we can read the
existing perspective out of the scene: in this way, by
using our eye and drawing vanishing point lines, we can
guarantee that any new picture elements we add are
consistent with the scene we started with.

Lifting the lid 1

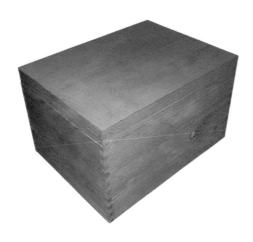

DESPITE THE HUGE AMOUNT OF IMAGES available through stock photography sites, there will come a time where you cannot find exactly the right one for your project. This is not always a problem, as we'll see in the following tutorial.

The image of the wooden box is perfect except it's closed and we want it open. Unlike the real thing we cannot simply remove its lid: the rear sides of the box don't exist. With a few selections and transformations we'll create the missing areas using copies of the remaining sections.

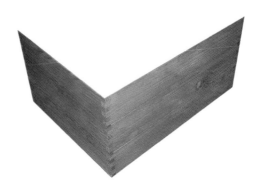

1 Our first task is to isolate the lid from the rest of the box. The Polygonal Lasso **L** is perfect for this. Create a selection around the whole of the lid. Press *ctrl* *Shift* *J* ⌘ *Shift* *J* to cut it away from the rest of the image. Hiding the layer shows the problem: we only have half a box.

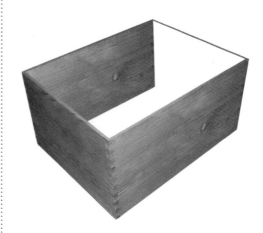

4 Make sure the box layer is active. Create a selection around the front side of the box. Press *ctrl* *J* ⌘ *J* to create a copy. Move this layer down the stack so it's behind the rest. Now reposition and distort it into place as the back side of the box.

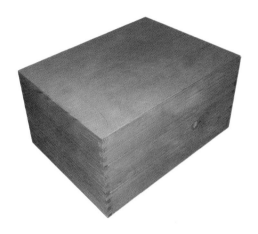

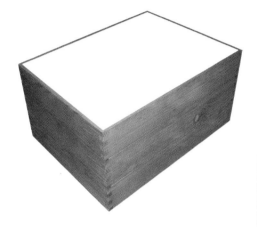

2 Make the lid visible again. Change the layer order so the lid is behind the box. Enter Free Transform *ctrl* **T** *⌘* **T**. Start by lowering the lid so its front corner lines up with the existing sides of the box. Hold *ctrl* *⌘*. Now distort the outer corners to match.

3 Next we'll cut a hole in the top. This serves two purposes: we can use the edges as a guide for the missing sides. It will also give them substance. Create a selection following the perimeter of the lid but a few pixels inside the edge. Press *Backspace*.

HOT TIP

It can be helpful to have a guide to follow when distorting in perspective. Sometimes you'll be able to use other areas of the original image. You can also create your own reference. This could form part of the object, as with the rim of the box. You can also use layers to create an overlay which can be turned on and off during the creation process.

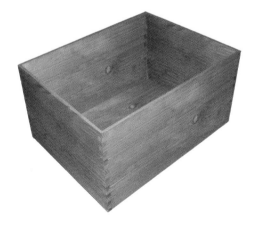

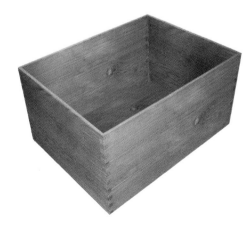

5 Repeat the last step to create the remaining side; remember to switch back to the box layer first. Switch to the back side layer. Make another copy. Again, move it to the bottom of the layer stack. Distort this to create the floor of the box.

6 All that remains is to add some shading inside the box. Grab the Burn tool **O**. Set the mode to Highlights. Use a large, soft brush to paint in some shadows; you'll need to switch between the layers. We only need a few subtle areas in this instance as the original lighting works quite well.

SHORTCUTS
MAC **WIN** **BOTH**

277

Lifting the lid 2

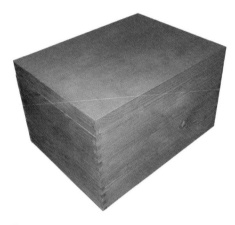

ON THE PRECEDING PAGE we opened a box by removing its lid completely. You may, however, decide that you want to keep it in the image, opening as though it were hinged.

This is not difficult to achieve. We can't, of course, simply pivot the lid to open it. This is two-dimensional artwork after all. Instead we'll use geometry in our favor. By flipping and rotating the lid, its angle is mirrored against the box. Once in place, we can use a variation on the previous technique to create the hollowed-out effect.

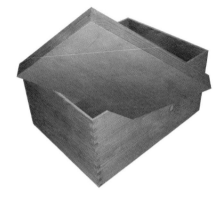

1 To avoid unnecessary steps in creating the open box we'll use the completed image from the last technique. The original lid has been selected and placed on a separate layer. The first thing to do is flip the layer. Do this by selecting Flip Layer Vertically under Image > Rotate.

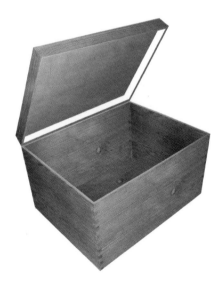

4 Use the Move tool **V** to push the panel toward the rear of the lid. This creates a recessed area. Don't place it too far back, we need to give the illusion that it has thickness. Again we can see the problem. The rear and side panels are missing.

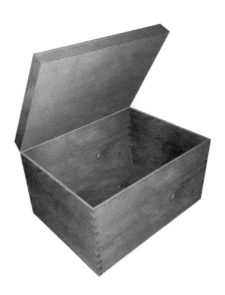

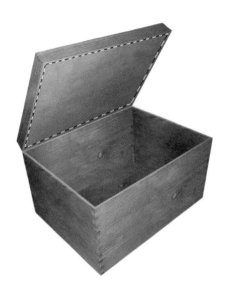

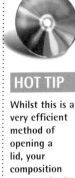

2 Use Free Transform to move and rotate the lid into place at the rear of the box. You'll notice it doesn't quite fit: it's too wide. Use the corner handles to squash the lid up a little so it meets the corners of the box. Make sure it meets the edge; you may need to rotate it a little more.

3 We could leave it at this stage. That lid looks a little heavy, though. Use the Polygonal Lasso to create a selection a few pixels within the edge of the lid's panel. Press *ctrl* *Shift* **J** **⌘** *Shift* **J** to remove the area and place it on its own layer. Drop it behind the lid in the Layers panel.

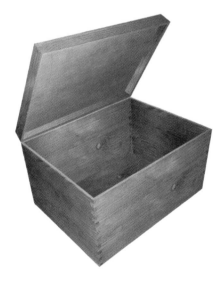

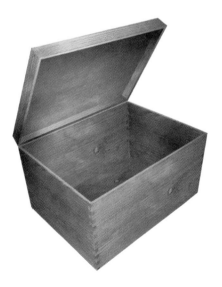

5 Click the lid layer's thumbnail to make it active. Select the top edge of the lid. Press *ctrl* **J** **⌘** **J** to copy it to a new layer. Drop this new layer behind the lid and panel layers in the stack. Use Free Transform to distort it into position. Repeat to create the missing right-hand side panel.

6 Select the Burn tool **O**. Set the mode to Highlights. Choose a large, soft-edged tip. Paint in some areas of shadow on the inside of the lid, particularly at the top and in the corners where less light would reach. You may also want to darken the inside of the box itself.

Tiling the floor

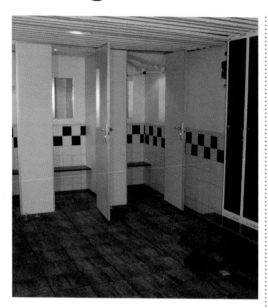

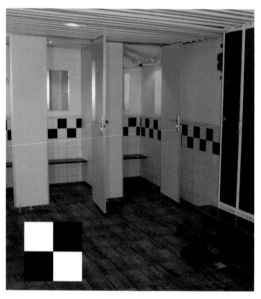

T HERE'S NOTHING LIKE A SPOT of redecorating to brighten things up. The old wooden floor of the changing room in this photo could certainly do with renewing. Let's replace it with something a little more lavish: a nice marble checker to complement the border on the wall, perhaps?

The effect is not as difficult to produce as it might seem. We'll create the pattern on a layer, using the Clouds filter to add the marbling effect. We already have the existing perspective to use as a guide so it's simply a matter of distorting the new floor into position.

You can, of course, use any pattern or texture with this technique. Perhaps use it to visualize ideas for decorating your room before you commit to a particular design.

1 Create a new layer. Grab the Rectangular Marquee **M**. Draw a selection holding **Shift** to keep it square. Fill this with black. Holding **ctrl** **alt** **⌘** **⟥**, click and drag the selection to create a copy. Place it next to the last square. Fill this with white. Repeat this twice more to finish the pattern.

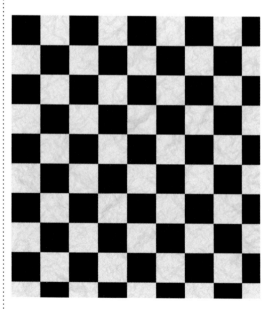

4 Add another new layer. Fill this with the Clouds filter. Apply the Find Edges filter from the Stylize menu. This gives us a nice marble-like texture. Set the blend mode to Difference. Lower the opacity slightly to reduce the contrast. Press **ctrl** **E** **⌘** **E** to merge the layers together.

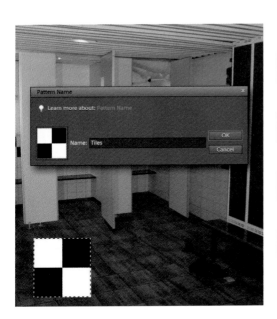

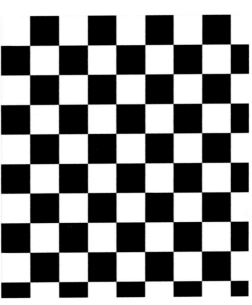

2 We'll use this to create a repeating pattern. Load the layer's selection. Select Define Pattern from Selection from the Edit menu. Give it a meaningful name for later reference and click OK. At this stage you can either delete the layer or hide it as it's no longer needed.

3 Create a new layer at the top of the stack. Press **Shift** **Backspace** to open the Fill dialog. Choose Pattern for the Contents from the drop-down menu. Select the tile pattern from the panel. Clicking OK will fill the whole layer with our new pattern.

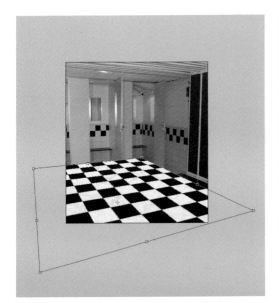

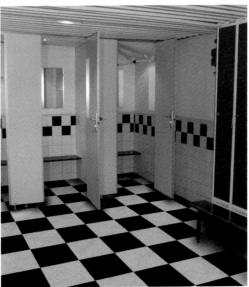

5 Now we have our new floor we need to distort it into position. Enter Free Transform. Hold **ctrl** **⌘** and distort the corner points to match the floor in the photo. You'll need to zoom out to be able to maneuver the left-hand side of the new floor into position.

6 We need to mask out the areas around the bench and the cubicles. This can be achieved by using the original floor as a clipping mask (see Chapter 3). A Hue/Saturation adjustment adds a slight color cast and darkens the floor down. Some shading is added to complete the effect.

HOT TIP

It can be tricky to get the perspective right when you don't have the whole area to match up to. Try to find as many points of reference as possible. In this image we have the lines of the original floor. The problem is they are hidden beneath the new layer. You can, of course, lower the opacity; a better solution here, however, is to change the tile layer's blend mode to Multiply or Screen. This will hide the white or black squares respectively, allowing us to accurately match up the visible edges.

SHORTCUTS
MAC **WIN** **BOTH**

Opening doors

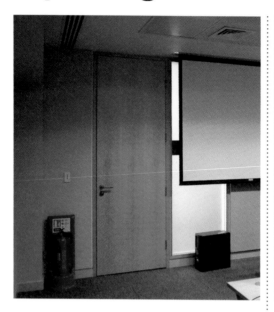

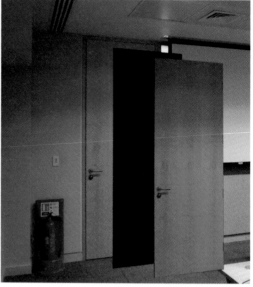

ONE OF THE NEATEST TRICKS we can play in Elements is to open a closed door. It's impressive to see it done, but here's the real trick: it's very easy to do.

The procedure makes use of the Free Transform tool, which performs perspective distortions with ease – and without us even asking anything of it. Distort a corner handle or two and the object in question will do its best to fill the space in a true three-dimensional manner.

In this tutorial we'll concentrate on opening the door and giving it some thickness so it looks real. The view through the door we'll leave as a gaping black hole; overleaf, we'll see how to fill this hole with a convincing view.

1 Use the Polygonal Lasso to trace the shape of the door, then use *ctrl* *J* *⌘* *J* to make a new layer from it. Load the door region by *ctrl* *⌘*-clicking on its thumbnail, then make a new layer behind it, filled with black. The three layers are shown here offset to show the stacking order.

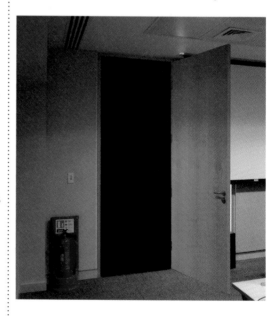

5 We can distort this new piece of door in a similar way to how we distorted the door itself, using Free Transform to adjust not only the width, but the height. The edge where the side touches the door should be slightly higher than the edge away from the door.

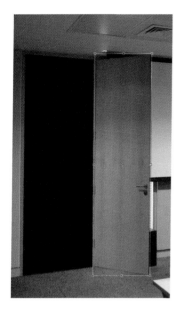

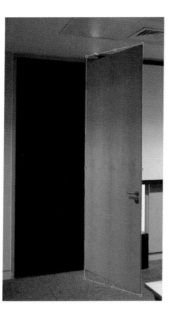

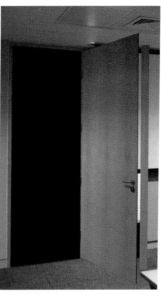

2 Enter Free Transform on the door layer using *ctrl T* *⌘ T* and drag the center-left handle to the right in order to flip the door so it's facing the other way.

3 Now for some perspective. Hold *ctrl Shift* *⌘ Shift* as you drag the top-right corner handle up; repeat this for the bottom-right handle, until the door looks like it fits the space.

4 To give the door some thickness, we'll need to add a side. Make a rectangular selection with the Marquee tool from the door itself and make a new layer from it; move it to the side.

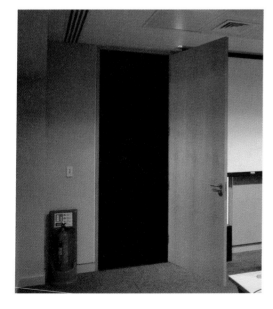

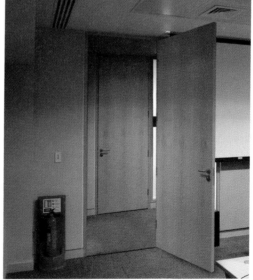

6 Brighten up this door side a little using Levels or the Brightness/Contrast adjustment – whichever you prefer. Here, we've also drawn in a lock mechanism, just for the sake of completeness: a rectangular selection was filled with a color sampled from the door handle.

7 Now, that all-important shadow. It's only a tiny amount of shadow, painted on a new layer beneath the door layer, but it makes all the difference to the realism of the scene. And how about copying the original room, grouped with the black layer, to make the view through the door?

Using perspective

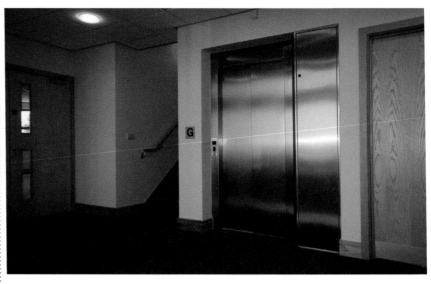

PERPSECTIVE IS ONE of the trickiest techniques to master in Elements. It's the factor that distinguishes convincing montages from those that just don't feel quite right. But, by following a few straightforward rules, it's possible to make perspective work for you, rather than against you.

The key to reading perspective in a photograph lies in using horizontal lines in the original image to calculate where the vanishing point of the image lies: once we've established this, anything we draw will naturally fit the scene.

1 In this photograph of an office hallway, we're going to remove the elevator and replace it with a corridor. At first glance, the task looks daunting. While there are plenty of horizontals here that are parallel to the wall facing us, there are very few at right angles to it. But we're fortunate in having that side wall, containing the doors, just in view: using these, we can read the perspective for the scene, which is enough to give us our vanishing point.

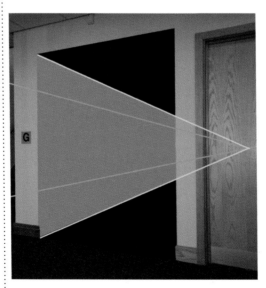

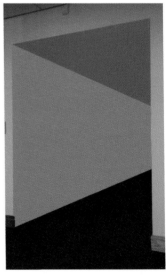

3 We can now draw two new perspective lines, to give us the top and bottom of our hallway. Start from the left corners and finish at the vanishing point. It's now possible to draw our first wall by using the Polygonal Lasso tool to follow these persepective lines, then filling the selection with a color to match the other walls. Group this wall layer with the black base layer we made in the previous step, so it only shows up where the two overlap.

4 We can now recolor the black layer to make a suitably colored ceiling. It's behind the wall layer, so the wall still shows up. To make the carpet, copy a section of the existing carpet and paste it in place, grouped with the ceiling layer but behind the wall layer. You may need to distort it to fit.

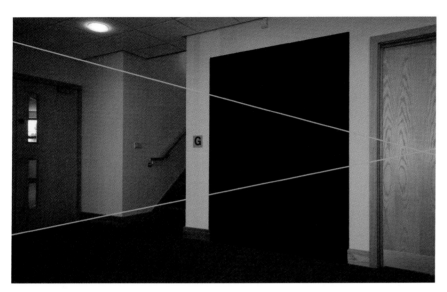

2 We'll begin by making a new layer. Then choose the Shapes tool, set to draw straight lines. Draw two lines that follow the strongest horizontals in the left-hand wall: in this case, the bottom of the doors and the very top of the wall. Where these lines converge, over on the far right of the image, is the vanishing point. Next, on another layer, draw a selection that matches the face of the elevator opening – going right down to floor level – and fill this with black.

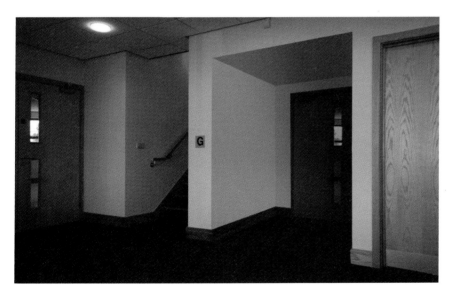

5 After drawing in the end wall, finishing off the scene is simply a matter of copying the elements we want from elsewhere in the picture. Here, we've taken a copy of the door on the far left and distorted it to match the perspective of the hallway.

A section of skirting board, taken from the far left of the facing wall, is copied and then stretched to run along the base of the new wall, and another small copy bent around the end wall. Finally, we made a new layer and added some shading to it with a large, soft-edged brush, to give the impression of the corridor darkening as it recedes into the distance. This final touch accentuates the sense of the corridor as a real space, adding extra realism to the scene.

HOT TIP

When we distort the copies of the original door in step 5, we run into a tiny problem: because the door wasn't viewed head on, we can't use the bounding box in Free Transform to match the perspective of the view. Instead, adjust the distortion so that the bottom of the door lines up with the bottom of the wall, then drag the top corner so that it follows the angle of the top of the wall, once again pointing directly towards the vanishing point.

Make your own jigsaws

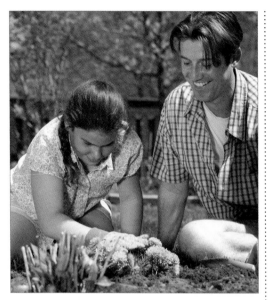

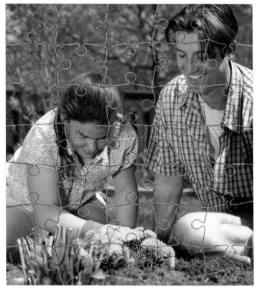

WITH ALL THE MULTITUDE OF FILTERS in Elements, it's perhaps surprising that, hidden among the stained glass and other effects, there isn't one for creating jigsaws.

Here's a technique that makes use of a custom shape that we've included for you on the DVD. Instructions for installing these shapes, as well as the other custom files, are in the root of the Goodies folder.

1 Choose the shape Jigsaw Portrait from the Cheat section of the Shapes dialog. Once the shape is selected, use the Shapes tool to drag from corner to corner within your image, so that the entire space is filled with the jigsaw pattern. You'll see it appear as faint lines as you do so.

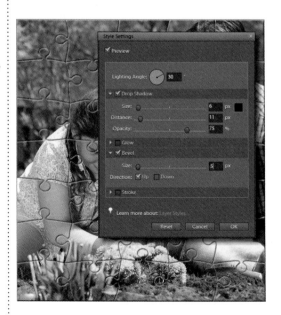

4 To give the pieces some depth, add an Emboss effect. Open the Style Settings dialog and reduce the size of the Emboss to about 5 pixels; add a slight drop shadow to make the pieces look more three-dimensional. You can play around with the Emboss settings until it looks right.

286

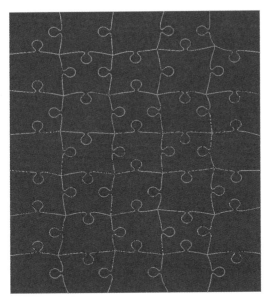

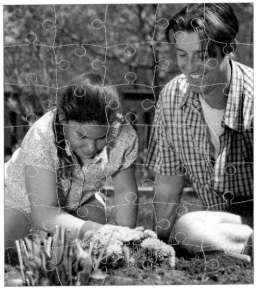

2 Once you release the mouse button, the shape layer will be filled with the default color – generally blue. We'll only be using this as a template, so there's no need to change the color of the layer: it won't appear in the final illustration.

3 Load up the shape layer's pixel area by holding `ctrl` `⌘` and clicking on its thumbnail in the Layers panel. Then return to the image layer and use `ctrl J` `⌘ J` to make a new layer from that selection. Hide the shape layer to see the image made up of jigsaw pieces.

HOT TIP

We've included two versions of the jigsaw on the DVD – one in portrait (vertical) orientation, the other in a landscape (horizontal) shape. Choose whichever one is most appropriate for the shape of the image you're working on.

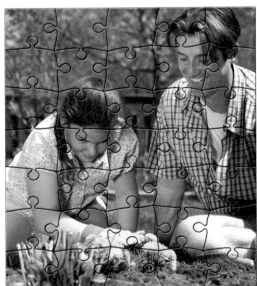

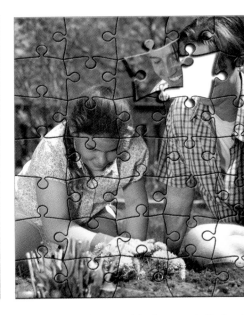

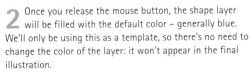

5 Now let's make the dividing lines clearer. Load up the selection of the shape layer again, then inverse the selection using `ctrl Shift I` `⌘ Shift I`; now everything except the pieces is selected. Make a new layer and fill the selection with black to make the lines between the pieces.

6 To take one piece out of the jigsaw, go to the lines layer we just created and click in one of the pieces with the Magic Wand. Return to the image layer and use `ctrl Shift J` `⌘ Shift J` to cut the selection to a new layer. Move it to the top of the layer stack and move and rotate it as you like.

SHORTCUTS
MAC WIN BOTH

Out of bounds

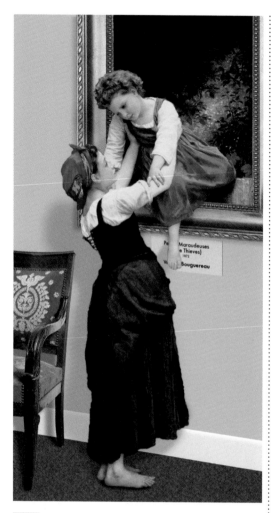

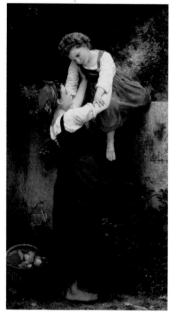

1 Here's our original painting. The format – one girl helping another down from a wall – is perfect for our purposes.

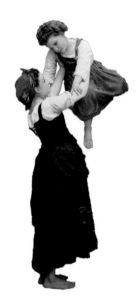

2 The first step is to select and copy the figures to a new layer, using a combination of your favorite selection tools.

THE 'OUT OF BOUNDS' TECHNIQUE is a popular one with Elements artists and it's not hard to see why: breaking a picture out of its frame makes for an arresting image.

The process can be as simple or as complex as you want to make it. Here, we'll look at a rather more detailed version of the trick, using not a photograph but a painting – *Little Thieves* or *Petites Maraudeuses*, by William-Adolphe Bougeuereau.

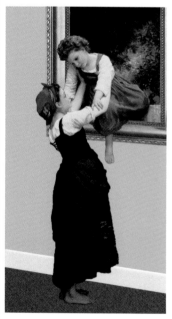

6 The carpet is added on a new layer: solid color, Gaussian Noise, then Gaussian Blur. We've also deleted the section of wall behind the painting.

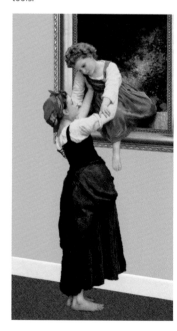

7 Use Shadows/Highlights to brighten that dark skirt and the Dodge tool to lighten the legs; then clone out the foliage on the skirt.

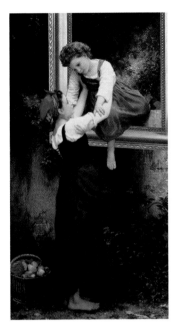

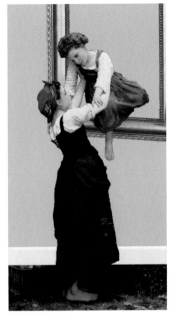

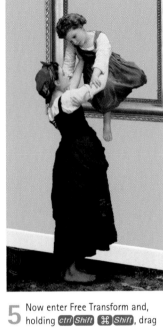

3 Now place the picture frame between the two layers, distorting it using Free Transform until it follows the angle of the wall in the painting.

4 Let's now add our own wall. Make a rectangular selection on a new layer filled with solid color; the skirting board is easily painted at the bottom.

5 Now enter Free Transform and, holding *ctrl* *Shift* ⌘ *Shift*, drag the bottom-right corner down until it matches the painting's perspective.

The real key to this technique lies in constructing a setting to match the perspective of the original painting or photograph. You'll almost certainly have to adjust the lighting, particularly in the shadow areas: here, the feet looked fine in the original painting, but were much too dark against the carpet.

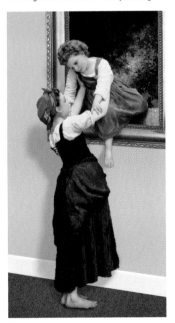

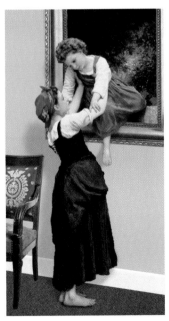

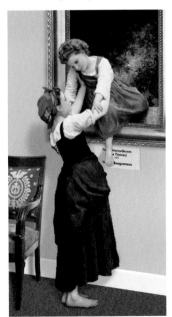

8 The shadows behind the girls give them some distance from the wall: use the techniques outlined in Chapter 5.

9 We've added a chair to give a sense of the room continuing out of the frame and to make that plain wall look a little less bare.

10 Finally, add shadows for the chair and picture frame. And while we're at it, we may as well include a plaque to the painter.

RGB or CMYK?

PICTURE THE SCENE: you've spent hours creating the perfect birthday card in Elements. It features a lovingly crafted cutout image against a bright green background, a dazzlingly bright red headline, and a contrasting blue caption. But when you print it out on your inkjet printer, the text looks dull and lifeless, and the background is far darker than it looked on the screen – despite having used the best quality glossy photo paper. What can have gone wrong?

The problem is the fundamental difference between what you see on the screen and what can be printed on paper. And it all comes down to two acronyms: RGB and CMYK.

RGB stands for red, green and blue, and refers to the colors used by computer monitors. In standard 8-bit mode, each pixel on your screen can display each of these three colors in 256 different levels of brightness. 256 is 2^8, or 2 multiplied by itself 8 times – which is what 8-bit means. By combining these three basic colors, each pixel can display 2^8 x 2^8 x 2^8 different colors – over 16 million in total.

We start with a black screen and the more color we throw on it, the brighter it becomes. These are known as 'additive' colors for this reason: we're adding light to blackness. When we add the maximum value of each of the three primary colors, we get white.

Printing ink on paper, however, works in precisely the opposite way. Rather than using red, green and blue, printers use cyan, magenta and yellow. But when we print, we start off with white paper; the more colors we add, the darker the result (just as you find when you mix paints together). These are known as 'subtractive' colors. If we add 100% of cyan, magenta and yellow together, we get black. Or rather, we don't; we get a muddy brown. That's why printers use an additional color, black, to deepen the shadows and strengthen the printed image. The four colors combined give us CMYK. Surprisingly, no-one seems to know precisely what the 'K' stands for. Most claim it means 'key', although that seems a poor substitute for 'black'.

When you mix the primary colors together, either on screen or on paper, you get some surprising results. On screen, mixing red and green makes yellow, red and blue make magenta, and green and blue make cyan. Do those colors sound familiar? They should do – they're the primary colors of printing inks. And, when printing, mixing magenta and yellow produces red, magenta and cyan make blue, and yellow and cyan make green.

So what does this have to do with poor quality printing? The trouble is that while your monitor is capable of displaying a huge range of colors, CMYK is capable of reproducing only a very limited part of that color 'gamut', as it's known. That's the reason why commercial printers use additional Pantone colors, chosen from swatch books similar to those you'd use to choose household paints. If you want a color that can't be achieved with CMYK, you need to use additional inks.

Some inkjet printers try to get around this problem by using six colors, rather than four. And this does expand the range slightly, but the unfortunate fact remains that not everything you see on your monitor is capable of being reproduced on paper.

What's the solution, then? Can't we just convert our images to CMYK before we print them and see what the difference is? Not in Elements, we can't, although we can in its big brother Photoshop. The ability to prepare print-ready artwork is one of the reasons Photoshop costs nearly ten times as much.

Avoid 100% green or blue, as these are the colors least likely to reproduce well; dazzling pinks are also problematic, although 100% magenta and solid red will work well. If a color combination on your monitor looks larger than life, then that's probably a good indication that you won't be able to print it. Ultimately, though, it comes down to experience: seasoned users get to know which colors will work and which won't. If in doubt, sample colors from your photographs rather than creating them from the Color Picker – you're much more likely to get printable colors that way.

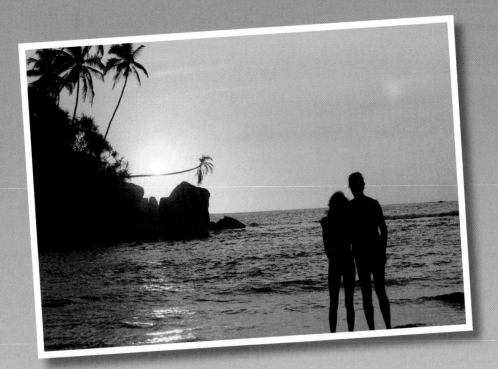

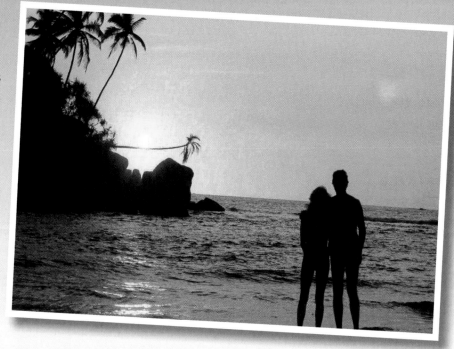

■ Two versions of the same vacation scene. The top one, as a Photoshop Elements file, takes up just over 4Mb of disk space. The one on the right, saved as a low quality JPEG file, takes up just 78K. Can't spot the difference? That's because Elements' innovative Save for Web feature can make huge size savings with minimal loss of quality.

12

Print and the internet

CREATING FANTASTIC IMAGES in Elements is one thing.
Getting it off your computer screen is another matter
entirely. As with most techniques, there are right and
wrong ways of doing the job.

In this chapter we'll explain how to save files for
speedy internet delivery, both for single images and for
animations. (We'll also look at how to create eye-catching
animations directly in Elements.)

We'll also show a useful technique for making your
printed results look far more like what you see on screen,
without having to get your printer or monitor calibrated.

Saving files for the internet

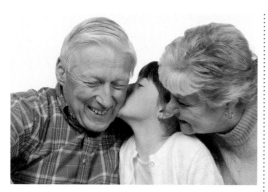

W E ALL WANT to share our photographs and montages with others, and the internet provides a simple, easy way to do just that. But rather than just taking your Elements file and uploading it to a website, you first need to save it in a format that web browsers will understand.

JPEG, GIF and PNG are the three most common file types. Elements provides a useful way to save images for web delivery: it's called Save for Web and you'll find it under the File menu.

Here, we'll look at what each of the three formats has to offer and see how to use the Save for Web dialog to get the best possible results from your digital images.

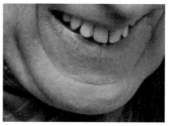

1 Here's a detail of our original photograph, enlarged so we can see the detail – but at 313K, it's far too big for internet delivery.

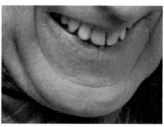

2 As a 256-color GIF image, we can see a little blockiness appearing in the white of the teeth: this image is a hefty 264K in size.

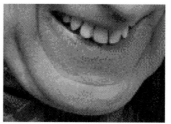

3 Reducing the number of colors in this GIF file to 64 reduces the file size to 168K, but we can clearly see the 'dither pattern' in the skin tones.

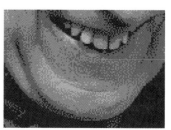

4 As an 8 color GIF, the file size comes down to 72K: it's now acquired the appearance of a poorly photocopied sepia print.

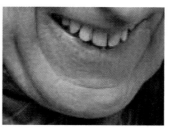

5 As a JPEG file with a quality of 50, this is very close to the original, but its size has been reduced to just 73K – fine for the internet.

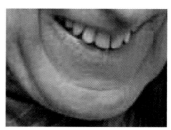

6 Taking the JPEG quality down to 20 produces some marked 'blockiness' and reduces the file size to 38K.

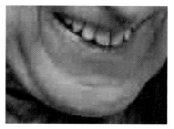

7 For the sake of comparison, here's the file at a JPEG setting of 0. The image is just about unusable, but takes up just 19K of space.

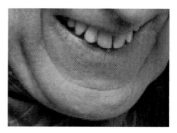

8 A 24-bit PNG file produces the best results, but at a cost: this file is a massive 604K – nearly twice the size of the original.

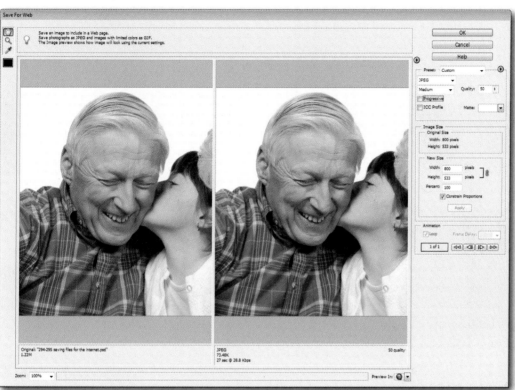

You may find that you have a particularly large image you want to save for internet delivery and you can't get the file size small enough – if, for example, you want to upload a large image to a site that sets a limit on file sizes. In this case, consider applying a little Gaussian Blur to the image before entering the Save for Web dialog: this will smooth out some of the fine detail and will go a long way towards making JPEG files far smaller.

The first step in Save for Web is to choose the file type. JPEG is best for photographs and GIF is best for areas with a lot of flat color, such as buttons and badges. PNG supports transparency, unlike JPEGs, and produces good quality – but at the cost of increased file size.

Unless you're creating page furniture for web pages, it's best to stick to JPEG format, as this will give you the best results. There's a trade-off between file size and quality: the better the quality, the larger the file will be, so the longer it will take people to download.

A JPEG setting of 50 or more will produce an image that's almost indistinguishable from the original file. The more complex an image, the larger the file will be: so a shot of a cloudy sky will produce a much larger file if there's an intricate fence in front of it.

As you drag the Quality slider, you can see the results of the JPEG compression in the right-hand pane (the left one always shows the original

image). If it's not showing an area you want to concentrate on, drag within the window to move it and both images will pan together. You can also zoom in using the Magnifying Glass tool at the top left to see an area of interest in detail.

JPEG files can be set to 'progressive', which means that they will load in stages, each pass producing a more detailed version of the image. This was an issue when most people had slow modems, but is now rarely used.

Beneath each image is a readout showing the file type, the size the resulting file will be, and the time taken to download it. Click the tiny arrow at the top right of the images to change the speed of download: the default 28K applies to old-fashioned modems, which are hardly relevant in the era of high speed broadband.

You can also choose to reduce the physical image size as well, using the New Size section (center right). This will, of course, reduce the file size as

well, but you need to be sure of the dimensions you want to end up with before playing with these numbers.

If you have a favorite combination that works well for your images, you can save it as a preset and then apply it to each image that passes through the Save for Web dialog. You can also choose to include ICC profiles, which aim to maintain consistent color: unless your computer has been calibrated to do this, it's best avoided.

The Matte box is used for saving GIF and PNG images with transparency: if you want to place images on a colored background in a web page, specify that color here and the transparent pixels will be blended with it. This is necessary because GIFs and 8-bit PNG files only support one level of transparency – on or off.

When you've chosen your settings, press OK and the standard file Save dialog will open. Be sure to specify a different name for your file to avoid overwriting the existing image.

Presenting your work

I F YOU WANT TO SHOW OFF your creations in printed form, Elements has a powerful photo-book generation engine with customizable layouts and themes. These can be printed on your own printer or, if you reside in North America, packaged off to be professionally made through an online service and delivered to your door straight from Elements. Non-US residents can still get a bound copy, of course: the Mac has inbuilt support for creating PDF files via its print dialog. For Windows users there is a free utility called CutePDF (www.cutepdf.com) which gives the same functionality; rather than printing to paper, it creates a PDF file which can then be printed as a whole. The best way to do this is through Lulu.com. They have an excellent range of media options and will work directly from the PDF file. There may also be local print stores that you can take the file to directly on a memory stick or CD.

This is the perfect way to show prospective clients what you're capable of in a clean, professional-looking portfolio.

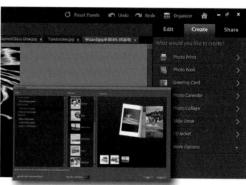

1 We've opened a set of images and clicked Create from the panel on the right. The Photobook option is at the top of the list. A dialog opens with a range of initial options. We'll choose Print locally with a size of 11.69 x 8.27 inches. The units can be specified via Preferences.

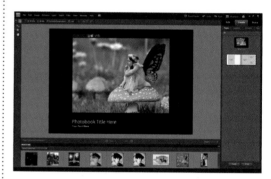

4 The toadstool fairy makes a good statement piece. We'll drag it in from the Project Bin. It's too large and most of it is lost outside the frame. If we double-click the image, we get the editing tools. Now we can scale and move the image around. Press *Enter* or click the green check mark to commit.

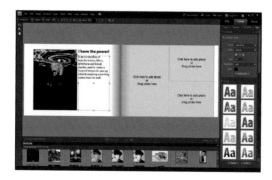

7 Go back to the Text tab. Click Add Text Block. A new text line will appear in the center. Move the cursor away from the text to access the Move tool. We can reposition our title next to the image and make it the image title. We can click on the page to add more text now if we wish.

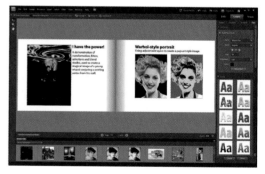

8 The layout of the facing page is not right for this particular book. This is easily changed. Click the Layout tab and select a new page style. We've chosen the 2-up photobook portrait. Simply click and drag it across to the page. Now we can add our images as before.

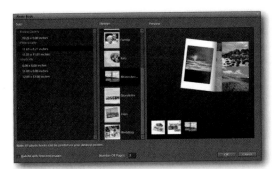

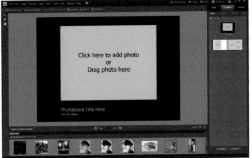

2 We have a set of templates to choose from. We'll go for Monochrome as it's a nice, clean design. Although we have preloaded our images, we'll deselect the option to Autofill as we want to choose where they are placed. We'll also start with only two pages. Click OK to continue.

3 After a short time the main screen will appear. Here we see the blank title page displayed. On the right is the project layout. There are only two pages, of course. We can add more as we need them. At the bottom is the Project Bin. If it's not visible we can open it from the Window menu.

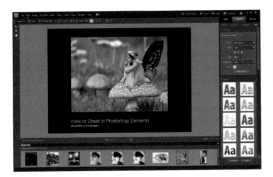

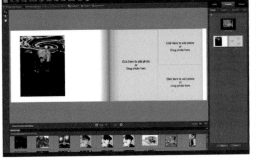

5 We can add a title and sub-text. Double-click on the text beneath the image. The panel on the right-hand side changes to the Text Panel giving us a host of font-related controls. We can also add more text areas if we choose. We'll keep the default settings and type out our title.

6 We can move on to the content pages now. Click the Pages tab at the top of the right panel. The first page has a single portrait section. We'll keep this and add a new image. We'll use the wizard photo here. Again, we need to scale it down to fit.

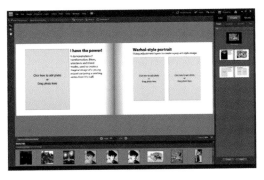

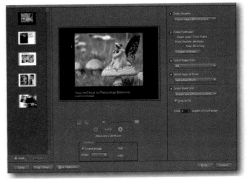

9 Now we'll add another page spread. Go to the Pages tab. Now click the green plus sign. A new spread will be created. The layout is a copy of the previous pages, including the text. The images don't get brought across, however. This can be useful if we want the same layout throughout.

10 We can save the book at any time. Elements uses a special type of file that retains all the information about the pages. When you next open it, all the settings will be as you left them. We can also choose to print the book. Click Print in the bottom right corner to open up the dialog.

HOT TIP

We've only scratched the surface of what is possible when creating photobooks. Aside from the standard layout and design options, you can switch to the Advanced Mode. This is almost the same as the full editor and gives you complete control over the individual layers that build up the pages.

SHORTCUTS
MAC WIN BOTH

Animated GIFs

MOVEMENT IS ONE of the characteristics that most distinguishes the internet from printed books. We can create short animations right inside Elements, using the Save for Web feature.

In this example, we've made a simple montage containing just five layers: the background, with the road and sky; the clouds; the car; the crate on the back of the car; and the shadow beneath it.

By moving each of these layers around and making a new composite copy as a separate layer, we can create our animation as a series of separate Elements layers. It's then an easy matter to string these together to make a moving image.

We can't show our finished animation in this book, of course, but it is on the DVD if you want to see how it looks when it's moving.

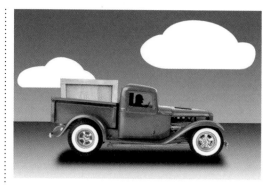
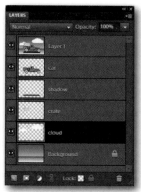
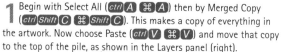

1 Begin with Select All (*ctrl* A ⌘ A) then by Merged Copy (*ctrl* *Shift* C ⌘ *Shift* C). This makes a copy of everything in the artwork. Now choose Paste (*ctrl* V ⌘ V) and move that copy to the top of the pile, as shown in the Layers panel (right).

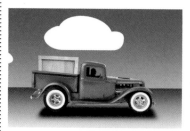

4 The same process once more: move the clouds and jiggle the car and the crate, then Select All, Merged Copy, and Paste. Remember to hide the previous composite copy by clicking its Eye icon in the Layers panel before you attempt to move anything. When moving the clouds, hold the *Shift* key to make sure you're moving them horizontally.

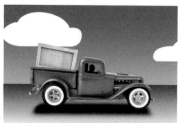

5 When we get the big cloud over to the far left (frame 4 in our animation), we need to make a copy of this cloud layer and drag it over to the right, so the small cloud is just creeping in from that side. This will allow us to make the animation run for ever.

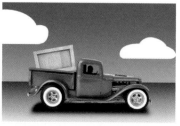

6 For frame 5 and for subsequent frames, we need to move both the original clouds layer and its copy. In Elements 5 and later you can select both layers together in the Layers panel, but it's just as easy to use *ctrl* E ⌘ E to merge the two layers together, so you can move them as one.

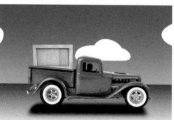

7 You can make as many frames as you like in your animation: we're using just six. In this final frame, the small cloud, which has been sliding in from the right, is now approaching its original position, and we can see the copy of the big cloud starting to make an appearance too. By duplicating the cloud layers in this way we're able to create an animation which appears to run seamlessly for ever.

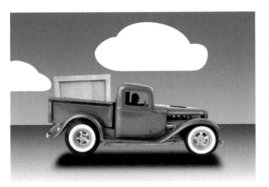

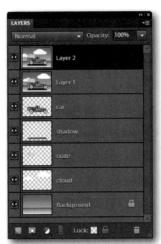

3 Now repeat the Select All, Merged Copy, Paste procedure as before, to create another new layer – and, once again, make sure it's at the top of the layer stack. Each of these new composite layers will form a single frame in our animation. Here's how the Layers panel will look after the second frame is complete.

2 That's frame 1 done. To make frame 2, first hide the first merged copy, then drag the clouds layer to the left a little way. Move the car up a fraction and rotate the crate to give the impression of them jiggling around as they move.

Although we've gone to some lengths to wrap the background clouds around so that the animation will loop convincingly, you don't need to do this with every animation. However you choose to animate your constructions, do be sure to save a copy before deleting all the original layers: Elements can only work with one layer equalling one frame of animation and you don't want to accidentally lose all your hard work.

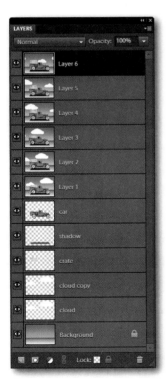

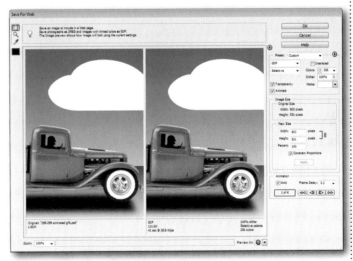

8 Here's how your Layers panel will look after all six frames have been completed. We now need to delete all the original layers – including the background – leaving just the six composite frames of the animation.

9 Now's a good time to save your document. But rather than overwriting the original, choose Save As and give it a different name: we don't want to lose all those individual layers that we've had to delete in the previous step.

Choose File > Save for Web to open the dialog, which will look exactly as it did on the previous pages. This time, though, check the Animate box near the top of the dialog window.

The number of frames in the animation is set by the number of layers in the document – one for each layer. But we can specify the time each

frame is to last for, as well as whether the animation will run just once or will loop for ever. This is the option we'll choose here: that's why we wrapped the clouds around in that way.

Adjust the Dither and number of colors, if you like, to reduce the size of the file; our example weighs in at over 600K, larger than a standard web animation would normally be.

Click the Preview button at the bottom to see how your animation will look in a browser: this is the first time you'll be able to see it moving. When you're happy with the timing, press OK to save the animation as a GIF file.

Easy print matching

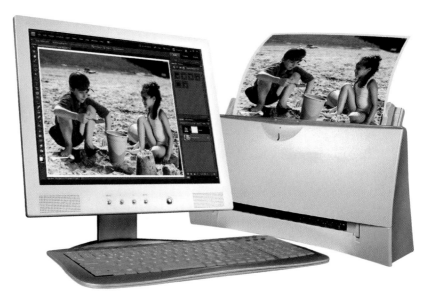

WITH COMPUTERS GETTING EASIER and easier to use, it's something of an irony that the biggest stumbling block seems to be when we revert to older technology – and that's in getting our images onto paper.

There's no real substitute for having your printer properly calibrated, perhaps investing in a monitor calibration device as well. But many of us don't have the money, the time, or the inclination to get this involved in our printing.

Instead, here's a simple workaround that may help to fool your printer into producing results that more closely match the image you see on your monitor. It's not 100% guaranteed, but the chances are it will fix a lot of print problems.

1 Here's the problem. You've downloaded your photos to your computer and you've adjusted them in Elements so that they look their best. But when you print them out, the results look quite different to what you see on screen: the prints may be darker, they may have a strong color cast, and so on.

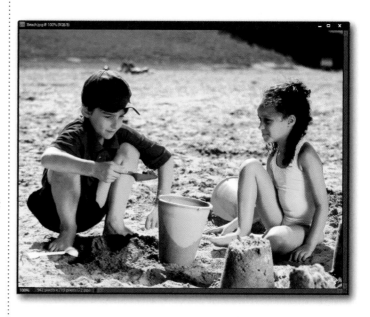

3 Back in the original file, make a new Levels Adjustment Layer. With this one, adjust the image – as seen through the first adjustment – to make your image look as close as possible to the original. By doing this, we're (hopefully) reversing the process of color change produced by the printer.

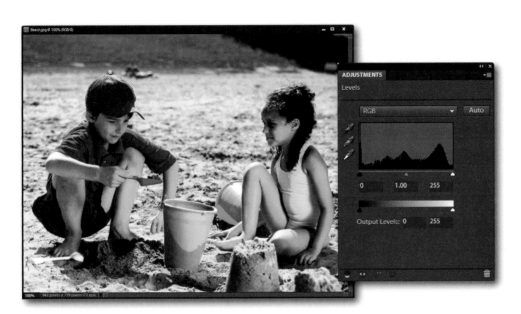

2 With the image you've just printed open in Elements, make a new Levels Adjustment Layer. Tweak the Levels settings to make the image on screen match the printout as closely as possible. What we're doing here is to simulate the color shift your printer will have upon the image, so we can compensate for it.

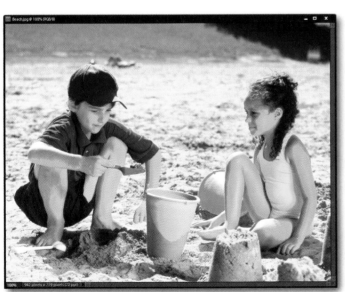

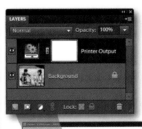

HOT TIP

You may find this technique produces too strong an effect, with a print that's skewed the other way. If so, try lowering the opacity of the Adjustment Layer until you get a result that works.

Once you're happy with the result, you can drag this second Adjustment Layer into any of your images before printing and it should help to compensate for the misdoings of your printer.

4 Now hide the original Adjustment Layer, leaving just the second. The idea is that by then printing this file, the printer will produce the same color shift it did before; and as we saw from the original Adjustment Layer, this should produce a print that's far closer to your original photograph.

5 Save your second Adjustment Layer by dragging it into a new, empty file. When you next print, drag it into the document for improved results.

Glossary

Actual size

Displaying the image on screen so that one pixel in the image exactly matches one pixel on the monitor. This is not the same as print size, which is determined by the resolution of the image.

Adjustment Layer

Special layers that perform non-destructive tonal and color adjustments to all or part of the artwork; they can be turned on or off and altered as required.

Aliasing

The opposite of anti-aliasing: no attempt is made at blending elements of the artwork to avoid jagged edges. This does have its uses: it can be used with very small fonts to avoid them becoming unreadable.

Alignment

A set of tools on the Options bar to force multiple layers to line up with each other using edges or centers.

Alpha channel

An area used to store a layer's selection information. This can be loaded and saved whilst the document is open; some file types can store alpha channels permanently with the image information.

Anti-aliasing

The method of creating a smooth transition between contrasting colors to avoid harsh, jagged lines.

Background layer

By default, this is the base layer upon which all others are added. Most operations can be performed on this apart from moving and applying styles.

Bitmap

The method of creating an image by adding individual pixels of a specific color in a two-dimensional grid. Most images produced in Elements use this process.

Blend mode

Used to combine the content of two or more layers by blending the upper layer with the layer beneath in different ways to produce a variety of effects.

Brightness/contrast

An adjustment method used for enhancing the strength of layers and images.

Channel

The area that holds the color information of an image. In Elements there are three channels: red, green, and blue, that are mixed together in varying amounts to define all the colors.

Clipping group

Hiding areas of the artwork by grouping two or more layers: the base layer acts as a mask template, its pixels defining what is visible on the layers above.

CMYK

Abbreviation for cyan, magenta, yellow, and black – the colors used for reproducing images in printed materials.

Color settings

A section of Elements' Preferences that set whether images are displayed for on-screen viewing or optimized for printing.

Compression

The method of reducing image file sizes using complex algorithms. There are two types: lossless, which does not affect the quality of the image, and lossy which sacrifices some quality in favor of smaller files.

Contiguous

This is an option for tools such as the Magic Wand: when enabled only the local area around the cursor will be affected; otherwise instances will be selected from the entire document.

Constrain

Forcing the direction of movement when using a particular tool, usually adhering to 45° angles. This is often used to ensure layers remain aligned when they are moved around the artwork.

Constrain proportions

When enabled this function maintains the dimensions when resizing an image, shape, or bounding box. When used with the Marquee tools it ensures a perfectly circular or square selection.

Cropping

Reducing the frame around an image to focus on an area of interest.

Depth of field

This is the area of the image that remains in sharp focus whilst the rest is left softer. The technique is often used to draw attention to a point of interest in the picture.

Desaturate

Removing the color information of an image leaving only grayscale tones describing the shadows, midtones, and highlights.

Dingbat

A font style that uses monotone images in place of standard letter characters. These can be anything from a simple symbol to a famous person's face. Being text, all the same effects can be applied as you would normally.

Displacement

A method of distorting an image according to the brightness values in an associated grayscale image file.

Distribute

A method of arranging layers to produce equal spacing between their centers or edges.

Dithering

The method of making an image appear to have more colors than it actually has by creating a patterned transition with a mixture of the available colors.

Dots per inch (DPI)

A measure of the output resolution of an image. On-screen images are typically displayed at 72 or 96 dpi whilst professional-quality prints are 300 dpi or sometimes more.

Feathering

The method of smoothing and blending a selection to avoid jagged edges. This differs from anti-aliasing as the edge is blurred against the destination rather than bridging using a gradient.

Filter Gallery

The dialog that lets you browse and apply individual filters or stack several filters together as layers to achieve different effects. These can be previewed prior to committing them to the image.

Gaussian Blur

A filter that uses a bell-shaped curve to give the impression of soft focus.

Gaussian Noise

A filter that adds random pixels in black and white (or in color) to create the effect of tight texture.

GIF

A lossy file format used in the early days of the internet. Today, GIF images are used for creating animations, a feature not possible with most other file formats.

Graphics tablet

A device connected to the computer that allows you to control the cursor with a pen-shaped stylus instead of a mouse. Many are pressure-sensitive, allowing much more accurate control of the tools.

Grayscale

An image composed of black, white and shades of gray, with no color component.

Hard Light

A blend mode in which midtone gray is invisible, leaving just the highlights and shadows on view.

Hue/Saturation

An adjustment method used for changing the color of layers and images.

Interpolation

This is the method of resizing up or down by adding or removing pixels. When upsizing, an algorithm works out the average between adjacent pixels and places new ones in between.

JPEG

A method of compressing images to take up less space on disk. JPEG files can have a variety of settings, offering smaller file sizes at the expense of some quality.

Layer

All images in Elements consist of at least one layer: they are equivalent to laying sheets of acetate on top of each other to build up areas of the artwork.

Layer linking

Layers can be linked together, allowing them to be moved and transformed as a single item. This is useful if you need to uniformly reposition or scale multiple sections of the artwork

Layer mask

Masks are used to selectively hide parts of the artwork by painting in shades of gray: black hides the area, white reveals it, and anything in between makes it transparent.

Layer style

These add effects to a layer without permanently affecting the artwork. Examples include: drop shadows, bevels and glows. These can be combined and their attributes adjusted to suit the image.

Leading

The adjustable spacing between lines of text. The term originates from the early days of printing when lead blocks were placed to keep the type separated.

Levels

An adjustment dialog for correcting and enhancing the shadows, midtones and highlights of a photo. They can be applied to the image as a whole or to the individual color channels for finer control.

Liquify

A powerful self-contained filter with which you can distort an image as though it were oil floating on water. This is very useful for flowing, organic substances and also for retouching photos.

Magic Wand

A selection tool that finds areas of an image of a similar color to the area in which the tool is clicked. Commonly used for selecting and removing backgrounds.

Marquee

This is the outline that defines a selection. It's often called the 'marching ants' because of its continuously moving dotted line.

Merge

The Merge Down command will combine one layer with the layer directly beneath it. Merge Visible will produce a single layer from all visible layers in the artwork.

Modifier keys

The keys ctrl, shift and alt that provide additional functions when held down in conjunction with certain tools, usually serving as shortcuts for switching between the tool's modes.

Non-destructive

A term used to describe an effect which does not permanently alter the image and remains editable, even after the image is saved and reopened.

Opacity

Determines how transparent the content of a layer appears: 0% is completely invisible, 100% is solid. Adjusting this value can be used for blending components of the artwork or for creating special effects.

Options bar

The contextual toolbar that sits across the top of the Elements window. This provides specific options and controls for the currently selected tool.

Out-of-bounds

A framing technique where parts of the image extend outside of the frame's boundaries; often used to emphasize the action of a photo.

Painting tools

Any tool such as the Brush, Clone tool, Smudge tool, and so on, that affects the area of an image over which it is dragged.

Palette

An area in the workspace containing sets of items such as styles, brushes or layers. These can be collapsed or hidden away when not in use.

Photoshop CS5

The 'big brother' of Elements, which offers superior controls and a range of additional features.

Pixel

A loose abbreviation of 'picture element'. The individual dots which make up a digital image; each can be one of the millions of colors available.

Pixelation

Visible degradation often caused by scaling the image larger than its original size. This is also used to describe the stepping effect when anti-aliasing is disabled.

Preset Manager

A dialog with which you can load, save and organize any brushes, gradients, color swatches and patterns you may have downloaded or created, along with the program's built-in presets.

Print size

A viewing mode in which an image is displayed at approximately the size it will print, using the current resolution settings.

RAM

Random Access Memory: the part of the computer that holds running programs and their data; for Elements this would be open images and the undo history.

Raster image

An image that is formed of individually colored dots (pixels). This is the most commonly used format for digital painting and photo editing.

Resolution

The method of describing the quality of a digital image by the number of individual pixels it contains. The higher the resolution, the more defined the areas of the picture can be.

RGB

Abbreviation for red, green, blue – the colors used by a computer monitor for displaying images.

Saturation

The depth and intensity of the colors in an image.

Scratch disk

A special area of the computer's hard drive reserved for temporary data storage when system RAM is running low.

Scrubby slider

An alternative method of increasing and decreasing the value of a particular attribute in some dialogs by positioning the cursor over the value and dragging right or left.

Shadows/Highlights

An adjustment method for recovering image data from the darkest and brightest parts of an image without affecting the midtones.

Simplify

Also referred to as rasterizing. The method of converting a shape or text layer to a regular bitmap layer; this can also be applied to layer styles to make them permanent.

Smart Fix

A simple method of automatically enhancing images that requires minimal technical knowledge on the part of the user.

sRGB

A color space devised to make graphic elements look better on computer screens. sRGB is a limited space that's best avoided for printing purposes.

Swatches

A collection of favorite colors and gradients stored in an easily selectable panel.

TIFF

A lossless image file format (see JPEG). Some digital cameras have the option of saving images in TIFF format.

Tolerance

This setting determines the precision of the associated tool. The higher the value, the larger the area of similar tones will be affected and vice versa.

Unsharp Mask

An adjustment that attempts to make the image appear crisper by enhancing the contrasting edges. The 'mask' element allows the area of the effect to be fine-tuned by means of a tolerance-like setting.

Vanishing point

Used when working or drawing in perspective: these mark the position on the horizon where two or more lines converge, for example as when looking down a straight road or railway tracks.

Vector graphics

A way of creating images using interconnected points, lines and curves generated by mathematical formulae. Unlike pixel-based artwork they can be scaled to any size without losing definition.

Visibility (layer styles)

Similar to changing a layer's opacity except it only affects the pixels of the layer, leaving the style itself untouched. The three modes, Show, Hide and Ghosted, turn the pixels on and off or render them semi-transparent.

Project files

This symbol indicates that you'll find an Elements file on the DVD to accompany the tutorial. They're in a folder called Tutorial Files and each one includes the starting point for each workthrough. The project files are sorted according to the chapter to which they belong and each file has a name that relates to the headline on that page.

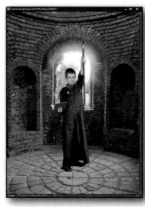

This symbol means that there's also a QuickTime movie on the DVD that shows the tutorial played out in real time. Sometimes it's easier to understand a concept when you see it acted out live, rather than just by reading about it. They're in the Quicktime Movies folder. To view them, you'll need the free QuickTime player from www.apple.com/quicktime, if you don't already have it installed.

Previous editions

Times change and Elements has not been left behind. Throughout the *How to Cheat in Photoshop Elements* series, we have done our best to keep the projects compatible with all versions of the program. Sadly, we cannot keep every spread in the book so we've transferred the older ones to the DVD in PDF format, along with any necessary supporting files.

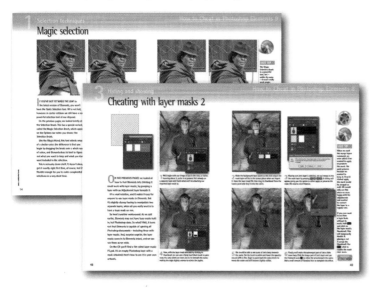

Shapes

The custom jigsaw pattern shapes, as described on page 286 are contained on the DVD. We've also included a small selection of stars so you can make your own starbursts to place behind text announcements.

To use them, open the Goodies folder on the DVD; there is a text file with instructions on where to place the files on the hard drive depending on which operating system you are using (Windows 7, Vista, XP or Mac OS X).

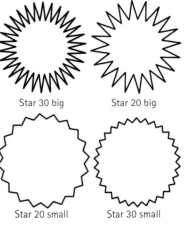

Star 30 big   Star 20 big

Star 20 small   Star 30 small

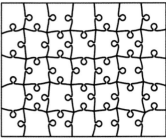

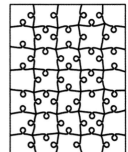

Above: Jigsaw Landscape

Left: Jigsaw Portrait

Layer styles

We've included a range of useful layer styles to complement those already present. As well as the neon text effects used in the book, we've added a range of inner shadows, some metallic styles and two new types of inner and outer glow, the difference being their blend mode is set to Multiply; this can be useful for creating shadows which are centrally placed, rather than offset to one side. The files and installation instructions can be found in the Goodies folder on the DVD.

Smart brushes

Smart Brush presets for the project on page 94 can also be found here. Refer to the text file on the DVD for details on how to install them for your version of operating system.

Gold paint

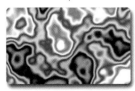

Silver paint

Metallic paint

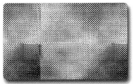

Diamond paint

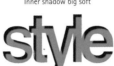
Inner shadow big soft

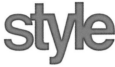
Inner shadow big softer

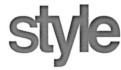
Inner shadow small

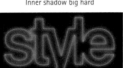
Inner shadow big hard

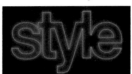
Inner shadow edge

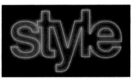
Inner shadow small soft

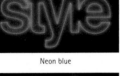
Neon blue

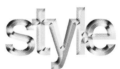
Neon blue 2

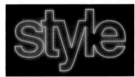
Neon pink

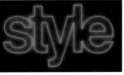
Neon green

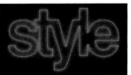
Neon red

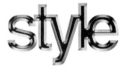
Neon yellow

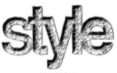
Metal bling

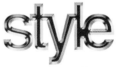
Metal chunky gold

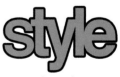
Metal chunky chrome

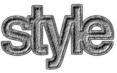
Metal rust

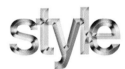
Metal chunky gold 2

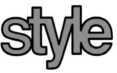
Metal chunky chrome 2

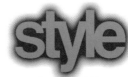
Inner stroke

Center stroke

Outer stroke

Inner glow multiply

Outer glow multiply

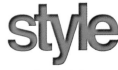
Bevel and shadow

Index

A

Add Noise filter 181
Adjustment Layers 36, 52, 301
   Levels 107
   Solid Color 119
adjustments
   Hue/Saturation 82, 175, 179
   Levels 72, 82, 241
   Shadows and highlights 74
   Threshold 101
age and youth 238
align and distribute 40
Andy Warhol 246
animated GIFs 298
Auto Levels 155
Auto Select layers 21, 27
Auto Smart Fix 63

B

background elements 54
Background Eraser tool 94
badges 216
bevel and emboss 221
blend modes 16, 36, 38, 109
Blending images 52
bling 92
blueprints 200
blur 103
bobbleheads 250
boxes 276, 278
Brightness and Contrast 72
brush creation 196
Burn tool 123, 152
buttons 216

C

Camera RAW 78
candlelight 122
caricatures 250
cars 212
chrome 212
clipping groups 56, 225
Clone Stamp tool 103, 177

Clouds filter 121, 155, 165, 199, 267, 280
CMYK 290
collage images 42
color correction 86
Color Dodge mode 161
Color replacement 85
color, selective 90
Colorize 37, 155
columns 224
compression 295
corner folds 131
Correct Camera Distortion filter 249
correcting perspective 162
creases 131
Create mode 296
creating brushes 196
Crop tool 62, 167, 176
curls and folds 152
cursor keys 19
curtains 172
curved surfaces 150
Custom Shape tool 34
cutout text 222

D

Darken mode 39
day into night 118
Define Pattern 177, 281
depth of field 104, 142
design 224
design, elements of 224
Detail Smart Brush 91, 93
Difference Clouds filter 135, 165, 185
Difference mode 39
Diffuse Glow filter 179, 248
Displace filter 157, 172
Dissolve mode 39, 190, 221
distortion 140
   Liquify 236
   perspective 144
distribute 40
Dodge tool 123, 152, 159
dogs 254
doors, opening 282
draw from center 6

dust 190

E

Elements interface 20
Ellipse Shape tool 146
Emboss 286
exposure 80
eyes, opening 244

F

faces, changing 232
Feather selection 19
Fibers filter 172, 175
file formats 256
Fill dialog 17, 18, 281
filling selections 17
Film Grain filter 184
filters
   Add Noise 181
   Clouds 121, 155, 165, 199, 267, 280
   Correct Camera Distortion 249
   Difference Clouds 135, 165, 185
   Diffuse Glow 179, 248
   Displace 157
   Fibers 172, 175
   Film Grain 184
   Find Edges 178, 280
   Gaussian Blur 62, 143, 195
   Glass 197, 198, 267
   High Pass 77
   Lens Flare 128
   Lighting Effects 194
   Liquify 151, 160, 175, 237, 238
   Mosaic Tile 17
   Motion Blur 98, 103
   Noise 191
   Offset 176
   Plastic Wrap 155, 189, 195, 250, 269
   Polar Co-ordinates 99
   Radial Blur 103, 127, 193
   Ripple 155
   Shear 150, 153, 157
   Smart Blur 251
   Spherize 159

Texturizer 57, 203, 215
Twirl 165
Unsharp Mask 77
ZigZag 154
Find Edges filter 178, 280
fire 120, 122
fireworks 58
flags 156
flames 120, 123
flowers 142
Frame Layers 30
free images 204
Free Transform 115, 126, 140, 144,
  151, 154, 281
fur, cutting out 254
Fuzziness 85

G

Gaussian Blur filter 62, 109, 143, 195
Gaussian Noise filter 180
GIF 294
GIFs, animated 298
glass 270
Glass filter 197, 198, 267
gold text 219
Gradient tool 99, 260, 263
graph paper 201
grass 51
grayscale 49
grids 224
Guided Edit 242
guides 42, 225
gutters 224

H

hair 239
hallway, creating 285
Hard Light mode 38, 117, 128
Hard Mix mode 38
heads, changing 230
Healing Brush 234, 238
High Pass filter 77
histogram 72
Hue/Saturation 82, 164, 175, 179

I

iconic portraiture 248
image compression 295
image size 226
image templates 64
images, free 204
inkjet printers 291, 300
Inner Bevel 57
Inner Shadows 223
internet, saving files for 294

J

jars 271
jigsaws 286
JPEG 256, 294
JPEG 2000 256

L

laptops 144
Lasso tool 8
layer masks 48, 50, 63, 241
layer modes
  Color Dodge 161
  Dissolve 190, 221
  Hard Light 117
  Multiply 221
  Screen 59, 200
  Soft Light 76
layer styles 32, 34, 208, 210
  carving 209
  chrome 212
  Inner Bevel 57
  neon 210
  Wow Chrome 199
layers 2, 30
  adjustment 36, 52
  align and distribute 40
  Auto Select 27
  background 25
  basics 24
  blend modes 38
  clipping groups 56
  constraining movement 27
  deleting 25

distribute 40
duplicating 26
Frame 30
Hard Light 128
hiding & showing 24
importing 28
mask 50
opacity 125
ordering 24
shape 35
Simplify 209
Smart Objects 30
styles 32, 35
transparency 25
layers, importing 28
layout 224
Lens Flare filter 128
Levels 72, 82, 241
Levels adjustment layer 107
lids, creating 278
lids, removing 276
Lighting Effects filter 194
lighting, stage 124
lightning 134
liquid, simulating 268
Liquify filter 151, 160, 175, 237, 238
Luminosity mode 39

M

Magic Extractor tool 14
Magic Wand tool 8
magical vortex 164
Magnetic Lasso tool 10
magnifying glass 158
Make Selection 147
maps 153
marbling 280
Marquee tool 6
masks 48
memory 44
metallic effect 93
models 104
molasses 268
montages 54
Mosaic Tile 17
Motion Blur filter 98, 103, 173

Multiply mode 38, 221

N

Natural Tone 90
neon signs 210
night, creating 118
Noise filter 109, 191, 221
non-destructive masking 48
notepaper 180

O

Offset filter 176
old paper 184
opacity 114, 125
Options bar 21
out of bounds 288
Overlay mode 39

P

paintings 288
panoramas 66
paper
  old 184
  parchment 184
  ruled 180
  tearing 182
paragraphs 225
parchment 184
Paste into selection 148
patterns 176
PDF files 257, 296
people, adding 240
people, removing 242
perspective 144, 162, 265, 277, 280,
  282, 284
photo-books 296
Photomerge 67, 80, 232, 242
Photomerge Style Match 88
photorealism 272
photos
  tearing 188
Photoshop 168
Place command 65
Plastic Wrap filter 155, 189, 195, 250,

269
PNG 257, 294
Polar Co-ordinates filter 99
Polaroid style photos 56
Polygonal Lasso tool 9, 55
pop art 246
portfolios 296
portraits 248
posters 130
printing 300
Project Bin 29, 243
pumpkins 214

Q

Quick Selection tool 12, 64

R

Radial Blur filter 103, 127, 193
rain 99
rainbows 98
RAW adjustment 78
Recompose tool 166
Refine Edge 12, 91
reflections
  complex 262
  in window 264
  simple 260
Replace Color 84, 87
RGB 290
Ripple filter 155
ripples 154
rotation 140
rubber stamp effect 196
rulers 225

S

sand, writing in 220
saturation 37
Save for Web 295, 299
scaling 140
Scene Cleaner 242
Scene, cleaning up the 242
Scotch tape 188
scratch disks 45

Screen mode 38, 59, 200
seamless 176
season shifting 86
Selection Brush 8
selections 6, 18
  circular 16
  draw from center 6
  elliptical 6
  expand 191
  filling 17
  Lasso 8
  Magic Extractor 14
  Magic Wand 8
  Magnetic Lasso 10
  modifier keys 6
  Paste into selection 148
  Quick Selection tool 12
  rectangular 6
  Save Selection 101
  Selection Brush 8
selections, tricky 146
selective color 90
sepia effect 88
setting up 20
shadows 18, 51, 74, 114
  on ground 114
  on walls 114
  soft, painting 116
Shadows and highlights 74
shadows, reflected 261
Shapes tool 285, 286
sharpening 76
Shear filter 150, 153, 157
Show Highlight on Rollover 21
silhouettes 106
sketch drawing 202
skies 94
slime 268
Smart Blur filter 251
Smart Brush 90, 92
Smart Objects 30
smoke 160
Smudge tool 50, 121, 254
snow 108
soft focus 248
Soft Light mode 39, 76, 185
Solid Color adjustment layer 119

Spatter brush 255
speed 102
Spherize filter 159
Spot Healing Brush 234, 239
spotlights 124
stained glass 126, 198
stitching 66
stone carving 208
storm, creating a 134
Stroke 181, 198, 220
style matching 88
sunsets 88

T

templates 64
text
    chrome 212
    neon 210
    stone carving 208
    Warp 216
Text Warp 215, 216
textures
    blueprint 200
    curtains 172
    dust 190
    notepaper 180
    old paper 184
    satin 178
    stained glass 198
    wax 194
    wood grain 174
Texturizer filter 57, 203, 215
three dimensional text 218
TIFF file format 256
tiled floors 280
Tiles 29
tilt-shift 104
tool tolerance 8
Toolbox 3
tools
    Background Eraser 94
    Burn 123, 152
    Clone Stamp 103, 177
    Crop 62, 167, 176
    Custom Shape 34
    Detail Smart Brush 91, 93

Dodge 123, 152, 159
Free Transform 115, 126, 140, 151,
        154
Gradient 99, 260, 263
Healing Brush 234, 238
Lasso 8
Magic Extractor 14
Magic Wand 8
Magnetic Lasso 10
Marquee 6
Polygonal Lasso 9, 55
Quick selection 12
Recompose 166
Replace Color 84
Selection Brush 8
Shape 146
Shapes 285, 286
Smart Brush 90, 92
Smudge 50, 121, 254
Spatter brush 255
Spot Healing Brush 234, 239
Type 217
Transfer Tones 89
transparency 17, 25
Twirl filter 165
Type tool 217

U

Unsharp Mask filter 77
upgrading 44

V

vanishing point 284
Vibrance 81
vinyl records 192

W

Warhol, Andy 246
watermark 34
wax 194
weight loss 236
windows 74, 264
wizards 162, 164
wood grain 174

work, protecting your 34
Wow Chrome 199, 213
wrinkles 131

Z

ZigZag filter 154